OLD MONEY

Nelson W. Aldrich, Jr.

OLD MONEY

The Mythology of America's Upper Class

ALFRED A. KNOPF *New York* 1988

Grateful acknowledgment is made to Alfred A. Knopf, Inc.,
for permission to reprint an excerpt from "The Comedian as the Letter C"
from *The Collected Poems of Wallace Stevens*.
Copyright 1923 and renewed 1951 by Wallace Stevens.
Reprinted by permission of Alfred A. Knopf, Inc.

Library of Congress Cataloging-in-Publication Data
Aldrich, Nelson W.
Old money.
Includes index.
1. Upper classes—United States. 2. Wealth—United States.
3. United States—Social life and customs.
I. Title.
HT653.U6A43   1988   305.5'234'0973   87-46079
ISBN 0-394-57036-7

Manufactured in the United States of America
First Edition

For

ANNA LOU ALDRICH

In Memory of

NELSON W. ALDRICH, 1841–1915
WILLIAM T. ALDRICH, 1880–1966
NELSON W. ALDRICH, 1911–1986

Triton, nothing left of him
Except in faint memorial gesturings,
That were like arms and shoulders in the waves,
Here, something in the rise and fall of wind
That seemed hallucinating horn, and here,
A sunken voice, both of remembering
And of forgetfulness, in alternate strain.

WALLACE STEVENS

Contents

Contents

Acknowledgments

I have spent more hours thinking about this book than I want to count. On the other hand, I do want to count the people who now and again spent them with me, talking and arguing about Old Money. To name them all would be to name virtually everyone I know, and as this is impossible, I shall name just a few, with the understanding that my gratitude is no less for the many.

First, I should like to thank three magazine editors: Lewis Lapham of *Harper's* magazine, who first persuaded me that there's nothing really to be afraid of in writing for publication, and nothing at all to be afraid of in writing about one's own class; Daniel Okrent of *The New England Monthly,* who gave me repeated opportunities to do just that; and George Gendron of *Inc.* magazine, who provided me with an invaluable chance to observe, close up, the quality and drama of life among the entrepreneurs.

Second, I want to thank certain friends and relatives, whose conversation and encouragement were vital to me at various times in the course of this project: Frances T. Aldrich, Paul Aron, Joseph Bazinet, Frederic Bradlee, James Chace, Alexander C. Cortesi, Timothy Dickenson, Frances FitzGerald, Margaret Gibson, George Gilder, James R. Hammond, Jr., Alan Heimert, Alison Humes, Valerie Humes, Wendy M. Jacobus, Deane Lord, Frances A. Maher, David McKain, Jonathan Miller, Edwin Morgan, Frederick S. Nicholas, Jr., Frank Niewiarowski, Alton Peters, Frederick Seidel, Charles P. Sifton, John Stockman, Katharine W. Tweed, and Alan Williams. To Elisabeth Sifton, who somehow managed to remain my friend after becoming my editor, my gratitude is almost inexpressible. As *Old Money* went through one crisis of representation after another, she never failed to reassure me on the most critical question of all, that there actually was something there to represent.

Finally, the matter of this book being what it is, unearned income,

I feel obliged to express my gratitude to these sources of indispensable financial support: the Charles Tweed Trust, the Camilla Davenport Trust, and the Massachusetts Division of Employment Security.

N.W.A., Jr.

Preston, Connecticut
January 1988

Introduction

Inherited wealth is a powerful given in the economic arrangements of American life. Effortlessly, through no merit of their own, some Americans come into greater and more varied opportunities, including opportunities to make more money, than the great majority of other Americans. Inherited wealth puts an egregious wrinkle in the nation's promissory claim to be a land of equal opportunity. One would have thought this might cause comment, if not outrage, but rarely in American history has there been much of either.

The exception is when inherited wealth appears as Old Money. Old Money is inherited wealth socialized, so to speak, and it appears in many guises. Some are loose-fitting, such as what appears to be the establishment, the eastern upper class, the patrician class, the bourgeois aristocracy; some are rather tighter-fitting, such as the Brahmin, the preppie, the clubbie, or the Summer People. All these guises of Old Money are controversial. Political intellectuals, for example, heatedly debate Old Money's influence on the dispositions of power, with pluralists maintaining that the class occupies merely one among many of the nation's command posts, and with ruling-class theorists arguing to the contrary, that Old Money is a field of binding energy that gathers the command posts' occupants into one body, coherent in culture and complicitous in policy. As one of them put it, "The flaw in the pluralist heaven is that the heavenly chorus sings with a strong upper-class accent."

The man must be tone-deaf; it should be enough for his purposes that everyone know the words to the song. Still, whatever Old Money's relationship to the powers that be in the United States, there is one thing that all sorts of people believe about it: that it is a social class. They believe that the class has certain peculiar sources of economic support and concern—its social property. They believe it is laid out along certain special parameters of belonging, with special institutional affiliations creating special social affinities. And they believe that members of the class can be identified by their adherence to certain norms of social behavior, such as accents. Beyond this, there's a good deal of dispute, but few people deny that there's some sort of social distinction in Old Money, or that there's some point in arguing about what that distinction is and what it means.

This book is about one such argument. It's an argument between two ways of imagining wealth, and of imagining oneself in relation to wealth, the Old Money way and the New Money way. In Old Money's imagination, wealth takes on many characteristics of real property, as many as it can bear in a capitalist system. Wealth is seen as an estate or a patrimony with a history and a posterity, literally or figuratively held in trust, and producing an income dedicated to specific social purposes: the support of a family and its cultural, social, and economic undertakings over as many generations as the family endures, or as the estate remains integrated and productive. Wealth in this view is a given, not something owned or possessed, which should be given on.

New Money conceives of wealth in the first instance as *money* (or credited money)—an abstract symbol as far removed from any referent in real property as the capitalist system can remove it, which is pretty far. There it becomes a measure and a tool of almost universal usefulness, and a reminder of almost infinite possibilities. New Money grasps this protean character of money more easily than the Old Rich grasp their inheritances. Its stance is insistently entrepreneurial. Everything is to be made; everything can be made. Nothing is given, not even the self. The entrepreneurial imagination thrives on possibility, opportunity, chances; and its preferred field of play is where these things, thanks to money and credit, seem most abundant—in the marketplace. The entrepreneur is a maker of markets: markets for the self, for the self's goods and services, for the self's ideas and notions, and for everyone else's as well, all the resources of nature and the cultures of man.

Markets and marketing provide the great preemptive metaphors of New Money's entrepreneurial vision. The entrepreneur is Market Man, a brilliant figure in that otherwise dismal composition known as Economic Man. And money, or credited money, is his medium: fluid, buoyant, and powerful, but otherwise as susceptible as water to whatever desire may dictate in shape, color, and taste. Wealth enters this view as a sort of sedimentary deposit of the flux and flow of market exchange. Mostly, though, it is just another form of money—stored possibility.

No one has ever met, socially or otherwise, the protagonists and antagonists of this book. The social imagination of Old Money and the entrepreneurial imagination of New Money are schematic renderings of tendencies to be found, to one degree or another, in all kinds of American Money, including No Money; and the conflict between them goes on within individuals as well as between classes of individuals. Moreover, the class conflict is not much of a contest. America, a New World, is dominated by the entrepreneurial imagination of New Money. Indeed, if it weren't for one circumstance, New Money might never take any notice of Old Money at all. This circumstance is envy.

Envy is so integral and so painful a part of what animates behavior in market societies that many people have forgotten the full meaning of the word, simplifying it into one of the synonyms of desire. It is that, which may be why it flourishes in market societies: democracies of desire, they might be called, with money for ballots, stuffing permitted. But envy is more or less than desire. It begins with an almost frantic sense of emptiness inside oneself, as if the pump of one's heart were sucking on air. One has to be blind to perceive the emptiness, of course, but that's just what envy is, a selective blindness. *Invidia,* Latin for envy, translates as "non-sight," and Dante has the envious plodding along under cloaks of lead, their eyes sewn shut with leaden wire. What they are blind to is what they have, God-given and humanly nurtured, in themselves. This is why envy is a sin, a sin against God or Nature or Fortune, to whom gratitude is owed for the gift of what we are.

Blind as the envious are to what they have, they are exquisitely observant of what others have: objects, traits, positions, and honors that, if they only had them, might fill up the void inside themselves. They seem to love these things. But envy swings back and forth between love and hate, admiration and resentment, wanting and despising, spinning this way as it is satisfied, the other way as it is frustrated, always in emptiness. Hence the humiliation and pain: It is humiliating to feel oneself empty, and painful to be denied what seems like fulfillment and self-respect. The envious are never more revealingly themselves than when vigorously denying their envy.

Envy greens both sides of the argument between Old Money and New. The Old Rich sometimes envy the New Rich their success, for example, even to the point of disfiguring themselves by striving for it. But the most flagrant and historic envy faces the other way. It goes without saying (except to certain economically insensate heirs and heiresses) that Old Money from time to time needs New Money's *money*— to shore up declining fortunes and to help support increasingly costly institutions. But Old Money also needs New Money's envy. Otherwise it is in danger of becoming a crypto-class, a group of people whose significance in any larger scheme of things, whose very existence, is known only to themselves. If Old Money is saved from this misfortune, it is thanks to the emulation, covetousness, or rancor of those among the New Rich who are tempted to become Old. Envy opens a dialogue that may or may not corroborate Old Money's valuation of its distinctions, but that certainly corroborates the essential thing, which is that such distinctions exist.

Are the Old Rich distinctively nonchalant about pursuing financially lucrative work? The argument here is lively. Many beneficiaries of ancient riches, myself disastrously included, affect a careless indifference to the financial rewards of our work, partly to satisfy certain class standards of self-respect, but partly, too, *pour épater la bourgeoisie.* By the same token, many self-made men, when asked why they pursue profit so avidly, offer deliberately crude, bottom-line explanations, again partly to satisfy class standards of self-respect, but also to do a little *épatage* of their own on the "idle rich." The point is that without envy—the envy of the hereditary rich for the alleged energy of their class rivals, the envy of the nouveaux riches for the ease and assurance of *their* rivals—this exchange of polemical poses would never take place.

The loss would be Old Money's, mostly. The New Rich hardly need the Old to corroborate their chief distinction: that they're rich. The poor do that, above all the poor man who shivers inside every newly rich one. The New Rich do perhaps need the Old to remind them that that's all they are—rich. But this is a reminder easily ignored in America, perhaps even dangerous to take seriously. Old Money, on the other hand, is a social presence conjured out of vivid memories and lovely aspirations, working together to create an impression of what can be done with money to transcend money. To be truly visible, however, this presence requires (besides money) considerable effort of the social imagination, and the Old Rich cannot rely solely on their own. They need New Money to believe in them, that they may believe in themselves, and that the argument may go on.

OLD MONEY

CHAPTER ONE

My Founding Father

"*We'll* never see the day, Nancy—never in the world—
never, never, never, child. We've got to drag along, drag along,
and eat crusts in toil and poverty, all hopeless and forlorn—
but *they'll* ride in coaches, Nancy! They'll live like the princes
of the earth; they'll be courted and worshipped; their names
will be known from ocean to ocean! Ah, well-a-day! Will
they ever come back here ... and say, 'This one little spot
shall not be touched—this hovel shall be sacred—for here
our father and our mother suffered for us, thought for us,
laid the foundations of our future solid as the hills!'"

"You are a great, good, noble soul, Si Hawkins, and I am
an honored woman to be the wife of such a man"—and the
tears stood in her eyes when she said it.

Mark Twain, *The Gilded Age*

I WAS ALMOST TWENTY years old when I realized that I was
entitled to a Roman numeral after my name, a "IV" instead of the
"Junior" I'd lived with until then. I'd found it rather humiliating,
that "Junior," and I knew that generationally speaking it wasn't even
accurate. There had been a Nelson W. Aldrich before my father: his
grandfather, the longtime (1881–1911) Republican senator from Rhode
Island, whom Lincoln Steffens had called "The Boss of the United
States." But I had been persuaded that Roman numerals, even a mere
III, were pretentious; better to be inaccurate, my father said, than to
appear a genealogical snob. Then, attending the funeral of my great-
aunt Lucy Aldrich at the family plot in Providence, Rhode Island, I
learned that there was one more Nelson in the line.

By 1955, when Aunt Lucy died, at the age of eighty-six, not many
of her generation, the Senator's children, were still alive. Uncle Ned,

3

Uncle Richard, Uncle Stuart, Aunt Elsie Edgell, Aunt Abby Rockefeller, all were dead. But my grandfather William, and his younger
brother, Winthrop, were still very much with us. They were at
the funeral; so were many of my father's generation, Aldriches,
Edgells, and Rockefellers, along with a sprinkling of their children. I
don't remember these people very well. Many of them I'd consigned to
that limbo of nonelective affinity (or hostility) which one reserves for
aunts, uncles, and cousins with whom, once or twice a year, one is
courteous.

I do remember the family plot, and I've seen it many times since.
Swan's Point cemetery is just east of College Hill, the commanding
height overlooking the city where Providence's oldest families have
their historic winter houses, and which it was the great triumph of the
first Nelson W. Aldrich to have conquered in his own lifetime. To be
sure, there wasn't much left of his property, not in Rhode Island. His
house on College Hill (Aunt Lucy's until her death) became the museum of the Rhode Island Historical Society; and his house in the
country had already been sold to the Roman Catholic Archdiocese. No
great sacrifice, certainly no falling off of the family's standing, should
be read into these events; merely the fact that his descendants, all but
Aunt Lucy, had long since abandoned Providence for bigger, more
glamorous cities in larger states. They returned only for funerals, to
this last portion of the Senator's real estate to remain, as one says, "in
the family."

The family plot is on an elegantly landscaped rise of land, screened
by hemlocks from more indiscriminate resting places around it. At the
highest point of the rise, fittingly enough for those to whom the family
owes its first great lift to eminence, are the monuments to the Senator
and his wife, Abby. We in the funeral party stood on the next level
down, where Aunt Lucy was to be buried alongside her brothers and
sisters. There were other levels below that, obscure in the shadows of
evergreens.

The service began. I bent my head and closed my eyes. When I
opened them again, I found myself looking down at a small headstone
of polished red granite, barely peeping above the turf. On it, to my
horror, was carved my name, "Nelson W. Aldrich Jr." I thought for an
instant that my father must have put it there, holding a place for me
in the family plot as he might have done at my boarding school or one
of his Boston clubs. Then I saw that the little headstone was inscribed
with dates, 1867–1871. A great-uncle, then: the Senator's firstborn son.

I felt a strange and wistful sorrow that the little boy had died before he could continue his father's line, an unbroken line of eldest sons, all Nelson W. Aldriches, down to the fourth, me as I might have been—and then beyond, on into what was for me, as I then was, the unimaginable future.

This was the first access of *pietas,* or something like it, that I had ever experienced, and for a long time it would be the last. The past was a strong motif in my upbringing, at least so far as my grandfather was in charge of it (which to a large degree he was), but it was history's accumulated weight and momentum, its tremendous determinacy, that he liked to reflect upon. "Originality," he would say, quoting I don't know whom, perhaps himself, "is only a failure of memory." My father was more liberal in awarding powers to the present, to our capacity to shape the future. But neither man cultivated in himself, or in me, that reverential sense of ancestral precedence which passes for *pietas* in many founded (so to speak) families.

The reason had to do with the founder. When I was a boy, very little was said about the first Nelson W. Aldrich. There was a biography of him in both my father's and my grandfather's libraries, and I remember being pleased and somehow flattered by the photograph of him in the frontispiece: how handsome he was, with his strong chin, his fine bold nose, and the sharp intelligence in his eyes. But I never felt any desire, nor did I get any encouragement, actually to read about his life. On the contrary, my father assured me that the book was dreadfully dull, a hagiography commissioned by the family, not worth reading.

Then, too, there was the curious toast to his brothers and sisters that my grandfather used to give at family dinners. He told their story, the tale of their rise in prosperity, and he played it off a peculiarity of the street names on College Hill that many of them are named for blessings. In his toast, Grandpa was able to trace the family's ascendancy from Hope Street to Benefit Street (the hope, you see, beginning to bear fruit) to other streets, other earthly felicities that I've forgotten, until they achieved their apotheosis on Benevolent Street (the benefits at last yielding a bounty of liberality and high spirits). The odd thing about this toast was that while there must have been some human agency, and some material heft, behind this ascension of Aldriches, Grandpa never named them.

What lay behind this silence I did not learn until I was sixteen. Arriving in Brookline, Massachusetts, on Christmas vacation from St.

Paul's School, I came to my grandfather's house by cab from the train station, dumped my bag and books in the front hall, and went out again, to a friend's house. What happened when I returned for tea may be explained by the fact that one of the maids, tidying up after me, happened to place my books on the hall table, where my grandfather happened to see them on his way to the library. It's also possible that I put them there myself, accidentally on purpose, with something like the eventual result in mind. However the books got there, when I came back to the house later that afternoon I heard my grandfather calling my name, rather sharply, and knew instantly that he wanted to talk to me about my vacation reading.

The books were *The Robber Barons,* by Matthew Josephson, *America's Sixty Families,* by Ferdinand Lundberg, and *The Communist Manifesto.* They had been suggested by one of those teachers, not uncommon at New England's boarding schools, who harbor ambivalent feelings with respect to the privileged social and economic position of their pupils. His name was Richard Day, and he subsequently became principal of Exeter; at the time, he was a freshly credentialed Ph.D. from Harvard and my American History teacher. He was a good teacher, rigorous but infectiously enthusiastic about his subject. He was also a brutal meritocrat. Within two months of our first meeting as a class, he had triaged all of us into the academically hopeless, whom he ignored; the mediocre, whom he set to learning Morison and Commager virtually by heart; and the meritorious, to whom he assigned special projects and independent reading. The meritorious could choose their projects freely, as I remember, but I think Mr. Day liked to point us in directions where each of us might stumble across some inherited but possibly unsuspected connection with a maker of the country's history. At St. Paul's School the number of such connections is fairly large, though most often concentrated in the business history of the Gilded Age. Mr. Day suggested that I might want to "look into" the career of Senator Nelson W. Aldrich. Josephson and Lundberg, he said, could tell me something of what he'd done; the *Manifesto* was for "perspective." Mr. Day was a mischievous man.

I came into the library and saw my grandfather sitting in his usual chair, to the right of the fireplace. He was in his early seventies then, a plump, smallish man with bright red cheeks, snow-white hair, and a little Foch mustache, which, like the rosette of *officier* in the Legion of Honor, was a souvenir of his service in World War I. As always, his mustache felt a little damp to my kiss (curiously, we kissed on the lips, my grandfather and I), and as I kissed him I noticed *The Communist Manifesto* open on his ample lap.

"Have you read this?"

"Yes, sir. Most of it."

"Well, that's all right," he said. "I suppose you know the old saw, don't you—how if you're not a socialist before the age of twenty-five you've got no heart, and if you're still one after twenty-five you've got no brains."

"Yes, Grandpa." Months before, during some argument, the same old saw had consoled my father.

"And that?" he asked, pointing to *America's Sixty Families* as though it were a filthy dog that had unaccountably settled down among the tea things.

"No, I haven't. Not yet."

It was true. I hadn't looked at either the Josephson or the Lundberg. But even if I had, I would have denied it. Mr. Day had teased me a bit about Senator Aldrich, a teacherly tease to whet my curiosity, but I gathered that if I really looked closely at my forebear's career, I might find certain irregularities in it, certain practices that were, if not precisely illegal, then not quite ethical, either. So I knew already that these were dangerous conversational waters I was on. But Grandpa, I noticed, was not angry. His face showed something worse than anger, a deep hurt surfacing after long burial. He looked like a man called on for the umpteenth time to give witness in a cause he no longer knew whether to believe in.

He said, "When you read it, if you must read it, just remember that your grandfather—no, he's your *great*-grandfather, isn't he?—did more for this country than all those muckrakers put together. He made sacrifices, great sacrifices. . . ." His voice grew faint with an inward quarrel, as though he'd be *damned* before he went through it all again, his father's accomplishments, his terrible ordeals. And for what? His voice picked up again: ". . . founder of the Federal Reserve system; why don't you look into that?" But then, abruptly, he leaned back in his comfortable chair and said, with just a hint of irony: "Let's talk about something more agreeable. How are you getting on in school?" He knew, of course, that this was hardly a more agreeable subject, but we talked about it for a few minutes until Marie, the downstairs maid, padded in and removed the tea things. My grandfather took up the evening *Globe* and was soon fast asleep.

I ran upstairs to my room and tracked "Aldrich, Nelson W."

through the indexes of *The Robber Barons* and *America's Sixty Families*. The first contained only one reference: "the masters of business who sat in the upper chamber of Congress (or Millionaires' Club, as it was humorously called) ... make up a long and distinguished roll which, to mention only a few, includes Leland Stanford of the Southern Pacific monopoly ... Henry B. Payne of the Standard Oil family ... among the professional politicians there were also shrewd former tradesmen or lawyers such as James G. Blaine, Nelson W. Aldrich ..."

I wondered what Mr. Day or my grandfather imagined I could make of that. Lundberg was far more generous. There were eleven references to the man whose name I had inherited (and some part of whose fortune supported me still):

> ... the late Senator Aldrich, who in his day was successively the legislative "whip" of first the Morgan, then the Rockefeller factions in the United States Senate ... the whole Rhode Island political machine, dominated by Aldrich and General Charles R. Brayton, was corrupt in every detail.... Brayton, Aldrich and Marsden J. Perry manipulated the [state] legislature, gave themselves perpetual public utility franchises ... worth millions to themselves. When Aldrich gave up his wholesale grocery business in 1881 to enter the Senate he was worth $50,000; when he died after thirty years in politics, he was worth $12,000,000.... "Morgan's floor-broker in the Senate" ... Whittling by reactionaries under Aldrich, however, made [the Pure Food and Drug Act] woefully ineffective.... Attempts to outlaw labor injunctions and a joint effort by Beveridge and LaFollette to form a tariff commission of experts were brought to naught by Aldrich and his hatchet men ... the dubious Aldrich ... [and so forth].

The effect on me of these allegations was instantaneous. I would not do my American History project on Nelson W. Aldrich; I would write on John Reed instead. A revolutionary seemed a more attractive figure than a "reactionary," and though I'm not sure I could have told you why at the time, it almost certainly had something to do with the fact that I had been persuaded, right then and there, that the reactionary—my ancestor, my family's founder—was quite clearly an old crook.

Pietas, as I say, was not part of my Aldrich legacy. Indeed, I cherished a certain scorn for people I met who expressed even the slightest respect for their ancestors. Of *my* "historic" forebears, I would say on such occasions that one was an old crook, while another—my favorite, a man on my mother's side of the family called Obadiah Greene—was so flagrant a womanizer that he was thrown out of the Plymouth Colony (not an especially puritanical place) for "persistent ogling in church," as the records put it. (Actually, I have no idea whether this story is true; I would tell it only to suggest that if all aristocracy begins with someone's natural superiority, as Emerson asserts, then I was happier to think of myself as belonging to an aristocracy of lust than to one of corruption.) In short, what my early glance at Nelson W. Aldrich had taught me was that ancestor stories are for unmasking, for provocation and *épatage*. It never occurred to me that they might be useful for anything else or inspire any other feelings.

I'm still not sure what those feelings might be, if not *pietas,* but I know that at least two of the Senator's descendants had them: Nelson Aldrich Rockefeller and his son Michael. A year or so before he died, drowned off the coast of New Guinea, I had a rather awkward meeting with Michael on the subject of our common great-grandfather. He had called me up, wanting to talk about his thesis topic. He was then in his senior year at Harvard, three or four years behind me, and majoring in American history and literature, as I had done. His proposed thesis topic, needless to say, was the Senator. He wanted to know what I thought of the idea.

I laughed—complicitously, as I recall. For of course I assumed that what he wanted to do with our great-grandfather was to expose his crimes. Indeed, I felt slightly ashamed of myself, and a little jealous of Michael, to think that a family member had come along who was not afraid to tell hard, unvarnished truths about his ancestor. Michael would do it. I had never felt such a rush of family feeling. And then, well into telling him about my own feckless pass at writing a paper about the old crook, I suddenly realized that "unmasking" wasn't what Michael was after. He was after revision, even rehabilitation.

"I want to look into his contribution to the Federal Reserve system," Michael said, echoing my grandfather. "I just think he hasn't been given the proper credit for it. It was his idea. He gave an awful lot of time and study to it, and as it turned out, the system that came out of it, it was really his. That's what I want to write about." This was the same thesis topic, he told me, that his father had written about at Dartmouth.

I hope I contained my contempt that afternoon, for I know now that it masked the first stirrings of a kind of envy I had of Michael, envy of a son, grandson, and great-grandson who believed he could derive something from his family's past that I could not. Nelson Aldrich Rockefeller had thought so too, as I learned much later. For example, he rejoiced that he'd been named for one grandfather, and born on the same day as the other. To him, these legacies were wondrous and inspiring portents of his own splendid future. He wrote his parents from Dartmouth in the year 1929: "It seems funny to think that today is Grandfather's 90th birthday and my 21st birthday. The 90 makes my 21 seem mighty small and insignificant, just like a sapling standing by a mighty fir tree. But the sapling still has time to grow and develop and someday it might itself turn into a tree of some merit. Who knows?"

Reading about his two grandfathers at college, he had to have learned of the criticism, the allegations, the calumny. His son had to have heard them too, and not just from me. Yet in 1959 Michael wrote to his grandfather John D. Rockefeller, Jr.: "On my twenty-first birthday, my father made known to me the trust which you have established out of consideration for me and my future. For this I am deeply grateful. It is unique and extraordinary that the third generation after Great Grandfather will be able to share in the privileges and wonderful opportunities coincident with taking responsibility over a trust which he made possible. . . . I will become that much more a part of a wonderful tradition, one which has already exerted a profoundly broadening and morally inspiring influence upon my upbringing."

This is nauseating. Yet behind the sapling and fir tree clichés of the father, behind the son's saccharine cant about privileges and responsibilities and morally inspiring influences, I think I hear something very powerful, and to me, now, appealing. It is an almost Homeric eagerness to succeed—succeed, that is, in the dynastic sense. "Who knows?" asked Nelson Rockefeller about the succession of generations, but I think he knew at least what Glaukhos knew:

> Very like leaves
> upon this earth are the generations of men—
> old leaves, cast on the ground by wind, young leaves
> the greening forest bears when spring comes in.
> So mortals pass; one generation flowers
> even as another dies away.

A "wonderful tradition," exclaimed the son, but perhaps the sappy phrase concealed the ancient boast:

Hippolokhos it was who fathered me,
I am proud to say. He sent me here to Troy
commanding me to act always with valor,
always to be the most noble, never to shame
the line of my progenitors, great men
first in Ephyra, then in Lykia.
This is the blood and birth I claim.

This is the real thing, this *pietas,* and it could be that the Rockefellers, modern men after all, never even approached it in their hearts. All I can say is that looking back along the line of their descent, they seem to have been able to take only what they wanted—a fairy tale that would give them the strength and courage to come into their own kingdoms. Clearly they did not want the truth. Years after writing his letter from Dartmouth, on his nomination to the vice-presidency, the closest Nelson Rockefeller came to the office he aspired to most of his life, he testified before Congress: "The example of my grandfathers made me feel a terrific challenge.... Grandfather Rockefeller was a leader of men. Grandfather Aldrich was completely different, a great man with the people." The characterizations are ludicrous and, in his Grandfather Aldrich's case, virtually the opposite of the truth. But perhaps the truth would have failed him as inspiration. Perhaps it would fail me too, but there came a time when I finally resolved, as Mr. Day had suggested, to "take a look" at the career of my forebear, the man who first bore my name.

Nelson W. Aldrich was raised in East Killingly, Connecticut, just across the line from Rhode Island. His father was a mill hand, indolent and charming, whose name was Anan. His mother was called Abby, and there were times when she could hardly believe that such a man as Anan had fathered such a boy as Nelson. He was bright, and so much more serious and ambitious than his father. At nine, in 1850, he took some money his mother had given him for the circus and with it bought a little book called *A Tinker's Son, or, I'll Be Somebody Yet*. Later he read Walter Scott—perhaps to learn what a Somebody was in the Old World. His mother told him what Somebodies were in the New World. He was descended from two of them, she said: from John Winthrop, the first governor of Massachusetts, and from Roger Williams, the founder of Rhode Island. What basis she had for making these claims is a little obscure, but Nelson believed them all his life. They may have explained what Anan obviously did not: that while the world might suppose young Nelson W. Aldrich to be a nobody, he himself knew otherwise. His blood told him so.

His mother sent him to Greenwich (Rhode Island) Academy, and then he went to Providence to seek his fortune. He began as a clerk in a wholesale grocery business, and he was still a clerk when he left to be a soldier in the Civil War. Four months later he was mustered out, sick, and was back in Providence, a clerk again and more serious than ever. He was going to the Lyceum now, and while he learned much in those instructive halls that would be practically useful to him later— parliamentary rules and tactics, debating, and the like—he also learned a view of life that struck him, certainly the indolent, ineradicable Anan in him, as a grim and fearful thing. He learned about Charles Darwin's theories and what evolution meant for human society—an intense and relentless struggle for advantage.

There were grounds for hope in this account of the way things were, especially for someone destined, as he felt himself to be, to take his place among his country's once and future founding fathers. But there were also grounds for a terrible anxiety. Engaged to be married (and doubly blessed in his fiancée: she was the wholesale grocer's daughter, and her name was the same as his beloved mother's, Abby), he wrote to his fiancée that he often felt as though he'd been "set adrift upon a sea of doubts and fears." He anticipated "catastrophe." He imagined himself prey to "all conceivable evils." With her—his future haven, his solace even then—he could freely vent his unhappiness. But he could not change it to happiness, or not for long.

His metaphors returned again and again to the fretful, random turbulence of the sea: "Alas! Disappointments come to us all. Our lives are continually twisted from the current in which we would like to have them run. . . ." Or again, it seemed to him that society was "a great Maelstrom of passion and excitement, where the life of a man or of a thousand are valued as a rush light. . . ." In such a world, He Himself having supposedly made it, even God was not to be trusted. Repeatedly, even after the power he sought seemed within his grasp, my great-grandfather could be horribly cast down by the suspicion that, after all, he may have been wrong about his destiny. God was to be implored: "if the Superior Creator *would* only *give* to my ideal creations, *would* make me always hopeful, never despondent . . ." Faith, and secretively approaching his goal of total control of the oil industry.) My great-grandfather, however, had a way out of that world—or what, with a little sham, flattery, and deception of the self, he could imagine was a way out. This was the way of political power. "Five years of this imprisoning alliance to traffic," he had written his wife around 1866, "and then I *will* be free. My commencement in business life has been, beyond my most sanguine expectations, successful, and if some dreams of my boyhood may never be realized, more *power* for good than I ever hoped for seems within my reach." It's not clear from the context whether he had financial or political power in mind, and his prediction was off by about another five years, but by the late 1870s, he himself being in his early thirties, the prisoner of "traffic" was well on his way to becoming one of its most powerful controllers.

He was also well on his way up College Hill, an extraordinary feat for someone of his background. (I mean, of course, his actual background, not the one he imagined.) The old families established on that height—Browns, Goddards, Iveses, Metcalfs, et al.—constituted then, as they still do, one of the most culturally and economically cohesive patriciates in the United States. Its wealth, anciently rooted in the "triangular trade" in slaves, sugarcane, and rum, was now strategically invested in textiles and other industries nationwide. (A young Goddard once told me, pointing to an ancestral portrait in the family dining room, that as an officer in the Civil War his forebear had bought up large tracts of land in the Middle West with government vouchers that his men had received in lieu of pay on being mustered out of the army. The land was still in the family portfolio in the early 1980s.) Membership in this patriciate brought with it much besides wealth, of course: complete domination of all educational and cultural institutions, ownership and control of the news media, exceptionally favored treatment at the hands of political and civic officers, all the legal and fiscal advantages that money and prestige can command, and vast and varied opportunities for further financial gain. All these assets were hereditary. There were, in fact, few other ways to get them.

Politics must have been one way; otherwise it's hard to imagine my great-grandfather abandoning, as from the late 1870s he increasingly did, his direct pursuit of dollars and cents. Until the 1930s, when Theodore Francis Green went from Rhode Island to the United States Senate as a Democrat (grounds, according to family legend, for Aunt Lucy to reject him as a suitor), the patricians of College Hill abstained from personal participation in politics. This had not been so before the however, he could put only in his own will: "I will ask, expect happiness; more, I *will be* happy."

By the mid-1870s, he might have called himself happy. His wife had brought him some money and, through the grocery business, a means of making more of it. Soon he also became a director of a small bank. It was not enough: his "ideal creations" seemed no more real than ever. As an American, indeed as an American of high destiny, what he wanted from America was simple enough: "Willingly or forcibly wrested from a selfish world, *Success!* Counted as the mass counts it, by dollars and cents!" One might ask where such a cry comes from—from the heart of the country or its bowels? But wherever it comes from, it is ever present, ever pressing. Founding fathers far more eminent than mine—Thomas Jefferson and John Adams—had predicted it after the Revolution: that the new nation would soon entirely give itself over to the pursuit of money. Adams's most prominent line of descent was clever enough to entwine itself with money by marrying it. Jefferson's had to make it: "Everybody was at work trying to make money," wrote Thomas Jefferson Coolidge in Boston in the 1850s, "and money was becoming the only real avenue to power and success both socially and in the regard of your fellow-men. I was ambitious and decided to devote myself to the acquisition of wealth." Almost a century and a half later, a new founding father, Lee J. Iacocca, defended the $20.6 million he took in compensation for his work at the Chrysler Corporation (while cutting merit pay for other employees): "That's the American way. If little kids don't aspire to make money like I did, what the hell good is this country?"

But for my great-grandfather, certainly for his "ideal creations," there were difficulties in the way of *Success!* They lay in the nature of business itself. Nelson W. Aldrich appears to have been one of those anomalous creatures of capitalism, a businessman who disdained business. His aim was the same as Coolidge's and Iacocca's, financial success, but as he expressed it with less gusto, so he pursued it with less fortitude. He felt "governed," he wrote once, he who was of the blood and sensibility of governors, "by the exacting, unfeeling, I almost said unscrupulous laws of business." Such fine sentiments were fairly commonplace—certainly in the class to which he aspired but also among some of the aspirants. John D. Rockefeller once wrote: "I feel now more than ever that the world is full of Sham, Flattery and Deception." (At the time, Rockefeller was on a business trip, guilefully, cunningly,

Civil War, and it would not be so after Senator Green, when it became a virtual custom of the state to send at least one, currently two (Claiborne Pell and John Chafee), Old Family members to the Senate. But in my great-grandfather's day the patriciate had left the defense of its political interests, and everyone else's, to others. They did so the more easily, perhaps, knowing that they were as well protected by the undemocratic nature of the system as by the loyalty of its personnel.

Many states in the United States have been as undemocratic as Rhode Island in fact, but few states have been so undemocratic in law. The last of the original thirteen states to ratify the federal Constitution, Rhode Island was also one of the last to ratify a constitution of its own. For more than half a century after the nation organized itself in Philadelphia in 1787, the state's politics were conducted under a royal charter given to "The Colony of Rhode Island and the Providence Plantations" by Charles II, amended by a few unwritten provisions. None of the latter touched the suffrage requirement, which remained what it had always been, ownership of land. In 1842, with the adoption of a written state constitution, the vote was extended to owners of personal property (males only, of course), but only if they were native-born. This was a crucial restriction in a state that, from the 1840s on, took in thousands of Irish, Italian, and French-Canadian immigrants to man its burgeoning industries. In 1888, voting rights were extended to the foreign-born if they owned property, and to the native-born even if they didn't. Again, however, there was an important restriction: To vote, the propertyless and the foreign-born had to register four months before an election, and they could not vote at all "upon any proposition to impose a tax or the expenditure of money."

The safety and eminence of the College Hill families was assured by other constitutional means as well. The governor was popularly elected but also, having no veto, quite powerless. At the same time, until the very end of my great-grandfather's political career, election to both houses of the General Assembly was governed by rules that assured maximum representation of the small, conservative, and solidly Republican towns and villages, at the expense of the growing, increasingly appetitive, and soon solidly Democratic populations of the cities. In the lower house, for example, the rules stipulated that while each town should have at least one representative, none could have more than one sixth the total membership, and this last was fixed at seventy-two. It was the same in the state senate, where the town of Little Compton, for example, with fifty-eight registered voters (in 1900), had the same representation as the city of Providence, with over twenty thousand voters.

For my great-grandfather, these conditions were almost perfect. One of his "ideal creations" (and I suspect the most cherished) had always been the dream that he might one day find himself, as he put it, "above the reach of circumstance, above the whirlwind of common passion." Not for a long time now has any sane man gone into American politics with a dream like that. But in Rhode Island for about fifteen years on either side of 1900, it seemed a feasible thing to do— at least for a United States senator, a Republican, and a man devoutly disposed to further the interests and foster the values of the leading citizens of his state. For such a man, the laws of politics could provide as sure and permanent a lift above the tumult of circumstance and common passion as the marketplace, with its "unscrupulous laws of business," ever could. The laws of politics placed his position, not even in the hands of a restricted number of voters, but in their representatives, the even more restricted number of assemblymen and senators in whom the federal Constitution (until 1913) vested the power to elect senators.

As my great-grandfather saw it, so far as I can tell at this distance, there were only two flaws in the arrangement. One was that he had a large and growing family, refined and imperious tastes, and very little money relative to his needs. This circumstance, as he took his seat in the Senate for the first time in 1881, he probably felt he could someday correct. But the other flaw was not so easily dealt with. This was that the whole constitutional apparatus he counted on to hold him aloft among "the honor'd number," like Rome's senators in *Coriolanus,* was not really all that dependable. Not only did it have to be shored up by an extraconstitutional political machine but the machine had to be extensively lubricated by bribes.

My great-grandfather, like many of his descendants, was a fastidious man—a prematurely fastidious man, I'm tempted to say. Indeed, he said it himself. "Oh, if I could only paint in words the visions that have passed before me during this one day," he wrote from Europe, where in the fullness of his success he loved to voyage. "If I could only catch and retain in tangible form the inspired life that has filled and surrounded me. Never before have I—as during these few days in Rome—lived so little in the present, the real." But immediately he corrected this wild abandon of his heart and forcibly reminded himself of harsher, more importunate claims on his imagination: "I have not,

I trust, forgotten my duties and relations to the few loved ones, to whom alone my thoughts and doings are of consequence. I know at best the dream is a short one. At home . . . I would have no right, *could not afford,* such dreams." We could, his descendants; but not he, not back there in little old Rhode Island.

Still, it may have offended him that the votes of at least twenty of the thirty-eight towns and cities whose representatives sent him to the Senate for thirty years could be bought outright or be decisively influenced by bribery. The polity was so corrupt that when in 1903 the governor issued a well-researched, evenhanded denunciation of both parties, the report was received by the General Assembly with no more alarm than if it had been written by the janitor. "In a considerable number [of towns and cities]," the governor said, "bribery is so common and has existed for so many years that the awful nature of the crime has ceased to impress. In some towns . . . the money paid to the voter, whether two, five, or twenty dollars, is spoken of as 'payment for time.'" It sometimes happened, in fact, that when an overconfident party manager would keep the bribe money for other purposes, or himself, the citizenry would rise up in rebellion. One town's voters were so enraged by a failure to pay them for their time that they elected a prohibitionist.

The best Senator Aldrich could do about this squalid situation was to keep it at a comfortable remove from himself. In Washington, tending to great affairs of state, he let General Brayton, the Republican machine's boss, handle the sordid details of the voters' market. Even patronage distressed him. As early as 1883, he refused to have anything to do with the award of postmasterships. To news of some sort of patronage squabble in Olneyville, he high-mindedly replied that he would "have to insist upon preserving the strict neutrality which I have hitherto maintained in this matter; and I feel sure that the slightest distraction from it now would be destructive of my peace of mind."

My forebear's noble disdain for the unattractive machinery that maintained him in office might have been no more than hypocrisy, except for one thing: it went hand in hand with a loathing for those whom the machinery exploited—the poor. Very early in life, there had worked its way into his sensibility an unmistakable fear of and repugnance for those he'd left behind him in his drive for success. Once, still in his twenties, he went back to East Killingly to attend a memorial service for a cousin who had died in Libby Prison. What my great-grandfather was doing at the service—or his cousin was doing in prison, for that matter—I would love to know. In the church where he'd gone as a boy, the old Calvinism and the new Darwinism came together in a vision of just what he'd been saved from, the origins from which he had evolved. His mother had told him the wherefore of his life; now he realized the whence, and it was grim.

> It was in the old church all unchanged since the days when my youthful self sat bolt upright upon its hard board seats, and heard with fearful wonder—without understanding—the unsparing denunciation of sin and emphatic warnings of the eternal punishment that threatened all sinners. . . . All except the church had changed. I knew hardly any one. Those which I had known as boys and girls were fathers and mothers; many prematurely old, most unmistakably entering into that dreary monotony of drudgery and toil from which they never could emerge.

"From which they never could emerge . . ." The phrase has the ring of a performative utterance, as though Calvin's God and Darwin's Nature are both proclaiming that the great mass of mankind is doomed to remain forever undistinguished and indistinguishable, anonymous, deformed, and hopeless, stirring only to labor, to couple, and to reproduce. Naturally, it was a necessary corollary of the people's fate—or so the Senator's ideal creation might have it—that the elect, the fittest to survive, should have a higher, nobler one. Just as it was the end of generations of most men to pass their days and years in drudgery and toil, so it was the end of a few men—and their descendants—to pass their days in happiness, above the clutch of contingency, far from the common anxieties of mere survival. For my great-grandfather, history was as teleological an affair as it is for any faithful Christian or Marxist. What the Senator believed was that history, evolution, and a saving grace found their end in him and in men like him, in his family and in families like his, down to the close of time.

There was a price to be paid for this historical salvation, and it was vigilance—vigilance, above all, against the resentment of those who never could emerge. Great-grandfather Aldrich had a dread of revolution. In Paris once (probably visiting my grandfather, who was studying architecture at the École des Beaux-Arts at the time), the Senator saw two men "of the middle or lower class" drinking absinthe in a café. That evening he wrote: "As I looked upon their dull wild stupor I wondered what dreams were evolved from the depths of the bitter glass. Multiply that scene and you have the possibility of the wildest revolution or the most terrible outrages." This demophobia, compounded of God knows what mixture of reason, anxiety, and guilt—survivor guilt, as we would say—was a commonplace of the day, and quite as virulent among the Senator's ideological enemies as it was among his friends and would-be friends in history's select class. Especially after the 1840s, when for imaginative purposes the Yankee poor practically vanished in the Irish, Italian, Jewish, and other ethnic poor, so-called Progressive novelists like Jack London and David Graham Phillips conjured visions of the urban mob that were identical to my great-grandfather's—identical, for that matter, to the visions in Henry Adams's *Education* or Mark Twain's novels and travelogues. Repeatedly, these writers evoked the poor in metaphors of disgust: in "hordes" and "swarms" of racked and verminous creatures, scarcely human except in their capacity to nurse a grievance. My family's founder had nothing original to add to this picture, only a lively sense of their shameless, insatiable (and wretchedly unreliable) purchasability.

It followed that Senator Nelson W. Aldrich, a politician in a democracy, had never, in any sense of the word, to be democratic. Nelson Aldrich Rockefeller may have seen in his forebear "a great man with the people," but the first Nelson W. Aldrich was *not* a great man with the people; he abhorred the people. In 1881, just elected to the Senate, he was cornered by a minion of the New York *Tribune*. The reporter wrote: "He has brilliant dark eyes which he fastens closely upon the person with whom he is conversing. His manners are genial and attractive." All that was true. Strikingly good-looking as a youth, well over six feet tall, with black hair and fine, balanced features, he grew into a man of imposing presence, with a flowing handlebar mustache and an erect posture. He was also intelligent, discreet, and reasonable. He had humor and charm. Just as important, he had an unequaled mastery of the minutiae of the nation's economic business. For thirty years, as chairman of the Senate Finance Committee, he was the principal author of all tariff legislation—the instrument of government economic policy in those days before taxes and the Federal Reserve. Yet for a long time the *Tribune* had said all there was to say, or all that was publicly available to say, about my family founder. "No, don't ask me any questions," the new senator had told the reporter, "let's talk about something else." For the next thirty years, he never gave a public speech outside the Senate, never gave interviews to the press, and seldom even wrote a letter. The conduct of the public's business, in my great-grandfather's view, was none of its business.

The only public whose company the first Nelson W. Aldrich ever sought, whose counsel he considered, or whose interests he chose to advance was the public of the "emerged": the patrician families of College Hill and their peers who existed in every well-established city in the nation. Primary among them was the man whom he admired over all others, J. P. Morgan. In Senator Aldrich's view, Morgan's great labor to bring order, reason, and gentlemanly cooperation to the country's chaotic, often ruinous industrial growth was a labor of history, as proper in means and certain in ends as the teleological evolution of families that brought Aldriches to College Hill and Morgans (a generation earlier) to the heights of Hartford, London, and New York. What history was accomplishing through Morgan was an oligopoly of superior wealth-producing institutions for an oligarchy of patrician men. It was Senator Aldrich's task to help these men and institutions by protecting them from troublesome free-market competition from abroad, and from rivalrous assertions of governmental power at home. He did help them, indispensably. He included them in every step of the painstaking process of legislation, going over every detail of the tariff schedules, any one of which meant millions of dollars gained or lost for an emergent monopoly, or "trust." The last step, steering the bill through Congress, he took himself. In the genre of politics he preferred—a politics of private consultation and discreet negotiation, as between men of honor—he was unsurpassed: competitive, delighting in feint and infighting, but generous in victory and forgiving in defeat. He was a consummate parliamentarian and a calculating student of human nature. "In pursuing personal power," a recent student of his career has written, "few men were more dedicated, and no one had a more sensitive feeling for drawing it from other men's self-interest."

For ten years, he must have thought that his ideal creation had come close to reality. He had power. He was free. There were times when he thought himself safe. He had as well the gratitude of the men and institutions whose interests he protected so paternally. One lobbyist wrote to ask for his portrait: "I should like to frame it where the wool manufacturers can look upon the features of the man who has done more services, in a more effective way, in their behalf, than any other man, living or dead." My forefather was a father of industries, of fortunes and empires without number! He should have been happy.

But then, in 1892, he announced that he would not seek reelection. The weaker reason was that the "disturbances to his peace of mind" back home in Rhode Island were increasing. He was being maintained in office by a mercifully distant but exceedingly unattractive "traffic" in votes. It was rather like what might happen in a family business— a laxative manufacturer, say—part of whose profits are deployed in support of the worthy endeavors and high social position of the family's favorite son, when more and more often this favorite son gets word from his asset managers that the business is losing market share. There was an irony in this. If Senator Aldrich's protective paternalism had borne fruit in growing industries, the fruit was now attracting "swarms" of industrial laborers, most of whom were being lured into the rival enterprise of Senator Aldrich's political enemies. In short, the Republican "traffic" in votes was under increasing competitive pressure from the Democratic "traffic," with unhappy consequences for my forebear's tranquillity.

The stronger reason for his decision had to do with another sort of asset—dollars and cents, the banal stuff with which the vulgar masses count *Success!* The Senator hadn't enough of it. By 1892, he was the father of eight children and the owner of two houses, one in Washington, the other at some felicitous address on College Hill. He had also acquired an almost Morgan-like taste for Old World *objets* and Old World travel. All this was very costly. This most reticent of men went so far as to confide in a Rhode Island businessman, Marsden J. Perry, that he was resigning from the Senate because his "independent" income, the income from his equity in the grocery business and the bank, was no more than $3,600 a year. (His salary as a U.S. senator was $5,000.)

Whatever his income, his confidence in Perry proved well-placed. The Senator was soon the recipient of a tantalizing offer from a small group of Rhode Island businessmen, Perry among them. (Another, as it happens, was another of my great-grandfathers, William Greene Roelker, a lawyer and state senator, who was a descendant of lusty Obadiah and my mother's maternal grandfather.) Briefly, what the Perry group proposed was to bring some order—that is to say, monopoly—to the rats' nest of independent street-railway companies in Rhode Island. The group needed Senator Aldrich's blessing. The new "trust," eventually called the United Traction and Electric Company (UTE), would require the cooperation of the state legislature to extend the long-term franchises and tax breaks needed for assured profits, and

Senator Aldrich, through General Brayton, controlled the state legislature. It would only be fitting, then, and a wonderful answer to my great-grandfather's need for lucrative employment, if, after his retirement, the Senator would assume the presidency of the new company.

What happened next was widely suspected at the time. Indeed, because of what happened, Senator Aldrich suffered a series of intense public exposures at the hands of muckrakers, Lincoln Steffens and David Graham Phillips among them, which cost him and his family much painful embarrassment. That they did not cost him any more than that—his social standing or his senatorial seat—can be explained only by the profound privacy in which he managed his affairs. It was impenetrable. Consequently, the charges against him could never be documented.

Now they have been. (Not by me, I hasten to admit, but by Jerome Sternstein, a historian at Brooklyn College.) What happened, first, was that one of the monopolies most dependent on Senator Aldrich's paternal concerns, the American Sugar Refining Company, better known as the Sugar Trust, took alarm at the impending loss of its most powerful political patron. Learning of the UTE offer, an agent of the Sugar Trust devised a scheme by which my family founder could share in the equity of the new company without having to give up his Senate seat. The agent, according to Sternstein, agreed to provide my great-grandfather (both my great-grandfathers, actually, and their partners) with up to $7 million in cash, the money to be used in the purchase and electrification of four profitable but inefficient horse-drawn trolley companies in and around Providence. The money would be paid back in forty-year, 5 percent bonds issued by UTE.

As the years went by, stock in the company did reasonably well, with the result that Senator Aldrich, having laid out no money of his own (not having had any), was soon worth many millions of dollars. At his death, these assets would come to something like $16 million, a magnificent accumulation for a full-time politician in that era. But they did not reach that height without further dubious exertions of his senatorial power. In 1902, the new millionaire was able to acquire some longed-for liquidity with the sale of UTE to the United Gas and Improvement Company, a holding company controlled by the Philadelphia traction magnates W. L. Elkins and P.A.B. Widener. What he didn't take in cash he took in stock; by 1906, when the stock of United Gas and Improvement was languishing and sale was in order, it was arranged through the good offices of Mr. Morgan's bank that Rhode

Island's trolley systems would be bought by the New Haven Railroad. This was not fortuitous. For some time, the relationship between Senator Aldrich and the bank had been close to the point of intimacy. A letter from a Morgan partner, Henry P. Davison, strikes the right tone:

> The enclosed refers to the stock of the Bankers Trust Company, of which you have been allotted one hundred shares. You will be called upon for payment of $40,000.... It will be a pleasure for me to arrange this for you if you would like to have me do so. I am particularly pleased to have you have this stock, as I believe it will give a good account of itself. It is selling today on the basis of little more than $500 a share. I hope, however, you will see fit to put it away, as it should improve with seasoning. Do not bother to read through the enclosed, unless you desire to do so. Just sign your name and return to me.

With the New Haven Railroad deal, however, my forebear seems to have acted with less nonchalance than this letter implies was his custom. Several years later, when the railroad was tottering (among other reasons because of bad investments), its president was summoned before an investigating committee and asked why he had paid such an unconscionably high price for United Gas and Improvement stock. Charles Mellen shrugged. "I was dealing with Nelson W. Aldrich," he said. "Do you think I got the stock at par?"

This was the sort of thing, quite as much as his patronage of monopoly and the "trusts," that caused my great-grandfather to become, along with his co-father-in-law John D. Rockefeller, one of the most vilified men in America. The story of the loan he took from the Sugar Trust appeared in *The New York Times* on 20 June 1894, under the headline:

SENATOR ALDRICH AND SUGAR
THE REPUBLICAN TARIFF LEADER OWNED BY THE TRUST
INDEBTED TO IT FOR FINANCIAL AID

Thereafter hardly a year passed without an article appearing in the reform-minded middle-class monthlies, going over the same data contained in the *Times* story. Typical of the rhetoric Senator Aldrich inspired in Progressive circles during the last twenty years of his career was an article by David Graham Phillips—called, crudely enough,

"The Head of It All"—published in *Cosmopolitan* magazine in April 1906. It began:

> He was born in 1841, is only sixty-four years old, good for another fifteen years at least, in his present rugged health, before the "interests" will have to select another for his safe seat and treacherous task.... In 1901, his daughter married the only son and destined successor of John D. Rockefeller. Thus, the chief exploiter of the American people is closely allied by marriage with the chief schemer in the service of their exploiters.... Before he reached the Senate, Aldrich had fifteen years of training in how to legislate the proceeds of the labor of the many into the pockets of the few. He entered it as the representative of the local interests engaged in robbing by means of slyly worded tariff schedules that changed protection against the foreigner into plunder of the native. His demonstrated talents for sly, slippery work in legislative chambers and committee rooms, and his security in his seat against popular revulsion and outbursts, together marked him for the position of chief agent of the predatory band which was rapidly forming to take care of the property of the American people.... Aldrich is rich and powerful. Treachery has brought him wealth and rank, if not honor, of a certain sort. He must laugh at us, grown-up fools, permitting a handful to blind the might of our eighty millions and to set us all to work for them.

Reading such passages, I wonder how my ancestor could stand them. Privileged creature that I am—attentive, indeed morbidly so, to the resonance of my conduct, its honor and weight in the world—it seems to me almost unimaginable that he could have carried on even a very *private* public life after acquiring a reputation such as that. I'm sure he managed to oppose the rhetoric of Progressives with his own rhetoric of teleological evolution. Still, he had to have known that much of the animus behind the attacks on him rested on a belief that was not so easily dismissed—especially by someone whose patrician destiny had lain for him like a sword in a stone. This was the belief that public office in a republic should not be used for private, material gain. This he had done, and I wondered how he could carry on with the knowledge that he had done it, and that people *knew* he had done it.

First, he must have known how very forgiving—or, what often amounts to the same thing, forgetting—America is with respect to its

Successes! He was a hero of the great American revolution, after all: the revolution that gets written in autobiographies, not histories; the revolution against the dead hand of the past that lies on each individual; the revolution that frees all Americans to make themselves *new* (if they can); the revolution, finally, that his so-called Progressive lower-middle-class enemies wanted so fervently to bring about in their own affairs. Of course, a quirk in his understanding of his past enabled him to see himself as in some sense the inheritor of his rightful place in the world—he who was the descendant of governors and founders—as well as the maker of it. This perspective may even have helped him redefine the money he took as merely an unexpected dividend on a legacy he'd done nothing to earn. To have claimed that he'd earned it, of course, would have been to admit that he'd been bribed—unacceptable conduct in a patrician. But regardless of how he saw his own story, as an heir's or as a self-made man's, he benefited, and perhaps expected to benefit, from the forgiving obscurity with which the New World shrouds the origins and protects the decencies of its New Men.

More decisively, there was a great overriding purpose to his career that must have been especially helpful, above all in his later years, as he bore up under his odious reputation. This purpose was not a paternal nurture of the nation's industrial might, nor was it the institution of a central banking system—the proto–Federal Reserve about which Nelson and Michael Rockefeller wrote their senior theses. (The latter scheme did occupy a great deal of his time from 1909 to 1912, and he was happy enough that throughout the many drafts of the plan it bore his name. In the end, however, his association with it had to be publicly denied. By 1912, his fame and power lay in such tatters, even in his own party, that Nicholas Murray Butler, the Columbia University president who was his friend and fellow Republican, felt bound to tell him that his name could no longer appear on the plan. In a sense, this was perfectly fitting: whatever contribution to the Federal Reserve system historians, or Rockefellers, may judge my forebear to have made, it will remain strictly private.) Private goods were what he valued most, and it was a private good that claimed most of his love and attention in the last years of his life. In fact, according to the family-authorized biographer, this good had been claiming his love and attention almost from the beginning:

Aldrich's absorption in his family was the basis in part of a purpose that was pointing to a far but sure objective. He wanted to found an

estate. His family feeling, his love of beautiful things, and an innate
class sense which was always strong in him, combined to give him a
fondness for the figure of a country gentleman. As far back as 1869,
he had fixed upon the location of his dream. Some day he would
own an estate on Warwick Neck. Years were yet to pass before that
lovely site was occupied by the house, the garden, the spacious living
of his country seat, Indian Oaks. But all that, though an unfulfilled
desire was a clearly perceived desire while the natural aristocrat was
hard at work learning the ways of Congress. . . .

What this "innate class sense" was is clear enough: a keen appreciation of "estate" in the full sense of the word. No nineteenth-century
natural aristocrat, certainly not one who had discovered his "nature"
by reading *A Tinker's Son* and his "aristocracy" by reading Scott, could
have failed to note that a man's status is closely connected with his
proprietary holdings. Status and estate, height and heft: they went
together. The estate that my great-grandfather built proclaimed him
at least a baron. It was (it still is) a ninety-nine-room château, reminis-
cent of Fontainebleau, but done in grim granite and slate, with a se-
verity of adornment that makes it seem less a château than a castle.
The whole estate, in fact, seems designed to withstand siege. Protected
by Narragansett Bay on one side, it was everywhere else encircled by
an iron fence, and all the necessaries of life were secured within. The
Senator had his own water tower and raised his own food; all provisions were collected in the barn, then carried by underground railway
to the main house. On the entire vast holding there were only two
points of delight, to my taste, both of them designed by my beloved
grandfather: one the water tower, a delicate obelisk covered in ivy,
from which the Senator might have surveyed, beyond the impenetrable
fastness of his landed estate, the entire extent of his estate in votes; the
other the ten-room boathouse, which looks rather like a collection of
Grandpa's best charrettes at the Beaux-Arts (not surprisingly, as he
designed the building while still a student). It was here that the baron
preferred to conduct—informally, privately—what we would call the
public business. "Here," gushed a writer for *Country Life* in 1919, a
few years after the Senator's death, "were held conferences with his
closest friends and colleagues; here too were enjoyed unsung but productive . . . gatherings which helped those in authority to bear the
burdens and carry on the tasks of their offices. . . . the very walls whisper of the state secrets they have heard, of decisions that have helped
mold the political fate of the world."

But there was more to my forebear's "innate class sense" than an appreciation of the imperative congruity of status and estate, the spatial dimension, so to speak, of one's social standing. He had an equally fine appreciation of the imperative of a standing in time. He might, after all, have chosen to found his estate in Newport. But Senator Aldrich felt about Newport much as Henry James did, that since the Civil War it had become a theater of "new" aristocracy whose "errors" were pitilessly exposed—"flaunted" might be the better word—in "the full modern glare." He was not an aristocrat, except perhaps in the "natural" sense. He was a patrician, and as such abhorred the careless swagger of the aristocrat and the provocative allure of his lady, almost as much as he abhorred the squalor and potential violence of the poor. Thus my family founder chose to establish his place several miles up Narragansett Bay from Newport, in an area that for more than a hundred years had offered "seats" to Rhode Island's oldest, most eminent families—Hoppins, Larneds, Russells, Utleys, Woods, Clarks, many of them governors of the state and leaders of the church. As early as the 1860s, he had begun buying up property as it came on the market, assembling the land carefully, lot by lot, as he might put together support for a tariff bill.

But much more lovingly. For it was here, firmly rooted in the land, carefully established on the plane of time, that my family founder determined to found his family. It was as though he'd brought some sacred fire to that place—a fire first kindled, to be sure, in his mother's imagination—and there resolved to keep it burning "above the reach of circumstance, above the whirlwind of common passion." He said as much in his will, in which the trustees of his estate were directed to

> keep the buildings ... in good order and repair ... to keep the walls, gates, drives, walks, and wharf in good condition; to care properly for the trees, shrubs, vines, plants, lawns, and renew the same from time to time; to maintain the water system on said estate; to heat the buildings thereon, and light them and the walks and drives; to operate the greenhouses and purchase supplies of all kinds, and generally to keep up and improve said estate ...

for twelve years, after which the trust could be broken and the property liquidated and divided up among his heirs.

Twelve years only? Reading his will, I ponder that figure. For of course it is a major part of my *pietas,* such as it has become, that I, the fourth of his line, should have one day "come into" this great estate. Twelve years was hardly enough time to have given even my father a crack at it, never mind me.

But such thoughts may only go to show that I am deficient where Aldriches (and some Rockefellers) are well endowed—in the social imagination of the family. "I express the hope," my great-grandfather concluded his will, "that my estate may continue in the possession of some members or member of my family." It was simply unimaginative of me to presume that the "estate" he had in mind here for his living posterity was exhausted in the land, buildings, and walls of his property. There was money, a more liquid estate but no less inviting to the social imagination; and there was status, some part of which is a play of that imagination on money. Money and status—more of the latter than of the former—remained in the possession of his family, and his money and status, along with his name, came down to me. Enough for *pietas,* and enough, too, to impose an obligation of *pietas,* which is to understand the "estate" I have inherited.

CHAPTER TWO

The Composition of Old Money

Next evening while he waited for her to come downstairs, Dexter peopled the soft deep summer room ... with the men who had already loved Judy Jones. He knew the sort of men they were—the men who when he first went to college had entered from the great prep schools with graceful clothes and the deep tan of healthy summers. He had seen that, in one sense, he was better than these men. He was newer and stronger. Yet in acknowledging to himself that he wished his children to be like them he was admitting that he was but the rough, strong stuff from which they eternally sprang.

F. Scott Fitzgerald, "Winter Dreams"

THE ESTATE I INHERITED from Great-grandfather Aldrich (among other forebears, not all of them so *nouveau* as he, but most of them quite as *riche*) may be described as Old Money. The epithet has at least the merit of being familiar, and of pointing to two major compositional elements that figure in most people's descriptions of an estate: wealth and time.

Wealth and time are alike, of course, in being almost perfectly abstract, and therefore wonderfully susceptible to the free play of a needy imagination. Old Money's wealth, for example, is notoriously elastic, sometimes expanding with pride or stupidity, sometimes shrinking with apprehension—of moochers, the market, or the richer. I remember lunching with a friend at one of his New York clubs, the Brook, and asking him what difference his inherited wealth had made

in his life. That it had made a difference seemed obvious to me: At
the very least, it had enabled him to establish himself as a writer without having to worry about meals, rent, and the costs of foreign travel.
"*Me?*" he yelped, looking about him with terror. "Good heavens, *I'm*
not rich!" Following his glance around the Brook Club table, laden
with an imperial ton of Georgian silver, surrounded by inheritors and
makers of fortunes much greater than his, I saw that under the circumstances my friend's hot denial was altogether plausible. In other
circumstances, it would have been sheer nonsense.

Time, the social antiquing required for New Money to become
Old, is almost equally elastic. I cannot say when, or even whether, the
first Nelson W. Aldrich considered himself to have "arrived" at the
patrician status he believed his birthright; my guess is that his position
was always a little shaky, even in his own eyes. It didn't matter: in the
eyes of most of his countrymen, even in the eyes of College Hill and
in Mr. Morgan's eyes, time began with his children. Yet it's a peculiarity
of this aging process that having begun with the offspring, it may run
so fast and powerfully that it pulls the parents along with it. This
phenomenon, outstandingly but not exclusively American, is known
as climbing up on the backs of one's children; and in my great-
grandfather's case it had astonishing results. In E. Digby Baltzell's influential *The Protestant Establishment,* for example, the son of indolent
Anan the mill hand is said to have been a "Brahmin." Peter Collier
and David Horowitz even go so far, in their best-selling account of
the Rockefeller dynasty, as to credit the Senator's mythic descent
from Winthrops and Williamses for John D. Rockefeller's odd conviction that in marrying my great-aunt Abby, his son John D., Jr., was
marrying *up.*

But there are other circumstances and purposes, for which the time
it takes to create Old Money just won't run fast enough. My dear
grandfather William, for instance, always seemed to me when I was a
boy the essence of what his father had not been—a Brahmin, indeed
a Boston Brahmin. The list of his clubs went on for inches in the Social
Register; his trusteeships were many and distinguished; old Beacon
Hill families and old Brattle Street families alike accorded him affec-
tion and respect. Then one day, when we had a brief exchange about
my future and I told him that after Harvard I planned to go and live
in France for a while, as he had done, he replied, "Well, I hope you'll
come back to Boston. Boston, the people here, they've been very good
to me. They will be to you too." The look of abject gratitude on his

face was horribly incongruous with the rather grand and acerbic character of the man I loved. I suddenly felt very queasy.

Time or wealth, "oldness" or richness of family—the question frequently comes up in Old Money circles as to which of these elements in people's perceptions of the class is the more important. To me, the answer has always been time: certainly now that time has left so little wealth in my own social portrait. Of course, there has to have been wealth. Without some intelligible, socially persuasive, and above all inheritable asset, there would be nothing for the imagination to work on, nothing to grow old. But once the wealth has been there, for perception, it needn't go on being there. Indeed, it must not go on being there; it must retire discreetly behind the veil of time and disappear like the Cheshire cat, leaving a smile. It is another good question— nervously discussed, in fact—how long a smile can be sustained without material substance behind it. But again the answer seems obvious enough: forever, so long as the cat knows, if only subliminally, that the social and aesthetic value of his smile is of economic value, and that he must not neglect it. Time, even Old Money time, can be money.

There is a very good reason for time to be, so to speak, pictorially dominant in the composition of Old Money. Time has always had to carry a large part of the rhetorical burden of justifying the key institution that makes Old Money possible—the inheritance of wealth. Inherited wealth is an especially egregious, because wholly unearned, source of inequality. Even in its purest, most abstract condition, where it does nothing for its inheritor but make him or her more money, wealth confers a certain superiority. At the very least, it confers an invidious distinction. But such inequalities do not for long go unquestioned in modern societies: certainly not in the New World. Here in America, inherited wealth must legitimate itself, and time, as often as not, is called upon to provide the legitimacy. Of course, time plays no part in the legal defense of the institution, except insofar as the property right at the heart of it, the testamentary freedom to dispose of one's property after death, is time-honored. But this legal defense exists within a cultural one, within a moral-aesthetic argument for inherited wealth, and for this argument time is the key.

Whether in my great-grandfather's generation, with Social Darwinism riding high on a moralized Calvinism, or three generations later, with much the same views still ascendant in what is called neoconservatism, "cultural" apologists for inherited wealth have persistently taken the same line: that inherited wealth, money that doesn't

have to be earned, buys its beneficiaries time—time away from the
exigencies of the marketplace in selves as well as goods and services,
time in which to cultivate "higher" values, which advance the cause of
civilization. William Graham Sumner, Yale's great expositor of Herbert Spencer's vision of Darwinism, put the argument for the Senator's
generation:

> A man of inherited wealth can gain in youth all the advantages
> which are essential to high culture, and which a man who must first
> earn the capital cannot attain until he is almost past the time of life
> for profiting from them.... hereditary wealth is the strongest in-
> strument by which we keep up a steadily advancing civilization.

The same view has been expressed more recently by Friedrich von
Hayek, the Austrian-born University of Chicago economist, who is a
favorite of American neoconservatives. They like his uncompromising
stand against the "serfdom" of state-sponsored public welfare, his re-
sourceful defense of a political economy of sink-or-swim freedom, but
they like even more the civilized understanding that he brings to the
conservative cause. Von Hayek appears like a blessing of Old World
realism on New World idealism:

> There is, indeed, good reason to think that there are some socially
> valuable qualities which will be rarely acquired in a single genera-
> tion but which will generally be formed only by the continuous ef-
> forts of two or three. Granted this, it would be unreasonable to deny
> that society is likely to get a better elite if ascent is not limited to one
> generation, if individuals are not deliberately made to start from the
> same level, and if children are not deprived of the chance to benefit
> from the better education and material environment which their
> parents may be able to provide.... Many people who agree that the
> family is desirable as an instrument for the transmission of morals,
> tastes, and knowledge still question the desirability of the transmis-
> sion of material property. Yet there can be little doubt that, in order
> that the former may be possible, some continuity of standards, of
> the external forms of life, is essential, and that this will be achieved
> only if it is possible to transmit not only immaterial but material
> advantages.

One weakness of these arguments is that they leave unanswered
the question of why on earth individuals, not members of von Hayek's

"better" elite, or Sumner's "instrument . . .[of] advancing civilization," should acquiesce in the existence of such a class. One answer—that they might aspire to join it—was given in the mildest, most tactful tones by my great-grandfather's distinguished contemporary Charles W. Eliot, the true Boston Brahmin (also, through his father's bankruptcy, a penniless one), who built Harvard from a provincial college into a great national university. Unsurprisingly, Eliot understood Old Money as exerting—very likely through such institutions as Harvard—a beneficent, educational influence on the rest of society.

> The family, rather than the individual, is the important social unit. If society as a whole is to gain by mobility and openness of structure, those who rise must stay up in successive generations, that the higher level of society may be constantly enlarged, and that the proportion of pure, gentle, magnanimous, and refined persons may be steadily increased. New-risen talent should reinforce the upper ranks. . . . The assured permanence of superior families is quite as important as the free starting of such families.

In short, society has two great interests to promote: One is economic, roughly speaking, and concerns the encouragement of "new-risen talent," including presumably the talent of making money. The other is cultural, the "refinement" of that new-risen talent through the influence of virtuous families—families, Eliot strongly implied, that attain their virtues (purity, gentleness, magnanimity, and the like) because they are allowed to "stay up" over many generations, over time.

Implicit in all this, of course, is a critique of whatever goings-on these Old Money families are supposed to stay above. Eliot delicately refrained from describing these activities. Henry Dwight Sedgwick did not. The scion of a very old Old Money family (whose most celebrated member was Edie, the Pop tragedienne of the 1960s), Sedgwick was a contemporary and friend of my grandfather's. In the 1930s, he wrote an apology (also a lament) for Old Money called *In Praise of Gentlemen,* which turned on an argument of Matthew Arnold's:

> Again and again I have said how the refinement of an aristocracy may be precious and educative to a raw nation . . . how its severity and dignified freedom from petty cares may serve as a useful foil to set off the vulgarity and hideousness of that type of life which a hard middle class tends to establish, and to help people see their vulgarity and hideousness in their true colors.

This may seem rather harsh stuff for an American to cite, still harsher to believe. With one stroke Sedgwick condemned the central worldly enterprise of nine tenths of his countrymen—all of whom, in that Depression era, would have been overjoyed to consider themselves engaged in a "hard middle class" type of life—to an existence of unqualified and contemptible ugliness. There have always been Old Money men in America, and some women, who are not afraid to call a pearl a pearl, and a swine a swine.

In my generation, the most noteworthy defense of Old Money in this vein was written by the man who conferred Brahmin status on my great-grandfather. E. Digby Baltzell is a member of an Old Family, and in *The Protestant Establishment* he takes on two tasks. One is to show that Old Money is what he calls a "caste"—that is, a class self-segregated by religion and ethnicity, and stubbornly closed to all out-siders, especially Jews, no matter how brilliant their "new-risen talent." Rather like President Eliot, whose words above he cites, Baltzell seems to believe that societies do well to strike a bargain with their ascendant families, according to which the ascendant will be allowed to stay "up," so long as they continue to make room for, and cast their benign influ-ence upon, the families who rise "up" after them. In this way, not only will the general tone of society be uplifted but established families will acquire the reinforcements of money and talent they need to remain, as it were, uplifting.

In some versions of this scheme, the educative contribution of the class is described as a kind of social discipline. Baltzell does not dwell on this, since it approaches too closely a justification of the door-slamming "exclusiveness" he deplores. But in the previous generation, this disciplinary function of the upper class was heartily approved by Herbert Pell, a leading New Deal Democrat of ancient lineage and vast riches, and the father of Rhode Island's current senior senator, Claiborne Pell. Herbert Pell's views of the hard hustle and hump of middle-class life may be judged from a story still told about him: that when a favorite niece of his one day joyfully announced that her new husband had at last found a job, Uncle Bertie replied, "Oh, my dear, I'm so sorry." The great gift of the gift of inherited wealth, in Pell's view, was freedom, and freedom ought to be put to better use—public service, for example—than holding down a "job." Moreover, Pell was confident that many unfortunate jobholders desired nothing so much, at the end of their tedious lives, as to join the company and enjoy the opportunities of the hereditarily free. And this desire, he argued, could be turned to the advantage of society as a whole. In a 1933 essay, Pell wrote: "When a man realizes that, if his career has been one of dishonesty, neither he nor his sons will be admitted to reputable clubs or to good society, he will probably be content to leave his children a smaller fortune and a better reputation."

Whether this discipline works is, of course, another question. It didn't work with my great-grandfather in 1892. It didn't work with the investment banker Martin A. Seigel in 1986.

> When it became known that Martin A. Seigel had received one of the many subpoenas issued in connection with the Ivan F. Boesky insider trading scandal last fall, the usually calm and polished Mr. Seigel was furious. The 38-year-old whiz kid investment banker complained vehemently that he was innocent and that a subpoena was standard procedure for a Government investigation. Besides, he fumed, the bad publicity was making it impossible for him to enroll his six-year-old daughter in a prestigious elementary school.

In view of Martin Seigel's story, it might seem that Baltzell's second task in *The Protestant Establishment* would be fairly easy: to show that emergent families are actually in need of uplifting. Baltzell points to more contemporary forms of hideousness and vulgarity than Seigel's. The "newly affluent," he says, lead

> a lonely and rootless expense-account life, centered around the most fashionable cafés of the moment.... pandering to the public becomes an obsession and self-advertisement an elite vice.... pornography has become polite, while vulgarity and smut ... have graduated to the educated classes who now syndicate their honeymoons, send out Christmas cards displaying pictures of themselves posing for beer ads, call hundreds of their "intimate" friends by their first names, and of course are willing and anxious to Tell All, not only on the psychiatrist's couch, but anywhere at all—in the living room and café and over the air.

The tirade, typical of Old Money at its most self-confidently contemptuous, varies from the norm only in allocating some of the blame for this repulsive state of affairs on Old Money people themselves. If the "newly affluent" are lonely, rootless, emotionally incontinent panders, pornographers, and self-publicists, one of the reasons is that Old Money has denied them access to their schools, summer resorts, and

clubs, places where they or their children might have learned to conduct themselves in a fashion more fitting their station in life. In other
words, if the successfully self-made are engaged in "a futile chase without end," as Baltzell says they are, it's because Old Money denied them
a goal, a wherefore for their hard and frantic hustling.

Equally characteristic of the Old Money line of self-legitimation is
Baltzell's description of what this "end" is. It is a kind of social space,
private and secure and well-appointed, resembling a gentlemen's club.
But what is it private, secure, and well-appointed *for?* It is not just to
provide a place for *arrivistes* to arrive. It is for authority, what Baltzell
calls the "privacy of aristocratic authority." (I would quarrel with the
qualifier: "aristocratic" to me suggests a perfect indifference to privacy
and a disdain of security. The aristocracy that he wants for America I
would call a patriciate. The term better captures the contained and
reasonable nature of the authority he seems to admire; it captures, too,
the well-protected, comfortable, and aesthetically agreeable environment he seems to fancy for its exercise.) Baltzell cites Walter Lippmann's piteous description of America's leadership class—as accurate
now, Baltzell believes, as it was in the 1920s, when the older, German-
Jewish Old Money man wrote it:

> They give orders. They have to be consulted. They can more or less
> speak for, and lead some part of, the population. But none of them
> is *seated on a certain throne,* and all of them are forever concerned as
> to how they keep from being toppled off.... They have been edu-
> cated to achieve success; few of them have been educated to exercise
> power. Nor do they count with any confidence upon retaining their
> power, nor in handing it on to their sons. They live, therefore, from
> day to day, and they govern by ear. Their impromptu statements of
> policy may be obeyed, but nobody seriously regards them as having
> *authority.*

This is the ultimate justification of Old Money, as Old Money men
would have everyone understand it: a purchase of generational time
and social space that serves poor, hustling, unattractive middle-class
society as a goal for its labors, a school for its manners, and a quiet,
safe, and pleasant withdrawing room for its authority.

The putative object of New Money's desiring—and of my inheritance whether I desired it or not—was already there by my great-
grandfather's day. It could be seen in the institutions Old Money established to give shape and agency to all this space in time, or time in

space. Old Money exercised guardianship over the distinctive tastes, fashions, and manners of its members in Society, its men's and (far fewer) women's clubs, its boarding schools, and its colonies of country and seashore estates. On those same meeting grounds, it also sought to control its members' friendships and loves. Through its hospitals, clinics, asylums, and churches, the class was pleased to see itself, and its women to some extent to occupy themselves, promoting the welfare of their fellow citizens. Through its schools, colleges, and universities, its museums, orchestras, and operas, the class could believe itself the chief sponsor and custodian of high culture. In the House of Morgan and hundreds of smaller banks in every city, it built patrician towers from which it could direct the investment of the nation's savings—a sizable part of them its own. Those primary institutions were also in place—Old Families and trust funds of Old Family money—by which the class might be maintained in perpetuity: reproducing itself, so to speak, by birth, adoption, and training, and supporting itself by generous and judiciously timed infusions of cash.

Finally, the class managed to breed a deviant, perhaps more truly aristocratic type of person: fearless of the people, high-spirited to the point of recklessness, with a penchant for the open exercise of personal power or the flamboyant display of personal idiosyncrasy, and fated to conflict with the patricians who bred them. Senator Aldrich might have pointed to any number of examples of this (to him) appalling faction within the class he aspired to—from Mr. and Mrs. Bradley Martin, perpetrators of one of the most publicized balls of the 1890s, to Theodore Roosevelt, who appeared to threaten so many of the trusts that had been the object of the Senator's paternal care. Subsequent generations of the patriciate saw even more foolhardy tarantellas danced before the mob, especially in the 1920s, and even fiercer-seeming threats to "the privacy of its authority," from Franklin Delano Roosevelt to John F. Kennedy. As my family founder might have demanded, admirer of Shakespeare that he was: Did they know what they were doing, these aristocrats, to "nourish 'gainst our Senate / The cockle of rebellion, insolence, sedition . . . / By mingling them with us, the honor'd number"?

To anyone brought up in the institutions of this estate, as I was, the most impressive thing about them is how much they really are what Eliot, Baltzell, and the others said they should be—*educational* institutions. Enemies of Old Money, from Andrew Jackson's presidency to Ronald Reagan's, have never tired of accusing its beneficiaries

of trying to subvert New World principles of equal opportunity with
Old World institutions of privilege. "What ... is this American system?" cried Orestes Brownson in Jackson's day. "Is it not the abolition
of all artificial distinctions founded on birth or any other accident, and
leaving every man to stand on his own two feet, for precisely what
God and nature have made him? ... What else is it that we are constantly throwing in the face of the old world?" Almost a century and
a half later, the same sentiments were expressed by Irving Kristol, a
voice of Reaganite neoconservatism as Brownson was a voice of Jacksonian liberalism. Arguing in favor of America's extraordinary com-
placency in the face of huge disparities of personal income—disparities
far greater than those tolerated in most other capitalist countries—
Kristol is at pains to point out that he is concerned only with self-made
income, New Money, not income derived from inherited wealth.
"[I]nherited concentrations of wealth," he solemnly warns, "can pose a
very special problem for a democracy. The primal nightmare of a democracy is the emergence of an oligarchy that would, through the
power associated with wealth, perpetuate itself, and eventually constitute a kind of aristocracy." This nightmare, he suggests, should be
dispelled once and for all: "We should discourage the inheritance of
large fortunes."

Kristol's and Brownson's readings of Old Money's intentions are
perfectly accurate so far as they go. But the most distinctive thing
about the institutional arrangements the Old Rich have established
over the years is not so much their sinister Old World character as
their ingenuous New World hopefulness. Old Money might found
favored boarding schools and colleges on Old World models, stock the
Great American Museum with Old World works of art, people its
imagination with an Old World family romance. Where else, after all,
were they to go for inspiration? But none of these features of the estate
should distract anyone from the profoundly New World purpose behind them, which is to change, to improve, to instruct, to *educate*. In a
sense, Old Money's intentions are just like every other American's.
Americans typically want nothing so much as to make themselves *new*,
an appropriate yearning in this New World. Old Money Americans
simply want to make themselves new in the most radical way a New
World can imagine, by making themselves Old. This requires long and
intensive training. From dancing class to the varied "lessons" of the
country club, the yacht club, and the Grand Tour, from Fay School to

St. Paul's School to Harvard, from the Porcellian Club to the Somerset Club and the Knickerbocker Club, from the summer place at Northeast Harbor, Maine, to the winter place in the firm, at the bank, and, most important, "on the board"—all these stations of Old Money life appear not only as constitutive of the class but instructive of it: as so many courses that have to be taken, so many credentials tested, so many qualifications proclaimed. Before it is a status, *while* it is a status, Old Money is composed of a curriculum.

A beneficiary's sharpest reminder that he or she is engaged in a curriculum is, of course, his or her required presence at certain schools. Old Money, as Senator Aldrich and Martin Seigel both knew, has its own (private) school system, which begins at innumerable "prestigious" elementary schools. It culminates at Harvard, not necessarily the actual university of that name, but a rhetorical "Harvard," Yale, or Princeton, some other college in the Ivy League, a school in the Little Ivy League, Stanford; or whatever college the social imagination may plausibly promote to the prestige of Harvard.

> The next regular step was Harvard College. He was more than glad to go. For generation after generation, Adamses and Brookses and Boylstons and Gorhams had gone to Harvard College, and although none of them, as far as known, had ever done any good there, or thought himself the better for it, custom, social ties, convenience, and, above all, economy, kept each generation on the track. Any other education would have required a serious effort, but no one took Harvard College seriously. All went there because their friends went, and the College was their ideal of social self-respect.

This magnificent nonchalance, even in retrospect, even from an Adams as brilliant (and Old) as Henry, would probably have to be affected today. It was very possibly affected then—the lament of Henry Adams's *Education* being, after all, that generational lines such as his could no longer hold against the new, unattractive energies let loose in America. And indeed there were developments at Harvard, even in Adams's generation, that were beginning to strain the "customs" that saw "generation after generation" of Old Money families following along on the same educational track.

The strain arose, then and now, from tensions between Harvard's two social functions, at least as Eliot defined them: to confirm the standing of Old Families, and to confer that standing on New Families. Since the time of Eliot—also of Henry Adams, who taught there, and of my great-grandfather, who sent one of his sons there—Harvard has understood its duty to Old Money as a duty to the class as a whole rather than to the generations of individual family members whose "custom" it has been to go there. This duty was to provide the class with "new-risen talent": lawyers, doctors, teachers, clergymen, architects; more recently, too, business professionals to help manage their investments, and government professionals to help protect them. Clearly, only a small part of this talent could be supplied out of the ranks of Old Money's descendants. Clearly, too, the class would be better served by greater talents than by lesser. Thus a commitment was made by Harvard's largely Old Money fellows and overseers, prompted by a succession of Old Money presidents, beginning with Eliot, to define talent according to high intellectual standards. High standards, however, mean recruiting teachers whose interest in their studies outweighs their interest in Old Money or its alleged virtues—purity, magnanimity, or whatever. High standards also mean favoring the admission of students whose interest in their studies matches that of their teachers. Here is the source of the strain. Again and again, the college's disposition in favor of the newly talented overrules its disposition in favor of the anciently talented (or rich), thereby each year inevitably derailing scores of Old Money family tracks.

All sorts of people, quite apart from the injured families, deplore this admissions policy. Vulgar ruling-class theorists, for example, are cheated of some empirical corroboration of their theories; fund-raisers in charge of "alumni giving" are frustrated in their tasks; and the hearts of all those who love "custom" for its own sake are grieved. However, Harvard, actual or rhetorical, is unmoved. Like Old Money, it takes a long, multigenerational, historical view of its mission, which reveals that the constant strain of its conflicting obligations to Old and New is constantly being resolved by its powers not just to confirm Old Money status but to confer it on its graduates. In other words, for every Old Money family lost to "custom," to the endowment, and perhaps eventually to the Old Money class itself, a New Family will be gained. For admissions officers, it's all a question of balance: between children of Old Money alumni—whose presence provides significant continuity in the "high" social composition of each entering class—and children of "talent." The actual Harvard has usually fixed that balance at around 20 percent of alumni children. They are called, fittingly enough, "legacies."

The (rhetorical) Harvard's power to confer upper-class standing is very often exaggerated. Norman Podhoretz, for example, has written of his passage through the ivied walls of another Cambridge:

> Aubrey [his servant at Clare College] neither knew nor cared that I was a boy from the provinces of immigrant Brooklyn, a member of roughly the same social class to which he belonged. So far as he was concerned—so far, indeed, as the whole of England seemed to be concerned—I was a Clare man and therefore a "young gentleman" to whom amenities, privilege, and deference were owed as by natural right.... It has been said that it takes three generations to make an aristocrat; my own experience would suggest that about three weeks are enough. That, at any rate, is approximately how long it took for all the [social] anxieties I had brought with me to England ... to evaporate: poof and they were gone.

Podhoretz is naive: It is never a good idea to take one's social credentials from people, like servants and headwaiters, who expect a large tip at the end of one's stay with them. For just as there is more than Harvard in the Old Money curriculum that born-and-bred beneficiaries must go through, so there is *much* more than Harvard in the curriculum that a would-be beneficiary like Podhoretz must go through. Of course, his naïveté very likely has an ideological basis: Neoconservatives who deplore inherited wealth cannot afford to believe in the central Old Money proposition that it takes time away from "making it" (the title of Podhoretz's memoir) to compose the qualifications for membership in the class. Perhaps Podhoretz has to believe in a three-week elevation to the aristocracy because he could not afford the time or the compromise of his ideological principles to believe in a three-generational one.

On the other hand, the "poof" effects of Harvard can also be too quickly discounted. Graduates without social imagination regularly do so; they seem incapable of appreciating the imagistic possibilities of having gone to school with Adamses, Brookses, Boylstons, and the like. Sometimes the poof effects are deliberately underplayed: Kennedys in politics, for example, like to present their "customary" passage through Harvard as a sign, simultaneously, of Old Money status and New Money talent. So do countless other (rhetorical) Harvard graduates; in most social situations, including meetings with the image in the mirror, the combination of merit and class is extremely attractive. But sometimes, too, the poof effects are subject to delayed reaction, as when a "new-risen talent" in early middle age suddenly wakes up to the realization that in the eyes of his colleagues and competitors, in the eyes of his children, in the eyes, even, of his old Old Money Harvard classmates, he is endowed with the flattering or unflattering attributes of people who, in college, he imagined despised him, and whom he despised in return.

Below Harvard in Old Money's educational system is St. Midas, Fitzgerald's name for the New England boarding schools, which I'll extend to "prestigious" elementary schools as well. These schools are in many ways more crucial to the Old Money curriculum than anything except the Old Family, for their influence falls on the child almost as early as the family's does, and perhaps even more decisively. European upper classes (except the English) entrust their posterity to state school systems, believing that their authority over their children, seconded by the inertial stability of the class structure, will prove strong enough to counter any social hazards their children may face at the *lycée* or *Gymnasium*. American Old Money families generally lack that confidence. The family structure is liberal—generously and elaborately "extended," full of proxies and substitutions, nonauthoritarian, and by means of its wealth capable of almost unlimited centrifugal or centripetal movement. Raising children in such a family is a little like throwing dice. Out they go into the world, and what comes up, socially speaking, hinges on whom they fall in with, on elective affinities so obscure they might as well be a matter of pure contingency. This terrible chanciness of the children's prospects lends a peculiar anxiety to what Tocqueville called America's "most imperious necessity, that of not sinking in the world." The family must do all it can to trick the dice: whatever money can buy, or influence arrange, to ensure that the children fall among people who are, socially and aesthetically, good influences.

The St. Midas boarding schools are crucial to this task. Schools like Groton and St. Paul's were once as isolated from potentially bad influences as Cuba, say, is from the United States. More so: Cubans can listen to American radio. At St. Paul's when I was there in the early 1950s, radios were contraband. There were many other things we couldn't have: no cars or motorcycles or bicycles, no playing cards or backgammon boards, no cigarettes or liquor or drugs, no sexual relations. Visits to and from the "outside" world were limited to a few weekends a year. Money was not banned, but it was discouraged; besides, there was nothing to spend it on. All this has changed now. The schools are coeducational; sexual relations do take place. Money circulates as openly and invidiously as it does everywhere else. Every object of consumer appetite is available for cash or swap: cameras, radios, TVs and CDs, twelve-speed bicycles, computers, calculators, Rolexes. The walls of student rooms, once bare of all decoration except for the photo of Dad by Bachrach, of Mother by Zerbe, are now swathed in the epicene textures of India prints; Mother and Dad have ceded place to posters of soulful girls in flowery fields; and in every dark corner of these warm nests, expensive electronics glow and hum.

Still, let there be no mistake, St. Midas is not to be confused with Riverdale High. This is so even though (the rhetorical) Harvard's ratcheting up of its intellectual standards of admission has forced the same standards on the St. Midas schools, with almost the same results for the relative balance of Old Money and New Money (actual or potential) in the composition of the student body. I say "forced" advisedly. As Fitzgerald noted as early as the 1920s, even the most resonantly Old Money boarding schools have always lain under the heel of Harvard. Whatever else old St. Midas does for Old Money, and it does a great deal, it must do one thing more: get the kid into Harvard. This gives Harvard tremendous leverage on the boarding schools' admissions policies, and failure to bend to that leverage—as did St. Mark's, for example—sooner or later results in the school's erasure from the Old Money curriculum. Nevertheless, none of these institutions bent willingly, and all still loyally enroll the maximum possible number of "legacies" that Harvard will let them get away with. These are patrician schools, after all, and demophobia is never far away. Moreover, though Harvard's leverage has made the schools more hospitable to a greater variety of social backgrounds than they used to be, though it has made them more sympathetic to a greater variety of personal "talent" than they used to be—music and fine art, for example, or science and math—they are still the most deliberately Utopian communities in the country. All their delicately assembled components—students; faculty; courses of study; extracurricular activities; above all, perhaps, what can only be called their moral teaching—are put together and maintained according to the most rigorous Old Money criteria of "good influence." The effects are very powerful indeed as ways to trick the dice, though not always with precisely the desired results.

After St. Midas and Harvard, Society is the most egregiously instructive element in the makeup of the Old Money class. This function

of Society has been repeatedly lost to public view behind its constitutive (or exclusive) functions and its theatrical functions, even now that
these last have largely faded away. For almost seventy years, roughly
from the time Theodore Roosevelt entered Harvard College in 1876 to
the time Franklin Delano Roosevelt declared war against the Axis in
1941, Old Money, acting on the stage of High Society, held the attention of anyone in America with a dash of social imagination. Newspaper editors and readers, gossips, novelists, and the whole gallery of
parvenus, arrivistes, and *nouveaux riches* (not to mention hustlers, humpers, and hideous vulgarians)—all were transfixed by the dramas of
inclusion and exclusion, the magnificently insouciant displays of social
power and buying power, that was High Society in its glory. If there
was ever a reason, apart from the Roosevelts, to suppose that America's
Old Money class was an aristocracy, a worthy successor to history's
other aristocracies, High Society might have provided that reason.

It was not, for one thing, at all shy of the public. In its day, High
Society was the principal means by which America's rich trumpeted
their *entrée joyeuse* into history. The Bradley Martins' notorious ball of
1896, for example, received extensive coverage in the press, both in
England, where their daughter was married to Lord Craven, and in
America. William Randolph Hearst is said to have told his editors to
give the event itself five full pages. Even the minutiae of the preparations were news: a foul-smelling furniture polish that for one day appeared to threaten the noses of the guests, a brief worry over the
flowers. Most of the attention focused, of course, on who was invited
and who wasn't, who had accepted and who hadn't. "James van Alen
Cannot Go!" announced a headline in the *Times.* People were mad to
know where the magic circle of Society was being drawn, and why.

High Society was prepared to tell them. F. Townsend Martin, the
aristocratic Bradley's rather more patrician brother, once wrote that it
was a peculiarity of his class that so many of its members craved the
approval, or at least the attention, of the crowd. He exaggerated, but
there is no question that there's a vision of greatness in the Old Money
imagination that can never be satisfied by the responses of an audience
merely of its peers. This vision is what Bradley's costume ball was
meant, in its fashion, to act out. As befitted "the heirs of all the ages,"
Townsend's wistful phrase for the estate *he* came into, the guests appeared in the garb of all the aristocrats who had preceded them in the
public eye. Townsend himself, for example, danced the *quadrille d'hon-*

neur with Catherine de Médicis and her Fool (Mrs. Stuyvesant Fish and Harry Lehr), the Dauphin (John Jacob Astor V), Prince Hal (Center Hitchcock), and an assortment of Old World princesses. Anne Morgan, the banker's bold daughter, came as a New World princess, Pocahontas, in a costume that the newspapers said had been prepared under the guidance of "Prof. Putnam of Harvard." The most expressive costume, however, was Cornelia Martin's; she came as Mary, Queen of Scots, and around her neck wore a thick bib of rubies that had once been Marie Antoinette's. Never mind the dreadful end these queens had come to: Mrs. Martin defied the omen of her clothes. Her party marked the beginning of an American century, socially speaking, whatever she wore.

The trouble with this theatrical aspect of High Society was not so much that it finally proved offensive to the public it was meant to impress. It did that. No sooner was the Bradley Martin Ball over than every pulpit, podium, and editorial page in the nation began heaping abuse on the host and hostess for flaunting their aristocratic pride in the face of a democracy, or their filthy riches in the face of decent wage earners and the worthy poor. So furious was the backlash, in fact, that the wretched couple were driven to England, never to return, leaving Townsend to go off and write a memoir imploring his class to cultivate the more patrician virtues of privacy, discretion, and good stewardship. Nevertheless, the fatal trouble with High Society was not that its aristocratic pretensions couldn't survive the outrage of a democracy; the fatal trouble was its innocence, which couldn't survive irony.

This is the significance of the sublime career of Mrs. Stuyvesant Fish, Catherine de Médicis, and Harry Lehr, her Fool. Mrs. Fish was one of *the* Mrs. Astor's successors as a leader of High Society; Lehr was her factotum, a successor of sorts to *the* Mrs. Astor's Ward McAllister. The careers of Fish and Lehr tend to be played down in upper-class memories of High Society, played up in everyone else's (E. L. Doctorow, for example, deployed them for sinister purposes in *Ragtime*). They were a questionable pair. As a social commentator of their own day wrote, with an indignation shared by all good (patrician) Old Money opinion:

> It is simply appalling to think of Mrs. Stuyvesant Fish becoming the leader of our society. In that case social life would become a long succession of monkey parties and equally undignified entertain-

ments. . . . It is dreadful to think of distinguished foreigners coming
over here and judging us by Mrs. Stuyvesant Fish's entertainments,
arranged with the assistance of Harry Lehr.

But of course it was precisely at sentiments like these, painfully "correct," constipatedly self-conscious, that Fish and Lehr, delighting in the
plaisir aristocratique de déplaire, aimed their ironic laughter. Marx was
not alone in seeing the repetitions of history appearing first as tragedy,
then as farce. Fish and Lehr gave their Monkey Party for a chimpan-
zee, which they sat at the head of the table, as well-dressed and well-
behaved as any "distinguished foreigner." They also gave a Dogs
Dinner—with a menu of stewed liver and rice, and fricassee of
bones—for at least a hundred of their friends' pets. But the giveaway
clue to what Fish and Lehr were up to came with their Servants' Ball
at Newport, where everyone dressed up as ladies' maids, valets, cooks,
chauffeurs, and footmen. Afterward, Mrs. William Leeds gave a "simplicity party," taking everyone in her yacht over from Newport to the
public amusement park at Rocky Neck, which she had rented for
the day.

But it was too late for simplicity. What Fish and Lehr were up to
was subversion. Their parties were *tableaux vivants,* devastating illus-
trations of Henry Adams's most famous witticism, that American society was the first in history to go from barbarism to decadence
without passing through an intervening stage of civilization. They
knew exactly what they were doing. "They say you have lost your
mind," Mrs. Fish once wrote to Harry, who had done just that. "Come
back to New York if you have," she continued. "None of our friends
will ever know the difference."

What happened to High Society after Fish and Lehr were done
with it—that is to say, after World War I—everyone knows who has
read Cleveland Amory's *Who Killed Society?* It joined with, then all
but vanished into, that rabble of gods, the Celebritocracy. It took some
time, this development. High Society lost its audience—first the tab-
loid readers, last the readers of *The New York Times.* As late as 1935,
for example, the *Times* sent five reporters, and devoted two full pages
of text and pictures, to the Harvard-Yale boat races, one of the most
public displays of Old Money's togetherness on the social calendar.
Even in the 1950s, when I was going to dances and coming-out parties
in New York, overjoyed to leave behind me the bleak, tightfisted little

affairs that were their Boston equivalent, the *Times* still accorded an astonishing amount of space to the rituals, scandals, and breedings of Old Money Society. With the rise of "life-style" coverage, however, even the *Times* lost interest in the public goings-on of the class. Without the *Times,* indeed, there were none.

The loss may have been the public's as much as Old Money's. Behind the legitimating rationale of an upper class is the proposition that the masses, no less than the middle classes, need a focus for their envy—a "radiant body," as Veblen called it—by which they may work out their "social salvation." High Society once served that purpose. Now the Celebritocracy does, and the change has had serious consequences. To be a member of High Society, or so it seemed, one had only to be rich, preferably having been born that way. But to take one's place in the ranks of Celebrity, one has to have accomplished something—discovered a wonder drug, played major league ball, committed an atrocity, cut a platinum record, been taken on by Leo Castelli. The difference is between an imagination that understands "social salvation" as the result of an accident of birth—beyond one's control but not perhaps beyond the power of prayer—and one that sees it as the result of some action or industry of one's own. Celebrity, in short, convicts nine tenths of its audience to a sense of failure; High Society condemned them at worst to a state of reverence, at best to a state of bitter resentment. Old Money might argue that society is better served if it is kept oscillating between reverence and resentment than if it's constantly reminded of its inadequacy. Neoconservatives, on the other hand, would argue the reverse. The coming of the Celebritocracy, they would say, is a wonderful development: the belated arrival of a free market in human beings, where the role of the public has been transformed from that of a largely powerless onlooker to that of a consumer whose choices control the composition of its own "radiant body." This is social democracy as a form of consumer sovereignty.

What Old Money lost or gained by the death of High Society is harder to say. Aristocratic-minded women lost a number of once dearly coveted command posts in the public eye. Patrician Society tends to be dominated by gentlemen, their ladies relegated to consort status, or at best to their own separate but equal quarters. High Society was dominated by women of such dazzling force of character that "lady" hardly begins to describe them. To their contemporaries like Ralph Pulitzer, the liveliest son of Joseph Pulitzer, the newspaper magnate and family founder, the women seemed sisters to J. P. Morgan, self-assigned the same mission in Society as the great banker had taken on in the economy:

> In a great doorway [to her ballroom], her triumphal arch, flanked by her married daughter, she stands, an imposing figure, instinct with formality and power. The stiff lines of her satin dress, the steady glitter of her diamonds, the rigid coiffure of her pale hair, the tautened crispness of her skin . . . her straight carriage, all show the born leader of women.

With the death of High Society, born leaders of women would have to go elsewhere to lead.

Lost, too, was the opportunity to teach people, openly and forthrightly, their place. Pulitzer has left a vivid description of how High Society used to teach this lesson at the opera in New York:

> The opera gives Society a point of contact, and thus of contrast with that horde against whose incursions it is its mission to defend itself. Society's reunion in the visible midst of its foes gives it an esprit de corps, a solidarity, which it could never secure or maintain by uninterrupted aloofness.

More or less uninterrupted aloofness, however, is just what the dominant patrician strain in Old Money wants. From that perspective, the death of High Society was all gain. "A lady should see her name in the papers on only three occasions: the day she's engaged, the day she's married and the day she's buried"—the old saying is as true for most gentlemen as it is for their ladies. The only exceptions arise on those occasions when the gentleman volunteers—as in fact he is trained to do—some strikingly honorable or generous action for his country, his city, or his college. Otherwise, in patrician Old Money circles, even aloofness is too public a posture for Society to take. Privacy's the thing. And courtesy—to maintain the privacy.

For me, though my generation knew it only by echo and anecdote, the loss of High Society was the loss of a realm of license, of abused privilege, of heady irresponsibility—all to be reveled in, or so I imagined, with the invulnerability of youth, good family, and (if needed) endless resources of cash and contacts. Temperamentally, I was born to that part of the estate, to what Fitzgerald called "the gay table." All my mother's family had sat there, it seemed: my beautiful, much-married mother herself and her sister, both of them raised in Europe; her mother, Eleanor Greene Roelker as she was, once married to a Hungarian count and therefore (to her intense satisfaction) the Countess Palfy; my mother's father, Harrison Tweed, once married to Michael Strange and therefore (rather unsatisfactorily) a sort of husband-in-law of John Barrymore; my glamorous upper-bohemian godparents, the Lewis Iselins; and others. I would have loved High Society.

Actually, however, I spent most of the years of my youth at "the sober table"; in other words, in New England. So do most children of Old Money. They go to school in New England; they spend their summers in New England; they are attached to cities that are more like Boston than they are like New York or Paris or Vienna; their sense of the past, both autobiographical and generational, is firmly rooted in New England. In "old" New England, after all, the foundations of patrician education were laid in this New World. Remove High Society from Old Money Society and what you have left is patrician New England Society, even when its institutions happen to be in New York, Philadelphia, Washington, D.C., or Chicago.

What patrician New England Society means, certainly to those who haven't been born to it, but also to some who were, is clubs. In the curriculum, club life begins with Harvard's undergraduate Porcellian, AD, and Spee clubs (here rhetorically standing for several others, of course, including those at other colleges) and culminates in any one or more of the men's (and ladies') clubs of the cities. Many of these institutions are vaguely meritocratic or honorific and always were: Boston's Tavern Club, for example, and New York's Century. Others are moving in that direction. Harvard's Old Money quota system is becoming the norm. None of these developments, however, has changed the clubs' essential function in Old Money's scheme of things, which is to furnish a place where inheritors of the estate, along with their most clubbable retainers, educators, and entertainers, may take refuge from the world of doing and simply be.

This is why, in the imagination of Old Money, there is a sort of hierarchy of clubs, marked off not so much by their "exclusiveness" as by their distance from the marketplace, especially from the marketplace of selves. Least distant, therefore least dear to the class, are the country clubs (also the yacht clubs) that Henry James, with some faint admiration, called America's only contribution to civilized social life. The first of these, so thought its founders, was the Country Club in Brookline, Massachusetts, founded in 1882, or about the time of the founding of the Groton School; another was the Eastern Yacht Club in Marblehead, Massachusetts, whose clubhouse was built in 1880. (Both these figured in the long list of clubs beside my father's and grandfather's names in the Social Register; as did the Somerset, Tavern, Century, and other distant institutions.) Country clubs and yacht clubs are "for the whole family," of course, and are key breeding grounds, so to say, of Old Money manners, recreational passions, and personal relationships. At the same time, and for that very reason, they are best described as Old Family proxies and properties: their Ivy League sailing and tennis instructors serving as proxy fathers, mothers, and nannies; their modest facilities (docks and moorings, courts, courses, and clubhouses) serving as outbuildings of the estate. Old Money "family" clubs usually reverse the balance of *luxe* between club and home found in New Money circles. The most typical Old Money country and yacht clubs, in fact, are positively primitive: a dock, a shack, and a distinctive pennant sufficing for Dark Harbor's Tarratine yacht club, for example; or a dozen clay courts and a nine-hole golf course making do for a country club. Like the families that belong to them, these clubs are very far from the marketplace indeed; but because most such (middle-class) institutions are actually breeding grounds of a hot commerce in goods, services, and selves, country clubs and yacht clubs do not have a very high standing in Old Money Society.

The men's clubs, and to a lesser extent ladies' clubs, do. Many Old Money gentlemen and ladies become very attached to their clubs. The appurtenances of the place, its comfortable chairs, its silver, its "good" pictures in the reading room, its silly little drawings in the men's room—these bind them to a common world of "things that will endure" as much as anything they have at home. Even more important is the warming recognition the clubman receives from members and servants alike—a recognition of his essential, almost spiritual belongingness. "Good morning, Mr. Oliver [Mrs. Oliver]," the porter says as he comes in to lunch. "It's been almost a year, hasn't it?" And the servant of the soul serves the body as well: "Would you like to use the facilities, Mr. Oliver, before going up?"

In the club a man or woman can be known almost as if such knowledge had been bred, not learned. A story is told of the late John Hay Whitney, for example, that one day he ventured into the bar of the Brook Club in New York. "Good evening, Jock," said the men playing backgammon. "Hello, Jock," said the men having drinks around the little tables. "What can I get you, Mr. Whitney?" asked the bartender, pushing forward a chit for Mr. Whitney's signature. There was nothing unusual about this reception. The same salutations would have greeted him at the Century, the Knickerbocker, and the Racquet Club, all of which he belonged to. The anomaly was that Whitney was not then, nor had he ever been, a member of the Brook. He had never bothered to have himself put up for it. But Jock Whitney belonged. It is in the nature of Old Money to belong. His chit would be taken care of.

Beyond this ineffable sense of belonging and recognition, however, the greatest blessing of Old Money club life is its removal, not to say aloofness, from the unattractive strains and dangerous disappointments of a middle-class world bent on "making it." High Society's aim, in Ralph Pulitzer's impressionable view, was always "to tantalize the vulgar into a more poignant envy, and to tone up its own morale for a more zealous self-defense." Such aims are abhorrent to the clubmen and ladies of patrician Society. The last thing they want is to tantalize the vulgar; nor do they want to tempt the vulgarity that lurks in themselves. This is why there are those age-old rules against "shoptalk" at the lunch tables, against bringing the same guest more than twice a year, against taking out pencils and papers even in the club library. Up they go at lunchtime or in the evening—busy men, many of them, with heavy patrician responsibilities—up past the smiling porters, up the splendid staircases, up to zones of quiet belonging, where, to repeat, they may simply be. Up in the reading room it is always six o'clock on an autumn afternoon. Old men slumber in burnished leather chairs. Up in the dining room there is conviviality but also serenity. Here it is considered bad form even to introduce oneself (one is supposed to *know*), and actually offensive to identify one's job or standing in the world. The dining room is a garden for the cultivation of the more delicate graces and virtues of the class, but above all it is a refuge from the ugly world outside, with its pleading, cajoling, sleeve-plucking, breast-thumping strivers and strugglers swirling through the streets in every town and city in the land.

All this peace and propriety is threatened now. The strivers in the street want in, badly. Some of them always have, of course, but in the last ten years or so there have been crucial changes in the public's perception of what goes on in there, changes that will force the doors, and disturb the tranquillity, of the honor'd number.

Even at the remotest point of their withdrawal from the public, clubmen (and ladies) have always been ambiguously invidious figures.

Look at the clubman who still figures in the cartoons of *The New Yorker*. He is clearly a man of leisure, the very image of satiety, of surfeit, of arrival and peace at the last. Yet just as clearly he is also a figure of almost passionate virility, which very few other sorts of old men are in America. The humor, of course, is in the tension between the images of pudgy impotence and bursting power. It depends on one's being just a little apprehensive of this preposterous old fogy with a big cigar: As he rants on, anathematizing Democrats, women, Andy Warhol, the younger generation, and Progress, he may actually have the power to crush them.

In the 1920s and 1930s, this double image of club life reflected the felt helplessness of the observer to *get in*. The "social" novelists of those days—Fitzgerald, Marquand, and O'Hara—returned again and again to the snob's agony of belongingness. As High Society disappeared, the more aristocratic heirs and heiresses of Old Money sauntered out into more fluid fields of good company. (The company, indeed, of these writers: Fitzgerald was proud to be friends, as he thought, with the Gerald Murphys and with Tommy Hitchcock; Marquand was triumphant to marry the niece of Henry Dwight Sedgwick, then the daughter of the much richer but equally ancient Hooker family of Connecticut; O'Hara found some small compensation for never having gone to Princeton or Harvard by marrying the former wife of a Bryan from Virginia and Yale.) However, out among these people, idling about in relatively unprotected social space, the Old Money aristocrats also drastically worsened the snob's agony. Inadvertently, for the most part, they made him realize the tantalizing difference between friendship and belongingness. Scott Fitzgerald and Tommy Hitchcock might be friends, but there was no way, even if he had gone to Harvard, that Scott Fitzgerald could belong to the Porcellian Club. To belong to the Porcellian Club it was not enough—it still isn't—that one be friends with a member. One has to have been friends with him always, and in that elusive past perfect tense of the verb *to be* the socially ambitious read their sad fate.

This being America, however, they did not accept their fate. From the 1960s on, a significant change came over the street view of Old Money's clubs and the envious mob began to mount a new kind of assault. It soon appeared that there wasn't anything comical or impotent or lovable about that old bastard up there, waving his big cigar around the reading room. His cigar was a lightning bolt and his club was a kind of Olympus. In a sense, Baltzell's dream has come true—as a nightmare. The new assault has nothing in it of a desire for rest and decorum, for a quiet place where established authority might restore its strength. *Getting in,* as the world outside sees it now, has no spiritual "end" to it whatsoever. On the contrary, it is a purely instrumental step. Being a member is to know the man with the big cigar, to possess his "inside" information, to plug into his network, to make use of his influence, and to boast of his acquaintance. In short, club life today is seen as invidious, not because it is a privileged sanctuary from the market but because it is an advantage in it.

This is the significance of the 1980s women's campaign to desegregate the great Old Money clubs of the nation. It's not just that the presence of women will introduce into those restful precincts the most unsettling marketplace competition of all—competition with and for the opposite sex. It's the grounds of the campaign. What the women are saying is that all those rules against talking business at the lunch table, all those charming conventions of the knowing and the known, all that graceful courtesy and moral peace at the heart of clubbability—it's all persiflage. Clubs are a bottom-line enterprise like every other in America, and clubmen as much hustlers and humpers as any of their fellow citizens.

If this view prevails, Old Money Society will be shorn of its last claim on a capital letter. Whatever else they were, High Society and the clubs were a highly visible way for the popular imagination to enter, as it were, the society of the Old Rich on terms the Old Rich set. Without them, the entry points seem everywhere and nowhere, like the society itself. But without them, too, the society seems not less but more: more of what it means to be an inheritor of an Old Money estate.

Old Money society with a small "s" *is* that estate, really: a round of people, places, and things that is different from other people's rounds. It might call for a "thick" description of the sort that anthropologists strive for in accounts of the estates to which people in traditional societies are heir. "Thickness" was certainly what the founding fathers of the class strove for, and still strive for. Round and round their children go, round and round they are supposed to go, generations of men and women succeeding one another on accustomed tracks of birth and breeding, education and occupation, friendships and potential friendships; the round laying down deeper and deeper patterns of sympathy and revulsion, affinity and fear, tastes and distastes—all those affections of the heart and dispositions of the will that constitute in the individual a social character, and in the group a social class.

"Thickness" has not been achieved. As Henry Adams wrote to Henry James, on reading the latter's account of *William Wetmore Story and His Friends,* Bostonians of the same class as they: "Improvised Europeans, we were, and—Lord God!—how thin! No, but it is too cruel! Long ago,—at least thirty years ago,—I discovered it, and have painfully held my tongue about it. You strip us, gently and kindly, like a surgeon, and I feel your knife in my ribs." That was in 1903. The thinness has gotten no thicker. It cannot, not in this New World. Of course, the whole geographical and affective pattern of Old Money movement—the social round of Old Family and old friends, of boarding school and Harvard, of summers on the Cape and winters on the Board (boards of trustees, boards of directors), round and round from the nursery to the family plot—eventually creates distinctive proclivities that are at least as strong as those laid down, say, in a small town in Georgia. But a New World is a place of possibility, of endless forgiveness and forgetting, of continuous renewal and revival. It is also a place of anxiety, oblivion, and degradation, though knowledge of this is usually repressed. A New World won't take thickness. The social thickness in an anthropological description is the thickness of traditional societies, Old World societies, indeed highly literary memories of Old World societies: the cities of classical antiquity, the countrysides of feudalism. It is the thickness of fate. Old Money envisages its social round, its curriculum, as laying down a fate for its beneficiaries, glorious or tragic, as the case may be, but fitting. But for that sort of story the New World has anger and contempt, for fate is the antithesis of freedom—the freedom of a New World where anything (good) can happen, where anything (good) can be *made* to happen. Thin, therefore, Old Money society is likely to remain.

The key element in the composition of Old Money society is the family: extensive, sloppily articulated, susceptible to warm affections and cool hostilities, and "tight" or "relaxed" almost on preference. One of the most striking things about it is the absence of clear-cut roles: in this, so unlike the middle-class family of social theory, so like the poor one. The Old Money family is full of "aunts" and "uncles" who aren't aunts and uncles, of grandparents who take the place of (even usurp) parents in the children's affections, of domestic servants and boarding-school teachers who do the same, and of cousins, infinite degrees of cousins. Joseph Alsop, the journalist and collector, once tried to define the social class that Franklin D. Roosevelt (and he himself) belonged to. After rejecting all the usual epithets—"upper-class," "aristocratic," and the like—he hit on the class of the "Who Was She?"s. It is true. On their social rounds, Old Money people are always asking one another, of some new wife of a friend, "Who was she?" Old Money society is in many ways a man's society, but for breeding purposes it can be extremely concerned with the female line.

Still, the best way to describe Old Money families is to call them families of cousins. Consider the family that Alsop was grappling with, the Hyde Park Roosevelts. Franklin's relationship with the Oyster Bay Roosevelts, and Theodore Roosevelt in particular, was genealogically remote, something like fifth cousins, but affectively close: to Franklin, who admired him intensely and emulated him as closely as he could, the President was "Cousin Theodore" until, through Franklin's marriage to Cousin Theodore's niece, he became "Uncle Theodore."

Money sometimes tightens these cousinships, sometimes relaxes them. For example, until Eleanor brought her not inconsiderable income to Hyde Park, no money coursed through the cousinship of the two Roosevelt families. But money, in a tangled sort of way, did link the Hyde Park Roosevelts and the Astors. Franklin, born in 1882, was the only child of James Roosevelt and Sarah Delano, James's second wife. (They had met at Cousin Theodore's house, the same house where Franklin would be married to Eleanor, in a wedding ceremony conducted by his old Groton headmaster, also in some sense his surrogate father, Endicott Peabody.) Franklin was named for an uncle of Sarah's, Franklin H. Delano, who was married to Laura Astor, daughter of William B. and *the* Mrs. Astor. The Delano couple was childless, so that in honoring Uncle Franklin the Roosevelts may have had some thought for an inheritance for their child, or some such helpful intercession on his behalf in the event that his father might suddenly die. It was not to happen, neither the inheritance nor the intercession, but the Roosevelt-Astor connection was there nonetheless.

A second connection was provided by Franklin's half-brother James Roosevelt Roosevelt, a man old enough to be his father. Like his stepuncle Franklin Delano, James Roosevelt Roosevelt was married to a daughter of Helen Schermerhorn Astor, *the* Mrs. Astor. Money did flow in this relationship, although when Helen died in 1893—in Vienna, where Grover Cleveland had posted her husband in return for his services to the Democratic party—there was some unpleasantness over the will. Their two underage children were left a small portion of the Astor fortune (in trust, of course, the income to be distributed at the discretion of the trustees), and James Roosevelt Roosevelt took the Astors to court, petitioning the judge to award each of his children $15,000 a year. The judge was stern. Moral issues were at stake—of the same sort, it seems, as those raised by the Bradley Martin Ball. "The income," he declared, "should not be dissipated merely to accustom the children to luxury. When they are of age they can do what they will with their own. In the meantime they should be taught the value of money and should be habituated to prudence and moderation rather than to extravagance in the gratification of every luxurious desire." He granted half of what the children's father had asked for, $7,500 a year per child.

The third Astor-Roosevelt connection was also provided by James Roosevelt Roosevelt. He was a trustee, presumably a generous one, of the gargantuan $75 million estate left to Vincent Astor when Vincent's father, John Jacob Astor V, the Dauphin at the Bradley Martin Ball, went down on the *Titanic* in 1912. In some ways, this was the most fateful connection of the two families, for in the years to come, Franklin and Vincent became not just "cousins" but friends.

This cousinly character of Old Money families and, after the Civil War, the increasingly national character of the Old Money social round, combined to give many observers of the class the impression that "the radiant body" was even older than it wanted to be: not a feudal or Greek aristocracy, not a Roman patriciate, but a primitive tribe. Thorstein Veblen had fun with this notion. More than half a century later, E. Digby Baltzell did not, and he is right not to, for tribal metaphors are racialist ones; embedded in the class's consciousness of itself, they have results that are more vicious than amusing. Consider, for example, the implications of referring to the Social Register as the "stud book," as people of my father's and grandfather's generation used to do. The fact is that Old Money has always been tempted to understand its curriculum as aimed, not at the composition of a class, but at the purification of a body. Social narcissism, one might call this temptation, and many Old Money beneficiaries are overcome by it.

In the main, however, Old Money families function much as other sorts of families do in fashioning their life projects. Even their most egregious task, providing a conduit for the inheritance of unearned wealth, differs only in degree from ordinary middle-class practices. Yet to the truly alert social imagination, the Old Money family adds up to much more than the usual patterned impact of psychological, sociological, and economic influences on the individual. Or "racial" ones. To this imagination, the essence of Old Money families is that it lifts its members above such contingent influences: up to a triumph of history, if you can conceive of such a thing, over time.

For middle-class families, the only time worth thinking about is expressed in the gerund, as in rising and falling, going and coming, making it or not making it. One's status is a promise wrapped up in a dream that may turn out to be an illusion, or not. To be middle-class in America is to be strung out somewhere between two futures: success too invidious to mention, failure too horrible to contemplate. The drawbacks of this time slot are obvious. Success and failure rarely happen to communities; they happen to individuals, thence to families. Yet when time is possibility, anything done, good or bad, can be undone. Thus whatever sense of place or community a middle-class family has may dissolve, given the all-powerful sense of time as possibility.

Equally obvious are the benefits. The children are free to carry out revolutions of independence against the circumstances of their birth and background. The charming Jacksonian hero of Hawthorne's *The House of the Seven Gables* expresses this wonderful sense of liberation implicit in the middle-class family when he cries out against the "old" tradition-bound Pyncheon family, which his fiancée comes from: "Shall we never, never get rid of this past?" And later: "To plant a family! The idea is at the bottom of most of the wrong and mischief which men do."

But of course families do get "planted," some of them by charming Jacksonian go-getters who fancy themselves, later in life, as family founders. As Senator Aldrich showed in the selection of a site for his estate, and of Winthrops and Williamses for his ancestors, even in this New World there is soil enough to plant a family in time. There was nothing new about what he sought to do; the only newness was in the world he had to do it in. Every emergent family in history has tried to transform itself in this way, giving itself a depth and stability in the past to counter the onrushing vicissitudes of the future. This has been especially true when the emergence is floated on something as impersonal and elusive as money. Roman plebeians, raised suddenly to the patriciate by some commercial coup, instantly began rooting around for gods of the hearth, divine ancestors like those their new neighbors had. In Tudor England, families that had grown rich by conniving at court found heralds who traced their ancestry back to the Romans, the Trojans, the Greeks—even, in one case, Noah.

It has been the same in the United States. The decisive sign that a major wave of family founding was carrying away the social imagination of the American rich came in the Gilded Age, when Tifffany's opened a genealogical service for its customers. The genealogies it provided were largely spurious. The better-advised or more self-confident of the Robber Barons, then as now, chose professional genealogists to find them a real baron perched somewhere in their family tree. But whether real or spurious, it hardly matters. The point is that there seems to be a sort of metaphysical reflex attendant on the winning of great wealth, as though the task were so dark and close and hidden that when at last the bright world breaks in on the laborer to tell him he has won, he must become a new man, requiring new parents, new ancestors, for him and his descendants. Out of this new oldness, this instant history, he fashions a meeting ground of heritage and posterity.

Money, needless to say, is required as well. If Tiffany's genealogical service provided a clue to the metaphysics of the Old Money curriculum, the founding in 1903 of the Bankers Trust, my forebear's old stock, provided a clue to its physics. The Bankers Trust Company was established (with the help of J. P. Morgan and his ally on the Senate Finance Committee) to take custody of the enormous New Money fortunes then being transmitted to their first generation of inheritors—that is to say, to Old Money status. In 1913, Joseph Pulitzer's *New York World* published a list of the largest fortunes in America. It was overwhelmingly a list of self-made men and, substantially, of dead men; twenty of the fifty-two names are preceded by the words "estate of." Marshall Field, E. H. Harriman, Russell Sage, Jay Gould, Solomon Guggenheim, H. H. Rogers, W. L. Elkins, Oliver H. Payne, Cornelius Vanderbilt, and many others of David Graham Phillips's "predatory band" had by 1913 passed on—their fortunes and their souls. Several of the fortunes caused scandals, so huge and so concentrated were the benefactions. Two of the largest, Payne's and Whitney's, a total of approximately $55 million, cascaded into the coffers of four people, Whitney's children, one of whom (albeit to their mutual detestation) had married a Vanderbilt—Gertrude, the sculptor and the founder of the Whitney Museum. Marshall Field's was the most stunning of these legacies. He left about $122 million to two grandsons, Marshall

Field III and Henry Field, who, at the time of their grandfather's death in 1906, were twelve and eight years old.

Most of this money was left in trusts of various sorts: per stirpes or per capita, revocable and irrevocable, and so forth, all bristling with stipulations, devisings, and "wishes" designed to meet any contingency. As a legal instrument the trust is ancient, far older than the span of time during which it could maintain the stability, cohesiveness, and integrity of any one fortune. Trusts may run for no more than the "lives in being" of the testator's heirs—usually two (more) generations—plus twenty-one years, plus the normal gestation period of nine months. That is a long time to influence the future, conceivably five generations into it; and at any point in the line of descent, when the trust's principal is triggered by a death, the inheritor can of course start all over again by establishing another trust. But the legal instrument itself goes back more than seven hundred years, to the thirteenth century. Its first use, ironically enough, seems to have been as a holding device for prayerful donations to the Franciscan order, whose vows of poverty forbade its members to "own" wealth. The trust, as many beneficiaries of Old Money have long since had cause to complain, was to "own" it for them. Thus, seven centuries thence, the Bankers Trust Company, whose purpose and profit it was to provide, in twentieth-century America, a financial home for these "owners" of trusts.

Old Money inherits trust funds, by and large. Not freely available capital, not income flexibly adjusted to need, not lucrative and powerful positions in the world, not "rents" or annuities or even dividends. It inherits all those things (and more: one acquaintance of mine once excused himself from lunch with the rather shamefaced admission that he had to go downtown to see his trustees about his "allowance") and of course it inherits them in amounts hugely disproportionate to the recipients' own personal efforts. But mostly what Old Money inherits is trust funds, unquestionably the most important material base for the curricular superstructure of the Old Money class, and in many cases one of the most fateful determinants of individual Old Money lives.

Beyond their trust funds, Old Money beneficiaries often come into what I think of as a kind of extended patrimony (on the analogy of the extended family), which is also held in trust. Basically, this extended patrimony radiates outward from a nuclear private property to more remote relationships with public property, or, as policy analysts might put it, from private goods to public ones. The good in question could begin with something quite insignificant: an island off the coast of Maine, for example, handed down in metaphorical (or actual) trust from generation to generation in the same family. But from there it is but a short leap of the imagination to the operations of the Maine Coast Heritage Trust, a state environmental group, where the beneficiary suddenly finds himself contemplating a rather different notion of property than "his" island evoked, a broader notion of trust, and a more comprehensive notion of posterity.

Of course, the definitional problems here can be excruciating. George Harold Edgell, for example, a relation of mine who was director of Boston's Museum of Fine Arts in the 1930s, once told my father that the best museum was the one seen by the fewest people. My grandfather, who was a trustee of the MFA in this period and tended, like many patricians, to avert his eyes from the future, would have replied to Cousin Harold that there was nothing to worry about: only the "fewest" people would ever want to go to a museum. Yet my father, a more aristocratic type and in his turn also a trustee, actually rejoiced in the mobs of people that in the 1960s began coming to the museum. In some families, then, the radiant pulse of the imagination from private to public may move in generational as well as autobiographical time. Much depends, of course, on how the Old Money beneficiary perceives his economic position, on the particular form of property at issue (a picture or a "view," for example), and on the vagaries of personal temperament. Then, too, the movement of the imagination can also run backward, from public to private; and it often does.

The best place to observe the extended patrimony is not in any specific family but in certain old cities: Philadelphia, San Francisco, perhaps, but above all Boston. And the best personage through whom to view it is that famous figure of Old Money probity the "Boston trustee." He is a composite figure, as I see him: part individual—the lawyer or banker who looks after "your" trust; part institution—the bank or firm that actually manages the money. Very often he is in capitalistic succession to the family founder: if not a descendant of the man himself, then a descendant of one of his close friends and business associates; and his function in each family is to liberate some of its members, and/or some portion of their wealth, for the maintenance and support of those institutions that the family considers part of its extended patrimony. Two Boston examples are the Saltonstalls and the Coolidges. In my grandfather's generation, the Saltonstalls sent one brother, Leverett, to follow his sense of trusteeship into public service, while a second, Richard, attended to the private patrimony on Boston's State Street. In the family of Thomas Jefferson Coolidge, despite the example of their most celebrated forebear, it was not people who got sent out into the public sphere but money. Year after year, generation after generation, Coolidges have felt "custom" bound to shift sizable hunks of their estates from the tightly held, sensibly managed world of private property to the rather more public, but no less sensibly managed, world of Harvard University, the Museum of Fine Arts, and other favored institutions of Boston's patriciate. Their imaginations follow, perhaps even lead, this shift. So, to the limited degree of sitting "on the board," does their presence. Coolidges are "Boston trustees" of much more than their own trust funds.

This system of patrimonial care and service was well established in Boston long before Thomas Jefferson Coolidge set out to make money in the 1850s. By the 1820s, in fact, a group of his predecessors in the Old Money class had institutionalized the extended-patrimony idea in a Newtonian machine of money production, money entrustment and investment, and money expenditure, a circulatory machine whose movement was supposed to be cared for by their heirs and assigns forever. These men later became known as the Boston Associates: Francis Cabot Lowell, Abbott and Amos Lawrence, Nathan and William Appleton, James and Patrick Jackson, Israel Thorndike senior and junior, and the other four-score men who laid the foundations of the industrial (as opposed to the mercantile) wing of the Boston patriciate. All of them, if not related to each other already, soon would be: Nathan Appleton became Thomas Jefferson Coolidge's father-in-law; Samuel A. Eliot was Charles Eliot's uncle and Samuel Eliot Morison's great-grandfather. Money flowed with this blood, needless to say, but it was the physics of the system, *how* it flowed, that was significant.

First, to produce the money there were the progressively organized textile factories in the nearby towns of Waltham and Lowell, followed in due course by exploitively organized factories in Lawrence, Haverhill, Manchester, New Hampshire, and elsewhere in New England. Then, to hold and manage the money (held in trust, needless to say), there was the Massachusetts Hospital Life Insurance Company, a "savings bank for the wealthy ... the best institution on earth," as John Lowell described it to Samuel Appleton. Massachusetts Hospital Life, though an insurance company, functioned much like what the (very rich) Old Rich of today know as the "family office." It was the headquarters from which the family's trust funds were sent out into the financial markets and from which, in carefully stipulated amounts, stipends were paid out to family beneficiaries, thereby making it unnecessary for them to send themselves out into any sort of market at all.

The movement of the money-circulating machine from the textile factories to the investment office (and back again: in the early days, Massachusetts Hospital Life invested large amounts of its entrusted capital in the mills its founders had also founded) was only the first. But there was another beat and pulse in the system, which sent assets and imaginations out toward the public. It was the declared purpose of the patrician founders of this system, and the practice of their inheritors, that some part of the family's income and savings should go to the care and maintenance of the welfare and cultural institutions of Boston. The very name of the "savings bank for the wealthy" points to one such institution, the Massachusetts General Hospital. Harvard College, and later its professional schools, was another. And as the nineteenth century went on, there would be more and more of them: the Symphony, the Museum of Fine Arts, the Trustees of the Reservations, and so forth—though never so many as to tax the prudence or unduly swell the ranks of the patriciate.

Already in my great-grandfather's day, the Old Rich had established nuclear and extended (private and quasi-public) patrimonies in every city in New England's sphere of influence; and in most that were not, from Philadelphia to New York to Chicago to San Francisco, they had established patrimonies and imaginatively extended patrimonies that looked the same as New England's. The results were impressive. Hospitals, museums, symphony orchestras, clinics, boarding schools and colleges, asylums, and "charities" of incredible variety were flourishing everywhere before the turn of the century. After it, in the presidency of their own Theodore Roosevelt, the class even went so far as to stake out what still seems an astonishing advance in its patrimonial concerns, the national park system, with its nearly incredible investiture of trusteeship in the state. Finally, after World War I (and the war's inheritance tax), the class set in motion the first great wave of "foundations"—thereby establishing yet another patrimonial gradient in the distance from private center to public perimeter.

To many Old Money beneficiaries, and in fact to many resentful observers of the class, these cultural and welfare institutions are the crowning achievement of the Old Money curriculum. For one thing, they provide the class with agreeable images of itself as it goes about on its social round. One is that of charity *in corpore,* of the upper-class lady on her round of "visiting committees" at hospitals, slum nursery schools, and the like. Sometimes the visitor gives more than a visit: A relation of mine, Margaret Chanler Aldrich, won the Congressional Medal of Honor for her work as a nurse during the Spanish-American War. Sometimes, too, it would have been better if she had given less, so insulting is her presence to the objects of her charity or so inadequate her gift. These "ladies bountiful" are derided, yet many of them, like Eleanor Roosevelt, rise above the derision. There is something touching about those who do in person, even if awkwardly, what they might have sent large amounts of money to do for them—and perhaps do better.

The other image is that of a class with an aura of antique beauty. With a handful of exceptions (like Abby Aldrich Rockefeller's efforts on behalf of the Museum of Modern Art and her collections of early American art in Williamsburg), the focus of Old Money's cultural trusteeship has been on art that is Old and from Old Worlds. It is as though, in order even to survive in this New World, the Old Rich (and the New Rich seeking to become Old) have had to grab on to every old work of art, every old piece of music, every old book, every old chair and table, every old style and fashion, and set them up as props, in every sense of the word, of their historical legitimacy. In 1912, for example, my great-grandfather managed to correct an oversight in the tariff schedule that imposed a duty on works of art—but only for those works that were certifiably "old." Even Nature, as preserved in the national parks of Roosevelt's time and the Nature Conservancy of our own, seems dear to Old Money primarily because it is "old." The whole cultural edifice of America still bears the imprint of that anxious antiquity set upon it by its Old Money founders and patrons. From the Civil War to the Cold War of our time, Old Money and its New Money "emergents" have been creating a museum: the Great American Museum, with its galleries, its concert halls, its libraries, its colleges and universities, its "great outdoors," whose purpose is to provide for objects and ideas an "end" as safe, as authoritative, and as aesthetically pleasing as the "end" that Old Money is itself supposed to provide for the terrible struggles of men in markets. For objects, at any rate, this museum works astonishingly well. In 1919, with the mortar still damp in its massive walls, Senator Aldrich's house in Warwick, Rhode Island, was written up in a popular magazine as though it were in fact, not just in imagination, an ancient baronial country house—a stately home of New England, less than a decade old but already touched with nostalgia.

These welfare and cultural institutions were a crowning achievement in another, more comical sense. As everyone noted at the outset of the effort to build them, it was as though America's rich class were behaving as kings and queens had done in the Old World (and as their successor states continued to do). In the New World's beginning, there had been no such things as museums and hospitals. For a very long time, the terms of the deal struck between the state and its citizens were so tightly interpreted as to forbid all but local governments and their public-school systems, and state governments and their public colleges and universities, from doing much to protect the welfare of Americans, still less to uplift their "culture"—except by fostering the free play of the marketplace or the emergence of monopolies, whichever seemed more effective. Thus, since the marketplace showers gold only on individuals, then only individuals (and their beneficiaries) are in a position to redirect the shower, at least a trickle of it, to protect the welfare and enhance the culture of their fellow citizens. The class's adversaries found this deplorable, of course, and questioned whether all those objects of Old Money generosity were genuinely for the public. But people on the whole applauded, and continue to applaud, the shower of gold.

This, then, is the curriculum (and curriculum vitae) of Old Money. Its object was clear from the beginning—the beginning of the class's historical time, the beginning of each generation's time in each "founded" family of the class, and the beginning of autobiographical time for each beneficiary in the family. Its object was, and still is, to create a social estate, endowed with inherited wealth (much of it in the form of trust funds), where anyone's social imagination might plausibly play with the idea of a "patrician," "aristocratic," "upper," or even "ruling" class. That's what Old Money *is* in the last analysis: the imagination working on money to create the impression of a social class that is different from other social classes.

Of course, by no means is everyone so struck by envy of Old Money's position in the world that he or she wants to enter it, or have his or her children enter it. Many Americans lack the social imagination to make favorable (or indeed unfavorable) comparisons between Old

Money's condition and their own. Many others would disclaim such an imagination on democratic principle. And for almost everyone, I suspect, even for those of us born to Old Money, the social imagination comes into play only intermittently, perhaps even subliminally, revealing the estate in a sort of stroboscopic light that is constantly changing in shade and intensity. Its color, naturally, is green—green with envy, green with hope.

Still, the entrances to the estate of Old Money are well marked. I have suggested two of them: service to the class and education in the class's favored institutions. (In a sense, the latter is only a means to the former: the would-be family founder goes to the correct schools and then wittingly or unwittingly goes on to be "of service" to the class.) The service might be to the class's material base or to its restricted or extended patrimony. My great-grandfather, albeit without a Harvard degree, cultivated and protected the industries in which Old Money invested its wealth from his seat in the U.S. Senate. Other men continue to perform the same service from somewhat less lofty positions in family offices, law firms, and banks. And generation after generation, some of these men and women are sufficiently struck by the enviability of Old Money status to want it for themselves and/or their children. Usually, if their services are important enough and their persons agreeable enough, they will "make it." Certainly their children will.

Some of the best-known patricians of my father's generation came into the estate by this gate. John J. McCloy, Jr., for example, was the son of a Philadelphia hairdresser who moved from Amherst and the Harvard Law School to the highest councils of the Old Money establishment, private and public, to end his days in the Wall Street law firm of Milbank Tweed. (One of the antecedents of that firm, incidentally, was the Harvard friendship of my grandfather Harrison Tweed and my great-uncle Winthrop Aldrich, and in Uncle Winthrop's subsequent rise to the top of the Rockefeller-controlled Chase Manhattan Bank, whose lawyers, in due course, Milbank Tweed became.) But the same sort of entry can be gained by providing more personal services than McCloy's. Teachers, horse trainers, gardeners, architects, art dealers, *fournisseurs* of all sorts, ski instructors, even a few gigolos and gold diggers: in each generation there will always be a few of them, too, who "make it" onto the estate of Old Money—sufficiently, at any rate, for their children to feel comfortable there.

Naturally, a good deal of pain is suffered in this process. Envy is itself a hurtful emotion: the desire not just to have what another has but to *be* that other, the form of desire that most agonizingly convicts one of one's own neediness, one's own inadequacy or emptiness. But it is also the form of desire that frequently inspires an arrogant, fearful refusal of what is desired to those who desire it. And understandably so. To know your *self,* not just your possessions, to be the object of envy is one of the most deeply disturbing experiences of social life. You don't even know for sure that you are in fact envied. The envier is not going to admit it: Envy is humiliating, therefore denied. Always and everywhere, then, envy carries with it the threat of the self's annihilation: the envious one will swallow you up in his love or kill you in his hatred.

Many kinds of people are envied. For example, Old Money envies the newly successful; being successful already, it is forever denied success. But the worst envy falls on those who are gifted—whether by beauty, intelligence, physical prowess, or some other accident of birth. Alas, there are Old Money beneficiaries who see their wealth as such a gift, and who use that perception to close off as many entrances to the estate as they can. Much of Old Money's aesthetic, as it were, its integrity as a work of the imagination, depends on the belief that membership in the class is a gift beyond achievement.

At the same time, however, this belief opens wide what is in many ways one of the most accessible entryways onto the estate, and the only one available to those who are merely, newly, rich. As Old Money is a gift to its beneficiaries, so the fastest way to the heart of the class is to give—give money to the welfare and cultural institutions that are Old Money's extended patrimony. Everybody knows about the potlatch behavior of America's very rich—all those museum wings and the paintings in them, all those campus dormitories and "nature preserves," all those productions of Romantic operas, all those operating rooms in hospitals—every one with the name of the donor beseechingly displayed in immortal bronze. Everyone also knows that a social imagination is often at work behind such gifts: the thought that the donation will be not only a down payment on the donor's immortality but a ticket of admission, for him and his family, to the society, perhaps even the friendship, of the institution's Old Money trustees.

Over the years, this conspicuous giving, which looks very much like conspicuous buying, has been the deserving object of sardonic humor (notably Veblen's). The danger in this humor, to Old Money at any rate, is that it attacks the class at the point where it most loves to be praised. The gift is at the center of Old Money's best sense of itself as a class. A graduate got close to the fount of this feeling in a letter that St. Paul's School reprinted in the alumni/alumnae bulletin some years ago (significantly, it didn't matter to St. Paul's that the letter-writer was talking about efforts to raise money for Harvard):

> I was lucky to come from a family that could afford to pay the full [Harvard] tuition. Even then, I knew that I was subsidized by the generosity of alumni who had contributed to their college, and who realized that they owed their college at least something when they took their place in the world. To not support one's college at least once in a significant way relative to one's capacity is suggestive of a "take and run" philosophy and that "one did it all on his own and owes no man anything." Even the most casual look at life will tell us that this is not an attractive alternative except for a limited few.

The whole moral of Old Money's gift ethos is in that paragraph (including a back-of-the-hand swipe at the vanity and greed of self-made men). There is the gracious acknowledgment of gifts from those who came before us, the sons and daughters of Alma Mater, and implicitly the sons and daughters of Pater Noster as well, our founding father. There is the eager recognition that an acceptance of a gift entails an obligation to give it on, "relative to one's capacity." There is the suggestion, too, that while the writer would not go so far as to arrogate the gift ethos to a class—those "lucky" enough "to come from a family that [can] afford to pay"—he would argue that such an ethos is especially fitting, and safe, for people gifted with a "place in the world." Finally, there is a hint that the heart of hearts where the gift ethos resides is a place of strangely fungible values, where aesthetic values blur into ethical ones, where "good form" conduces to "the decent thing," and the "good deed" looks remarkably like "the beautiful gesture."

The gift ethos is felt everywhere that Old Money makes its presence felt. The result can be sublime but is often ridiculous, as when Cornelia Martin told the press that she was giving her ball to provide "an impetus to trade," which was just then languishing in a depression. Either way it points up a key distinction sought by the class: that it is sometimes what the middle class is never: a group of people, friends and potential friends, who rise above (or even sink below) the dreary constraints that define Market Man. Old Money would not deny the law of reciprocity, which is said to be the most severe of those constraints: tit for tat, this for that. What it exists—and loves—to cherish is a longer, looser loop than the tight little shuttles of the marketplace: the gift nexus over the cash nexus. Old Money, given money, is to be given. It is not lost on the beneficiaries of Old Money that to arouse envy and to disarm it, there's no better way than giving.

Why anyone should want to make his or her way onto the Old Money estate—by giving, service, or education—is a question whose answer is so simple that I sometimes wonder why more people don't try to get there. The basic existential condition of most Americans is to be at some distance from a new beginning, from square one, or at least to be back there. Americans are "players." They are strugglers and strivers, humpers and hustlers, heroes and villains, rabbits and turtles, performers and nonstarters, winners and losers and also-rans in the great game, the great race, the great battle of life. These players are all alone there, at best accompanied by a spouse, at worst close pressed by "tough" competitors; and they are constantly on the move—backward and forward, in and out, up and down. All this movement may look like a game to the players, but to the Harvard- and Hotchkiss-educated economist David Birch, now at MIT, it looks more like what happens on the roadway for space rockets leading from the assembly shed to the launching pad: on a solid roadway, the rocket's great height would cause it to sway, eventually to crash; on a roadway of crushed gravel it moves in stately majesty. This is the American economy: a vast apparatus of production and consumption kept going by tiny movements—which of them voluntary?—of millions of Market Men.

This grim metaphor is not, fortunately for the royal progress of the economy, a common one. The common one is the game, the race, the battle. Yet it, too, seems grim at times, even to the players who win, because it has no end. The news, constantly fed back by the relative winners to the relative losers, is supposed to come as a consolation, reassuring everyone that the brave declaration of independence they took on square one has committed them to the unremitting pursuit of happiness, not the attainment of it. In this endeavor, the message is: There are no winners, no losers—only players endlessly playing.

The message is true. And it being so, I should have thought Old Money a very haven in a heartless world, a haven, moreover, more attractive than the cramped little family affair of the Victorian compromise. Old Money is an extended family with extended properties, both of which have been lifted, thanks to inherited wealth and some

imagination, into the serene atmosphere of generational, even historical, time. Up there, this harsh, wild linear movement—social, geo-
graphic, and economic—subsides into circles radiating from the
individual center to a patrimonial circumference and back again. The
only line is the one that describes itself through time: a line above
circumstance, as my great-grandfather put it, above the common passions of men.

Yet the beauty of this work also rests on some values that Victorians and other moral majorities ascribe to the family, the values of
belongingness and order. In the haven of Old Money, it looks as if
everyone belonged and everything were in order. Old Money inherits
a lineage; many of us vaguely, some of us resoundingly, inherit a recognizable name. To others, this must seem like the inheritance of a
destiny—at the very least something like the sword in the stone, a
shortcut to identity. Old Money also comes into club memberships,
"legacies" at schools and colleges, ever-widening circles of friends and
possible friends, lovers, and marriage partners. This is its minimum
"place in the world"; at the maximum (as for Theodore, Franklin, and
Eleanor Roosevelt), that place might *be* the world. To others, this inheritance may seem to offer boundless love and social security. Further-
more, unlike Victorians and moral majoritarians, Old Money comes
into all this without having to give up any freedom. The estate of Old
Money is vast and varied, with plenty of room to move around on, and
plenty of delightful reasons to do so.

Lastly, it could also seem to others as though Old Money inherits
a kind of spiritual security, as well as a social and economic security.
For it has sometimes been possible to discern in them a glimpse of that
old regime where all the elements that compose human society—from
peasant to king, priest to bishop, artisan to patrician, knight to lord
—were linked with bonds of mutual allegiance, like the brilliant
and glorious chandelier of heaven suspended from the Hand of God
Himself.

CHAPTER THREE

Class Acts

Dick Humbird had, ever since freshman year, seemed to Amory a perfect type of aristocrat. He was slender but well-built—black curly hair, straight features, and rather a dark skin. Everything he said sounded intangibly appropriate. He possessed infinite courage, an averagely good mind, and a sense of honor with a clear charm and *noblesse oblige* that varied it from righteousness. He could dissipate without going to pieces.... People dressed like him, tried to talk as he did.... Amory decided that he probably held the world back, but he wouldn't have changed him.... He was not a snob, though he knew only half his class. His friends ranged from the highest to the lowest, but it was impossible to "cultivate" him. Servants worshipped him, and treated him like a god. He seemed the eternal example of what the upper class tries to be.

"He's like those pictures in the Illustrated London News of the English officers who have been killed [in World War I]," Amory had said to Alec.

"Well," Alec had answered, "if you want to know the shocking truth, his father was a grocery clerk who made a fortune in Tacoma real estate and came to New York ten years ago."

Amory had felt a curious sinking sensation.

F. Scott Fitzgerald, *This Side of Paradise*

PERHAPS I HAVE painted the estate I inherited from the Senator, my family's founder, in bolder forms and colors than the facts of the matter warrant. That sidereal chandelier suspended from the hand of God, for example: something more than social imagination is needed to hang an American upper class on that metaphor, something more like hallucination. Whatever else it may be, the estate to which I was born is not a First Estate, not a Nobility. It's an array of tutorial institutions and exemplary roles designed to encourage the flourishing of a particular vision of the good human life, above the reach of market circumstances, beyond the clutch of vulgar and craven passions. But there's one aspect of this estate that justifies an allusion to heavenly bodies. It is that the characteristic presence of its heirs and heiresses in the social world, and their distinctive settings in the material one, are meant to be beautiful.

What sort of beauty depends, naturally, on the observer. Guardians of the class's self-legitimating task of social uplift, men like Charles Eliot, Herbert Pell, and Digby Baltzell, would clearly prefer that observers fix their gaze on the moral as well as aesthetic beauties of the class. Just as clearly, however, this preference is seldom fulfilled, and almost never by those whose view of the Old Money class is most strongly colored by their fervent desire to be seen as members of it (my great-grandfather being an historic example). Such people have no difficulty discovering beauty in the way the Old Rich compose themselves for the world's regard, and feel no shame in yearning to be included in the composition. What they seldom understand is that the process of assimilation is supposed to require greater changes than simply a more attractive adornment of their persons or a more lovely arrangement of their possessions. Not for a long time now has anyone understood "the good life" (Old Money's or anybody else's) as having a moral or political dimension; it's all a question of style, of a *life style*.

The question then arises, how to determine what, at any given moment, the preferred objects of Old Money taste actually are. Fortunately, there are connoisseurs of these questions. Mark Hampton, a brilliant New York interior decorator whose knowledge of the subtleties of social class is as sophisticated as his knowledge of fine fabrics and furniture, told me once that in the course of his career he has learned to distinguish three kinds of good taste:

> I think good taste sometimes appears like a talent—for singing prettily, say. Perhaps her grandmother sang, and her mother, but you don't have to suppose a genetic inheritance. Background and breeding will do. Then there's a somewhat arid *learned* good taste. One can almost hear the poor creature flipping the pages of *Architectural Digest* and *House and Garden* in her mind. Finally, there's an irregu-

lar, intuitive sort of good taste—a personal taste. It's sometimes more difficult to work with such people, but it's always more fun. Their responses are so surprising.

The class contexts are pretty clear. The "background and breeding" sort of good taste I would guess Hampton associates with upper-class antecedence: "learned" good taste he probably sees as a product of middle-class striving; while "personal" taste he doubtless believes to be the result of one of those random descents of the gift, which even the most class-ridden societies are obliged somehow to account for.

For expository purposes, the very best connoisseurs of the special beauties of Old Money life usually turn out to be people such as Senator Aldrich, who were born at just the right distance from the manor: close enough to be able to study the basic elements of the design, but not so close as to take it for granted; far enough to see the setting in flattering perspective, but not so far as to reduce its beauty to a blur. This is the great value of the memoirs of William S. Paley. Born to a provincial manor (Chicago, then Philadelphia), to a suspect race (Jewish), and to substantial wealth (his purchase of the embryonic radio network that became CBS was financed by an advance on his inheritance), Paley's introduction to the aesthetics of the good life began in much the same way as Mark Hampton might expect of one of his more "learned" clients—with magazines. As a young man in Philadelphia, he was an avid reader of *Vogue, Harper's Bazaar* and *The New Yorker.* In those slick manuals, the young entrepreneur of a new industry studied the forms and gestures (not to mention the purchases) required of the young entrepreneur of a new self.

Aesthetically, however, the self and CBS were two separate spheres of discrimination. In his memoir Paley is frank to admit that the sense of style required to market the network came rather more naturally to him than the style required to advance his person. To program CBS for success, he had only to listen to the promptings of his body. Again and again, he locates the source of his inspiration in his gut, in his nervous system, or in his instincts. The taste that saw *Amos 'n' Andy* as witty, *The Beverly Hillbillies* as amusing, *Cavalcade of America* as touching and informative, or *CBS News* as providing serious and substantial news for the citizens of the republic, this taste, we learn from his memoirs, is the taste Paley was born with.

But just as surely as Paley's viscera told him how to present a winning schedule of radio and television programs, they sometimes proved false in telling him how to present a winning self. Visiting Paris in the 1920s with his parents, Paley bought what he evidently believed was a thing of perfect upper-class beauty, a seventeen-thousand-dollar Hispano-Suiza, and engaged a chauffeur to drive him around in it. In Paris, both chauffeur and car seemed to set him off nicely, but back in Philadelphia the chauffeur began to appear inappropriate, somehow, for someone so young. He got rid of him. Then the car proved troublesome. Beautiful and attractive as it was, it was not beautiful in quite the right sort of way, nor was it attracting the attentions of the right sort of people. Ordinary passersby on the street stopped to gawk at it, perhaps to reach out and touch it. Soon, sadly, Paley got rid of the Hispano-Suiza.

Paley is proud of the contribution that CBS (and by implication he himself, as a tasteful programmer) has made to American society. When he writes of *CBS News,* the tone of his prose takes on the orotund solemnity of Walter Cronkite himself. But he is obviously most pleased by the memory of all those "shows," all the "home entertainment," that he has sent into American households over the years. Yet soon after Paley learned a thing or two about upper-class taste, CBS seldom got brought into *his* home. No sooner had he arrived in New York, a bachelor with a devoted valet and an alluring apartment, than he realized that it would not do to mix his business life and his social life, his associates of the day (many of them necessarily devoted to various aspects of marketing) with his companions of the evening (many of them so far removed from marketing as never to have known what it is). Later, married and with children, he kept up the *cordon sanitaire* between the two stylistic domains. He recalled that in his youth his father used to discuss the affairs of the Congress Cigar Company, source of the family fortune, around the family dinner table. Paley never did that with CBS. Not, apparently, in front of the children. Much like my great-grandfather before him, Paley seems to have had a sure sense that the world in which he founded an industry was a very different place from the world in which he hoped to found a family.

The dinner table, his own and others', was also a good place to further his education in upper-class aesthetics. As an engaging and sociable man, as well as a rich and influential one, Paley quickly entered the round of social entertaining (so different from CBS's home entertainments) that he'd longed for in the pages of *Vogue* and *Harper's Bazaar.* In the process, of course, he soon acquired the sort of friends and acquaintances, many of them Old Money, whose example and instruction would help him in the future to avoid such solecisms as tooling around in a chauffeur-driven Hispano-Suiza. Like so many sensible New World social climbers—like my great-grandfather, for that matter—he was especially impressed with the sort of taste cultivated by the Old Families and Old Money of the Old World. In England during World War II, for example, Paley was delighted to go down to Ditchley, the estate of the Tree family, by then wonderfully restored by massive infusions of Marshall Field's wealth. There he learned the rudiments of the great operating principle of the upper-class aesthetic—*sublimation.* Looking around him at Ditchley, the clichés of Old Money taste seemed to rise spontaneously to his lips, such qualifiers as "understated," "casual," "rich but not ostentatious," combined with such resonant concepts of time as "tradition" and "owned by the same families for generations." What seemed to have impressed him the most, however, was his realization, however dim or informed I don't know, that the furniture and paintings he saw so casually scattered about in this house were "of museum quality."

Two generations earlier, Paley would have had little choice in what he could do, back in the New World, with the tastes he was acquiring in the Old. Before World War I, one had to build one's own country house—improvise it, as Henry Adams would say (and as my great-grandfather did). But by the 1920s and 1930s a young entrepreneur such as Paley was able to perceive an actual New World legacy of country houses. In his memoir, he vividly describes a place in Manhasset, Long Island, which he visited one weekend in the 1930s:

> We drove only a few hundred yards down the road and turned into spacious grounds of a lovely old country place. The main house was white clapboard, quite old, very simple, with an elegance and beauty which struck me as being just right.... As I wandered about the house and grounds, I could not but think that this house on these grounds represented the kind of home I myself might like to own and live in one day.

Paley had always shown a perfect awareness of his place in a line of corporate or technological succession: that his "house" of electronic journalism and entertainment would succeed (or usurp) the "house" of newsprint. His first wife was so enveloped in this dream of historic succession that she appears in the memoirs as, simply, "Dorothy Hearst, wife of Jack Hearst, who was the son of Mr. and Mrs. William Randolph Hearst of the famous newspaper chain." (No satisfaction for the "Who Was She?" class here.) The same sense of historic fittingness could have inflamed Paley's desire for the Manhasset place, for Kiluna Farm, which is what it was called, belonged to Ralph Pulitzer, part heir of another "famous newspaper chain."

Paley bought the Pulitzer place and lives there into his late eighties. Sometimes, it is true, the desired effects of his self-setting were lost on visitors. To Lady Diana Cooper, for example, the appointments at Kiluna Farm seemed anything but simple. "A little table in your bedroom was laid as for a nuptial night, with fine lawn, plates, forks, and a pyramid of choice-bloomed peaches, figs and grapes. In the bathroom were all the aids to sleep, masks for open eyes, soothing unguents and potions." Lady Diana noticed everything, not omitting her host's appearance, which was "physically a little Oriental and very attractive." Still, she was depressed by his "luxury taste. . . . [T]he standard is unattainable to us tradition-ridden tired Europeans." But such are the tired reproaches of Old Money everywhere, even American Old Money. Paley should have been flattered; in such people's eyes, success always looks like a succession.

In time, Paley's taste became sufficiently self-assured so that he could venture a few forays into modernism. His memoirs show him to be proud of commissioning Eero Saarinen to design a new headquarters for CBS; proud, too, of his collection of modern painting and of his rise to the chairmanship of the board of the Museum of Modern Art. These moves would not have been undertaken if the object in view had not been already certificated as "of museum quality." Even so, I suspect he would never have made them if it hadn't been for his growing acceptance and ease in the company of Old Money. His career in collecting, for example, began in the late 1930s under the tutelage of that "natural patrician" Averell Harriman, who in one summer introduced him to Impressionists in Paris and bird-shooting in the Little Carpathians.

It wasn't until 1947, however, that Paley might be said to have secured a firm seat in the class. That was the year he married Barbara Cushing Mortimer, one of the three famous Cushing sisters, daughters of Massachusetts General Hospital's renowned neurosurgeon Harvey Cushing, each of whom was more gloriously lovely than the others, each of whom had a nickname cuter than the next: Minnie, Betsey, and Babe. They had all married well, these girls, all of them to Old Money: Minnie to Vincent Astor, then to James Fosburgh; Betsey to FDR's son James, then to Jock Whitney; Babe to Stanley Mortimer. Paley was next. His emotions at the joining of this union may be judged by the title he gave to the chapter of his memoirs in which it takes place: "Triumph."

In acquiring the hand of Babe Paley, the great programmer finally realized, at least to his own satisfaction, what might be called the program of his own life. Self and setting, mirror image and social image, all had been made new—more accurately, made *old*. In the two long, lovingly detailed paragraphs in which he describes the furnishings of his CBS office, chosen with Babe's help, the word "old" is insisted upon with some frequency, varied only by "antique" and "traditional." The room even manages to look "lived in." But the real triumph of this room is that here Paley came into his own as an instrument of upper-class taste. No more flipping through the pages of magazines to discover what beauties appeal to him. The learned discriminations are natural discriminations now. The old "gut" has been replaced by a new, a finer "gut." How can we tell? We can tell because of the apparent effortlessness with which he, with Babe's help, has created this setting for himself. He tells us, pointedly, that "the first-time visitor might well believe it all came together out of some sort of carelessness." There it is, the key word in the familiar vocabulary of Old Money's most characteristic stance in the world: the casual, easy pose of the ineffably self-assured, the effortlessly *attractive*. With that word, we know that Paley had arrived.

When I was at St. Paul's School, the word most of us would have chosen to describe Paley's memoirs is "pathetic." "Pathetic" is the kindest thing we had to say for people who tried too hard to be "attractive," who tried too hard, that is, to be like people who didn't have to try to be anything: people like us, people who already *were*. There was always a touch of vindictiveness in the way we tossed off that word "pathetic," and I daresay there still is. For people like Paley remind us of what we would rather forget. His effortful carelessness, his labored casualness, his heavy-handed understatement, all call attention to what it is that we—authentically enough, because affordably enough—are all so casual and careless about, what it is that we are understating. He reminds us of the object of all this repression: the hideous, vulgar figure of Market Man.

In Paley's memoirs, as in Old Money lives, Market Man is conspicuously absent in any number of ways. One that's very significant is the way Paley scants the world of fashion. Fashion is a problem for Old Money, and even more so for any aspirant to Old Money. On the one hand, it is wonderfully alluring, possessing the natural appeal of novelty; and the rich, whether Old or New, are well positioned to respond to novelty wherever it crops up, which is everywhere: in the fine and decorative arts, in resorts, restaurants, and ballet companies, and in the people (celebrities or protocelebrities) who make the art, design the clothes, run the restaurants, choreograph the dances, and so forth. On the other hand, fashion presents Old Money (New Money only if it is trying to become Old) with the singular difficulty of having to figure out what, in all this welter of novelty, is of "museum quality."

The casual, most distinctive, and in some respects most invidious method of dealing with this difficulty is to ignore novelty itself. It is no coincidence that the two American cities most widely known for their hereditary upper classes, Boston and Philadelphia, are the two most notorious for their hostility to fashion. My grandfather's disdain for originality as "a failure of memory" was perfectly characteristic of his circle. Patricians of those old towns never go anywhere unless they've "always" gone there, never know anyone unless they've "always" known them. Fashion never troubles them. Sometimes, indeed, it seems as though anything they do not inherit they do without, buying only the very plain food on their plates. Cleveland Amory tells the story of the Boston lady whose beautiful and otherwise well-furnished Beacon Hill house was bare of rugs, simply because her mother hadn't left her any good ones. The story is a paradigm of one response to the problem of finding "museum quality" in fashion: Have nothing to do with it. I remember once going to Naushon Island in Buzzards Bay, a "country place" not much smaller than Manhattan, which has been "in the family" of Boston Forbeses—that is, in trust for Forbeses—since before the Civil War. The house I stayed in was a somewhat severe H. H. Richardson cottage of twenty-two rooms. The ambience, though "old" and "simple," was as far removed from Kiluna Farm as one could get without becoming actually squalid. Paint peeled from every wall and ceiling; it was a kindness to call the furniture rudimentary; the kitchen seemed well equipped for making sandwiches; everywhere was the odor of mold, carried along by brisk drafts of damp sea air.

No automobiles disturbed this idyll; none are permitted on the island. Forbeses walk or go by horse, or sail. Museum quality is assured on Naushon: the buggies, the sailboats, even the Forbeses, whose clothes look as though they, too, had been handed down to them by their mothers and fathers, are all certifiable antiques. On Naushon, only the horses look fashionable.

Forbeses, however, are patricians, and the distinctively aristocratic sector of the Old Money class cannot dismiss fashion so easily. To ignore it, they believe, is to deny oneself too much fun, too much beauty, and perhaps power as well. Moreover, the "museum quality" problem can be readily dealt with by cultivating the people who can be counted on to know this quality when they see it, or to make it when they want it. I mean the intelligentsia—the critics, professors, dealers, curators, magazine and book editors, arts journalists, and other such connoisseurs, whose business it is to make such judgments. One may also cultivate the producers of the artifacts, entertainments, and services contending for a place in the museum—artists, writers, architects, decorators, singers and dancers, couturiers, gardeners, restauranteurs, and the like. (The producers can't be trusted to judge their own work, of course, but they can provide critical insight into everyone else's, some of it occasionally positive.) The presence of these people in (and often of) many Old Money circles in New York and Cambridge, for example, distinguishes the society of those cities from that of much of Boston and Philadelphia, and all of Providence, Rochester, or Hartford.

But it is a risky thing they do, these Old Money aristocrats of fashion. The risk goes way beyond the peril of buying something, or reading something, or applauding something that isn't of museum quality. Fashion is appalling to so many Old Money beneficiaries because it carries with it a dreadful reminder of the incredible force and fluidity of the marketplace. Entering any world where fashion is an element, the Old Money participant risks entering a trade or, even more repulsively, becoming a "heavy player" in the trade. One might, for example, become a flack for one's own financial investments in this or that artist or restaurant or dress designer. Babe Paley flirted with that danger every year she appeared on the Ten Best-Dressed Women list; as it was, she embarrassed her children at the Brearley School.

Again, the easy solution is to retire completely: to decorate one's setting or person entirely from the attic, as patricians typically do, or from other people's attics, as Paley did. This safe course brings risks of its own, however, both to the overall culture and to Old Money's paternalistic pretensions to lead it. Long ago, in my great-grandfather's day, the brilliant Old Money aristocrat John Jay Chapman scorned the prudent patrician withdrawal from the cultural fray as leading to a culturally disastrous hypocrisy:

> In our ordinary moods we regard the conclusions of the poets as both true and untrue—true to feeling, untrue to fact.... Most men have a duplicated philosophy which enables them to love the arts and wit of mankind, at the same time that they conveniently despise them. Life is ugly and necessary; art is beautiful and impossible.... The practical problem is to keep them in separate spheres and to enjoy both.... Such are the convictions of the average cultivated man. His back is broken, but he lives in the two halves comfortably enough.

But it's not only the man's back that is broken; it is the culture's. Patricians are not much distressed by this. Both my Aldrich grandfathers would have thought the two cultures an inevitable consequence of "emergence": one culture for the emerged, like them, like Bill Paley and his children; and another for everyone else, like the viewers of CBS television programs.

Aristocrats of the class take a characteristically bolder course of action. With their allies among the critics and artists, they assume a deliberately exemplary stance toward the marketplace. They "find" and "discover" things; they model things for everyone else, and thereby, or so they hope, influence national taste. In matters of personal appearance, this opportunity to exercise leadership seems to have arisen in the 1920s, the decade of the first mass movement of the middle classes into colleges and universities. Zelda Fitzgerald pretended to be unhappy about what happened then:

> The flapper is deceased. Her outer accoutrements have been bequeathed to several hundred's girls' schools, and to several million small-town belles, always imitative of the big-town shop girls via the "novelty stores" of their respective small towns. It is a great bereavement to me.

She is joking, surely. If she liked the flapper "line" on herself, she should have been delighted to see it on every other girl. She had only to move on to something else, parading her precious distinction for a while before once again passing it on to the less adventuresome. The result should be gratifying: the maintenance of a certain minimum aesthetic tone in the whole society. Herbert Pell noted the same phenomenon in 1938: "Thirty years ago, it was comparatively easy to recognize a rich man by his clothes and the distinction among women was patent to the most careless eye. Now it is difficult to distinguish the average New York office worker from the daughter of a millionaire." Pell couldn't have been happier. It was a perfect example of what an Old Money class was supposed to do: elevate the tone of society and thereby justify itself. My father found the same pleasure: not about fashions in clothes (though I would swear he was the first man of his class to wear a pink shirt) but about fashions in art. Through the Institute of Contemporary Art and later the Boston Arts Festival, my father and a number of other Old Money and would-be Old Money Bostonians tried to give their fellow citizens a taste for modernist art. The effort caused a rift between him and his patrician father, which the two of them, for most of their lives, could barely bridge with courtesies. Nevertheless, my father adored trying to move people in this way, to persuade them to love the things he thought lovable. If fashion is a genie that makes markets, including art markets, move, then Old Money and its allies feel obliged to persuade the genie that what *they* want is better than what the masses (think they) want. The risk remains, of course. Fashion leaders come very close to an actual descent *into* the marketplace, where no Old Money beneficiary likes to be. But the risk of not taking that risk may be even worse. As Chapman sensed a hundred years ago, it is the risk of being aesthetically irrelevant.

A more conspicuous absence in Paley's memoirs, and so a more conspicuous clue to the repression of Market Man, is the absence of any mention of money. Almost never do he or his wives *buy* anything: They "discover" their treasures in antique stores or "find" them in galleries. The process is one of ingestion, not purchase, the consumer's equivalent of a programmer's "gut reaction." But Old Money taste is always agnostic with respect to money. The whole point of inculcating the peculiar aesthetic of the class is to lift its habitat above the quick and nasty transactions of the cash nexus to the exalted plane of disinterested delight.

Another reason to avoid mention of money is that the chink of coin often works unfortunate changes in other people's envy. The task undertaken by the Old Money curriculum is to teach beneficiaries how to *manage* envy, not merely how to arouse it. Children of wealth learn to do this early on. Inviting friends home from school, for example, they find themselves having to explain how it is that the living room looks like the Louis XVI room at the Metropolitan Museum, or what a "conservatory" is. Mark Hampton once told me about an Old Money client who cried out in panic at a proposal he dared make for her dining room.

> "I can't have those *boiseries,*" she said. "I mean, they look so expensive. What will Suzie say when she comes home from Radcliffe?"
>
> Or if it isn't Suzie radicalized at Radcliffe, it's the little boys that Tommy brings home from Collegiate. I've had clients who are afraid that their children might trash the place. Maids are much worse than *boiseries,* of course. No decent little liberal wants to bring his friends home from school when the first thing they're going to see is eight octogenarian Irish ladies padding around the house in uniforms. One of them might be somebody's grandmother, for God's sake!

In time, the children will either leave the house or learn to cope with their friends' envy. But the first rule of envy management is to understate, to the point of repression, the facts of dollar value. Money is democratic. Everybody wants it and it often seems as though everyone were getting it. Money envy can inflame the ugliest proclivities of the hustling world. What beneficiaries must learn to do, therefore, is to redirect envy away from the democratically available powers of money and toward the rather more "exclusive" powers inherent in their own inimitable taste.

Finally, money is repressed the better to highlight the ethos of the gift. One notices this aspect of the matter in relation to collecting art. America's Old and would-be Old Rich have usually collected beautiful things for reasons simultaneously self-centered and public-spirited. Their collections beautify their surroundings, ennoble their acquisitiveness, and enhance their reputations for sensitivity and judgment. And for the New Rich seeking to become Old, collecting is a way of making oneself socially attractive to custodians of the extended patrimony. But the rich also collect out of a breeding in, or crude aspiration toward, the gift ethos, with its central impulse to make a gift of what has been given. They might pass on their collections to their own descendants, of course, but this is rarely done in America. Old World collections were accretions; here, even among the Old Rich, they have always been accomplishments, and individual ones at that. Without primogeniture, then, there is no way for a collector to pass on his accomplishment intact, to enter history arm in arm with beauty, except by giving his collection to one of the institutions that care for Old Money's extended patrimonies. But mention of dollar values spoils all this. It reminds everyone of a hundred different vulgarities they'd rather not think about, vulgarities that the presence of art was meant to dispel. It reminds them of the art world's flagrant commercialization: the noisome rabble of greedy dealers, spoiled painters, corrupt critics, and unctuous museum directors that the art market spawns whenever, as in the last two decades, *art moves*. It reminds them of that most outrageous betrayal of the gift ethos, "deaccessioning." It reminds them of their own anxious aspirations to put together a collection of "museum quality." It reminds them that some people consider their gifts nothing but a tax dodge and their accomplishment nothing but an act of purchase, a jiggle in the movement of a market. Mentioning dollar values around a work of art, in short, amounts to a massive return of the understated. It spoils the careless effect. It will not do.

After their settings, the classiest acts by which the Old Rich reveal themselves are matters of an attractive personal presence: postures, demeanor, gestures, speech, manners, and other clues of personality and character that tell those of us who are interested in putting people in the places where, socially speaking, they belong.

Of course, to describe the particular significance that Old Money gives the word "attractive" is to risk making comparisons that most people, in a supposedly egalitarian nation, find odious. Perhaps that's why Paley did not attempt it; not in his memoir anyway. But I imagine that Paley on his social and corporate rounds behaves as many Americans do, certainly Old Money Americans. Like a curator on a visit to a strange museum, I'm sure he repeatedly engages in making the discriminatory judgments that mark the passage of a social connoisseur. Like the rest of us, he is probably wrong in some of his attributions. And like us, he may even feel guilty at treating people like this: questioning their authenticity, comparing their aesthetic values, submitting them, in a society where everything is supposed to be possible, to the terrible finality of the pigeonhole.

Still, I'm quite certain he does it. And I am certain, too, of what he looks for. It is the equivalent in behavior of Old Money's "understatement" in things. Paley knows what that is. It's in the title of his book. Other tycoons crudely emblazon their memoirs with the name they made for themselves: Boone! Iacocca! Paley's is called, somewhat pathetically, I'm afraid, *As It Happened.* The negligent note is just right, and all social connoisseurs claim to detect it or wish to strike it. Whenever Old Money's characteristic presence is described, the critical vocabulary returns again and again to the same family of words—casual, careless, nonchalant, insouciant, easy, unstudied, natural, effortless.

In Arthur Schlesinger's account of the life and times of Franklin Roosevelt, for example, he has the tiny, acne-scarred figure of Louis McHenry Howe gazing down from the gallery of the Albany statehouse at Roosevelt, then a state senator. "If Howe could not have this careless magnificence himself," Schlesinger writes, "then at least he could identify himself with a man whose qualities he so much prized." Fitzgerald, after having Dexter Green people the room with the men who already love Judy Jones, has him reflect on their carelessness: "he knew that to be careless in dress and manner required more confidence than to be careful. But carelessness was for his children." J. P. Marquand has one of his envious Dexter-like snobs reviewing his inadequacies: "I did not have that intangible radiant inheritance that makes for carelessness and joy, or that heaven-sent serenity and regardlessness for others' rights which was so beautiful yet cruel. It touched me, but I did not have it. Bill was the golden boy, and Sue the golden girl."

What's invidious about these careless people is their sense of composure, as though they were perfectly integrated in spirit, mind, and body. Nowhere in their makeup, it seems, are there any of those embarrassing dissonances of motive, those deformities of character or bewildering blanks in sensibility, that afflict the more common run of men and women. Seymour St. John, Choate's long-time headmaster, caught the essence of this quality in a phrase: "the sheer restfulness of good breeding," he called it. Such people are whole where others are in pieces; they are smooth where others are coarse; they are broad where others are narrow. Above all, they are confident, fearless, gallant—the adjectives fell like rose petals around the three Roosevelts, for example, and John F. Kennedy—when everyone else is weak, hesitant, fearful, or ashamed.

At the center of this curious stillness there appears to be an impalpable sense of latency, a sort of polyvalent potentiality. "'Tis the perpetual promise of more than can be fulfilled," Emerson said of the idol being created here, nicely isolating the reasons for envying it. The observation also explains why envy of these people so suddenly lurches from longing to resentment. For this "divine assurance," which is what even Veblen claimed to have seen in them, speaks of pagan gods: It has no moral value whatsoever. "Careless" people have the fascination of pure aesthetic form, waiting on events—some prince's kiss, some trumpet's call—to bring it into a single, perfect, compositionally beautiful actuality. There is even a curious purity to the sexuality of these figures, as though everything that rises, even the genders, must converge. The template presence of Old Money is alternately or indistinguishably male and female. "Golden" girls and "golden" boys, Basil and Josephine, they might be brothers and sisters, so closely do they resemble one another. Each stands there, equally "handsome," equally "beautiful," each perceived as being in a state of sexual latency that is in some eyes terminal, in others on the verge of arousal.

Fortunately for everyone concerned, however, amoral carelessness is not the only clue to the presence of Old Money. There are at least two others, marking a clear movement from aesthetics to ethics: the social graces and the social virtues.

The social graces are fine manners, the arts of courtesy. They have a tough time in middling America. As in the work of Mark Twain, most famously, they're the object of a constant three-way battle between their prissy promoters, their derisive detractors, and their doughty practitioners. But criticism of fine manners is by no means peculiar to Americans; it is an ancient practice and always ticks off the same two points: that manners can deceive, and that they're simply a way of putting some people down and others up.

Veblen made the second point when he characterized the social graces as "an expression of the relation of status—a symbolic pantomime of mastery on the one hand and subservience on the other." The iconography here is Egyptian, Byzantine, Gothic—that is to say, static. And it does undoubtedly represent some of the more primitive fantasies of the class: its nostalgic yearning for "human" social ties—slavery, for example, or the mutual allegiance of knight and lord, priest and bishop—in which the cash nexus, contracts, freedom of appetite, and all the other paraphernalia of Market Man are made to freeze or go away. But the last thing Market Man wants in his everyday manners is a mimicry of "mastery" and "subservience." Mastery and subservience are end points, the *results* of conflict. Market Man wants manners that reflect a different arrangement, in which no fixed positions are presumed and there is no end to the struggle to create them. Market Man wants what is known as *common* courtesy, manners that answer to his need for some minimum of system and predictability in his endless conflicts: some signs that there are limits to the suffering that can be inflicted on losers and on the power that can be awarded to winners. Manners in such a society must be like a boxer's gloves, or a magician's, or the velvet caress of a clever woman.

Basically, all that Old Money can do to refine this common courtesy is to endow it with the appearance of art. Emerson caught this aspect of the matter when he described the social graces as "music and sculpture and picture to many who do not pretend to appreciation of those arts." Anyone who has seen real courtesy in action knows what he means, though I suspect it's the art of the dance (not much appreciated in Concord) that comes most often to mind. Courtesies are movements, dispositions of the body as well as (sometimes) of the mind and spirit. They are required to get oneself in and out of a room properly, to introduce oneself (shaking hands, looking the other in the eye) and to introduce others, to greet people, to make them feel comfortable in one's company, and to send them on their way.

What gives these movements the aura of art is that they are designed to please, perhaps even to delight. And they do. Old Money's "old-fashioned" courtesy delights by putting anxious, enterprising strivers at their ease, or by distracting the defeated from their losses. Much of the celebrated charm of all upper classes—in the eyes of lower classes anyway—stems from their ability to bring others close to the healing touch of their own ineffable presence in the world. This ability to put other people at their ease, to make them happy *with themselves,* is a great gift in the Old Money ethos of the gift, and the only really personal one. Its highest form is reached by those inheritors, mostly but by no means all aristocrats, who manage to bestow a kind of delight almost everywhere they go, as though they exclaimed, on meeting some vain contender for success, "Why, you're as good as I am!" In a society where the usual expression of egalitarian sentiment is a sullen "I'm as good as you are, any day!" the upper-class form can fall like a blessing.

John Jay Chapman offered an explanation of this gift: that the

upper classes could close, even as they marked, the social distance between themselves and others. "Come down to it," he wrote his half-
Italian, half-Boston Brahmin, and wholly Romantic wife, Minna, "and
you find the paradox that only aristocrats are truly democratic in their
social conduct and feeling. They only are simple—they have nothing
to gain and nothing to lose, and have the freedom and simplicity of
human beings." Chapman was an extremist: Mad Jack, he was called
by some of his stuffier clubmates. He was often led to take a much
more aggressive view of the responsibilities of Old Money in a democratic society than Eliot, Pell, or Baltzell ever took. Aristocrats should
not be content to be "democratic." Aristocrats should discipline the
commercial classes, never losing an opportunity to remind them how
disfigured by fear and greed they really are. This was the function of
aristocrats: not only that they should be above economics, where freedom and simplicity reign, but that by their easy, natural, and democratic manners they should remind everyone else of what they are
missing.

It goes without saying (Chapman refrained from saying it) that
Old Money's courtesy often pays astonishing dividends for individuals
and for the class. Again and again, someone will find himself in the
company of some reverberantly Old Money personage—a Rockefeller,
say, or a du Pont—and then return to his own social circle with the
amazing news that the personage is "really a great guy, just like you
or me." (The same news gets passed around in Old Money circles when
the personage in question is a success of some sort: a celebrated painter,
or athlete, who also happens to have a modicum of good manners.) It's
a ludicrous by-product of envy that we impute to the rich or successful
the worst possible disposition toward ourselves, and are then surprised
and overjoyed when they prove to be even faintly agreeable. Chapman
did not mention this benefit of his aristocrat's manners, I suspect, because the thought of it was beneath his dignity, reminding him that
manners, even with all due credit to their giftedness and aesthetic
delight, are hopelessly instrumental, "economic" ways of presenting
oneself in the world. Every child of wealth knows as well as any other
that "it pays to be nice."

The blessing they seem to bestow when they are nice is known as
charm. Franklin Roosevelt had it, for example, and knew how to use
it to perfection. I think of the day when Senator Huey Long of Louisiana came to visit him in the White House. It was in 1935, when the

New Deal's first recovery programs seemed to have stalled, and the Kingfish wanted to try one more time to get the President to redistribute the nation's wealth from the rich to the poor. (Huey particularly had in mind FDR's friend and cousin Vincent Astor.) This was not the first time they'd met. Two years earlier, Huey had been invited to Hyde Park for lunch, arriving in a white suit, an orchid shirt, and a pink tie, a costume that provoked the President's mother to whisper, loudly: "Who is that awful little man sitting next to my son?" It is not known whether Huey heard this remark; he would not have been wounded if he had. Huey liked provoking the rich, especially the rich and well-born. For his meeting at the White House two years later, in fact, he had his provocations all planned in advance. He was going to sit there and do anything—quote the Bible, Plato, statistics—he had to do to persuade the President to his point of view. He even planned to touch him. Not with his hand: Huey hated touching people with any part of his body. He would use his fedora. He would tap out his arguments with a hat.

Roosevelt for his part planned to touch Huey where he hurt, by telling him that he would no longer be consulted on federal patronage in Louisiana. The President had already dispatched the IRS to inquire about the senator's interest in the Win or Lose Oil Company. (This was the source, incidentally, of the inherited wealth of Russell Long, Huey's only son, one of my great-grandfather's successors as chairman of the Senate Finance Committee, and a man whose life was proof positive that many inheritors of wealth, and their parents, have no use whatever for the curriculum of Old Money.) But Roosevelt's IRS move had to remain a secret, lest he be accused of abuse of power. To keep the interview going his way, he would have to make do with the patronage threat and his own formidable charm. And never, perhaps, had that charm been put to a greater test. Huey sat there in his white suit, fedora in his hand, and he talked and talked, more and more passionately, and every once in a while he would take the hat and gently, just for emphasis, hit the President on his crippled knees.

It wasn't happening. The suit, the hat, the bulbous little man in the suit, with the hat—they just were not there. That's the power of charm. It can make the world seem the sort of place it ought to be. It can even, sometimes, convince the world to behave accordingly. But mostly what it does is to hold the charmer in a sort of magical social space, where he can go on functioning, calculating, and (if need be) planning his revenge. Schlesinger sees Roosevelt in this ghastly moment as surrounding himself with "a ring of cool and gracious phrases."

Brooke Astor, Vincent's third and last wife, and the able inheritor of his foundation, uses almost the same language to describe her own manners:

> If people are rude to you, pay no attention, they simply don't know any better. . . . Why argue with rude and aggressive people? It simply weakens and eats away at the spirit. . . . As a child, I was made to feel that I should create an atmosphere of goodwill around me. It is . . . in a strange way, a defense. It is a moat of still but deep water, that keeps one in tranquil isolation without appearing to.

Men have drowned in that moat. After Vincent died, little more than five years after they were married, and she became an heiress of one of the most famous fortunes in America, she was suddenly faced with people who were "totally different from the way I had seen them before. I became, overnight, a person to be manipulated, talked to, and asked to behave in a way that was completely contrary to my character. It surprised and hurt me deeply. . . . I had never before seen the claws and teeth of men climbing the status ladder." But that's what moats are for: to make sure that no one ever gets their ladders anywhere near one's walls. Ideally, no one ever catches on that there *are* walls. So it was with Roosevelt's ring of cool and gracious phrases. When Huey left his meeting with FDR, he told the press that he'd been persuaded that the President and he were working for the same goal—he, Huey, "shouting" for it, he admitted, but the President working for it too, in a more "cultured" way. He was wrong, of course, as he soon found out.

All charms eventually lose their power; some charms do not work at all. Old Money beneficiaries forget this at their peril. The trouble with Old Money's social graces is the trouble with all arts: They may or may not express the actual moral disposition of the artist. What manners mimic is not "mastery" and "subservience" but dignity and respect. Always at issue, however, is the question whether there's any substance beneath the seeming. The recipient of a courtesy can never be sure whether the gift expresses the actual sentiments of the giver— her "real" respect for you, for example—or masks quite opposite feelings. Courtesy is a performing art, and it has never been wise to confuse performative excellence with moral excellence.

The social graces may always have a touch of traitor in them, or a touch of the tease. FDR was often accused of personal betrayal, bitterly (and sometimes rightly) so. And I suspect that Brooke Astor may often be accused of being a tease, though with what accuracy I can't say. Yet perfidy like theirs is as common as dirt in the business world—in the worlds of politics and foundations too, for that matter—where it passes as a normal part of the daily struggle for advantage. Why should possessors of Old Money be judged by different standards? The answer is obvious: Different standards are expected of them, not least (one may hope) by themselves. Inconstancy, phoniness—these should be beneath them, if for no other reason than that they can afford to rise above them. Deception and disappointment: in French, the same word is used for the two experiences; in FDR's White House, and perhaps among supplicants to Brooke Astor's foundation, a single experience frequently evoked the two words. To repeat what Emerson said of the presence of such people: "'Tis the perpetual promise of more than can be fulfilled." To be "attractive" is to be fated eventually to be resented. It's enough to make some beneficiaries of Old Money want to chuck the whole effort.

Yet that mimicry of dignity and respect cannot be dismissed so easily, or ought not to be. The mutual giving of dignity and respect, phony though it may prove to be, makes the social graces the transitive operations they are, shuttling Old Money back and forth between aesthetics and ethics. I have a story about my beloved grandfather that illustrates what I mean here. I came back to this country from France in the summer of 1961, when Kennedy was entering the glory days of his presidency (or so it seemed to me at the time). So far as I knew, my grandfather's allegiance to the patrician wing of the Republican party—the Lodge, Rockefeller, and (adoptively) Eisenhower wing— had never wavered in the years I had been away. Yet I suspected that it had suffered some strains in the 1960 election, and this suspicion emboldened me to ask him how he had voted. (Normally, he and I did not discuss politics, or art, for that matter: I had no wish to fall out of his good graces, as my father had done.)

My grandfather thought for a moment, as if what he was going to say surprised him. "Well," he said, "to tell the truth, I rather wanted to vote for Kennedy. He's been here to the house, you know. Your uncle

George, I think, used to bring him around when they were at school together. He seemed an extremely attractive fellow."

I could fill in the pause at the end of the last sentence: "for an Irish Catholic." Like most Bostonians of his class and time—any time since the 1840s, actually—my grandfather loathed the Irish. The children of any other ethnic group—Jewish, Italian, German, blacks (though I don't think he knew any blacks)—my grandfather was more than happy to consider for friendship or potential friendship, provided they met certain Old Money class criteria. But not the Irish. Thus for him to find Jack Kennedy "attractive" was something of a triumph for the Old Money curriculum that the President had followed: for Choate, Harvard, the Spee Club, ample trust funds, and a winning presence.

But Grandpa could not bring himself to vote for the boy. "I couldn't do it," he said with a touch of regret. "I've been a Republican all my life. I just could not vote for a Democrat. On the other hand, I must confess that I couldn't vote for Mr. Nixon, either. He's so very unattractive, don't you think? Good heavens, how can one vote for a man who has to shave three times a day?"

This is a characteristic passage of Old Money's imagination. It's as though the lift of hereditary wealth carries its beneficiaries to a plane of consciousness where everything below, their own conduct as well as everyone else's, seems a matter of form. "Good form," they say, speaking now of a woman's table manners, now of her helping an old gentleman into dinner, now of her easy, graceful acknowledgment of the truth despite great temptation to tell a lie. Born and bred in Old Money circles, one learns to think of the good and the beautiful as the same, really, and that there need never be any awkwardness about doing what is right. One learns that ugly moral behavior is a contradiction in terms, as unthinkable as a stumbling ballerina or a nauseated doctor. Thus in a sense the social graces are the social virtues. They are where *virtu* and virtue come together, where sin and solecism combine.

Still, distinctions must be made. The social virtues have ethical value, as even a mere list of them suggests: modesty (understatement), personal and institutional loyalty, truthfulness, generosity and gratitude, and the elements of sportsmanship—magnanimous winning, cheerful losing, and fair play. One can make the point in another way, by drawing the distinction between "character" and "personality." In nurseries, at St. Midas schools, at the rhetorical and actual Harvard, at country clubs and yacht clubs and gentlemen's and ladies' clubs, even face to face with one's father or mother—wherever an attempt is made to inculcate the graces and the virtues, the graces are said to belong to personality, the virtues to character. Personality is always addressed to an audience. It's the figure we cut in public, actions asking for aesthetic judgment. It's what Paley and others might call "style"—preferably a personal style. Mentors of the Old Money curriculum have insisted for generations that people like Paley may become so concerned with cultivating a personal style that they omit the next step, which takes them toward a virtuous character. Character concerns the figure we cut in public *and* in private, moral actions demanding moral judgment, addressed ultimately not to an audience but to duty, tradition, God, some notion of the good. Paley's memoir has hardly a word to say about his or anyone else's character; my great-grandfather left no views on the matter, either: Character may be one of those concerns that can't be cultivated in one generation.

Old Money might be delighted to hear that this is the case, for it would then be plausible for the class to declare that it had an "exclusive" on loyalty, truth-telling, sportsmanship, and so on. But of course these virtues are readily available to any member of the human race, and to claim otherwise, publicly, would be disastrous. The most the class claims, again publicly, is that it holds these social virtues in trust (as it does so much else), and that the virtues are better off in their care than in any other group's. Even Market Man frequently admits he can't afford them. Old Money can.

Moreover, as the Old Rich from time to time concede, Market Man has his own social virtues: industry, single-mindedness, energy, tenacity, alertness, and the intellectual courage to face facts and calculate risks and benefits. He has his own form of imagination, an entrepreneurial one that gives him the ability to imagine how he might satisfy other people's needs while simultaneously satisfying his own, and his own ethos, the spirit of competitive self-reliance. Market Man has not been well regarded as a human type, not even by his most persuasive apologists. Adam Smith thought him selfish and vain, David Ricardo thought him liable to the worst sort of folly, and John Maynard Keynes would not have sought his company at dinner. Even so, though in making wealth he might not serve the cause of the social virtues, still less the graces, he does serve society. Indeed, he makes it possible.

Against these worthy but asocial virtues, Old Money's might almost to have been contrived to play like dark against light. Personal loyalty to old friends is a good example of this odd chiaroscuro. Old

Money people pride themselves on nurturing the sort of friendships—among men, among women, even (lately) among men and women—that they believe don't have a chance to develop in the hustling world of Market Man. The beneficiaries of the Old Money curriculum come into a social life in which they can enjoy the freedom and mobility of middle-class social life, the stability of the social life of the poor, or some combination of the two, as they wish. But the keys to this given is the loyalty of one's friends—the old friends who go back to summers in Maine, to the years at St. Paul's or Foxcroft or the dining halls and clubs of Harvard. Among one's friends (as much as, or more than, in money) are the foundations of that belongingness, that social security, which is the envy of all New Money wishing to become Old. Represented in those friendships, too, is everything that Old Money knows of class consciousness: common memories, shared tastes, discipline (peer pressure)—all the mutual impositions and presumptions of a social class.

These friendships were one of the deliberate objectives of Endicott Peabody in founding Groton. Himself, educated at an English public school, a bowdlerized version of which he wanted to recreate at Groton, Peabody had the idea that it was thanks to such schools that the English possessed "a genius for friendship." He was thinking of the sort of friendship celebrated in Tennyson's "In Memoriam," and he was delighted to note that "this same tendency is discovered among the boarding schools of our country." William Amory Gardner, a classics teacher at Groton (also a member of Harvard's Porcellian Club and the best man at John Jay and Minna Chapman's wedding), might have cited Plato's *Symposium* as the most illustrative text for the friendships he valued. (There are always several such teachers at St. Midas schools.) Miss Charlotte Noland of the Foxcroft School may never have heard of the *Symposium* or "In Memoriam"—she was not a literary woman, fancying instead a curriculum of equestrian sports, military drill, and good works for her girls—but generations of Old Money women learned at Foxcroft and other St. Midas girls' schools the same fiercely loyal, sometimes romantic friendships that Peabody and Gardner thought one of the great benefits of a boarding-school education.

Schools were not the only setting, nor Tennyson and Plato the only texts, for such relationships. Other Old Money people would point to the *Song of Roland* and the friendships of war; still others would cite the clubby friendships celebrated in John Buchan's novels, or the cool but somehow enduring ones of Evelyn Waugh's men and women.

American writers were late to explore the dramatic possibilities in these friendships, but loyalty is a constant theme in J. P. Marquand's work. All his Old Money men, it seems, just before suffering a fatal cramp in the waters of social change, can be heard to sigh, "There is such a thing as loyalty, isn't there?" The theme is also to be found in James Gould Cozzens's novels, and it is the entire focus, along with envy, of one of America's best boarding-school novels, John Knowles's *A Separate Peace.*

Market Man cannot know these "old" friendships, thinks Old Money, either their sufferings or their joys. Friendship is a gift, a mutual giving, for which time and security are needed to give and receive. They are needed to build up a thick bed of shared associations, stories and anecdotes, prejudices and proclivities; and most important perhaps, for trust and tolerance. In the marketplace, there is little trust (*caveat emptor*), and tolerance only for "merit," for people whose company confers power, service, or some other form of advantage. Under such circumstances, how can friendships flourish? Where merit rules, people are forced into critical assessments of their own and everyone else's worth, and the measure is all too often economic. The problem with meritocracies is that they are epistemologically totalitarian: The knowledge they know how to arrive at, and what to do with, is economic knowledge—knowledge about consumption and production, about wants and the satisfaction of wants. Noneconomic knowledge, such as the kind revealed to friends or in a gift relationship, is revealed only in the most fleeting light. In meritocratic markets of the self, for example, like the upper and middle managements of corporations, people are thrown together to struggle and scheme together, occasionally to get a little rest and recreation together. At best, they become comrades. But they do not become friends. The relationship is improvised and intense, like the relationships of soldiers or athletes, which is exactly how these people see themselves. Comradeship seldom survives the occasion that gave it birth, seldom even survives quitting time. It evaporates on the commute. True, comrades are made again the next morning, or on the next level up (or down) the corporate ladder; Americans are the most gregarious people on earth. They have to be: they have no friends.

With economic life subdued and Market Man kept down, an Old Money beneficiary should be able to regard human "merit"—a person's high use-value to the enterprise, whatever it may be—as he does any other form of excellence, with delight or indifference. Wellington's famous remark on the Order of the Garter—that merit hasn't a damn thing to do with it—is frequently cited by critics and apologists of Old Money's social exclusivity, but the citation misses the point. It's not that Old Money beneficiaries don't give a damn about merit but rather that they may be so far above the exigencies of economic life that they *needn't* give a damn about it. Merit makes its way in the world by renting itself out in some marketplace or other, by being of use. And very rich Old Rich families, especially those that make forays out into public life like some of the Rockefellers and Kennedys, hold in semi-feudal thrall dozens of lawyers, intellectuals, confidential secretaries, and other men and women of "merit"—all for their use-value. They may even make friends with them. But there is no economic necessity behind these relationships, not on Old Money's side. Inheritors of wealth, simply put, do not have to use people.

This explains one of the most astonishing features of Old Money social life—astonishing, at any rate, to those who were not born to it. I mean its tedium. The "old" friendships that are the object of Old Money's loyalty and the agency of its belongingness may be a splendid reproach to the fleeting comradeliness or exploitativeness of Market Man's relationships, but they can also be boring. "Boring" is the commonest word in Old Money's social vocabulary. But the insult is mild compared to those that are hurled at the Old Money class from outside—that it's "stuffy," "old-fashioned," "pompous," and "stupid." They're all richly deserved, the inevitable reward of a social group that often prefers to inherit the company it keeps rather than choose it. But most Old Money beneficiaries do not mind either the insults or the company. There are a few who keep their old friendships as a sort of social base paint to give stability and structure to the overall portrait, against which they compose figures of fun and novelty, even interest (in both the best and the worst senses of the word). But most of the Old Rich are not so adventuresome. Weighed down by patrician responsibilities, worn out by their endless reconnoiterings of the patrimonial perimeters, they want nothing more at the end of the day, or on weekends, than to sink back into the restful, loyal, and private company of people they've known, as they say, "all my life."

As a virtue, loyalty is vulnerable to the skeptical question: loyalty to what? But no such quibble can be raised against the social virtue of truthfulness. Truthfulness is perhaps the centerpiece of "character" as

Old Money teaches that concept. It comprises everything the mentors of the class mean by openness, honesty, candor, and integrity. It comprises everything too, needless to say, that the mentors of Market Man deliberately ignore. Teachings like Mark Twain's Colonel Sellers's have no place in the Old Money curriculum:

> I've got some prodigious operations on foot; but I'm keeping quiet; mum's the word; your old hand don't go around ... letting everybody see his k'yards and find out his little game.... Now there's an operation in corn that ...[s]ome New York men are trying to get me to go into—buy up all the growing crops and just boss the market when they mature—ah, I'll tell you it's a great thing.... I haven't promised yet—there's no hurry—the more indifferent I seem, you know, the more anxious those fellows will get. And then there's hog speculation.... We've got quiet men at work ... mousing around, to get propositions out of all the farmers ..., and other agents quietly getting propositions and terms out of all the manufactories—and, don't you see, if we can get all the hogs and all the slaughter houses into our hands on the dead quiet—whew! it would take three ships to carry the money.

Inheritors of wealth do not have to bluff, mislead, or mouse around in commodities markets. They do not have to offer people phony or trivial services on the service markets. They do not have to start businesses in any kind of market, indeed, and need not nurture the enterprises by lying to creditors, cheating on taxes, and deceiving bankers. They do not have to run any business by exaggerating the "quality" of the product. Finally, they do not have to hype their selves. Of course, secrecy and deception are neither absolutely required in order to survive in the marketplace nor unknown among the Old Rich. But they are not an *expectation* of the Old Money class. On the contrary, of all the moral beauties that the Old Rich love to contemplate in themselves, truthfulness is perhaps the most honored.

At St. Paul's School, a story is still told that perfectly illustrates the standards of truth-telling the school expected of bred-in-the-bone children of Old Money. The event took place under the rectorship of Samuel S. Drury in the spring of 1924, just before graduation. A rumor reached the rector that half a dozen sixth formers, including some class officers, had celebrated their forthcoming deliverance from school at a *fête champêtre,* complete with cigars and champagne, somewhere on the school's sixteen-hundred-acre campus. (Drury was the sort of headmaster, I should point out, who once strode up to George W. Hill of the American Tobacco Company, visiting his son at the school, and struck a smoking Lucky Strike from his hand.) On this occasion he summoned the boys to his study and asked them one by one, on their honor, whether they had ever, at school or on vacation, smoked tobacco or drunk liquor. One by one, on their honor, they told the truth. Yes, they had. Drury thanked them for their honesty, then expelled them all. By nightfall they were gone.

Ever? At school *or* on vacation? No headmaster today would presume that his jurisdiction ran any further than the school grounds, if that far, nor take on himself the onus of being both judge and jury in a student disciplinary action. But the point of the story is not in the headmaster's theocratic powers but in the shared presumption that the only conceivable response to a leading question was the honest and forthright truth. More important, the truth must be volunteered. It should not be necessary to coerce it, or make a deal with it. Like so much else in the world of Old Money, it must be *given*. The Fifth Amendment has no place in the more private precincts of the Old Money class. Even at today's boarding schools, the privilege against self-incrimination is considered *infra dig*. Disciplinary cases are now reviewed by a faculty-student committee; the accused is allowed an "advocate" of his or her choice; the committee then passes judgment and recommends a punishment to the headmaster, who usually accepts it. But these changes since Dr. Drury's day are intended not to protect individual rights, which in Old Money circles are assumed to be in good hands anyway, but rather to distribute responsibility for enforcing the rules of the community outward and downward to include all its members. And in this process, a forthright admission of the truth is still the course of honor.

Generosity and gratitude, especially toward institutions, also count among the highest of the social virtues of the Old Rich. In the gift ethos, of course, nothing could be more fitting or attractive. Children of Old Money are taught to be grateful from birth—indeed, *for* their birth—for having been brought into circumstances that were so very, very advantageous. The circumstances are never detailed; the wealth that purchased and arranged the circumstances is never mentioned. "Always remember, dear," I can hear my grandparents and parents saying to me, "that you have a lot of advantages that others don't— your health, a good education ... Well, I mean, how many children have all this ... ?" The voice fades as the arm stretches out over the

Louis XV furniture in the drawing room, out the French doors to the small *parc* in (of all places) Brookline, Massachusetts. What did it mean, this silence, just when one wanted some particulars? Perhaps the thought occurred to them that if the child knew his "advantages" he might become spoiled. Perhaps an ancient superstition struck them: that if the gods overheard what they were saying, they might snatch it all away. About money, Old Money has many reasons to be mute.

So gratitude tends to be focused on the institutions in which money is "refined." First among these is the Old Family itself, usually as incarnated in the grandparents. Perhaps no group of Americans is so deeply (or so properly) grateful to their elders as are the grandchildren of the Old Rich. It was for the grandparents that most of us mastered the social graces. They were the "old" audience for whom we learned and before whom we practiced our "old-fashioned" manners. "Remember to be on your absolutely best behavior, dear," one was told. "We're going to Grandma's for dinner."

After the family, gratitude focuses on all those institutions—the schools, colleges, clubs, museums, welfare "charities," and the like—that compose the class curriculum. And now, of course, gratitude may be discharged with something other than courtesy. One cannot give money to one's grandparents, but one can give money to other institutions, and which better than those that gave one's money and one's self a certain social and cultural significance?

The time has long gone for the Old Rich when gratitude and generosity could combine to produce that true largesse which occasionally marked giving in my great-grandfather's day. Largesse harks back to those eras, nostalgically remembered, when upper classes not only had riches but were riches incarnate—when their wealth was not only inherited but, so to say, inherent in them. And it was important that the benefaction should fall with just a hint of randomness, like a god's. Largesse could be only approximated in a New World, of course, but there were men who tried. J. P. Morgan, my great-grandfather's idol, tried:

> Harvard Medical School wanted to build a new group of buildings in Boston for its Medical School. Morgan liked the idea. Harvard was a good place; his son Jack had gone there [he himself had gone to Heidelberg] and the result seemed satisfactory. President Eliot was an excellent man. Medicine was a good thing, and the Harvard Medical School well spoken of. So when Morgan was approached

for a gift he said he would be glad to see the plans for the new group
of buildings.

[It is said that] John D. Rockefeller had taken six months to have
the school investigated. Morgan, when two or three representatives
of the school came to see him . . . walked in, watch in hand. "Gentlemen," said he, "I am pressed for time and can give you but a moment. Have you any plans to show me?"

The plans were unrolled.

Said Morgan, moving his finger quickly from point to point, "I
will build *that*—and *that*—and *that*. Good morning, gentlemen."
And he departed, having committed himself to the construction of
three buildings at a cost of over a million dollars.

Nowadays that kind of overflowing inner plenitude is extremely
rare among heirs and heiresses of Old Money. In fact, it may have been
possible for Morgan only because most of his money was New, made
by him, not inherited, certainly not held for him "in trust." New
Money is always more capable of largesse than Old Money. The money,
having been made by those who possess it, is in some sense an exten-
sion of their own personal powers, not an issue of some mystical marriage of blood and lucre. New Money can liberally overflow, in other
words, because the source and the fountain are one and the same.

It is quite otherwise with Old Money. As every fund-raiser and
development officer in the land knows—for that matter, as every poor
relative in the land knows—Old Money is dry money, its sources remote and well hidden, and its fountains well guarded. Understatement, patrician privacy, the trust-fund mechanism, and the family
foundation (if there is one) require this state of affairs. But just as
important, each Old Money family's version of the gift ethos also requires it. Year after year, fund-raisers make the same vain effort to get
money out of some Old Family, only to be told that the family's phil-
anthropic or charitable or cultural or educational "dollar" has already
been spoken for; indeed, has been spoken for ever since the founding
of the fortune. The Old Rich pass on customs of giving to such-and-
such schools, hospitals, museums, and so forth much as they pass on
customs of making those institutions a length of their track through
life. I'm sure there are families who inherit the custom of giving to a
symphony orchestra, say, who never attend a concert; or who continue
to give to Harvard or St. Paul's even after their children are rejected
for admission at these schools. Nevertheless, there's overlap between

the generational commitment of a family's material resources and the autobiographical commitment of its human resources. Gratitude, after all, is supposed to work both ways: from generous giver to needy institution, but also from socially significant institution to needy giver.

Perhaps the most charming of Old Money's social virtues is modesty. In the form of self-deprecation, for example, it charms away the uglier forms of envy, which is why ironic or self-mocking humor is so common among aristocrats in public life. John F. Kennedy was a master of it. "I'm the man who accompanied Jacqueline Kennedy to Paris," he told the people of France when on a triumphant tour through Europe. "I thought he needed the legal experience," he told the American people when criticized for appointing his younger brother attorney general. Katharine Graham, on being elected president of the Associated Press, amused fellow members by saying, gratefully, "We inheritors like to do something on our own." It is a sign of extraordinary virtue, somehow, that a man whom the envious would credit with every reason to be vain and arrogant turns out, in fact, to take lightly any superiority he may have over the common lot, purifying the situation of resentment with a laughing reminder that life, as everyone knows, is unfair. The laughter is essential. If Nelson A. Rockefeller could never persuade the Republican party to nominate him for the presidency, it was partly because his earnestness in the pursuit of power aroused fears that he who had been given so much solemnly believed that he deserved the rest.

But modesty also serves the cause of perpetuating a family's riches. Childishly, impulsively, the aristocrat in every beneficiary wants to thrust his ego out into the public world, where it might strut and boast of its good fortune like a hero of the *Iliad* (all but the modern world's favorite hero: the wily, prudent, protopatrician Odysseus). But "carelessness" on the Homeric scale can be afforded by only the most generationally secure of upper-class families in traditionally stable societies; and Old Money families are not that. The code of the gentleman (and the lady), and behind him the code of the courtier, and behind him the code of the Roman patrician, may be said to have been erected on the perception that the best way to deal with the ruinous aristocratic appetite for power and glory, not to mention more depraved appetites, is to indoctrinate the beneficiaries of inherited wealth with a sense of modest self-restraint. A gentleman does not put himself forward, a lady does not "look out loud"; a gentleman does not vaunt his prowess or his resources, neither does a lady revel in her beauty or her clothes. Gentlemen and ladies, having the power to hurt, will do none of it, intentionally.

If there is any form of behavior in which all Old Money's social graces and virtues find their ultimate performance, it is in sportsmanship. Nothing so becomes an upper class, aesthetically and morally, as the control of its aggression, and that's what a sporting code is for. The best example of this is the relative apportionment of luck and merit by and to the winners and losers of any contest. Sportsmanship calls for victors always to credit their good luck and their opponents' bad luck for the way things turned out, while it demands the reverse of losers: that they take responsibility for the outcome—"No, no, I played badly; that's all there is to it." In this way, winners are prevented from forcibly depriving losers of more than was at stake in the competition (such as their pride), while losers are prevented from violently taking back what they've lost. And *within* the game, sportsmanship demands the same self-restraint—no "fighting dirty," no cheating, no "taking advantage." It's a question of fine manners curbing the powers of the class while adorning its presence.

Some of the most powerful and flattering images in Old Money's gallery are to be found in the annals of sportsmanship. This is probably inevitable, given the nature of the American society against which it tries to distinguish itself. In a competitive, self-reliant New World, where everything and everyone have to be made, it is not enough, even for Old Money, that its most distinctive conduct should simply exist, totally careless, like a collection of antiquities in the Great American Museum. If its conduct is to be seen as truly "ascendant," in President Eliot's word (the only position from which one might hope it would influence the conduct of others), then its avatars or trustees must from time to time prove its ascendancy by allowing it and themselves to be tested against other forms of conduct and other selves. The contests occur wherever Old Money finds itself in competition with Market Man and people possessing entrepreneurial virtues, and they invite invidious comparison. Sports are not the sole arenas in which they take place, only the most dramatic and the earliest in the autobiographical experience of the class.

Time was called on a round, [Theodore] Roosevelt dropped his guard, and Hanks landed a heavy blow on his nose, which spurted blood. Loud hoots and hisses from the gallery and floor, whereat

Roosevelt's arm was instantly flung out to command silence, while his alert and slender figure stood quiet.

"It's all right," he assured us eagerly, his arm still in the air to hold the silence; then, pointing to the time-keeper, "he didn't hear him," he explained, in the same conversational but arresting tone. With bleeding nose he walked up to Hanks and shook hands with him.

The hoots and hisses from the (Harvard) crowd, the future President's outflung arm commanding silence, the generous gesture of forgiveness—morally and aesthetically, the scene is almost perfectly done. As well it might be: The writer is TR's great admirer, his "brother" in Harvard's Porcellian Club, the novelist Owen Wister. But other, more learned observers of Old Money, such as Arthur Mizener, also know the iconography of sportsmanship when they see it:

Sports require great physical gifts and some moral ones, like courage. Moreover, if the player is a serious sportsman, as Hobey Baker [the great St. Paul's and Princeton athlete and World War I fighter pilot] was, they may also demand considerable magnanimity. When Hobey Baker limped into his opponents' dressing room to shake hands and thank them for a wonderful game after he had been ruthlessly hammered all evening long, it was not because he was a fool or even because he was a man gritting his teeth and carrying out the sportsman's code. It was rather because that code was so deeply ingrained in him that he was incapable of treating an opponent according to his mere deserts; always he treated him according to his own honor. On the rare occasion when he was forced to admit he had been deliberately fouled, he was driven to tears.

Neither Wister nor Mizener makes the invidious comparison explicit, but it's there in the image of sportsmanship as forbearance. Roosevelt forbears to take advantage of a momentary but unfair moral ascendancy his opponent has handed him, thereby even more solidly establishing the ascendancy of his (upper-class) character over his opponent's (lower-class) character. Hobey Baker not only forbears to retaliate against his opponents but rises above them, as if unable to believe that people could behave so badly. Wister and Mizener also note the deficiencies of character in their heroes' opponents, but they do not really blame them. Blame would be unsporting. Sportsmanship is the performance of disinterested delight—the amateur spirit, as it's called in sports—under tremendous temptation to perform otherwise.

Mizener suggests kinds of invidiousness that are no less dizzying for being commonplace. Consider the explanation he offers for why Hobey Baker behaved the way he did in the locker room, and why his opponents behaved the way they did on the rink. The least invidious explanation he could have given would chalk up unsportsmanlike, un-gentlemanly, ungracious conduct to differences in taste. As Oliver Wendell Holmes, Jr., the Porcellian Club's (and TR's) representative on the Supreme Court, once remarked: "if a man says, 'It is all very well to talk about being a gentleman, what I want to do is succeed,' it is hard to give any other answer except that our preferences differ." The Justice, I am sure, was being too kind. Nevertheless, there is a utopian liberal school of thought that would have all cultural ways of being in the world become matters of free choice. One may elect to be a sportsmanlike Old Money person or an entrepreneurial New Money person, just as one may elect to be a hippie or a yuppie. This is a predominantly New World school of thought, but some of its greatest enthusiasts are Old World converts, immigrants of the entrepreneurial imagination. Jean-François Revel is one:

> The cultures of the past, although they differed among themselves, created individuals who resembled one another. Henceforth—and the process has already begun in the United States—individuals, on the basis of their affinities, will regroup to create cultures which will no longer be wholly conditioned by a system of production. We tend to forget too quickly the despotism exercised by our traditional cul-tures—the prisons which we called villages, tribes, parishes, corpo-rations, and families.

No hero of entrepreneurial freedom, setting out to make his way, his name, and his fortune in the world, could have put it better. To such a man, his neighborhood, his ethnic group, his church, his workplace, and his family are all "prisons"—dead hands of the past holding back the greening possibility of the present, museums of the Old holding back the tremulous promise of the New. To such a man, everything is a matter of choice. Choice is all he's got, the only thing that saves his independence from being a rejection, his freedom from being aban-donment, and himself from being horribly alone. Such a man might well conceive a choice between gentlemanliness and success to be a simple matter of preferences, like choosing one's "life-style."

Justice Holmes did not agree. Nor did Arthur Mizener. What Mizener suggests in his little vignette is that Baker's opponents lack something that Roosevelts and Bakers possess in abundance. Middle-class audiences today might call this something "class," as in: "He's got a lot of class" or "That was a class act." But the epithet begs more questions than it answers. Mizener is more specific. With President Eliot and others, he calls Hobey Baker's "class act" an act of magnan-imity. He is very clear what he means by that virtue, pointing out that it is not what passes for magnanimity in marketplaces or meritoc-racies—giving to a man "according to his mere deserts"—but a greater deed than that, on a longer, looser loop of reciprocity. Just as important, he is also careful to show where Baker got this virtue. It does not develop like Paley's taste; Baker did not learn magnanimity from a magazine. No, Mizener wants his readers to know that Baker was one of those in whom the code was "deeply ingrained." The phrase is ordinary enough in the context, yet its invidiousness is breathtaking. It is a thing beyond learning, far beyond purchase. It is a secret of nature, like the grain in the wood.

"Deeply ingrained," like "good breeding," is a concept that it's best not to examine too closely. But it is a key to the overall chiaroscuro effect created by the presence of Old Money, by its carelessness as well as by its social graces and virtues, in a world largely arranged by Market Man. It is an artistic effect, in two senses. In the first place, its appeal is largely to the aesthetic side of the social imagination, which wants to see beauty in social arrangements and behavior; but in the second place, it raises the usual questions about artistic intention. Does the class intend to create this effect? Who knows? Sometimes yes, some-times no. Now here, now there. The intention behind the effect may be as stroboscopic, a matter of intermittent need or desire, as is its perception. But we certainly know that the effect is created and that people do see it: the Old Rich, the New Rich, and the not rich at all.

The effect is one of *precedence*. The Old Rich somehow manage to convince people, including themselves, that they were there before anyone else, that they knew how to best present their settings and themselves before anyone else, that they have "always" moved to the measure of the social graces, that they have "always" belonged, that their friends have been friends "forever," that they did the right thing before anyone else even learned what the right thing was. If the proper tense for Market Man is the future conditional, the proper tense for Old Money is the past perfect. Whatever it is, they had it, did it, knew it, savored and appreciated it, knew how to do it, before you did. This is the significance of all the metaphors borrowed from organic nature, including "natural," with which the behavior of the Old Rich is so often qualified. They stake, or accede to, a claim of autobiographical and generational priority, primacy, perhaps even preemption and (if there were such a thing, in contrast with arrogance) prerogance.

Of course, it is undeniable that Old Money's money was made, by definition, before New Money's money. Its families were known for being rich before New Money's families were, and before No Money's families probably ever will be. But it is also believed that Old Money's beneficiaries know things—tennis, table manners, foreign and ancient languages, good pictures, fine music, French wines, the little harbors of Penobscot Bay, and famous, powerful, and brilliant people (called "contacts")—before anyone else does. Precedence here suggests a distinction between *gnosis* and *techne, connaissance* and *savoir-faire,* knowledge and know-how.

About travel, for example, one might ask what is so enviable about having been brought up, as my mother and aunt were, in Vienna, Paris, London, Trieste, Dijon, and a castle in the Little Carpathians? They didn't find it enviable in the least. Yet lots of people do, apparently. In the *Times,* John Leonard once lamented the turn of fate that foreclosed his being raised in all the capitals of Europe, where he could have "made friends with the Louvre . . . instead of [having] an apprenticeship according to whose austere terms one learns how to climb out of the lower middle class and purport to be a gentleman." This is what the effect of precedence can do. For people like Leonard, the rich and wellborn, having always been there before them, will always be ahead of them. Jack Chapman would have agreed with him. To Samuel Drury of St. Paul's, Chapman wrote in 1917:

> Elizabeth's [his second wife's] account of St. Paul's is like St. Francis' idea of heaven—all glowing and jolly, merry, joyous, and the boys at play, on the field, and at meals, and in their rooms. . . . All this social element, and free talk and development, at St. Paul's is your influence. . . . My own independent studies long ago convinced me that *social life* was at the bottom of every form of art, and that the deadness and feebleness of our social life in America was at the cause of our artistic incapacity. So perhaps you're getting a good cold-frame

started, and perhaps in 400 years something will emerge—pictures
or something.

Chapman believed that art reveals itself to love (the amateur spirit
again) and there can be no love without some kind of social feelings
for its object: feelings, he might almost have said, of social equality.
This is what Leonard feels he misses, I daresay, in not having made
friends with the Louvre in his youth.

Grace is the greatest artistic effect of the Old Money class. It even
reminds some people that there may be other artists at work in our
social arrangements besides man and nature. Grace is the true and
final end of the Old Money curriculum and the deepest message in the
presence of the Old Rich. If the curriculum is only a learning experience after all, if breeding is no more than an accident of birth, if
precedence is merely lucky timing, if the trust fund is just money, and
unearned money at that—then grace is the great salvific, redeeming
these crude constructions with the sublime metaphysic of the gift. The
gift ethos is central to Old Money culture not just because in the New
World, in the absence of royalty and aristocracy, there were only rich
people to give, and to be given Old Money status in reward for giving,
all those schools, museums, hospitals, parks, and entitlements that
grace the nation. It is central because gifts speak of grace, and grace of
gifts. That's the root of the word: Grace is a gift, the unbought, unpurchasable, unearned, and unmerited grace of life.

Needless to say, these claims and effects of the Old Money presence
do not go down well with other Americans. On the contrary, for every
flash of the stroboscope that reveals Old Money as attractive, another
reveals it as offensive. It offends egalitarian principles and democratic
ideals, republican dogma and capitalist ideology. At infrequent times,
the class's presence has incited some Americans to un-American
thoughts of class war. But most often, the response is to wage a more
subtle war of class demoralization. That response begins by pointing
out that Old Money's vaunted precedence can also be described as
pretentious, presumptuous, and preposterous, and that its grace may
be merely gratuitous. In short, it begins with the charge that inheritors
of Old Money are lightweights.

CHAPTER FOUR

The Revenge of Market Man

We crept along on our hands and knees until we were pretty close, and then looked up. Yes, it was a man—a dim great figure in armor, standing erect, with both hands on the upper wire—and of course there was a smell of burning flesh. Poor fellow, dead as a doornail, and never knew what hurt him. He stood there like a statue—no motion about him, except that his plumes swished about a little in the night wind. We rose up and looked in through the bars of his visor, but couldn't make out whether we knew him or not—features too dim and shadowed.

Mark Twain, *A Connecticut Yankee in King Arthur's Court*

C LASS WARFARE HAS many fronts in the United States—debtors against creditors, industrial labor against professional management, philistines against intelligentsia, and the poor against the middle classes—but none is so rhetorically lively as the front between the patrimonial haves, or Old Money, and the entrepreneurial haves and would-haves, or Market Man. It might be thought that their conflicts are serious enough—continuity versus change, for example, or a social versus an economic imagination of wealth—to justify an occasional outbreak of physical as well as rhetorical violence. But this has happened only rarely. One instance, however, involved a class enemy of my own family. It occurred late one morning in January 1911. The victim was David Graham Phillips, the muckraking assailant of my founding father, Senator Nelson W. Aldrich.

Phillips had awakened that morning as he always did, to take the first of his many daily baths, to dress himself as fashionably as his Princeton-educated taste allowed, then to saunter out into Gramercy Park, the enclave of Old New York where the promptings of his social imagination, fueled by his earnings as a popular novelist, had led him to live. He was on his way to the Princeton Club to collect his mail.

He did not arrive. Not far from his doorway, a man stepped up and shot him dead. The man was called Fitzhugh Coyle Goldsborough, and he was the scion of a socially prominent old Washington, D.C., family. His motive, it appeared, was to save the Goldsborough honor, which Phillips had besmirched in one of his novels—or so Goldsborough believed—beyond any other form of redress.

If revenge was indeed the murderer's motive, no one would have been more astonished to hear it than Phillips. The writer's opinion of people like Goldsborough, the opinion that got him killed, was that they were hopelessly effete. In his books, they appear "self-intoxicated, stupid and pretentious." They are "a polo-playing and racing and hunting, a yachting and palace-dwelling and money-scattering generation; a business-despising and business-neglecting, an old-world aristocracy-imitating generation." They are also "Nancy boys," recognizable as such by the usual clues: perfume, lisps, and limp wrists. Not the sort of people, in short, who are easily stirred to deeds of violence.

And not the sort of people their founding fathers were, either. Phillips, middle class and middle western as he was, actually had a rather well developed Old Money notion of the goal of New Money's struggles to succeed, but the imagination that made him a best-selling writer focused with almost sexual awe on the giants of enterprise that strode through his time. Indeed, virtually all the writers of popular fiction in the Progressive Era—Jack London, Theodore Dreiser, even Mark Twain (though in his case with truly ghastly ambivalence)—were fascinated by the "predatory" men, as Phillips described my great-grandfather, who were gathering the country's property unto themselves, to "take care" of it and to "set us all to work for them." These heroes of capitalist endeavor were not very different from the men (and women too) who found fortunes and families in the "dynastic" novels and television series of the Reagan era. The entrepreneurial imagination cuts them from the same cloth: ruthless, crude, greedy for power and wealth, but strong and proud and purposeful, paragons of Darwinian fitness and Free Market power.

These are the telltale broad strokes of Market Man's revision of

Old Money's iconography, the opening moves in his complete reversal of Old Money's invidious comparisons that show themselves as enviable, the New Rich as pathetic. Are the Old Rich graceful, careless, nonchalant? The entrepreneurial imagination sees them as lazy, flaccid, effeminate. Is their taste as casual as their manner? The young lawyer Samuel Rosenman, according to Arthur Schlesinger, Jr., "noted with skepticism [FDR's] soft collar, the loose tweed suit, the patrician carelessness of dress and manner." Are they beautiful in their social graces? Market Man sees their beauty, if he sees it at all, as an incapacity for the necessary toughness that's required to confront difficulties in a competitive world. Market Man will not notice the usefulness of courtesy, its possibilities for treachery and the tease, or for getting other people to do your bidding; to notice would be to credit both manners and men with too much power. The most the entrepreneurial imagination can see is that the social graces seem to operate on the Old Rich like a stuffed shirt, paralyzing them; or like a silk shirt, caressing them into a state of terminal languor. It is the same with the virtues the class believes so precious—loyalty, modesty, magnanimity, generosity, sportsmanship, and so on. They appear, if at all, as signs of stupidity, of a lack of realism. It is the same, too, with the class's more rarefied points of pride—their vaunted precedence, their grace. The historical precedence claimed by the Old Rich seems invisible, in a world where the only precedence is the perpetual precedence of the now, a history of new beginnings endlessly begun again. Whatever grace Market Man sometimes sees, he sees only as a faintly ridiculous etherealization of the character, a sort of thermal updraft spiriting the children of the rich up into a pretty nursery in the sky.

Four charges dominate Market Man's revenge on the preposterous pretensions of the Old Rich: that they are weak, that they are stupid, that they are without wants, and that they are degenerate. A fifth charge, equally persistent, is kept in reserve in the event that the Old Rich counterattack with some plausible demonstration of their value, and the good influence of their virtues. The response is easy: "Yes, maybe, but you're so rich and socially secure that you can afford it."

Weakness first. Every child of Old Money grows up under a barrage of verbal snowballs impugning his or her personal powers. A rich kid is a kid who can't

boil an egg	change a flat tire
comb her own hair	fight his way out of a wet paper bag

wear the same sweater twice	bicycle to school
balance her checkbook	go out with the guys
wash the dishes	tie his own shoelaces
take the subway	mow the lawn
do the laundry	stand up for his rights
eat with her fingers	stand being hurt
lift a finger	stand on his own two feet

And of course the reason they're so weak—the reason thrown at them from the time they take their first little steps out into a more public world, if they ever do—is precisely what the carefully cultivated presence of Old Money has been trying so hard to repress: their unearned, unmade, unmerited, undeserved inherited wealth. If the children of wealth *can't,* it's because their money did it for them, the little yellow eunuch that is their slave and proxy self.

Worse, the children who *can't* become the adults who *never could have.* This deliberate perversion of the past perfect tense of precedence is a favorite thrust of Market Man's revenge. Is he the president of a great bank? Has he got the best collection of Fabergé eggs? Is she chairperson of the board of trustees? Did he/she get into Princeton? Did she/he marry the handsomest boy/girl in the class? Was he made a partner at an astonishingly early age? Did his polo team, his yacht, his campaign for the Senate, win a famous victory? Does she have many influential friends? Does he have the best staff in Congress? What can that beautiful man possibly see in her? Over and over again, the Old Rich hear someone murmuring, "If it weren't for his/her money, he/she could never have ..." There is almost no achievement for which inheritors of wealth can give themselves credit that isn't also credited in some way, directly or indirectly, to the powers of their money. This is perhaps the worst nightmare of all, that at the end of their lives even the most "successful" of the Old Rich will have to confront a derisive accuser, perhaps in the mirror, who looks on all their works and sees nothing more than the brave but pathetic efforts of a heavily subsidized mediocrity.

The same accuser, of course, holds in reserve that terrible charge "He can afford it," dismissing not only everything the beneficiary does but everything he or she most proudly *is.* Does he tell the truth, come what may? Does she refuse to "take advantage"? Do they remain loyal and generous to their old schools, chums, retainers? Do they put friendship above calculations of merit? Perhaps, replies Market Man, but so would anyone who had that kind of money.

And it's no good arguing that the Old Rich might well be much worse than they are, the opposite of what they're proud of being. Because of course they *can* be rude, insolent, cruel, arrogant, insensitive. *Le plaisir aristocratique de déplaire:* What is that? It's like their vaunted eccentricities—simply another luxury that only they can afford. Market Man is no more shaken by Old Money's vices than he is impressed by its virtues. The Old Rich can get away with anything—nice or nasty, it hardly matters.

Stupidity, the second charge, is another form of weakness, but Market Man loves to rub it in separately. Are the Old Rich stupid? Listen to a counting of the ways:

Well, one thing I know—they're mythologically stupid, or categorically stupid; like jocks are stupid, or fashion models.

They're too stupid to help themselves. You know, like the heir who falls among thieves and loses his fortune in a shell game. Or like that favorite object of neoconservative scorn, the rich liberal. John V. Lindsay was a perfection of the type.

I think of them as bestially stupid. As in Jefferson's description of the aristocrats of Versailles before the Revolution: a menagerie of sleek, fat, sensual animals, he thought, all body and no mind. I've never met a nice rich American playboy. There are none, I think. There are only nice rich American drunks. So sad, so stupid. Or take those Locust Valley louts like Tom Buchanan in *Gatsby.* The final clubs at Harvard, the dining clubs at Princeton, the country club at Piping Rock on Long Island and the Green Spring Valley Hunt Club in Maryland, every horse show and yacht race in America, are filled with people like that. Muscle-bound dolts in Brooks Brothers suits, grunting over their oars on the Schuylkill River; women who take fewer baths than their horses, and who are just as stupid.

Intellectually stupid. They're well educated, but you can see the feebleness of their minds in the conventionality of their responses to any intellectual problem. They are incapable of the strenuous discipline of the intelligence that yields interesting responses to the world.

. . .

I don't know, the ones I've met are just plain dumb, no street smarts. But what do you expect of people who've got it all already?

To the entrepreneurial imagination, there's a very good reason for all that mental and physical flab they see in the Old Rich. It is that Old Money is not hungry. It doesn't *want*. I remember reading an astonishing rendition of this argument in an article about football players who had gone from the Ivy League to the pros. It seems that the biggest problem these men have to face is the toughness problem: how to persuade their coaches and teammates that they're mean and aggressive enough to play competitive ball. Of course, the fact that they have any problem at all on this issue is wonderful testimony to the poof effect of Harvard, Yale, and Princeton. (Few, if any, bred-in-the-bone Old Money athletes go into the pros.) But it is the explanation of the problem that's intriguing: It always comes down to the same thing, that Ivy Leaguers wouldn't be hungry enough to be tough.

Where there is no motion, as in the idol of carelessness fashioned by Old Money, there must be no want. Why should there be? Haven't the Old Rich been fed with a silver spoon, their sustenance handed to them on a silver platter? Market Man has a whole thesaurus of epithets that speak of the surfeit, the wantlessness, of the Old Rich. Some of these insults refer to the middle-aged or elderly: They are stuffy, pompous, smug, complacent, bloated, self-satisfied fat cats. Others refer to the young, who are indolent, lazy, pampered, fat-bottomed brats.

Even where Market Man sees motion in the Old Money picture, he cannot imagine it being a fully intended, willful, and significant *action* unless it is prompted by obvious want. I once worked as a reporter on the Boston *Globe*. Reporters are supposed to be tough. Reporters are supposed to be hungry to get the stories. I worked hard, I got stories. Yet people frequently came up to me, looking slightly puzzled, and asked, "What do you want to be a reporter for? I mean, you don't need to put up with all this, do you?" I was asked the same question when I was teaching fifth grade in a school in Harlem, in New York. "What are *you* doing here?" people would wonder. "How did you get from Harvard to Harlem?" Suddenly, for an instant, my being there seemed to me not only inexplicable but, most devastatingly, not quite *real*.

The charge of unreality is a transvaluation of Old Money's claim to grace. Grace is a note, a finishing touch, not quite real because not really necessary. The charge of degeneracy, on the other hand, is a transvaluation of breeding, the quasi-biological aspect of the claim to precedence.

> There are a few cases like that of the Morgans, where great ability seems to have found its residence in father, son and grandson. But what of the Goulds, the Astors, the Vanderbilts, the Goelets, the Thaws, the Brokaws? And what of the thousands of lesser names known only locally? In many cases there seems to be a total reversal of character, if not a sweeping family degeneracy.

This particular diatribe was composed by a middle-class, middle western polemicist against the evils of inherited wealth, H. E. Read. It appeared in 1916, five years after David Graham Phillips was shot for voicing similar sentiments. Degeneracy had been long in the minds of all opponents of Old Money, as well as many of its friends and beneficiaries. "Shirtsleeves to shirtsleeves in three generations" is a watchword of capitalism all over the world (in England and on the Continent, it is "clogs to clogs"), and as a prophetic utterance it carries the weight of all the weakness, all the stupidity, all the surfeited appetite that Market Man sees in inheritors of Old Riches. But degeneracy played an especially prominent role in the class polemics of the Silver Spoon Age, a period I'd put between the time Teddy Roosevelt was graduated from Harvard (1873), say, and the time Hobey Baker was killed in the skies of France (1918). In those days when eugenics was as widespread a concern as genetics is today, it seemed obvious that the debilitating effects of a virtually inanimate life would somehow seep into the genes of the Old Family and from there into the gene pool of the whole Old Money class. There were grim racialist and racist ramifications in this thought, especially as it affected many Old Families. But in the work of people like Phillips and Read, or even in their successors like Scott Fitzgerald and Ferdinand Lundberg, the charge of "sweeping family degeneracy" was a figment in the imagination of a class war, not a race war.

One of the ways degeneracy still makes itself felt is in the imagery of sexual identity and sexual appetite that people derive from their view of the Old Money presence. The formal requirements of Old Money's imagination—which resulted in those beautiful men and handsome women of the *Illustrated London News,* the drawings of Charles Dana Gibson, and (most noticeably today) the advertising of Ralph Lauren—reappear as limp-wristed, wasp-waisted, hairlesschested Nancy boys, or as dark, broad-shouldered, flat-chested, commanding Tom boys. The men get the worst of it. In Phillips's day, for example, the men of Old Money were seen as passive and pretty, with soft, slender bodies, pettish temperaments, frivolous tastes, and squeamish sensibilities. (Actually, the most famous of these rich kids was a dog: Buck, in Jack London's *Call of the Wild*.) By contrast, as with Maude Brewster in London's *The Sea Wolf*, the women of Old Money are apt to be splendid creatures: long-legged, frank, athletic, and far braver than their brothers. Sexually, moreover, they are waiting for arousal by some muscular ruthless predator—a man like the author, one supposes, in his wildest dreams. Later, in quite another view (Thomas Beer's in *The Mauve Decade*, for example), these women reappear in society as Titanesses, successors of *the* Mrs. Astor, predatory, ruthless women who manage their husbands and emasculate their sons. After that sort of degeneracy, as everyone knows, a sweeping family perversion cannot be far behind.

Degeneracy is one insult that doesn't get thrown around as much as it used to, except by neoconservatives, who fancy they see it, in the form of liberalism and softness on communism, sapping the entrepreneurial strength of the entire upper middle class. But weakness, stupidity, and satiation, those other missiles of the class war against the Old Rich, are still very much in service.

So are invidious comparisons. In a memoir of Clare Boothe Luce, for example, Wilfrid Sheed summed up the strenuous career of this highly successful woman by comparing it to the careers of two first cousins of Old Money, Alice Roosevelt Longworth and Eleanor Roosevelt Roosevelt. "Alice Longworth and Eleanor Roosevelt could embroider received positions," writes Sheed, his metaphor a needle of scorn. "Clare Luce hammered hers out of nothing." Sheed, like Jean-François Revel, comes to the New World from the Old, in his case from Great Britain, a nation galled and stupefied for centuries by a social imagination not unlike Old Money's. While improvised Europeans like Henry Adams complain of the thinness of American culture, improvised Americans like Revel and Sheed actually applaud it. A more neutral visitor might wonder whether there was anything to choose between the presumed precedence of the Old Rich and the arrogant assumptions of the New. Does anyone "make it on his own"? Does anyone come from "nothing"? It matters more, surely, what pattern was embroidered on the received position, what kind of life was hammered out of nothing.

Many Americans, born on these shores of the imagination, may be less than enthusiastic about the moral merits of the entrepreneurial life. Most of them, after all, spend their lives hammering away at the same nothing Mrs. Luce did, but without her success. Still, in any forced comparison between Old Money and the entrepreneurial heroes and heroines of Market Man, there is no question about where the balance of their sympathies would lie. America is not a classless society, and it does make a difference to Americans how people come by their success. It makes a difference not so much for their judgment of the individuals in question—Clare Boothe Luce or the Roosevelt ladies— but to their own morale, to their own perception of their chances for success. Like a lighthouse, the American imagination of wealth is always flashing. With respect to wealth, the shore still looks like that of a New World, its virtues organized by the imperatives of competitive self-reliance, its imagination fixed on the entrepreneurial task of making something—a name, a fortune, and a self—out of nothing. That's what the green light reveals: not only hope and envy but an abstract conjunction of time and space—the beginning, the start, the outset.

Such a vision obviously has little room or respect for an inheritor of wealth. A child of riches is not at the beginning of anything. He or she is all outcome, ending, goal. And not of his own efforts or her own dreams, but of someone else's. An inheritor is a mere *effect*—the creature and dependent, the accidental and largely unfortunate consequence of someone else's success in the race, the contest, or the market warfare of life. The inheritor is also an effect of other factors. He is an effect of the laws of private property, which dictate that someone must own property after the person who "made" it has died. He is an effect of tradition and custom, which dictate that family members are probably the best people to be given this ownership. Finally, he is an effect of public policy, which permits these laws, traditions, and customs to govern the distribution of wealth in America—and with it everything that money can buy.

This ought to present a problem. If the institutions of inherited wealth—testamentary freedom, for example, and multigenerational trust funds—are responsible for the distribution of the buying powers of money, then one might suppose that Market Man would constantly monitor the pattern of distribution to make sure that it fell fairly evenly over the population, and to howl for a change of policy if it did not. But it has not, and still does not. Recent studies show that in 1981, after almost a century of steadily increasing wealth-making by middling Americans, the top .08 percent of the population still owned 20 percent of the nation's wealth, a far more uneven distribution than that of income. Yet only three times in the history of the Republic—in the Jacksonian period, in the Age of the Silver Spoon, and during the Depression—has Market Man sent up a heartfelt cry for the government to change the laws that permit such inequities. Estate taxes have been instituted, usually to help pay for wars, but not until recently have they caused a major inconvenience to the transmission of wealth down the line of the generations. Significantly, it was the overwhelmingly entrepreneurial, New Money regime of Ronald Reagan, acting perhaps in response to Irving Kristol's 1974 demand, that inflicted grave tax damage to the ancient aims of the trust fund: to keep an estate intact and "in the family" for as many generations as possible.

The Silver Spoon Age provides the richest trove of entrepreneurial rhetoric against inherited wealth. It was a time when the middle-class readers of Phillips's fiction had begun to feel that the waters of opportunity had been dammed up in vast reservoirs, reservoirs very like the actual ones being built at the time, their stores of life-giving chances held back by masonry eight feet thick, their pumps protected by medieval battlements, the whole preserve closed off to all but the predatory band of founding fathers and their weakling children. This was the significance of the "trusts" issue, not only the kind that the patrician Aldrich and J. P. Morgan nourished and that the more aristocratic Roosevelt and Holmes tried to "bust," but the kind that Marshall Field, for instance, left to two prepubescent boys. The scholar Gustavus Myers put the entrepreneurial case against Field's $122 million legacy in a series of brilliantly evocative metaphors. Field, he wrote, "welded his fortune into a compact and vested institution. It had ceased to be a personal attribute and become a thing, an inert mass of wealth, a corporate entity. This he did by creating . . . a trust of his estate."

That was and still is the entrepreneurial indictment of inherited wealth. The phrase "an inert mass of wealth" perfectly captures what happens to the American landscape of opportunity when Old Money's claim to precedence appears to ring true. All that shimmering possibility looks compacted and put away somewhere, where the would-be self-made man can never get at it. Much more important, the phrase "personal attribute," which the little Field boys' wealth emphatically was not, locates property rights just where the industrious striver wants to have them—as close as possible to the person of the property holder. This gives him a philosophically respectable justification for his view that inheritors are weaklings, and a reason for his deep suspicion of their right to inherit. So long as a man can claim the money he makes as a "personal attribute," he can be wholly secure in his rights to it. He fixes on that primal scene of "making it," the moment in space and time when "all the world was America," as John Locke put it, and a man's rights in property were founded on the labor that he (or his servant; Locke was careful to allow servants) invested in it. What could be more inalienably right?

By the same token, what could be more wrong than the rights of inheritors? Even the law recognizes it. Myers and other critics of inherited wealth rarely insist on the point, but not since the Dark Ages, if then, have children born under Anglo-American law enjoyed an indefeasible claim on their parents' estates. (This is not true in continental Europe or in Louisiana, where Roman and Napoleonic law protect a child's birthrights, sometimes amounting to a claim on a third of the parental estates.) In most of the United States, the only rights of inheritance are *faute de mieux*: when the parent dies without making a will, or when it can be shown that he literally forgot the children, or when she or he was made to forget them, so to speak, by unsound mind or the undue influence of somebody else's mind. In other words, blood descent enters the picture only in the absence of some free and uncoerced declaration of the property holder's will: the exercise of his wealth-maker's right to do what he wills with his wealth. Even entail and primogeniture, the two major legal limitations that in the American South hedged what the owner might call "his" property, are more eloquent of the powers of testators than they are of any rights of inheritors. "Entail" comes from a French word meaning to tailor, but the tailoring in an entailed estate was done primarily to fit the needs and ambitions of the testator, not his heirs. Southern entailments were not unlike Boston trust funds. Both were designed to keep an estate (and its beneficiaries) safely above the worst hazards of the marketplace. Primogeniture gets thrown in, primarily in the agricultural South, as a special cut of the tailoring intended to maximize the *lift* of the assets, so to speak, by keeping them all together in the care of one heir or heiress. But even if the entailment worked to the benefit of the heirs, which was by no means always the case, it most emphatically worked the will of the founding father. Thus the idea of "family money," so dear to the hearts of the Old Rich, is a fiction—a sentimental fiction, not even a legal one. In the law, individuals, not families, own money, and they own it only by right of "making it" or by the will of the maker of it.

One solution to the offense of "inert" masses of wealth, an extremely popular one during the Depression, was the proposal that Huey Long tried to get through FDR's ring of cool and gracious phrases. Share Our Wealth, as Huey named his program, was as simple as a snapping turtle. It called for a capital levy on all personal fortunes beginning at $1 million—1 percent on $1 million to $2 million; 2 percent on $2 million to $3 million; and so on up to 100 percent on all fortunes over $100 million. At that rate, to take an example that surely occurred to Huey if not to FDR, Cousin Vincent Astor's fortune (assuming it to have been about $60 million in 1935) would have been summarily reduced to a mere $24 million. In addition, SOW proposed a limit of $1 million a year on "earned" incomes and a ceiling on inheritances somewhere between $1 million and $5 million. Thinking about what could be done with this money once the government had collected it, Huey could be as indecisive as a boy in an ice cream parlor. In his speeches, he would ramble on about rivers and harbors, the national defense, price supports for farmers, support for the aged, and, above all, higher education. (This was one of Long's big differences with Father Coughlin, his rival in soak-the-rich oratory. Coughlin loved to lambaste "the vested interests of the intellect" as much as the rich, and the Jews more than either of them. Long didn't have much against the Jews, and he respected people of intellect.) Finally, however, the spending proposal that won the most support for Huey all across the country was a scheme that would give a five-thousand-dollar grubstake to every American family in the land.

This was oddly like the scheme sketched out a hundred years earlier, in the Age of Jackson, by Orestes Brownson. Brownson saw what many of the founding fathers had seen, that dense and narrow concentrations of wealth posed just as great a threat of "aristocracy" to the Republic as concentrations of power, dignities, and privileges. In fact, where wealth concentrated, power, dignities, and privileges would not fail to follow, even in this democratic New World. Consequently, "for the good of Humanity," Brownson advocated abolishing inherited wealth. In his scheme, properties "vacated" at death should be redistributed (perhaps by liquidation; Brownson goes a bit hazy on this problem) equally to all the children in the family when they reached the age of twenty-one.

Brownson was at pains to argue that his proposal was not communistic. Far from it. To entrepreneurial imaginations like his, it is the institution of inheritance that is communistic—the "primitive communism of family life," as Marxists, for different rhetorical purposes, later called it. That's because the "very essence" of property in the entrepreneurial view is that it is, as Brownson said, "individual, peculiar, exclusive." Inherited property is family property, sentimentally if not legally, and thus an offense to God and man—the former having endowed the latter with "an original, an innate sense of property." Thus it was no part of Brownson's plan that the state, like some protective parent, should make sure that all its twenty-one-year-old beneficiaries use their inheritances wisely. That would violate the principle that each individual is responsible for her own fate, or, as the Republic's founding document has it, his own pursuit of happiness. Brownson's equalized heirs and heiresses were free to waste their legacies or make a fortune with them: "the idle and the profligate" and "the industrious and the thrifty" must be left to their own personal powers and attributes, to swim or sink, succeed or fail, or (as Huey's oil company declared) win or lose. Society has no right to interfere with how people use their assets. As Brownson wrote, "it is not the inequality introduced by differences of character, of talent, or aptitude for the accumulation of property that we object to; but that which is created by the laws."

This bold antagonistic individualism runs through the whole entrepreneurial critique of inherited wealth, from Brownson to Phillips to Irving Kristol. The entrepreneurial imagination is an individualistic one, just as the Old Money imagination is a social one. Old Money imagines man in society, embedded in (not to say fated by) family, class, and history, affiliated and identified with social institutions, and gratefully endowed with inherited powers and received positions, for which he is responsible and with which he must do the best he can, for himself and his posterity. The entrepreneur has an image of man alone, stripped down to "nothing," without money, parents, or past, having only powers and prospects: his own personal powers pitted in constant, heroic, but lonely struggle, and the free, untrammeled prospects of a spacious (not to say thin and empty) New World. Posterity in this image is like the future, conditional.

Perhaps there is nothing invidious in this contrast, apart from the money. But there is no question which is more attractive to most Americans. The key document in America's view of inheritances from the past is Thomas Jefferson's celebrated dismissal of the past's "dead hand."

> That our Creator made the earth for the use of the living and not of the dead ... that one generation of men cannot foreclose or burden its use to another; that a preceding generation cannot bind a succeeding one by its laws or contracts ... —these are axioms so self-evident that no explanations can make them plainer; for he is not to be reasoned with who says that non-existence can control existence or that nothing can move something.... The laws of civil society, indeed, for the encouragement of industry, give the property of the parent to his family on his death.... And it is also found more convenient to suffer the laws to stand on our implied assent as if positively re-enacted, until the existing majority repeals them; but this does not lessen the right of the majority to repeal whenever a change of circumstance or of will calls for it. Habit alone confounds civil practise with natural rights.

Jefferson's assertion of the rights of the entrepreneurial I-here-now over Old Money's we-there-then is one of the bravest ever uttered. It also had highly autobiographical origins in Virginia's law of entail in Jefferson's day. There was nothing in that law to say that an estate had to pass on to its inheritor bursting with profitability and unencumbered with debt; by Jefferson's time, in fact, many estates were exhausted and debt-ridden. Jefferson's inheritance from his father-in-law certainly was. But if entail was intended to preserve an estate from liquidation *by* the market, it also prevented it from being liquidated *in* the market. Men like Jefferson and his numerous legal clients found themselves in the position of an inheritor of a family business whose market is failing, whose debts are crushing, and who can't sell the business to pay his creditors and go on to something else. Entail, in other words, could weigh down an inheritor as easily as it could lift him up. This was a dead hand indeed, and loosening its grip by abolishing Virginia's laws of entail was one of the proudest accomplishments of Jefferson's life.

But this founding father's hostility to the dead hand of the past went much further. (Would it have gone so far if he had had a son? Would it have gone so far if he had made a success of his nail factory? The founding of it, Jefferson wrote a French correspondent, pleased him as much as a title of nobility pleased men of the Old World. It was of course manned by slave labor.) Entailments were written in wills; wills are a form of contract; contracts, too, could be construed as dead hands of the past freezing the lively enterprise of the present. If a dead man has no right to bind his property unto the next generation, why should a living one have the right to do so for the next decade or two? It was this logic that led Jefferson to his most notorious exercise in the mathematics of natural law. The natural term of any contract, he once laboriously calculated, was nineteen years: no more, no less. After that the property would revert to some sort of state of nature, there to be contested—better yet, *made*—all over again for another nineteen years. Orestes Brownson and Huey Long, like many sons of this founding father, were weaker men than he.

Jefferson's scheme was madness. But it was a madness peculiar to the entrepreneurial, rich New World. The entrepreneurial imagination of wealth is dominant in America not only because it speaks to real human aspirations—for freedom from the past, for the right to choose and pursue one's own form of happiness—and speaks of noble human values, our persistent refusal to hand over responsibility for our own lives to others. It is dominant also because it illuminates a world that really, materially, does exist. Whatever "nothing" there may be in most Americans' backgrounds, there's "something": rich country, a country rich in opportunity. Americans really do believe that the here-and-now is the first moment in the rest of their lives. And the United States really is spacious, promising, and rich enough to support that belief.

Consider, in possibly invidious contrast, the precedential Old World text with which Jefferson bolstered his sentiments on the dead hand of the past: Blackstone's passage on the one right that Anglo-Saxon law acknowledges in matters of inheritance, the right to bequeath:

> There is nothing which so generally strikes the imagination and engages the affections of mankind as the right of property, or that sole and despotic dominion which one man claims and exercises over the external things of the world, in total exclusion of the rights of every other individual in the universe. And yet there are very few that will give themselves the trouble to consider the original foundations of this right.... We think it enough that our title is derived from the grant of the former proprietor, by descent from our ancestors, or by the last will and testament of the dying owner; not caring to reflect that ... there is no foundation in nature or in natural law why a set of words upon parchment should convey the dominion of land; why the son should have the right to exclude his fellow crea-

tures from a determinate spot of ground, because his father had done so before him; or why the occupier of a particular field or jewel, when lying on his death bed ... should be entitled to tell all the rest of the world which of them should enjoy it after him. These inquiries, it must be owned, would be useless and even troublesome in common life. It is well if the mass of mankind will obey the laws when made, without scrutinizing too nicely the reason for making them.

The passage is a masterpiece of casual elegance, Old World even in its tone. The whole business of inheritance is just too absurd, the great jurist seems to be saying, not only the rights of children to inherit but the rights of fathers to bequeath, though it's best not to talk about such things in front of the servants. It's Old World also in its vivid concreteness. Jefferson's abstract prose is just the opposite, the phrases so spacey they might have been composed on the open ocean just before the landfall at Jamestown or Plymouth, or somewhere on the Great Plains of the Middle West. Blackstone's writing is studded with telling detail: total exclusion, despotic dominion, the dying owner, spot of ground, jewel, death bed.

More important is the difference in character and scene. If there is any live action in Jefferson's contemplation of the dead hand, it's in the phrase "encouragement of industry." Blackstone, on the other hand, calls up a richly figured drama with real fathers on real death beds, scribbling words on parchment, letting fall the jewel, abandoning the field, dying; and real sons actively defending what has been given them, by excluding all their fellow creatures from enjoyment of it. But there's no "industry" here; certainly no Lockean mixing of labor and soil to *make* that "determinate spot of ground." There's not even any commerce. He talks of a "grant of the former proprietor"; it might have been purchased; it might also have been a gift.

Blackstone's imagination of wealth still obtains in large sectors of the Old World. There it is hard for people to conceive of any kind of wealth other than inherited wealth: Old Money, as inert as a jewel, as determinate as a spot of ground. Wealth-making therefore is largely perceived as a zero-sum game: Anyone who's "making it" is making it at someone else's expense. That's why until very recently only Marxists viewed the entrepreneur with real approval and gratitude. Only they saw him as a creator of wealth, the progenitor of powerful means of production which in the fullness of time would be inherited, as it

were, by History's youngest and most favored child, the working class.
Every other ideology saw him as a thief (Proudhon), a Scrooge (Dick-
ens), a creature of greed, vanity, and exiguous morality (Adam Smith,
Balzac), a usurper of the aristocracy and a pauperizer of the working
classes (Tory paternalists), or a Midas (the Midas of folk wisdom, who
starves to death). Behind this baleful view, of course, there is a keen
appreciation of the revolutionary force of capitalism. What could be
more revolutionary than an image of wealth—the entrepreneur's image—in which opportunity, possibility, the main chance, throbs like
the pulse of desire itself? In the Old World, it's hardly surprising that
many people seem to believe that Old Money is the only money. It's
the best money: the most stable and the most human. In some minds,
it is also the most available. All it takes is a revolution.

But in the New World, most people still seem to believe that all
it takes is a little entrepreneurial imagination, some of Jefferson's "industry" going to work. That's why attacks on inherited wealth have
been so fantastical, so halfhearted, and so ineffective. So long as there's
money to be *made* in America (enough for the imagination to feed on
anyway), there's no need to make it at the expense of those who inherited it. That's also why the graceful, precedential presence of Old
Money is only an intermittent thing in a New World. Most of the time
it is no obstacle to anyone's pursuit of happiness.

Nor will it be so long as the Old Rich are weak. Their weakness
is a hedge against the possibility that the entrepreneurial struggle may
be a zero-sum game after all. If limp wrists have no grasp, patrimonies
will drop from them like scented handkerchiefs. Weakness, wantlessness, stupidity, even degeneracy—the insults express some measure of
wishful thinking for a painless, nonrevolutionary expropriation of Old
Money's wealth: something like Bill Paley's takeover of Ralph Pulitzer's Kiluna Farm or Jack Hearst's wife. If Americans cannot have a
relaxation of the dead hand of the past, as Jefferson, Brownson, Long,
and Kristol have wished, then they can have the next best thing: heirs
and heiresses with limp wrists. The imagery of weak, stupid, degenerate inheritors makes for a nonviolent, nonpolitical social arrangement whereby the children of the rich can be counted on to return to
some convenient state of nature (to regress to the mean, as we say
today), leaving their riches for tougher, smarter, stronger men and
women. These are America's true revolutions, hundreds of thousands
of tiny revolutions in the lives of individuals, all confirming that each
generation will start afresh, each individual will fight alone on his own

two feet, armed only with the marketable merits given him by nature or by nature's god.

It would be too much to say that the children of Old Money believe all the insults leveled at them. They believe them exactly as they believe the other effects of their curriculum, or the imputations of admiring envy: that is, as much as they believe in their precedence and grace. They believe intermittently. There's no better illustration of this than the stories they tell of the chauffeur and the big car.

Almost every child of Old Riches has two kinds of chauffeur story to tell: one of glory and one of embarrassment. In the first, they recall how wonderful it was when they went to the theater with their grandparents, for example: the big car swooshing up to the entrance, the man with the umbrella opening the door, the crowds of people standing around gawking—why, they felt like movie stars or heads of state! The stories suggest thunderous hoofbeats, the headlong rush of coaches through the streets of the city:

> Six stallions, say, I can afford,
> Is not their strength my property?
> I tear along, a sporting lord,
> As if their legs belonged to me.

Cars or coaches are the picture, as one historian put it, of "the arrogance of wealth, with all its independence and carelessness." They are the picture, too, of the magnificent sovereignty of the consumer, measuring his glory in command over the products and services of others. These are not exactly the images that Old Money likes, ultimately, to create in public, but for the children they bring a sense of triumph.

Later they bring excruciating embarrassment. Once, unthinkingly, I let my grandparents' chauffeur drive me back to my Harvard dormitory in the family's Mercedes limousine—a folly of my grandfather's, and of the company's, that spent more time in the shop than on the road. I managed to slip into Eliot House without being connected with the car, but I never risked it again. Always thereafter I'd ask the chauffeur to let me out by the Charles River. Adam Hochschild came into this legacy of embarrassment earlier than I did, autobiographically speaking, perhaps because he went to a day school, while I was at boarding school. In his memoir of growing up rich, he writes:

I began to dread rides in the family limousine, a long black Chrysler. When William Hanley [the chauffeur] took me to school in it, I slid down in the front seat, trying to stay out of the view of the group of my classmates who bicycled to school each day along the same route. I timidly tried to talk to Father about this. He listened solemnly— he always heard me out, never interrupted anybody. But when I was finished, he declared,"Well, Adam, I just don't think having a car like that is anything to be ashamed of."

His father, it is worth noting, was a man much closer to the Old World than his mother was. His mother understood his embarrassment but would not contest his father's will in the matter of letting the boy bicycle to school. "Eventually," he tells us, "I got William to drop me off several blocks from school, where no one could see me."

This kind of chauffeur story has a thousand variations. George Plimpton, who disclaims any experience of growing up rich himself, first caught a glimpse of what it must be like in a chauffeur-driven car. It was in the mid-1930s, and he was attending St. Bernard's School, a New York day school that prepares young boys for one of the St. Midas schools (or for Andover and Exeter, depending on the family's susceptibility to the Old Money or the entrepreneurial imagination). Plimpton's awakening came on a Friday afternoon when he and his schoolmate Arthur "Punch" Sulzberger, heir presumptive of *The New York Times,* were being driven out to the Sulzbergers' country house in Westchester County. The mid-1930s was a relatively unabashed era with respect to servants. (The annual Field Day at St. Bernard's, for example, featured a short sprint, with prizes, known as the Chauffeurs Race.) Still, Plimpton never forgot the odd sense of discomfort that came over him on the trip when their chauffeur had to stop the car and get out to fix a flat tire.

"Shouldn't we help him, or something?" Plimpton remembers asking his friend.

"No," said Punch, "we'd only be in the way."

The two little boys sat back quietly in the soft pearl-gray seats, and in a few minutes the car began to rise beneath them, bearing them up in short, regular jerks. Through the rear window Plimpton could see the chauffeur, his coattails snapping in the rush of traffic, his black cap on the trunk, as he laboriously pumped the jack. The boys must have felt they weighed a ton, or no more than a feather.

Chauffeur stories perfectly illustrate the disturbing ambivalence—

to put it crudely: grace, or weakness; precedence, or degeneracy of mind and body—that is as much a part of the legacy of Old Money as trust funds. Of course, there have always been robust constitutions among the children of the Old Rich, which seem proof against any debilitating doubts as to the scope and heft of their personal powers. No one was more robust than Theodore Roosevelt, for example, or more frankly class-conscious. From Harvard he once wrote his sister that he stood nineteenth in his class in academic achievement. He would clearly rather have been first. Still, he was proud to note that "only one gentleman stands ahead of me." (The other seventeen were undoubtedly "base specialists," as his contemporary Jack Chapman would say.) But the fact that his own class didn't give him much competition was no surprise to TR. He could probe their weaknesses better than David Graham Phillips: "fellows of excellent family and faultless breeding," he called them in another letter, "with a fine old country-place, four-in-hands, tandems, a yacht, and so on; but, oh, the hopeless decorousness of their lives!" Edwin Morgan, a friend of mine who went to Groton just before World War II, and whose brother Temple went to St. Paul's, once described to me the peculiar image St. Paul's boys cultivated in those days:

> Many of those boys, especially those who fell under the influence of Craig Wylie [a master there, later an editor at Houghton Mifflin], were imbued with an absolutely poisonous combination of romantic Christianity and Pater-like aestheticism, physical chastity and mental sensuality, Charles Kingsley and Oscar Wilde, Tennyson and Beardsley. There was something truly sinister about the way fellows like Temple used the word *attractive*. It was poison they were getting up there, *pure* poison, you might say.

Twenty years later, when I was there, St. Paul's boys were still described in the same terms (not entirely to our displeasure) by Groton boys, just as Groton boys were described in the same terms by Exeter boys, and Exeter boys in (almost) the same terms by high-school boys, and so on out into the farthest reaches of the entrepreneurial imagination, where all boarding-school boys are described, without distinction, as a bunch of fairies.

Usually, though, the child of Old Riches cannot so easily split his ambivalence, and project the inconvenient part of it out onto other members of the class. It's in the grain; comes with the breeding. Part of the problem is the magically Protean nature of money itself. Given a certain insensitivity (or robustness) of character on the part of the buyer, money can buy a lot more than six stallions or a chauffeur and a long black car: if not intelligence, then the assistance of intelligent people; if not personal power, then the power of position; if not personal beauty, then beautiful settings and beautiful company; if not perfect decency, then the services of a good lawyer; if not complete security, then effortless mobility; if not the ability to love, then the chance to be loved; on and on. It is foolish to deny the powers of money. Fitzgerald, describing preparations for the escape from the diamond as big as the Ritz, has the daughter of the house delightedly exclaim to young John, the visitor from Hades: "'We'll be poor, won't we? Like people in books. And I'll be an orphan and utterly free. Free and poor! What fun!'" She's in the grip, obviously, of the rich kid's version of the entrepreneurial dream. "'It's impossible to be both together,'" replies John, "grimly. 'People have found that out. And I should choose to be free as preferable of the two. As an extra caution you'd better dump the contents of your jewel box into your pockets.'"

At the same time, however, money refuses to be assimilated to the self. It comes closest, as I've said, to the self who made it. But to the self who inherits it, his money remains adventitious, wholly other, like a chauffeur in a limousine. Thus, intermittently, it is believed that "legacies" do not get to Harvard on their own two feet: The chauffeur got them there, the Mercedes, their grandparents, the honest gains of two great-grandparents, the ill-gotten ones of two others. And the "legacy," intermittently, thinks so too. It would be the same if the "legacy" were beautiful: Everything he or she did or was could be accounted for by his or her beauty. This is one reason why, almost as often as they see themselves in chauffeur-driven cars, children of Old Money see themselves as beautiful. As an inheritor said not long ago:

> Having money is being like a beautiful woman in a romantic novel: you are always wondering whether men are loving you for your body or your soul. You develop all sorts of finely tuned antennae that try to detect whether somebody is being nice to you because he really likes you.... You look at people more suspiciously; you distrust warm gestures. You look for the little signals that show their real intentions. If you finally decide, "Hey, he really likes me for something I've accomplished," it feels terrific. But if that friendly approach finally turns into a pitch for money, or a hint that one is

coming, you get that old sinking feeling: your money has caught up with you once again.

To be beautiful is to run the gauntlet of desire from lust to love; to grow up rich is to run the same gauntlet from greed to need. Shakespeare's Timon reminds all the rich, New and Old:

> Who would not wish to be from wealth exempt,
> Since riches point to misery and contempt?
> Who'd be so mocked with glory? Or so live
> But in a dream of friendship?

There's a half-true answer to the half-true assumptions behind Timon's question, and every child of wealth knows it. It is in the hard swamp-Yankee logic of the beautiful woman in Robert Frost's poem who knows that wealth is a more dependable asset than beauty or knowledge or even being "true"; this is the logic of the real end of the struggle, which is death:

> Better to go down dignified
> With boughten friendship at your side
> Than none at all. Provide, provide!

In the end, the most disturbing thing about money is its abstractness. Like an ink blot, it allows one to see anything in it; like statistics, one can do anything with its numbers; like the deep blue sky, it has no limit. This is what makes it so wide open to the imaginative powers of want, and this is also what brings the inheritor around again from weakness to strength. For while the abstractness of money allows anyone to *imagine* whatever one likes in it, the same abstractness works similarly on the imagination of inheritors. Even within the forms laid down for them by the curriculum, there are all sorts of imaginative things they can do with their money to *possess* it, to make it at least appear to redound to their credit. Many specific lessons of their training are designed for this purpose. And of course inheritors have one more power over their money besides imagination. They own it. In the end, despite the muggings they endure, the children of Old Riches usually keep their chauffeurs and their long black cars, even if they also keep them out of sight.

The ambivalence that beneficiaries feel toward their money's pow-

ers and their weaknesses—or is it their powers and their money's
docility?—may be intermittent, but it is troubling and formative.
It issues in bizarre acts of defiance, like the one that an acquaintance
of mine, let's call him Marshall Jones, said he used to indulge in:

> If they took it [his money] all away, I think what I'd most regret is
> not being able to sleep late. Too bad. The thing I most enjoy about
> this deal is my differentness. At one time I was so exultant in my
> differentness that I didn't do anything. I didn't have to do what they
> did, so I didn't do anything. In this way I painted myself in a corner
> where I got lonesome and bored. I'm trying now to become a mem-
> ber of the human race. Still, that's what I'd miss the most, being able
> to sleep late.

Jones was given an odd introduction to the powers of his money. Most
parents of the Old Rich cannot bring themselves to talk to their children about their forthcoming inheritances; they let the trustees or
money managers do the job, invariably in a dry, abstract manner, like
a sex lecture in school. Jones's father spoke to him about his money
only once, when the two of them, the boy barely in his teens and on
his first trip to Europe, stood solemnly in Highgate cemetery by the
grave of Karl Marx. "Boy," his father told him, "that man predicted
that a major part of the world would end up slaving for wages. Well,
boy, you're never going to have to be a wage slave."

More often the inheritors' ambivalence issues in a kind of mocking
self-reproach over one or another of the specific insults leveled against
them by the entrepreneurial imagination. My old friend from St. Paul's
and Harvard, the late Hugh Jeremy Chisholm, used to laugh at his
lack of even the basest form of appetite—the consumer's:

> There's nothing I really *want,* no *thing.* I just piss my money away.
> It would never occur to me, say, to save a little from my income one
> month, and then go out and buy something I really wanted the next
> month. Instead, I'll spend six nights of the week in restaurants,
> spend maybe a thousand dollars, and then see a picture I like and
> not be able to afford it.

But over and over again the ambivalence revolves around the issue
of weakness—how the powers of the money seem constantly to subvert personal powers. One inheritor has said:

The older I get, the more I see how pervasively having money has influenced me.... Like, I've always been proud of being very laid-back. I don't get hot under the collar at meetings. I don't usually get embroiled in office politics, and so on. But now I see that a lot of that comes from the expectation that I'll always get my way because I can buy it. A rich person doesn't need to be a scrappy infighter ... you don't learn those skills in rich families.

Sometimes, when the worm turns, the Old Rich kid tries to become everything that his upbringing was designed to prevent—a member of the entrepreneurial class. On the male side, George Bush has provided a wonderful example of this quislingism. His party having ceased to have any use for patricians like himself, he once went so far as to declare, "They say I'm a patrician. I don't even know what the word means. I'll have to look it up." In the same interview, however, he inadvertently revealed not only that he knew at least one meaning of that epithet, but that he deserved to have it thrown at him. "It's a shame for the presidency to have that little guy in there," he said of Jimmy Carter. "He's got no class. And I don't mean in a social sense." Another time, he said that, yes, he'd had a little help from his family in putting together his Texas oil venture, but that basically what he'd done out there was to "make it on [his] own." It doesn't work. The American imagination of wealth, especially the *nouveau* Republican form of it, will not be gulled so easily. Bush's efforts to portray himself as a hero of Market Man may save him from being called a weakling, but at the price of being called a wimp. There are female quislings like Bush, so-called corporate professionals who claim to be daughters of their own deeds, but there aren't many of them. Among women of Old Money, the usual form of self-degradation is less pathetic than Bush's. They are the only women in America who can happily abandon their androgynous upper-class imagery for lifetimes of domestic bondage with "manly" entrepreneurs or, depending on their physical assets, for rather shorter careers as sex objects. To them, as sometimes to the Bushes of the class, this strange *nostalgie de la boue* may actually appear as a liberation.

That's one way of resolving the complex fate of being born into the Old Money class: to pretend that it never happened, or that one never learned anything from the experience. There are worse ways. Many children of the Old Rich are so ill-bred, or so maddened by the taunts of weakness they hear wafting through the windows of their chauffeur-driven cars, that they grab the wheel and start driving their inherited money powers like a tank through the crowd. This is the most squalid degradation of which Old Money is capable, what mentors of the class call "being spoiled." When they wake up in the morning, or when they stop pissing their money away, the Old Rich are under constant, almost irresistible temptation to use their money as the dominant imagination of wealth would have them use it—aggressively, individualistically, vulgarly, almost as though they had made it themselves. "Goddamn it!" I once heard a sporting lord scream at his polo team, composed of three paid professionals (paid by him) and himself, the weakest of the lot. "Pass me the ball! I *own* you bastards!"

For the most part, however, the ambivalence is never resolved, the complex fate never evaded. Poor little rich girls tormented over whether they're loved for themselves or their money are not the figures of popular amusement they once were, nor are the sad little Fauntleroys who buy the friendship of "regular guys and gals" with rides on their yachts. Yet the anguish of loneliness and confused identity that lies behind these caricatures is still a fundamental part of Old Money life. There is a nationwide support group of inheritors called the Dough Nuts ("We all have lots of dough," one of them explained to me, "and we're all a little nuts"), which meets periodically throughout the year, in secret, in understated resorts, to talk about their inherited wealth—what it does to them and what they can do with it, for themselves and (in keeping with the gift ethos) for others.

> I'll never forget what a thrill it was for me the first time I was in a group of people talking about inherited wealth. There were ten or fifteen of us, and we went around the room, with each person saying where her or his money had come from, and the problems they had dealing with it. At first, it struck me as ludicrously funny, a bit like an Alcoholics Anonymous meeting.... But ultimately the whole thing was enormously moving to me.... Being able to talk about it with others gave me an incredible charge. I remember the weekend meeting finished up with a big party, and I danced like crazy even though I don't usually dance at all.

There is, of course, the drastic solution to the chauffeur-and-limousine problem—Christ's. Inheritors of wealth can always sell all this stuff that's making them weak—go liquid, as their money managers might say—and give it to the poor. Few do, and not just because the stuff is locked up in inert masses of trust funds. For there is one thing that money buys that they will not do without; the thing, anyway, that they say they would most regret if they didn't have money: their freedom and independence.

In theory, of course, all Americans regardless of wealth are heirs to the blessings of freedom and independence. In myth, too. After all, the most enchanting of America's stories of liberation is about a scruffy, destitute kid called Huckleberry Finn, who floats down the river on a raft and then, when that glorious trip finally has to come to an end, lights out for the territories. There's no end to the territories; no end, either, for freedom and independence. That's the American way. Even so, even though Old Money *is* an end, of sorts, and even though its beneficiaries are much richer than Huck Finn, they dispose of quite as much, if not more, freedom and independence. The hereditary rich, we say, are people of "independent means," with "independent incomes"; they have, somewhat archaically, "an independence."

A common charge against the hereditary rich is that they are not an upper but a *kept* class, like the courtesans and catamites of more ancient regimes, like the welfare poor of our own. The charge is imaginatively beguiling and economically accurate, but the analogies are misleading. For however catamites and courtesans may have been kept, and however the welfare poor are kept, none of them has ever been kept free. The hereditary rich are. One meaning of a trust-fund inheritance, in fact, is that its beneficiaries are virtually forced to be free. Unless the trust is accompanied by a family business, which is in most cases only inheritable by one of the siblings, it makes almost no demands on its inheritors. What is inherited with a trust fund—more likely a collection of them, all timed to go off like time pills on certain birth- and death days—is not anything like a farm or a business. Nor is it like certain potentially lucrative (and eminently inheritable) arts and professions, such as acting or politics. Each of these carries with it, as part of the inheritance, an obligation to do something, not simply to be somebody. Each of them is also a more or less coherent collection of assets that it makes sense to call a "real" estate—the farm's land and machinery and cattle, the business's market value, cash flow, goodwill, and loyal employees, the family's good (or at least publicly recognizable) name among colleagues, fans, or constituents. But a trust fund is not quite an estate in that sense, and demands few of the attentions of "real" estates. It is a shapeless, ever changing assortment of paper properties—the so-called well-diversified portfolio—which becomes intelligible and manageable only by being reduced to the abstract measure of its dollar value. It brings with it nothing to do, no necessary functions to fulfill, no roles to perform, no duties or obligations to carry out. There is nothing to do but bank the income and, once every generation or so, appoint someone to put the principal out for the highest returns they can get in the financial markets.

It is true that the Old Money curriculum does strongly encourage inheritors to assume certain responsibilities for their near and extended patrimonies. It is also true that assumption of these responsibilities can take many forms: money management and investment banking, for instance; or curatorial duties and trusteeships in the Great American Museum, especially the Art and Nature wings; or more aristocratic ventures out into the public world, such as politics or certain kinds of *pro bono* advocacy. It is even true that many of these activities look remarkably like jobs, which means that they probably even satisfy the entrepreneurial notion of work (if not of market-making work). Still, there is all the difference in the world between taking on a worklike activity out of one's own free choice, as one's gifts and affinities might suggest and for no longer than duty or interest might continue to call, and taking on the same activity out of economic necessity. Beneficiaries of trust-fund freedom do not have to work.

So the first freedom in the gift of a well-diversified portfolio—the gift, as the envious sometimes call it, of fuck-you money—is freedom from work. Huck Finn's liberation is an everyday option for many beneficiaries of Old Money. One of my St. Paul's School alumni bulletins, for example, contains an intriguing item about Allan Mac-Dougall, a Huck Finn of the form of 1967, who was reported to be "sailing in the South Pacific aboard his 48-foot German Frers design ketch. He expects to cruise New Zealand waters early in 1987 and then head for Australia, where he may work for a few years." I must confess that my careless Old Money heart lifts in joy whenever I read this sort of notice. I feel reassured that there are still men and women gallant enough and true who might, just might, dare ask whether some forms of work are better not done at all, or whether others shouldn't be put to a social measure of *what for?*, not simply an economic measure of *how much?* One cheer for Allan MacDougall. There are possibly some worthier patrician things he could be doing with his freedom, and certainly some braver aristocratic things, but for the moment at least his carelessness appears to be doing no harm.

I am aware, of course, that work is what most people have to do to save their lives. It is what many people do to save themselves from humiliation. And it is what some people do to satisfy more elaborate needs and wants. As a measure of economic value, work shades into a measure of social status, of civic worth, of spiritual heft. In the entrepreneurial view, work is also the world's best policeman, preventing idle hands from getting into mischief or worse. It is the world's best therapist as well, forging identities and relationships with other human beings out of "nothing." Where the entrepreneurial imagination rules, people think that without work they would go mad. Even love cannot save them. Love is too chancy a thing to count on to hold one's self together.

Apologists of work, looking for a fortunate side to the Fall, often argue that work is one domain, more widely available than love, where people can get out of themselves, escape the prison house of self. But this is true of only three or four kinds of work: intellectual or spiritual work, craft or art work, and labor. For millennia of human history, these were almost the only kinds of work there were. But now much of the postindustrial labor force is engaged in work that is none of these things: service work or highly organized corporate marketing and sales work—including the marketing of self. Service work and corporate market work depend on the so-called social skills: being nice, being persuasive, manipulating people well, and so forth. But what is required is not an actual niceness, not the conviction behind the persuasiveness, not even a true desire to manipulate, but an effective simulation of these qualities. The self, in other words, has quite literally become the modern worker's stock-in-trade. This means the contrary of losing oneself in one's work. It means that the worker is driven back into the self, obliged to monitor its performance against his superior's assessment of it, juggling it between the needs of the job (the boss, customer, client, passenger) and his own hopes and desires, looking for some "space" where the true self can be safe and real again.

Who wouldn't say *fuck you* to that, if one could? Who wouldn't say *fuck you*, for that matter, to the other tyrannies of everyday life— the officiousness of bureaucrats, the arrogance of lawyers, or, should misunderstandings arise, the oppressions of the police? All kinds of money, obviously, can smooth away these shackles on our freedom, not just Old Money. But as with so much else, Old Money was free of them first.

Yet there is a serious drawback to being freed of necessity. It is a specific instance of the drawback attendant on freedom in general. At least on any existential account of the way things are, people get rid of the yoke of necessity only to be saddled with the burden of choice. For the Old Rich, this onerous burden is the beginning of the subtlest thrust of Market Man's revenge. The insidious and deadly weapon is the economic metaphor of cost. With it, it becomes possible to understand fuck-you money as enabling its beneficiaries to make choices without paying costs for them. The result is more freedom than most people, no matter how socially imaginative they are, can stand.

Most people make choices when they give up something of value in order to get something else of value. What they give up is the cost of the thing—money, time, opportunity, effort, or attention. But it's a cost only if it matters to them. Cost is not a figure; it is an experience of pain, the pain of loss in a world of scarcity. There is only so much of *this* to pay for *that*. How much it pains one to give something up is how much it costs one.

For Old Money, however, the *coup de grâce* of this logic is still to come. Market Man (and not he alone) argues that this pain cost is the source and sustenance of all values that get vested in things, activities, even values themselves. Costs have to be paid; unless they are, the thing is valueless. Modern folklore is filled with reminders of this central tenet. "No pain, no gain," people tell each other. And it's not a one-shot deal, either. Pain costs seem to be required to hold values up even after they've been paid. To take something for granted, it is said, is to lose it, as people lose their own paintings through not seeing them anymore. What is pernicious about this line of reasoning is how easily it can be turned against Old Money's precious ethos of the gift. Blessedness may attach to the giver of a gift, at least if it costs him something. But woe unto the receiver of it! For him it will have no value.

With that curse of costlessness, Old Money's cherished transcendence of the marketplace begins to look like a transcendence of the human world itself. Most curses hurl the victim downward. Not this one. Market Man's final blow against Old Money is to curse it with weightlessness. So tenuous is their purchase on human reality, the Old Rich might as well be bodiless apparitions in space—or featherweights in the back seat of a long black car.

There's no end of corroborating evidence for the effectiveness of the curse; Old Money's family albums are full of it. Their characteristic behavior with money, for example: now absurdly mean, now idiotically expansive. I think of the tactless price consciousness of one's rich relatives: "My dear, fabric is just so expensive these days; why, I've taken to buying mine on the Lower East Side!" One's relative has a ridiculously tight "budget" that will be flouted at the first flicker of desire, but for now it is serving its purpose, which is to impose a factitious sense of cost on her choices.

The spendthrift is also reacting to costlessness, in this case by trying to scratch the acquisitive itch until it hurts. It never happens. Spendthrifts buy and buy and buy, but it costs them nothing. It costs nothing for Mrs. Onassis, say, to enter a boutique, admire a blouse, and then buy it in all eight colors. It cost nothing for William Randolph Hearst to spend $1 million on art and antiques and to be conned on virtually every purchase. He once complained bitterly at having to pay $900,000 in taxes on his mother's estate but then saw a sign in Sloane's window advertising "the most expensive carpet in the world." He bought it for $40,000, had it shipped to his warehouse in the Bronx, and never saw it again. He is supposed to have put together "collections" in 504 different categories of arts and crafts, but when half of them were sold at auction—the trinkets covering two full acres of Gimbel's floor space—they brought in half of what he had paid for them. Spendthrifts like Hearst enthrall consumers. For if consumers are "torrent birds" (as Plato unkindly called them), people absorbed in their own alimentary and excremental cause, then spendthrifts might appear to be fowl of the same feather, flying point for the flock. But they're not. Consumers pay the cost of their feedings in foregone options; spendthrift inheritors do not. Moralists describe them as spoiled and selfish; therapists suggest they are addicts, trying to fill the void where their selves should be; but for Market Man they are simply the Old Rich, fighting their way back down into the economic world of scarcity—spending, spending, spending in the vain hope that one day they'll feel the pinch of cost, and bleed a little.

Market Man also knows how to link up cost and the infamous side of the icon of carelessness. Old Money has little idea of what to do with things of market value except to get them off the market and into some sort of museum, there to remain the objects of curatorial concern and aesthetic delight. With everything else, it is careless; not to say wasteful, frivolous, and neglectful. My friend Jeremy Chisholm once bought a gold Cartier tank watch for several thousand dollars, then spent weeks trying to get it metallurgically treated so as to turn the housing black. The aesthetic of this project was a pretext for a bit of malicious camp. He wanted to thumb his nose at the *nouveaux riches* who were buying the watch by the boxful at the time, and at Cartier for encouraging them. But when Chisholm discovered there was no way of turning gold black, he gave the watch to his stepson, who lost it.

The bizarre buying behavior of the hereditary rich may look like a feeble effort to make some palpable contact with their purchases. People who pay prices without also paying costs connect with the marketable world like feathers; they feel no pain, at most only a tickle of pleasure. This brush with economic realities has serious consequences for society, Market Man would argue. It loosens the tight little circles of market reciprocity into something like the long relaxed loops of the gift, with lamentable results in lost efficiency, energy, and substance. It also has serious consequences for the Old Rich themselves: Paying the cost, bleeding a little, is a source not only of enjoyment but of possession; for those to whom everything is given, however, nothing shall be possessed.

Their market behavior is not the only, or even the most significant, area in which, Market Man is pleased to point out, Old Money's costless lives have pernicious consequences. Costs may be front-loaded, like those entailed by (most people's) purchases, but there are also costs as consequences. The hereditary rich don't have to pay those costs, either. Fuck-you money is also bail-out money.

Think of debts. For most people a debt is a loan. To Old Money, however, debts frequently appear (if they appear at all) in the guise of punishments for fiscal misbehavior. This interpretation was apparently quite common in the Roosevelt family, the Hyde Park branch anyway. Eleanor had occasion to write to her husband about one of their sons:

> Something has to be done to make F. Jr. realize it is dishonest not to pay bills. I suggest you ask him to list all he owes. Pay it yourself and then take out of his allowance, $100 a quarter. Tell him he *has* to live on his income, no going to "21," etc. until he earns his own money in toto and has no bills. Forbid Granny [the President's mother] to give him anything except his Xmas and birthday presents beyond his allowance, and that to be cut in proportion as his earnings make it possible. . . .

Needless to say, the President never said a word to Granny about imposing a negative income tax on his son. Even if he had, and she had, it wouldn't have made any difference. Children of wealth can always find someone to bail them out, if not indulgent parents or absent-minded trustees, then rich wives (Franklin junior married Ethel du Pont), club stewards, provident brothers and sisters, loyal friends, sycophantic snobs, and so forth. If worse comes to worst, they can always go to a bank.

Parents, in fact, are usually the last resort for debt-ridden children of the Old Rich, and even the most rigorous (which the Roosevelts were not) seldom have the heart to let their children feel the full wrath of their creditors. Dishonesty is a harsh accusation for a mother to level against a young man who runs up a tab at "21." If Eleanor Roosevelt had really believed her own charge, she would never have allowed anyone else—the newspapers, for instance—to make it public. It would be too embarrassing a reflection on her and her husband as parents, and on the whole "old" family. If FDR had refused to help and Granny had cut him off, Eleanor would have bailed out her son herself—and with an income of about $61,000 a year (by 1940 partly earned, partly "independent"), she could afford it.

Debts belong to a larger category of consequences that an unearned income can soften or evade. As punishments for delinquencies—the earnings, as it were, of profligacy—they belong in the same category as going to jail for one's crimes, another form of desert that rich kids seldom have to face. But there's a whole host of consequences that can't be described as punishments but are equally painful and equally purchasable: I mean the consequences of risk, all those risks attendant on any exercise of choice under conditions of uncertainty. For most beneficiaries of Old Money under most circumstances, the risks they run in investing time, feelings, efforts, intelligence, and/or unearned money in anything—whether people, places, ventures, or things—are nowhere near so great as the risks run by people whose wealth cost them something. Jobs, houses, spouses—there's hardly a chancy undertaking whose consequences, should they turn out bad, the hereditary rich cannot sweeten or annul with their cost-free riches. Fitzgerald's mournful remark about there being no second acts in American life is inaccurate under most circumstances, but it is certainly inaccurate with respect to the hereditary rich. They may enjoy as many acts as their energies can sustain and their money can afford.

In family albums, however, the results of the relatively risk-free environment in which Old Money makes its choices can be rather disturbing. For many beneficiaries, a life spent without having to take the risk of paying the cost of consequences is, quite simply, an inconsequential life. Witness this report from, I would guess, a Dough Nut:

> I remember at one of these meetings of this group I belong to, where people with inherited wealth talk about how they deal with it, one guy said something that set everybody in the room nodding. He said, "Sometimes I feel as if everything I've done in my life has been a hobby." I think that's the crux of it right there, what money does to most people who have it. It takes away a certain drive. I don't mean that people with money . . . just loll around on beaches all day. No, they work. But you look closely and you see they tend to work part-time, or split their energy between several different things, or flit from one job to another, or go to school for years and years. I think our whole society is geared so totally around trying to make money that it takes someone who has their head totally together to be able to work full steam when they don't need the money. I mean work with the same drive and energy and ambition as someone who is poor and for whom that job is the only possible path to success. A rich person always secretly expects that success is going to drop down on him or her from the sky, without any effort required, the way the money did.

In this rich kid, the Old Money imagination is clearly more than half dead; his amateur spirit has left him, and the spirit of the gift is evidently about to depart. In the next scene one would expect to see him reborn as an entrepreneur.

But the inconsequential life can produce a worse effect than the sensation of being a hobbyist, especially when the cultivation of the social graces and virtues transforms the beneficiary's experience into a series of reflections in Narcissus' pool. This is a common outcome of an Old Money upbringing, and it is a disaster. My friend Chisholm redeemed the disaster with humor and insight, but even in that it might be alleged that he was evading the cost. He said to me once, in the course of a long evening's review of his life:

> When I was at St. Paul's I dreamed of being a great poet or philosopher. I can't remember dreaming of a career in the sense of working along a path or process, only of being something. After college I got a job entirely on my own in an investment banking firm in Australia. Then I went to Columbia Business School. Then I worked at Lazard Frères for a while, then I managed a department store's pension fund. I drifted out of all these jobs. I've never engaged. What has

been passed on to me by my father is not a way of life but a life-style. I am thirty-seven years old and I can afford not to work and I don't know what to do with my life. . . .

What do I mean when I say that I drifted out of these jobs? Well, first of all, I begin thinking that the job I have is interfering with something else I want to do. I never have a very clear image of what that is, mind you, only an image of myself doing it. But it's enough to start me rationalizing myself out of the job I'm currently in, whatever it is. After all, when you have no deep convictions in life, all that's left is rationalization. For instance, when I quit that job at the store—my God, but this is strange!—I had taken a house in the country, and one day I decided I wanted to be a cowboy. I know, it sounds crazy. It *was* crazy. What happened was that the image of myself as a pension-fund manager began to blur, while the cowboy image began to gain definition. And so one day I quit and went out west and bought a ranch.

This had happened before. When I was at Lazard's, I had this image of myself as a banker. Every morning I'd get up and look at myself in the mirror in my banker's suit and see a banker. I'm speaking literally here, you understand. Then one morning I didn't see the banker anymore. I saw the banker suit, but in it there was *nothing*.

What was happening to Chisholm, psychologically speaking, I don't know. But in terms of Old Money's imagination, what was happening was a fall from grace—a fall into empty space. Money and beauty and the upper-class decencies, he had them all. But they combined to waft him off into some nightmarish apotheosis, out into zones of weightlessness where the self loses shape and substance and finally vanishes altogether. The same thing happened to Marshall Jones, though he makes it sound more a matter of will, a willed inconsequence.

I had this inability to isolate what the money really was. Or an unwillingness. I owned it. He did give it to me. But did I have the sense that I could do anything I wanted with it? I don't know. I did boring things. I found them boring at the time. I went around asking myself why I felt so powerless. It was because of the money, I thought, the immense amount of power that was stored up in it. I felt over-amped.

Maybe it was because I'd served no apprenticeship. I graduated from high school in the early 1960s, went to Williams, dropped out

just before graduation—doing well, too—enrolled in the [Colum-
bia] School of General Studies, quit; went to the NYU film school,
quit; worked in film for a while, quit; went back to the School of
General Studies, studied geography, linguistics, historical geography. . . . I feel I'm a space traveler. I felt that way quite early in my
life. Floating around on a sea of information. B.B.—Brigitte Bardot
or Brooks Brothers—they're equally unfamiliar, strange. I like to
cultivate the strangeness, the sensation of it. It's my identity.

So there it is, the revenge of Market Man. Beneficiaries of Old Money
never feel the bite of costs and consequences, but only at the risk of
feeling like hobbyists, like rocketmen; or they lose their selves in the
mirrored image of their clothes. They evade the economic laws of
scarcity, saving themselves from the pain of preferences foreclosed, but
only at the risk of never fully possessing what they own. Their money
enables them to be saved from many of the consequences of their actions and, relatively speaking, from risk itself. This last is unquestionably the greatest risk of all—a metarisk, so to speak. The Old Rich
argue that the charges of weakness against them, and the etherealized
identities they sometimes feel, are more than compensated by the rewards they win in grace, beauty, and mobility. But there seems to be
no compensation for rising above risk.

Every serious choice that a man or woman makes is a leap, more
or less frightening, into contingency. Not to make those choices, not to
open oneself to misfortune and the fear of misfortune, is a tempting
option, but one gives in to it at the risk of never living a fully human
life. The hereditary rich can give in to it, and insofar as they do, they
lose that much of a wholly lived life. They do not connect, they do not
engage, they do not possess the richness and complexity of experience.
They are doomed, as Townsend Martin once observed, long after the
quadrille d'honneur at his brother's ball, to futility.

> I regard futility as the real nemesis of [Old Money]. It turns our lives
> to nothing; it makes of our fairest garden a desert; it robs us, in our
> very cradles, of our lives, our liberties, and our happiness. It leaves
> us groping about in a world of shadows, longing for the substance,
> dreaming of realities we can never know, wishing always for change,
> sighing always for worlds that are out of our reach.

Old Money people are fated to pass their lives forever out of touch
with the common ground, where others all walk on their own two
feet.

CHAPTER FIVE

Three Ordeals

"Oh, jest not, palter not, delay not! I am worn, I am
wounded, I can bear no more. Take me to the king, my father, and he will make thee rich beyond thy wildest dreams.
Believe me, man, believe me! I speak no lie, but only the
truth! Put forth thy hand and save me! I am indeed the
Prince of Wales!"

The man stared down, stupefied, upon the lad, then shook
his head and muttered, "Gone stark mad as any Tom
o'Bedlam"—then collared him once more and said with a
coarse laugh and an oath, "But mad or no mad, I and thy
Gammer Canty will soon find where the soft places in thy
bones lie, or I'm no true man!"

With this he dragged the frantic and struggling prince
away and disappeared up a front court, followed by a delighted and noisy swarm of human vermin.

Mark Twain, *The Prince and the Pauper*

T HERE ARE THREE WAYS by which Market Man's imagination of wealth may prevail over Old Money's. In one, Old
Money capitulates, surrendering its social graces and virtues,
including the spirit of the gift, to the more powerful entrepreneurial
ethos of competitive self-reliance. The denouement here, substituting
as it does one way of looking at the world for another, spells the end
of the class.

Market Man also prevails when the Old Rich act out all the bad
things he says about them. This is probably the most common outcome. Entrepreneurial values reflect deep human longings—to over-
throw the fateful momentum of the past; to make things new,
including the self; to be solely responsible for oneself. They also do

what a New World called them into being to do: they help make wealth. But capitulation to these values is not a realistic option for most beneficiaries of Old Money. They go against the grain, deform the breed, and in the end fall under the bane of futility. On the other hand, acting out the most pejorative things their enemies say about them is a real option. Held aloft by costless wealth, floating along on the envy of the crowd and their own astonishing presumptions, the Old Rich may all too easily describe a trajectory through life that, graceful and composed though it may be, is not in touch with the common ground of reality. Their bodies lack traction, their spirits lack consequence. Nothing they do makes any difference. Their noblest gestures, most beautiful arrangements of self and setting, greatest accomplishments, are all quite reasonably attributed to their unearned money. Deprived of the pains and pleasures of risk, they lose a large part of experience itself. The denouement here involves what John Jay Chapman feared for the class—a loss of social relevance.

Old Money may be defeated in a third way: by the indirect attack of Market Man's after-hours consumerist imagination. The hostile forces here are in the pay of entrepreneurs, but they are not identical with them. They are the flacks: the advertisers, trendmongers, and pop demographers of the media, designers of Market Man's purchasable goal of a "life-style." The attack takes advantage of a tragicomic flaw in Old Money's curriculum, the fact that its image of virtue is so often obscured by its image of beauty. True virtue may indeed be beautiful, but not with the "attractive" sort of beauty cultivated by Old Money. Yet, as we have seen, it is a premise of the justification of inherited wealth that the curriculum composed from that wealth should be attractive and indeed to some degree purchasable. Why else would the middle classes trouble to aspire to it? It was no part of the plan for the curriculum, however, that the whole thing should be imaginatively reconstructed into a "package"—nonchalance sold along with "naturally tailored" suits, magnanimity arriving in the mail with every L. L. Bean catalog, a sense of fair play included in the warranty of each Volvo station wagon. Poof! And poof to you! With that, Old Money is transformed into an upscale feeding pattern, a market with "good demographics."

A quisling surrender to entrepreneurial values, a free fall into irrelevancy and inconsequence, or a metamorphosis of the class into a flock of torrent birds are the three great disasters most feared by the mentors and more conscientious members of the Old Money class.

Needless to say, a good deal of imagination and money has gone into devising ways to prevent them.

Imaginatively, the task is not difficult. There are clues to the proper preventives in the story of every prince and princess who ever lived. All of them were made to suffer a series of ordeals to test "the soft places in their bones," like Mark Twain's little Prince of Wales. True, children of all families, royal or not, have to undergo ordeals. Establishing oneself in a kingdom is not a task for the hereditary rich alone. Nor are the hereditary rich the only ones to see this task as a matter of undergoing tests of their fitness to rule. Still, there is a difference between Prince Edward's relationship to his kingdom—or Christ's, for that matter—and the relationship of Oedipus or the children of Cymbeline to theirs. Princes and princesses who know and declare who they "really" are, and what their kingdom is, usually encounter different experiences in the course of their ordeals than princes and princesses who have to make (or find) their selves and kingdoms along the way. For both, the course lies over hard ground, which tests and trains them in the qualities necessary for self-rule and rule of others (if any): courage and judgment, determination and resourcefulness, justice and mercy, and so on. Beyond that, the hard ground takes them through somewhat different woods. Self-makers (or finders) have to suffer the agonies of not knowing, of spacey possibility, of endlessness; while the knowing (and the known) have to suffer the agonies of derision and the temptations of flattery, and run the gamut of envy from admiration to resentment.

There's another difference, which is that the ordeals of the known and knowing seem to have been arranged for them, like so much else. All ordeals require being deprived of the equivocal supports of home, either by exile or by a voluntary venture into the world. They involve witches and ogres and terrifying obstacles: monstrous things, but pushovers, if truth be told, compared to the shadowy figures and obscure tasks that children must contend with among their parents and siblings. There's a traditionalism—mandatory, fateful, institutionalized—to the ordeals undergone by rich kids. It's as though the children of the rich, who will one day never have to suffer the costs of anything, must now be made to suffer the costs of everything, without hope of escape. This front loading of the costs may account for another strong peculiarity of Old Money ordeals: their epic genre. I don't mean their grandeur (everybody's ordeals seem grand), or their status as myth (everybody's ordeals are mythic). I mean the past perfect tense in which they're composed, and the sense of greatness—their own, their family's, their class's, their nation's—which seems inimitably perfect, irretrievably past. But only seems so. Past though the epics are, they are still told as much to inspire (inspire our children, inspire our own maturity) as to justify our ascendancy. Even so, there's no question that the telling of them may also bring about the very opposite of inspiration: the dying sigh of nostalgia.

THE SCHOOL ORDEAL

Brooke Astor has given posterity a charming vignette of herself at a moment of great decision, when she resolved to send her son Tony off to boarding school. He was about ten at the time.

> After a couple of summers at Portofino away from other American children and ruling over the apartment in New York, I decided that Tony was getting spoiled and should go to boarding school, where he would not have everything his own way. I remember so well how I first spoke to Buddie [the boy's adoptive stepfather] about this. We were swimming at Paraggi when I said, "Buddie, I think that Tony should go to boarding school." Buddie lost a stroke or two, and when he recovered said, "When do you want him to go?" "*Now,*" I answered, "and as you are leaving for New York next week, you must find the school." ... When we left [Tony] at the school, he and I cried a bit, but I knew that he was as happy as a sheltered small boy could be away from home, and I felt that it was a character builder.

Astor's decision, like everything else involving the Old Money curriculum, is open to a good deal of contestable interpretation by people not born and bred to the class. And boarding schools, especially St. Midas boarding schools, seem to arouse a richer range of interpretations than most upper-class institutions. (Wider too: I've met all sorts of Americans who don't know the difference between Andover and St. Paul's, Choate and Groton, but who nevertheless have strong views on the nature and purpose of these schools.) For some, boarding schools seem more like a kingdom won than a proving ground on the way to a kingdom. They see vast country estates, with ponds and streams lacing a landscape of verdant lawns and deep woods of evergreen and birch. They see buildings of brick and stone, softened with ivy—dormitories, libraries, galleries, laboratories, gymnasiums, dining halls, hockey rinks, every facility to improve the mind, exercise the body, and lift the heart. And they see boys and girls absorbed in performances of one sort or another—speaking up in class, dancing or painting, clashing furiously on field, court, or rink, working in the lab, singing in the choir. Sometimes, not often, they see them going off by themselves into the dark woods.

As this yearning vision turns resentful, which it often does, the country estate becomes a country club. The epithet is a cliché of rancor. Now the schools are seen as playgrounds for the children of privilege, whose parents can buy their way into Harvard, Yale, and Princeton— they, too, playgrounds. Or else they are seen as elaborate "fitness centers," where fat, stupid, and neurotic rich kids get special help to enable them to compete with—and, more often than not, defeat—the slim, clever, and wholesome kids who have to "make it on their own." The "country club" sneer has been available for many years: Woodrow Wilson of Princeton and Samuel Drury of St. Paul's apparently discussed ways of countering it as early as 1912, when the future President came to speak at the school's graduation exercises. It has lost none of its appeal since, despite the fact that a taste for country clubs now seems to have trickled down to virtually everyone in America.

Another view of boarding schools puts aside the *optique* of envy and replaces it with that of pity. How cruel it seems to send young people, barely adolescent, away from the loving encouragement of their mothers, the firm guidance of their fathers, the lively rivalry of their brothers and sisters, the reassuring solidarities of their local communities. How barbaric it seems—or weirdly communistic—to give one's children into the care of strangers, people who might not have their best interests at heart but have only the interests of some larger group, or some broader idea.

This interpretation rests on rather wishful assumptions about the sorts of families and communities that most Americans come from. Still, it gets close to the deepest purpose of the boarding-school ordeal as Old Money's imagination understands it. The Old Rich have always known that rich families are not good places to grow up in. Childish minds are disposed to have everything their own way, in Astor's phrase, and Old Money knows that rich childish minds are likely to get it, especially in a society more than half convinced that everything can be bought. Three sorts of people come of this: those who are weak and don't know it (bullies and, in the derogatory sense, princesses); those who are weak and do know it (Fauntleroys and poor little rich girls);

and those who are strong and don't know it (wimps of both sexes). To make sure one's child becomes none of these is what boarding schools are for.

But not all boarding schools, or not all in the same way. One method is to expose the child to a simulated real-world, sink-or-swim America at one of the Academy schools (so called to distinguish them from the St. Midas schools), such as Andover or Exeter. The purpose of an Academy education, admirably fulfilled in such well-known graduates as George Bush, George Gilder, and Pierre ("Pete") du Pont, is to indoctrinate the children of the rich as early as possible in all the values and virtues of competitive self-reliance, almost as if they, too, could be self-made men and women. To accomplish this purpose, there would be tough teachers, well trained in their disciplines and in the harsh elitism of Puritan New England. And there would be tough competition from a large selection of middle- and lower-middle-class kids determined to "make it" into Harvard, Yale, or Princeton. The effectiveness of this program may be judged from a survey of its graduates published by Exeter in the mid-1960s. Asked what they got out of their years at the school, an astonishing number of alumni gave answers like the following:

> I will always be grateful for the absence of any indulgent paternalism.

> Each day after lunch during my first year, I went back to my room and cried. . . . My memories of Exeter are a series of bitter engagements with life, but without them I would never have matured.

> To have survived Exeter's terrors is to achieve a sense of masculinity and of mastery over one's fate that enables one to stand alone.

> She was a rough tough old baggage, more like the second who hoists you into the ring by the armpits when the bell rings. She made you face it alone, which, in the end, is the way all things must be faced.

Such testimonials are the beginning of entrepreneurial wisdom; the end of it too, unless some vision of Old Money (or failure) should interpose another end. Academy schooling can of course lead to New Rich impostures quite as bad as Old Rich prepostures. Academy educations toughen up rich kids with competitive self-reliance, but at the cost of a denial of the gift ethos, and a dangerous denial of the social element in the well-lived life.

In the last several decades, there has been a certain convergence of atmosphere between the Academy and the St. Midas schools, with the latter acquiring a strong dose of the entrepreneurial imagination, the former a mild dose of the social. Nobody seems able to give clear-cut reasons for this development. The coming of girls is mentioned, softening the Academy schools' teaching of competitive self-reliance, while the ratcheting up of Ivy League admissions standards has forced St. Midas children to work harder. Another factor is undoubtedly the ascendancy of so-called Reagan conservatism and the effects of the so-called Reagan recession. In any event, the convergence is far from complete, and until it is, distinctions will have to be made. And from Old Money's point of view, they will continue to be made in favor of St. Midas.

One cannot be definitive about the fundamental design of so richly figured a group of institutions as the St. Midas schools. It may even be foolhardy to try, especially when one's feelings are as ambivalent as mine are about St. Paul's. I have a vision of the atmosphere at school that will never leave me. It is a vision of the chapel, and in it I see hundreds of students sitting shoulder to shoulder, thigh to thigh, packed tight in long pews that run the whole length of the dark vaulted tunnel and vanish at last in the white-gold light of the altar. The chapel is cold and fitfully illumined, but we are hot. Our breath steams in the cold air. We are perfectly still. Then out of the dark and the cold comes the voice of the rector, the sound of a wave receding over a stony beach. He reads: "O Lord, support us all the day long, until the shadows lengthen, and the evening comes, and the busy world is hushed, and the fever of life is over, and our work is done. Then, in Thy mercy, grant us a safe lodging, and a holy rest, and peace at the last. Amen." Then, with a wild pealing of Dionysian pipes, the great organ breaks the stillness with a recessional, and we, like figures released from the frieze of a sacrificial parade, file out past the rector in his throne, through the anteroom of the temple with its little cluster of abashed latecomers, past the Angel of Death clasping to her naked breast the swooning hero of the school's Great War, and out into the hard bright glare of sunshine on the snow.

It is a vision, for me, of almost unbearable social density, and of terrifying personal consequence. It seemed to me that everything we did—the way we played games, the neatness of our rooms, our marks (in those days posted publicly and ranked), the stylishness of our sports jackets, the reply we gave to Mr. Smith's greeting, and things far more intimate than these, every movement of our souls—had a kind of uncanny resonance, like the nightly boom-zing-zing-zing of black ice expanding on the Lower School Pond. At the end of my fourth-form year I begged my father to let me transfer to Exeter. He had no objection and told me to go ahead and arrange it. I never did. I couldn't get up the initiative, thereby proving I didn't belong there. It was not some deviant entrepreneurial imagination that had prompted me to change, only a rich kid's longing for a way to say Fuck you, a yearning for the lazy river, for peace at last.

My vision is very morbid. Social density and personal consequence are precisely what the St. Midas ordeal is all about, but I wasn't meant to take it so hard. Students have taken it harder, of course, and no doubt still do. At St. Paul's in the 1870s, for example, John Jay Chapman went out into that forest of evergreen and birch to erect an altar. What gods he worshiped there, Hebrew or Greek, no one could imagine, but he soon left the school. The school never left him, though. Later, when he was at Harvard Law School, he thought he saw Percival Lowell make a pass at his fiancée, Minna; he struck his imagined rival in a rage, then returned to his rooms off Brattle Street and put his hand to the fire until it withered and blackened in the flames. Taking personal social responsibility for one's actions was never meant to go so far as that, certainly. On the contrary, it is the purpose of the ordeal to teach one to take it gracefully, eagerly, with high spirits and keen intelligence.

Samuel S. Drury, rector of St. Paul's from 1911 to 1936, never attained the fame of Endicott Peabody of Groton. (For that matter, neither did any of his students.) Perhaps this was because Drury had a more complex and troubling character than Peabody's, and a less attractive personality. Shabby genteel in origins, a Harvard-educated retainer of the class rather than a full-fledged member of it, Drury never got over the envy (by no means rare among St. Midas teachers) of the steward for the objects of his stewardship, the master for his pupils, the twice-born for the once-born. Peabody wrote once to the parent of a penniless Groton boy: "The most important consideration is that if he should remain at Groton he would be associating with boys whose means are for the most part greater than his are likely to be. This is only a slight disadvantage in the case of boys of substantial character but in [your son's] case I think it might make for serious harm." Such brutal simplicity was impossible for someone of Drury's background and intelligence. In his diary he railed against the people he'd been "called" to educate:

> [The school] must not become a place of fashion, an exclusive retreat where like-minded sons of like-minded parents disport themselves.... Our function is not to conform to the rich and prosperous world which surrounds us, but rather, through its children, to convert it....
>
> Our danger is that ... the school will become just one more factor in the luxury of modern society, St. Blanks, where the children are boarded for a season, like a golf or yacht club, a ministering servant to a pleasureable necessity.

Peabody, by contrast, was the social equal, if not superior, of everyone connected with Groton. He was also a man perfectly composed for a youth to admire: handsome, straightforward, powerful and athletic in presence, a man of deep and simple convictions, a father just in judgment and strong to save. In fact, he might well have served as Drury's beau ideal for the sort of man a St. Midas school ordeal was designed to send forth into the world. As it was, Drury chose David— the Old Testament's and Michelangelo's:

> And Saul armed David with his armor, and he put an helmet of brass upon his head; also he armed him with a coat of mail.... And David said unto Saul, "I cannot go with these; for I have not proved them." And he took his staff in his hand, and chose him five smooth stones out of the brook, and put them in a shepherd's bag he had, even in a scrip; and his sling was in his hand: and he drew near to the Philistine.... Then said David to the Philistine, "... This day will the Lord deliver thee into mine hand; and I will smite thee and take thine head from thee...."

For Drury, David is the very type of "trained physical competence, relaxed and alert, nowhere gross or ashamed; the responsive instrument of noble deeds ... quietly free of airs or arrogance." He affirms not only a kind of material chastity, disdaining to take advantage of anything he hasn't earned, but also the noblest and most dramatic impulse in the spirit of the gift, the gift of self. In Drury's view, and St. Midas's generally, the purpose of an education is to develop ardent spirits that don't need to be told what to do, that leap to defeat wickedness and ugliness in philistines as eagerly as they volunteer to defeat wickedness and ugliness in themselves.

David is also the ideal type of the Renaissance man—friend, poet, warrior, ruler, a man more Greek than Hebrew, really, more pagan than Christian. This, too, is a central aim of the St. Midas ordeal: to mold all-round men and women—amateurs, generalists, disinterested lovers of excellence and the good wherever they may be found and cultivated. ("Base specialists," in Chapman's contemptuous phrase, are discouraged.)

This is done primarily by curricular imperatives and, more subtly, by trying to inculcate an ideal of performance—striving for one's "personal best," in the usual phrase—instead of the more common ideal of winning. This is not easy. An ideal of all-round personal performance is less immediately attractive than the binary, win-or-lose view, which arranges human endeavor with a clear-cut bottom line. The win-or-lose ideal can be devastating, but it allows for time-outs, practice sessions, grudge matches, and changes of field, and it makes it easy for the player to slough off responsibility onto the arrangement itself. "I'm just playing the game" is one expression of this cop-out, or "That's the way life is." Still more important, it enables everybody to blame outcomes on anyone or anything but themselves.

The all-round personal performance ideal, by contrast, arranges human lives around metaphors of government, and a democratic self-government at that, with all the facets of personality and character having their equal and moderate voice. This is its chief weakness and chief strength. For while the powers of performative self-government may be virtually totalitarian—both in the absoluteness with which they place responsibility "where it belongs," on the performer, and in the scope of their surveillance—at the same time they remain firmly seated in the self. No "objective" measure, no gentile or barbarian authority, may judge the governance of this one-man, one-woman city. The performances, yes; the results of self-governance, yes; but whether they are indeed the best the person is capable of, no. That is for the Old Rich to decide, alone in their upper-class city of one. Many well-subsidized Huckleberry Finns issue from this ideal of performance, many odiously "careless people," and many brutal tyrants (of the self and others), all the inevitable errors and casualties of the ideal's horrible gravity.

A boarding school is a nine-month, twenty-four-hour-a-day agon of personal performance. It's not enough to play good football or field hockey; you also have to play squash well, and soccer well, and basket-ball well. It's not enough to capture Veronica for the school prom or Archie for a date at the pizza place; you also have to be popular and respected by all the rest of the boys and girls, the teachers, the rector— and, so far as is possible, to show yourself in the favor of the gods as well. It's not enough to be good at math and science; you also have to be good at English and history and languages—and write for the lit-erary magazine, and perform in the school string quartet, and debate in interscholastic debating contests, and tutor kids less "advantaged" than yourself, and stun your friends with your wit, and charm your teachers, and fuck off with panache, and show school spirit, and get into Harvard, Yale, or Princeton.

Other boys and girls go home at the end of the day or disappear into the streets. Alone or with their buddies, they can have some pri-vacy. There's a lot of privacy on the streets and in the spacey freedoms of the American family. They can even get help—from the family anyway. Other American families are as rich in personal and financial resources as Old Money families, some of them richer, and they give their children all the help they and their money can provide. But in a boarding school there's no privacy, no money, and no help, except from the larger family of the school itself. There's no dreamy solitude, no slack time, no lazing around. One's entire life is spent in public, per-forming.

David's aesthetic attractiveness to anyone who feels he can afford it is clear. One sees remnants of it still in the amateurish "general edu-cation" demanded of all students admitted to "the community of ed-ucated men and women"; that is, to the rhetorical Harvard. This vision of all-round education has splintered into mere "distribution requirements" under the tremendous centrifugal pressure of an eco-nomic system that rewards faculty for digging ever narrower, ever deeper tunnels of specialization. The result is a professional deforma-tion so great that the school can no longer agree on what the demands of a "general education" should be, and couldn't meet them if it did. In public colleges and universities, the pressure is intensified a thou-sandfold by middle-class students following urgent economic necessi-ties of their own: to specialize in business, for example. Even at the rhetorical Harvard, as confidence wanes in the content of a well-rounded education, so does confidence in its value.

This is unfortunate, for it leaves the David ideal without much extra-familial institutional support except at St. Midas. The loss may be serious, as the ideal has always had great polemical value against the philistines—which is to say, against those who attack Old Money. In America, the entrepreneur can appreciate his great moment (his moment of opportunity) as a moment of equality and therefore, in some sense, a moment of justice. American democratic ideology encourages this belief: it is the justice of starting-line equality. But a few democratic ideologues go further, arguing that arrangements must be made so that there may be something like justice around the finish line as well. In this view, there is a kind of violation of the natural fitness of things when the successful entrepreneur is rewarded by huge, disproportionate amounts of protean, transformative, desirable money. Great injustices come of this, says the tiny band of finish-line egalitarians. They're easily recognized: the ugly old man with the beautiful young wife, the aesthetic cretin with a wonderful collection of paintings, the woman with the thoroughbreds who can't even ride, the undemocratic politician in a democracy. And of course, with all the heirs and heiresses of this loot, the injustice is the more flagrant: *they* didn't even make the money themselves.

David goes some way to blunt the attack on the injustice of hereditary inequalities of wealth. In the first place, the boarding school's isolation from the economic world, combined with its fierce indoctrination in the spirit of performance, gives rich kids the sense that they are accomplishing something on their own. It's impossible to exaggerate how strong the yearning for this can be among children of the rich. Kathy Cronkite, the daughter of William Paley's prize newscaster, once did a survey of young men and women who, like herself, were the children of celebrities. "If there is one universal feeling," she reported, "it is, 'I want to be accepted on my own merits or fall on my own failures.' This is the biggest thing—to be accepted for yourself, or rejected for yourself." At an Old Money boarding school they would be. St. Midas boys and girls are among the most ruthless (noneconomic) meritocrats in America. Sooner or later the child of even the most resonant celebrity could feel that he has stood, unaided by his parents' money or influence, on his own two feet. The difficulty, indeed, comes with those credulous youths whose need to believe in their independence is so urgent that they imagine they've pulled themselves up by their own bootstraps.

Second, some degree of David's ideal all-roundedness is bound to become a reality. The entrepreneurial mind has words for this accomplishment—"amateur," "dilettantish," even "pathetic"—and children of the Old Rich hear them all the time. Still, polemically there is no more effective ideal than the Greek one of balance and moderation. It helps the woman with the famous library, for example, if she can also read, just as it helps the art museum trustee if he knows something about pictures, or the owner of an ocean-racing yacht if he can navigate, or the sponsor of a polo team if he can hit the ball once in a while, or the lady bountiful at the hospital if she understands the difference between Medicare and Medicaid. All-roundedness is a sort of preemptive strike against the injustice argument, a way of staking a claim to possess—through love, understanding, and enthusiasm—that which was merely inherited. It is also effective when an Old Money beneficiary is pushed out into the public world by a sense of patrimonial responsibility—to trusteeships, for example—beyond the resources of his or her private patrimonies. Even the poorest Old Money inheritors may still get a seat on the board on the strength of their St. Midas training—their eager willingness and disinterested, amateurish wisdom.

But the David story does not end with David's victory over ugly Goliath—the giant whose coat and spearhead alone weighed thousands of "shekels of brass." Rather, as everyone knows, it ends with David installed in the palace with thousands of shekels of his own, lusting after Bathsheba in her bath, then sending her husband off to his death that David may add her to his possessions. "This tragic retrogression," Drury used to intone, "wherein we see a soldier first attacking, then vanquishing, then ceasing to attack, then coming strangely to resemble, the enemy, we can trace both in persons and in groups. Is it, we must ask, the tendency of David gradually to resemble Goliath?"

It is indeed, or all too easily can be. The beau ideal of the Old Money class leads the imagination to the self, not to society. St. Midas schools need an epic conjuration of a heroic society to balance the personal heroism of the David story. The children must be given a deep, lasting, and (if necessary) painful consciousness of the wider relevance of their performances. Without indoctrination in that consciousness (a social conscience, it used to be called), St. Midas would not be an Old Money ordeal.

If the social ideal at St. Midas has a text, in the sense that David is a text, it is America herself. But St. Midas encourages an imaginative experience of America that is somewhat peculiar. It is America as the Athens of Pericles' funeral oration. No words ever spoken provide a more complete catalog of Old Money's concerns and conceits, a more challenging justification of its giftedness and belongingness.

America as Athens, Athens as Pericles understood it, the whole palimpsest as Old Money understands it, begins with the heritage passed down to us by our ancestors, they who have "dwelt in the country without break in the succession from generation to generation" and who "spared no pains to be able to leave their acquisitions," and Athens herself, free "to us of the present generation." The oration ends on the same note of generational continuity, with an invocation of the city's posterity and a reminder that "never can a fair or just policy be expected of the citizen who does not, like his fellows, bring to the decision the interests and apprehensions of a father."

Except that it *really* begins with the anxiety of envy and disbelief:

> On the one hand, the friend who is familiar with every fact of the story may think that some point has not been set forth with that fulness which he wishes and knows it to deserve; on the other hand, he who is a stranger to the matter may be led by envy to suspect exaggeration if he hears anything above his own nature. For men can endure to hear others praised only so long as they can severally persuade themselves of their own ability to equal the actions recounted: when this point is passed, envy comes in and with it incredulity.

There is envy toward the end as well: "The living have envy to contend with, while those who are no longer in our path are honored with a goodwill into which rivalry does not enter."

But at the *very* end, we are "citizens." The St. Midas social ideal is an ideal of citizenship. Economics has its place in this city, hidden away with the slaves who do the work. Poverty and obscurity of social condition have their inhabitants here, but these misfortunes exist to be overcome by "merit." No one in this city lets his poverty "tempt him to shrink from danger" or his wealth "unnerve his spirit." Each citizen may freely court risk and consequence, without which the good life is not fully lived. Honor, glory, and respect—the ground for these gifts of human togethering is "service to the state," not accumulations of private gain. Gain is of no consequence.

To be sure, there is some anxiety about this last point in our city. Old Money heirs must be told again and again that "we cultivate refinement without extravagance and knowledge without effeminacy," that "where our rivals from their very cradles by a painful discipline seek after manliness, at Athens we live exactly as we please, and yet are just as ready to encounter every legitimate danger." With our refinement, so with our generosity: it must not be construed as a sign of weakness: "It is only the Athenians who, fearless of consequences, confer their benefits not from calculations of expediency, but in the confidence of liberality." So, too, with our nonchalance. Our antagonists must know that it is a sign not of present weakness but rather of future glory. Wealth is not an issue in our city; only words and deeds are: the words to redeem our deeds from meaninglessness, our deeds to give weight and traction to the words. They matter because words and deeds are public, inevitably so, while wealth (if any) is private, hidden, a thing of base necessity that keeps us from the necessity of debasing ourselves, that keeps us *free*.

This is the constitution of the city of Old Money, the Athens of Old Money's America. It was Groton that in fact provided the country with the most numerous and splendid examples of Old Money citizenship: aristocrats like Franklin and Theodore Roosevelt (the latter by adoption: Peabody asked him to be a Groton master; all his male children went there; he was a frequent speaker there) and patricians like Francis Biddle, Averell Harriman, and the Bundy brothers, McGeorge and William. But St. Paul's provided the most articulate, also the most drastic, understanding of the requirements of Old Money citizenship. It almost had to be drastic, issuing as it did from the somewhat overheated Greco-Hebraic mind of John Jay Chapman:

> It is thought that the peculiar merit of Democracy lies in this: that it gives every man a chance to pursue his own ends. The reverse is true. The merit lies in the assumption imposed upon every man that he shall serve his fellow men. This is by the law of his being.

This law is the paradox of the gift: that only by giving their gifts away do the gifted come into true possession—of their gifts and of themselves—and, as Pericles pointed out, into true ascendancy over the recipients of those gifts.

If Chapman is any guide, and he is, then a St. Midas America is not a liberal society. Most Americans understand a liberal society in the light of the pursuit-of-happiness clause in the Declaration of Independence, with happiness a personal condition to be freely and individualistically pursued and, for the most part, economically gained. St. Midas hasn't much use for happiness. It is a society that hasn't much room for Huck Finn or for his little twin with the fuck-you money, and it looks with contempt on the entrepreneur resolved to make a self and his own private fortune. Happiness suggests contentment, rest, satiation, and, in the end, corruption—precisely the evils that the collective experience of Old Money knows to be dangerous for its beneficiaries. More to the point: except in some drearily additive sense, Old Money knows that individual happiness is of no more serious weight and consequence than, say, a fat trust fund. St. Midas is a purposeful tutelary community: designed and self-governed so as to promote the flourishing and punish the fallings-off of good lives in a good society. The ordeal's deepest purpose is to inculcate the notion that Old Money's gifts (including a St. Midas education) are insignificant unless displayed, performed, or otherwise given in and for the public world. In the Athens of America, one must participate in the life of the city, to the end and purpose of becoming a better, weightier, more consequential person.

The St. Midas challenge to the Declaration of Independence also calls into question the so-called right to liberty. In the actual experience of a St. Midas ordeal, there is no right to liberty at all, certainly not for the permissive liberties opened up by wealth. There is only the rather aristocratic liberty to choose among various forms of the good life. The trouble is, of course, that where permissive liberties are scorned, as they are at St. Midas and in the Athens of Old Money generally, even aristocratic liberty is in jeopardy. Liberties depend on tolerance, tolerance depends on magnanimity and liberality, and both of these are crucially dependent on confidence, on courage and high spirits. Liberty is therefore always at the mercy of fear, and fear (for the good, for people's ability freely to choose the good) is endemic in all intentional communities, even those intended to be liberal. St. Paul's School fell into a tyranny through fear. Twenty years ago, it had become an anxious, constricted little place held together by mostly empty rules, regulations, and rituals, and a shared taste in sports jackets. In 1969, Congressman Gerry Studds, then a master at the school, with sixty-odd members of the sixth form (including the sons of Secretary of Defense Robert McNamara and Secretary of the Army Stanley Resor), conducted an extraordinarily successful student rebellion. When it was over, with dress codes relaxed, more minority students and girls enrolled, the curriculum enriched, and one rector changed for another, the school discovered that it had had nothing to fear in the first place.

The fear will return to St. Midas and to the other imaginary cities of the Old Rich. Rich democracies always find much to fear. (Thucydides' Athens fell into tyranny through fear.) The citizens see themselves threatened on every hand by envy, disorder, covetousness, violence, and subversion. Their ancestral inheritance itself threatens them: their riches, the social virtues they have built upon those riches, above all their magnanimity and liberality—the sources of their tolerance and thereby of their liberties. Suddenly, in a spasm of fear, tolerance constricts, and every deviation from the most familiar patterns of the good life appears as a sign of weakness and effeminacy, or defiance and rebellion, all signifying the terrifying immanence of loss.

One cannot exaggerate Old Money's fear of loss. It poisons their most salient virtues, and it poisons the whole aim of their schools' Periclean ordeal, which is to induce in their children a gift of the self to the public world. The anxiety of the trust-fund rich over the market, the fear of the clubman for his privacy, the dread of poor little rich girls for bounders and cads, the uneasiness of the contented in the face of the hungry—all these apprehensions settle easily into one of the most persuasive convictions of the Old Rich: that the world is out to take advantage of them. Liberties are not safe in such hands. Not that they are altogether safe in the hands of the brave rich, either. Peabody banned Kipling's *Stalky and Co.* from the Groton library. Theodore Roosevelt applauded Justice Holmes's endorsement of the forced sterilization of imbeciles. Franklin Roosevelt tried to pack the Supreme Court, and forced American citizens of Japanese descent into concentration camps. John Kennedy on the eve of the Bay of Pigs threatened the freedom of the press. It is not fear that's at work here, but the opposite: Old Money's certainty that it knows, and always has known, what is best for the city.

Yet liberties are certainly no more safe in any other imaginary city of the New World. In the city of Market Man, the citizens' attachment to them is entirely individualistic, opportunistic, and economic, and rapidly breaks down whenever there's a breakdown in prospects for making it. Moreover, the bravest Market Man is often the most frightened. It's as though his drive for economic gain required so much courage that there was none left to face the liberties that their new lives could afford them. So, turning away from Old Money as a goal, they flee into religious fundamentalism, or Moral Majoritarianism, or ethnic sentimentality, keeping alive some sort of reassuring bond to the certainties—in other words, the tyrannies—of their old lives. There is pathos in this, but no safety for liberty. Actually, of course, there is no perfect safety for liberty anywhere.

The St. Midas schools have a difficult time maintaining the ordeal as it's supposed to be. They must burn away what Chapman would have called the "selfishness" of the students without at the same time burning away their courage and high spirits. They must establish a social conscience without social conformity or, worse, political tyranny. They must uphold the ideal of the generalist, the amateur, with no support from the larger society whatsoever. Harvard and other Old Money colleges are strong in the defense of the all-round ideal, both as an attainment of the individual (the mandatory core curriculum) and as the glory of a society (the diversity of students, the variety of their academic and extracurricular passions). But elsewhere, even within the class, there is an unremitting pressure to conform to the basest entrepreneurial imperatives of specialization, concentration, and professionalization.

The St. Midas schools, trying to maintain an aristocratic utopia in a market society, strive to keep David and Athens—two ancient ideals of the Old World—in a New World. There is no question about how they have accomplished this task. Most of the time, for most of the Old Money class, they have failed.

THE ORDEAL OUTDOORS

Nature worship today is laying the spiritual and institutional groundwork for the closest thing to a widespread social religion (as opposed to the individualistic religion of success) that Americans have ever had. Nature is sacred to millions of people in America: to bird watchers and conservationists, hunters and environmentalists, fishermen and ecologists, mountain climbers and landscape painters, health freaks and holistic medicine men. Her text is gospel to hippies and Thoreauvians, whale watchers and Melvilleans, even to the Emersonianly self-reliant. Americans go outdoors, and seek the company of outdoor people, largely in response to the same set of images that moves the Old Rich to go outdoors. They see Nature restoring them to mental and physical balance, to a sense of personal integrity—innocence too, perhaps—that elude them in their "other" lives. And these images of Nature are dialectically related to images of wealth: wealth as corruption, wealth as luxury and materialism, wealth as consumerism.

Old Money's pretensions to having a special claim on Nature are fairly sound. Historically and circumstantially, vast amounts of privately owned land are the preserve of the Old Rich. Then there's the relative freedom from economic necessity: The children of Old Money can easily abandon Athens and make their lives in the country, and many of them do. They can afford it, being happy to pay the political cost and knowing that the economic cost is borne by others, mostly.

Then, finally, there is the ordeal: Nature as an occasion for a testing and proving of one's strength, and Nature's noblemen as the guides and mainstays of those who pass through it. There is something distinctive in the urgency with which the Old Rich approach their ordeals with Nature, as though the nightmare of futility were about to engulf them forever and their only salvation lay in throwing themselves, *in extremis,* on the rough mercies of the wilderness. Once again, the epic tone in the way they recount their ordeals locates the experience back in time, far enough for inspiration or nostalgia.

Mrs. Oliver Harriman, for example, loved to go fishing with her husband and later wrote of it as if they had voyaged on the *Pequod* and she alone had been left alive to tell the tale:

> [T]he choppy seas around Newport are a drastic test of one's endurance. Many a man's pride has crumbled in the treacherous waters near Point Judith. . . . [C]rossing the Atlantic in the season of midwinter tempests seems mild to those who have scudded and careened through the whitecaps and thundering breakers that vex the bleak coast of Block Island. . . . Returning to the enamelled beauty of Newport, one feels like a whaler of old, coming back after a three-year voyage of incredible hazards to his cozy native village. Bridge and golf are rather bloodless pursuits to a real fisherman who has been battling with the elements and dragging his prey out of the yawning depths of old ocean.

In the libraries of the Old Rich, shelf after shelf might be filled with accounts such as Mrs. Harriman's of invigorating contests with the elements. Some fine amateur writing is to be found there: not only travelogues and ships' logs but histories and novels. The first great saga of the West, Francis Parkman's *The Oregon Trail,* had its origins (in the 1840s) in the adventure of a frail young man of Boston's old mercantile patriciate who left that Athens of America in search of his health. The first "Western," or what was alleged to be the first, Owen Wister's *The Virginian* of 1902, began in the same way. Theodore Roosevelt's two-volume history *The Winning of the West* was not only one of the best works of that paragon of the David ideal, the fruit of a youthful ordeal in the Dakota Badlands, but also one of his more successful efforts to recoup, financially, the inheritance he had lost in his cattle ranch. Accounts of agons with the sea are equally numerous in the Old Money library: William F. Buckley, Jr.'s, Philip Saltonstall Weld's, and Rockwell Kent's.

In the old days, the ordeal with Nature began with a breakdown in the rich kid's health. From Francis Parkman's youth to my own a century later, when it was still believed that asthmatics might breathe easier in Arizona than in Boston or New York, the West has been Old Money's sanitarium. Owen Wister's story is typical. As a boy in Philadelphia, he had shown signs of being musical, a gift much encouraged by his grandmother Fanny Kemble. His father was complaisant, for a time. After St. Paul's, Wister was allowed to study music at Harvard, where he graduated *summa cum laude,* and after Harvard he was allowed to go abroad to study with Liszt. But that was the end of it. No sooner had Liszt written to Fanny Kemble that her grandson had a talent *"très prononcée"* for composition than his father immediately recalled him to America and set him to work at the Boston brokerage house of Lee, Higginson & Co. Wister languished, fretfully computing the interest on 2.5 percent bonds by day, lounging around Boston's Tavern and Somerset clubs in the evening. Weakness, degeneracy, and futility lay ahead; that, or "materialist" corruption. He thought of the law then, as so many children of Old Money had done before and have since, as providing a respectable patrimonial station above the vile conflicts of the marketplace, and as not disfiguring the David ideal. But from all these evils (except the law, which he practiced desultorily for many years) he was saved by a breakdown. Weir Mitchell, one of the foremost "alienists" of the day, recommended a trip west to restore his health. It did that and more. It gave him a vocation, writing, and a subject to write about.

Parkman did not get his health back in the West, but most of the upper-class neurasthenics who followed him came home more or less cured of what ailed them. Nature even briefly blessed John Jay Chapman, who loathed his "cure" as a farmworker in Canada in the late 1880s. Like the Greeks he adored, Chapman found physical work oppressive: "The worst of this day-laboring," he wrote his mother, "is one's sense of infringement of personal liberty—like a galley slave." He also noted the comic but pernicious effects of labor on the imagination. "Soft chairs to sit on, enough to eat and nothing to do. As you look up from a shovel, these things seem to be the only things worth having in life,—to sit in the shade on a piazza without effort—this is what I chiefly desire and is what the laboring classes envy the leisure classes for." Still, as therapy it worked: Chapman had no further trouble with his eyes after his ordeal with the shovel.

The question is, how did it work? There was an element of Old World romance in these New World adventures—the suggestion, indeed, of an *aventure*. They might have been knights, the rich youths who went forth into those wildernesses of contingency. And the risks and consequences to which they gave themselves might have been knightly tests: proving their social graces and virtues in noble trials and tribulations. Out in the Dakotas, Roosevelt spent more time slaying animals than any hero of Chrétien de Troyes ever did, but the most memorable episodes in his ordeal concerned those staple ingredients of the romance plot: getting lost and meting out justice to evildoers—in his case, horse thieves. Endicott Peabody as a young Episcopal clergyman went out to legendary Tombstone, Arizona. Owen Wister's personal *aventure* out West I don't know, but in *The Virginian* he composed a perfect set piece of a *proving* of the social virtues. Beset by a bunch of unwashed villains, one of whom has just called him a liar, the handsome Virginian replies with exquisite nonchalance: "When you call me that, *smile!*" Cowed, the low-life scum slink away. For generations of Old Money children, the scene offered a flattering image of how, by mere presence alone and with no loss of grace or virtue, they might one day subdue the "delighted and noisy swarm of human vermin" that sometimes surrounds the little princes of this New World.

The romance of the West had also, of course, a hint of empire. Until the Spanish-American, First World, Second World, and Cold wars supplied America with a facsimile of an overseas empire, one disappointment of being born into its upper class was that the nation provided no place in which to test the resolution and hone the skills of a *ruling* class. The West was all there was, its Indians and outlaws serving for "natives," at least so long as it remained "Wild." But the essential thing was the rural simplicity of the place and the dodginess of the people, which, it was believed, threw into flattering relief not only the straightforwardness of the rich Easterners but their cosmopolitan sophistication as well. There was even a chance, out West, that people might take them for Englishmen.

As a field of romance and empire, the West was closed off to Old Money on 23 May 1911. This was the day that TR, then taking a swing through the West as a possible Progressive candidate for the presidency, sat down and wrote a letter to Wister that spelled *finis* to what had been for him a life-giving adventure.

> [T]he west . . . I knew so well has absolutely vanished. I realized this more fully than at any other time when we stopped at what used to be a homeless siding—near which I had spent thirty-six hours fighting fire, with a wild set of cow punchers, a quarter of a century ago, and which I had once passed leading a lost horse through a snowstorm when I got turned around and had to camp out—and found a thriving little prairie town with a Chamber of Commerce and a "boosters' society," of which the mayor was president.

There it is again: the market, happily closing a field of Old Money exploit and opening it to entrepreneurial exploitation. Ever since, Old Money's encounters with the Nature it knew in the West have been increasingly cast in the rhetoric of a funeral oration, part elegy for the men and landscapes that fell to market forces, part exhortation to preserve what remains of the inheritance. In short, as far as the West is concerned, the physical and spiritual ordeal has given way to a political cause.

But ordeals both physical and spiritual can still be found elsewhere. Above all, they can still be found where Mrs. Harriman found hers: on the ocean. The following passage about FDR, by Gerald W. Johnson, suggests what may be learned from an ordeal on the ocean off Campobello Island in New Brunswick, Canada:

> For a boy who is destined to become a statesman, especially in a democratic country, learning to sail a small boat . . . is admirable training. There he will learn, early in life, that he cannot alter the rules, that his will counts but can never be supreme, and, most important of all, that the very forces that destroy the fool are the forces that sweep the wise man on to victory. There he may learn at the same time self-respect and the stern fact that there are limitations upon all human endeavor. There he will learn that while Nature

rewards wisdom and skill with unerring justice, she has no regard whatever for good intentions.

I am not sure about Nature's "unerring justice." This most pathetic fallacy belongs to the entrepreneurial, not the social, imagination. With that correction, however, Johnson's panegyric offers a clear insight into the deepest purposes of the ordeal by Nature as Old Money families like to imagine it.

As with the two other ordeals, school and war, the presumption is that through a willing exposure of the self to the forces of luck, good and bad, little princes and princesses will be led to develop a sense of personal power and consequence, and thereby acquire pride, but not overweening pride. The balance is tricky to strike, and in the case of "future statesmen," vital. (Johnson's book on FDR, for example, was written primarily to reassure his countrymen that the upper-class President hadn't the temperament or training of a dictator.) The important point is risk; more accurately, it is the connection between risk and luck, between human effort and random contingency, between the individual will and imagination and what the Greeks called *tyche,* or what the Old Rich tend to call reality.

Not they alone. All subsidized classes—students, the elderly, soldiers in peacetime, tenured professors, writers with advances, and so forth—tend to place reality where they are not; that is, where risk is: contingency, luck, that which they can't do anything about. Harvard's undergraduate newspaper, *The Crimson,* carries a section of wire service reports on national and international affairs, called "The Real World." For Old Money imaginations, reality gets realer and realer as things get riskier and riskier, more and more out of control. This is the great quest of so many of the young Old Rich, a doubly subsidized class, who long to live their lives *in extremis.* The figures they cut are cartoons of the class: the backgammon players risking their inheritances at the racquet club, the racing car drivers playing with their lives at the track, the drunks and druggies, like my late friend Harry Phipps, who prefer a crash on the firm ground of death to an angel's free fall through life.

All these careers are degenerate perversions of the ordeal by Nature. They are degenerate not because the reality they seek is loss of fortune and life, though that's part of it. Mostly it's because the *entré* to these ordeals is money. It takes money to gamble, to race cars, and to travel all over the world in search of the highest high. It also takes money to sail boats in Campobello Bay, of course, but the stuff can be better repressed there somehow, out on the cold blue water. And the boats are not really so very expensive. Old Money never suggested it could stage a natural ordeal on board one of J. P. Morgan's *Corsair*s or one of Vincent Astor's *Nourmahal*s. Such vessels provided the luxury of oceangoing Newport cottages, not the experience required of an ordeal. If *tyche* was to do her work, she would have to do it under circumstances of material deprivation.

This was certainly what my father was after, when he went cruising every summer in Maine. The whole month he was away, he would never go ashore if he could help it; my stepmother was in charge of getting provisions to him. He also made a point of bathing in the ocean—a quick dip before breakfast: and he a man who, if he had ever gone to Florida, would never have gone swimming there. I think he liked to imagine himself as a latter-day Sieur de Champlain exploring the granite coast of Mount Desert Island, and with as little use for money. It was Arcadia he sought on those cruises. Arcadia is always the site of Old Money's ordeal by Nature. It is an Eden, but not the prelapsarian Eden of ease and plenty, of ignorance of costs and consequences; indeed, it is just the reverse. Arcadia is a place where there is no surplus, where subsistence makes equality possible, and where alertness to costs and consequences is an absolute necessity. Arcadia makes Eden's riches look like Hell.

The most exemplary account of a rich American's trial by "old ocean" is Kipling's *Captains Courageous*, published in 1897, the story of Harvey Cheyne, a spoiled sprig of wealth who has the "notion that the better part of America was filled with people discussing and envying his father's dollars." Harvey's ordeal begins with a fortunate fall off a steamship and into the hands of a Gloucester fisherman named Disko Troop, captain of the *We're Here*, and it ends with Disko's restoring him to his father at the end of the season, a man at last—richer too, by about twenty dollars of his own hard-earned money. What's significant about *Captains Courageous* is that Nature's role in the ordeal is far less forceful than man's. The true agents of little Harvey's regeneration, or his rescue from degeneracy, are "real" men and "real" work.

Perhaps I make more of this story than it merits. If so, it's because of an afternoon early one September many decades ago when I was sailing my boat off Gloucester, probably my last sail before going back to my ordeal at St. Paul's. A huge, rusty, and stinking fishing boat came by, and the crew, white teeth in tanned faces lined up along the rail, whistled and hooted at me to sail closer. I came right up to her and there was a lot of joshing back and forth, they telling me to tie up and come with them to the Banks, me telling them to jump ship and sail back to Marblehead with me. They didn't and I didn't, of course, but if I had, it would have been a *Captains Courageous* fairy tale come true. It would have been the perfect summer job.

What the perfect summer job means to Old Money, Harvey finds out soon after he is hauled aboard the *We're Here*. It means labor among laboring people. "The boy had rowed, in a ladylike fashion, on the Adirondack ponds; but there is a difference between squeaking pins and well-balanced rullocks—light sculls and stubby, eight-foot sea-oars." The difference, again, is in reality and the weightiness of one's felt presence in the world. Not economic reality or weight, needless to say: Old Money's romance with risk and real men does not recognize vulgar market risks and realities. There's no such thing as market manliness. If there were, the Old Rich would be pulling strings every summer to get their children jobs as assistants to used-car salesmen or commodity brokers. What gives Harvey's work its reality, and him a boost toward manliness, is, first, its physical pain and, second, the social class of his fellow workers: "At the end of an hour Harvey would have given the world to rest; for fresh, wet, cod weigh more than you would think, and his back ached with the steady pitching [of the dory]. But he felt for the first time in his life that he was one of the working gang of men, took pride in the thought, and held on."

Dean Acheson, the somewhat dandified future secretary of state, had a perfect summer job too, and responded to his ordeal with much the same emotion as Harvey's. In the summer of 1911, wires were pulled by his mother's family to get young Dean, recently graduated from Groton, a job as an axman on the Grand Trunk Railway, then being laid across northern Canada. The hard work exhausted his body and lightened his spirit, but it was the men he worked with who mattered most. This boy, who was to become the object of almost universal detestation by self-making and self-made Americans, cherished the gift given him by those men. They gave him a "new eagerness for experience," he wrote in his memoirs. "The simple extroverted pattern of their lives had revived a sense of freedom amidst uncoerced order. They had restored to me a priceless possession, joy in life. Never again was I to lose or doubt it."

It may be doubted whether working-class people would describe their lives as "freedom amidst uncoerced order." The ordeal by Nature and Nature's noblemen, like any formative experience, is primarily a work of the imagination. Charles W. Eliot, for example, once wrote an admiring account of a Down East all-round man (jack-of-all-trades) whom the Harvard president knew from his summers in Northeast Harbor. In his seventies, John Gilley discovered a lucrative market for home-grown vegetables among the summer people, and set his unmarried daughters to raising them. But in Eliot's memoir, Gilley emerges as a figure of epic enterprise, like Odysseus:

> From their sea-girt dwelling they could see the entire hemisphere of the sky; and to the north lay the grand hills of Mount Desert, with outline clear and sharp when the northwest wind blew, but dim and soft when southerly winds prevailed. In every storm a magnificent surf dashed up on the rockbound isle. In winter the low sun made the sea toward the south a sheet of shimmering silver; and all the year an endless variety of colors, shades and textures played over the surfaces of hills and sea.

This is the same imagination, working now on an Adirondack "guide" named Archie Miller, that led Douglas Burden to write, as of some Hobey Baker of the forests:

> [T]his rugged attractive man—half Indian, half Scotch—was the personification of grace and artistry. His precision with the axe, his finesse with a canoe, his ability to travel great distances through the brush, always knowing just where he would come out . . . were legendary. . . . I was eager to emulate him, especially to learn how to find my way alone in the woods.

And it is the same imagination, working on the same landscape, that bewitched Mrs. Malcolm Peabody, who once told me that: "Our real life was here in Maine. We used to come to Northeast Harbor on the twentieth of June and stay until the end of September." Mrs. Peabody was, to the "Who Was She?" class, the granddaughter of Francis Parkman, daughter-in-law of Endicott Peabody, mother of four well-known Old Money children (a New York socialite, a socially conscious minister, a former Democratic governor of Massachusetts, and a former delegate to the United Nations), and grandmother of, among other good citizens, the writer Frances FitzGerald. She was herself, late in her long life, a prominent agitator for the civil rights of black people. She was also a very different person from Douglas Burden.

Burden's background was preposterous even to himself. He once re-called wandering around his grandfather's house in the Berkshires as a child and happening on a note that the old gentleman had written and left in the visiting-card bowl: "Borrowed from Emily," it read, Emily being his wife, "$1 million." He remembered, too, that from another grandparent's house, this one in New York, a servant would emerge each Christmas with a twenty-dollar gold piece for every po-liceman on the block—twice the value of the tidbit that lay at the bottom of Douglas's stocking.

Yet both these Old Money backgrounds, prudent patrician or care-less aristocratic, required the same sort of Nature, peopled with the same natural men. Burden's Archie Miller was one of a long line of guides for the children of the rich, helping them to find their way through the dark woods on their own two feet. Eliot's John Gilley became the "captains" of a later day—Captain Wedge, Captain Stan-ley, Captain Black—who taught Mrs. Peabody and others how to sail the Aegean of the Gulf of Maine. For me, in Marblehead, it was Buster Dixie, who had been boatman on *Armida,* my grandfather's yawl, and crewed for my father when he raced his eight-meter boat in the 1930s. One spring vacation, the most memorable of my life, I worked for Buster at the Little Harbor Boat Yard, getting the rich people's boats ready for launching in the summer.

All these natural men, "natural aristocrats" indeed, are of the same family as Disko Troop. It is a family much like Old Money's, formed more by fortune than by appetite, more by tradition than by opportu-nity, and just as "old." Their ancestry goes back to Chiron and John the Baptist, to Falstaff and Jeeves, and includes all those nameless god-mothers who instruct the heroes and heroines of fairy tales on how to come into their kingdoms. Like the dangerous woods and perilous seas where they are at home, these men and women answer the most poi-gnant longing of the Old Money mind—the longing for authenticity, their own and the moneyed world's.

Labor Day, mixing memory and the promise of summers to come, is the perfect day for recounting the epic of ordeals by Nature and her noblemen. But now, in the last couple of generations, a new thing happens on Labor Day. More and more of the summer people do *not* go back to the city. They stay in Arcadia. Most of them are elderly: scores of them in every seaside village from Stonington, Connecticut, to Seal Harbor, Maine, and in every inland village from Red Hook, New York, to the Northeast Kingdom of Vermont. In some measure, they stay out of scorn for the South. Florida, the islands of the Caribbean—that's where entrepreneurial money, ugly money, goes to die. In the North, Old Money's tough old bones have a chance to live forever. Most important of all, they see a chance to make a factual truth of a poetical one. "Our real lives were here in Northeast Harbor," said Mrs. Peabody. She spoke truly, an imaginative truth. Wintering over, Old Money has a chance to hold on to that truth.

The grandchildren are also not leaving. All over the Northeast, Northwest, even Southwest—wherever the social and natural landscape can be understood as "old"—they are staying, these scions of inherited wealth. And they are working. A few of them are middlemen, brokering yachts and houses as their fathers brokered stocks and bonds. More often, they do artisanal work, the sort of thing they learned on their summer jobs. They're in marinas and boatyards, or construction, or some kind of agriculture, growing something special like mushrooms, or making cheese, or farming the sea, lobstering out of Marblehead, fishing out of Rockport. Some make the transition to craft work: pottery, furniture, textiles, cooking, and so forth. Others push boldly on into the image-making arts: painting, sculpture, photography. They are all looking to do something with their hands, something palpable, something, as Burden put it, to "get your teeth into," something to fill "a certain vacuum in our lives."

If that is what they are seeking, the decision to winter over in the summer place is perhaps the boldest leap into contingency that these trust-fund outdoorsmen will ever take. The whole adventure is beset with perils of ghastly irony. There is the peril, for example, of "going native." Many year-round summer people, as the locals call them, are persuaded that the reality they crave can be achieved only by their being accepted as one of the locals. This is usually impossible. The distinctions between native old families and summertime old families produce some of the most delicate and painful dramas in American social life. The summer folk love the natives: love them as they love their nannies, their views, and their Winslow Homers. What the natives feel for the summer people is harder to describe. Perhaps it is love, as the summer people hope, or love moving toward envy. More likely, it is what the summer people fear, envy moving toward hate. But whatever it is, it is not acceptance. A further irony awaits those who pause to look at the native world before leaping to join it. They discover that reality, among the natives, is the marketplace, and many of these real men and women are avatars of Market Man. Maine, or New Mexico, or Montana, is not Arcadia but America.

But staying aloof has its perils and ironies too. Behind their walls and fences, like my great-grandfather's at Warwick, Rhode Island, Old Money people may protect their class identities along with their privacy. But they do so at the price of betraying everything they were supposed to learn from their ordeal by citizenship at St. Midas. And they will be punished. Not only by the reproaches of whatever tatters of social conscience may be left them, but by the marketplace as well. Politics is the only realm of endeavor that can contest the forces of the market. The social religion of Nature, which began with rich kids going outdoors for their health, ends in political action against the market—the condo developers, the shopping-mall impresarios, the army of entrepreneurs whom Old Money (and not Old Money alone) imagines to be despoiling Arcadia. Grown-up rich kids, wintering over, ignore this political action at the risk of losing everything that made them decide to winter over: the newfound simplicity of their lives, their year-round authenticity, and the views from their windows.

But joining this political action, they risk losing the lesson of their epic cruises along the coast, their epic forays in the woods—something to do with scarcity being the mother of equality. Environmental political action is a child of scarcity and must sooner or later come to terms with equality. That is the great challenge facing Old Money activists: to recognize that for all its vulgarity, the outdoor market responds to wants very much like their own, and that it is better to respond to them imaginatively, democratically, with all due respect to Nature and her noblemen (if any are left), than to deny them tyrannically. The challenge is to move beyond the door-slamming politics of the environmental haves against the environmental have-nots, and toward a recognition that Nature is a gift that must be passed on not just to some abstract "future" but to posterity, human beings, citizens like themselves. There is no question about how the preponderance of the Old Money class has responded to this challenge. Most of the time, under most circumstances, it has failed it.

THE ORDEAL UNDER FIRE

Victor Emmanuel Chapman was born in New York City in 1889, the first child of John Jay and Minna (Timmins) Chapman. His given names—an Italian king's, a Savior's—managed to suggest simultaneously his mother's birthplace in Italy, the struggle of that ancient civilization for national liberation, and his father's fierce hope for mercy at the hands of an angry God. The life of this child of Old Money unfolded among scenes of great natural and tasteful beauty, and though it was repeatedly touched by catastrophe, it ended, as he and his father most devoutly desired, on a note of crowning sacrifice.

When he was six, a dark-haired boy, gentle but moody, already tall and powerful for his age, his mother died in childbirth. When he was twelve, vacationing in the Italian Tirol with his father and stepmother, Elizabeth Astor Chanler, his little brother Conrad drowned before his eyes. Near the inn where they were staying, a river came down out of the mountains in a torrent, then eddied out into a pool that might have been made for swimming, then rushed on, foaming over rocks, to the plain below. Conrad's body was not recovered for two days. Of the lost child, their father would say that he was "shy, brilliant, blond, handsome as a prince." Of Victor and that terrible day, he would say: "Here was grief indeed and the world lost once more, for a morbid child with no apparent talents and a gift for suffering."

Victor grew up at Rokeby, the Chanler family's estate in Dutchess County on the Hudson River, then at Sylvania, a house his parents commissioned Charles Platt to build for them on Chanler lands in Barrytown, New York. Summers he went to Dark Harbor, an island resort in Maine's Penobscot Bay. Twice in his boyhood, catastrophe came close again. Once he saved a playmate from the same death that had taken his brother; he pulled the boy out of the water with a shotgun. Another time he leapt between two railroad cars to save his half-brother. He was showing a talent, his father might have said, for rescue.

He followed his father to St. Paul's, as his half-brothers would do later, and to Harvard, from which he was graduated in 1913. In August 1914, he was in Paris studying—rather desultorily, it seems—at the École des Beaux Arts. War came as a deliverance. Within weeks of joining the Foreign Legion he was in the trenches, happier than he'd ever been. "He chopped, hacked, and digged," a fellow legionnaire recalled later, "hour after hour without pause. The captain noticed him. 'Say, you there, were you a ditch-digger in private life?' 'You're off, there,' said a by-stander, 'he's a millionaire.'"

Yet even at the front he could not dispel the persistent sensation that the reality of things was eluding him. On 3 December 1914, he wrote his parents: "At Creil we saw a dozen wrecked houses; but one gets no better impression by being on the scene than by looking at the post-cards strung up in the Boulevards of Paris." The impact of bullets against his *"abri"* affected him no more, he wrote, than the "lap, lap, lap of little waves against the side of my sailboat." A machine gun sounded like a "motor boat rounding a bend." Even a bombardment by heavy artillery seemed a fairy-tale horror: "a distant explosion, a low whistle growing stronger and louder ... a roar as of an emancipated genie, and the wind wafts aways the rest."

He saw frightful things in the trenches. His unit was shelled for a hundred days straight. One of his comrades remembered afterward that Victor had carried a wounded friend, a Polish mathematician named Kohn, to the first-aid station, holding him as easily and gently as he would a child. He was sobbing. "Save him, sir," he implored the surgeon, "and I'll give you a hundred thousand francs."

But later, the front having been quiet for weeks, his ardor went slack and he became restless. He wrote his father that he was beginning to feel like an *"embusqué,"* a shirker. Then, too, since Kohn's death he'd had no one to talk to. There was a fellow called Farnsworth, apparently: "beans by inheritance," nevertheless "a Grotonian" and a class behind him at Harvard. But Farnsworth was in another platoon and not much interested in talk. "It takes two to enjoy the scene," Victor wrote, "to study the character of the soldiers, etc." Repeatedly he turned inward, exploring for hard truths: "Perhaps after all I am doomed to be unhappy for I have the insight not to be content with things as they are, [but] lack the necessary force, or push, to make them otherwise."

He had the push to get himself transferred into aviation (asked by the French induction officer why he wished to fly, he replied, accurately enough, *"C'est plus dangereux"*), and from there his family had the pull to get him into the Lafayette Escadrille, the elite fighter squadron. February 1916 found him stationed at Luxeuil-les-Bains, a resort town in the Vosges. He adored flying. "It is all a question of balance, ..." he wrote his parents, "as one sails a boat, now yielding, now opposing; and, as in the case of a sailboat, the most difficult manoeuvre is making a landing." The Vosges Mountains, he said, reminded him of the view from Dark Harbor across the bay to the Camden Hills.

It was relentless, the power of this ancient summer language to waft him so effortlessly above the "real." He sensed where it was taking him: "This flying is much too romantic to be real modern war with all its horrors. There is something so unreal and fairy-like about it, which ought to be told ... by Poets, as Jason's voyage was." Yet he was helpless to stop it: the words winged him higher and higher. "There is my fish and prey," he thought, as he pointed his plane down toward the German plane, shooting down on him out of the sun. (At this sport, as at no other, he performed well: Before the end, he had four German "kills" to his credit.) Another time, neither hunter nor fisherman but a natural naturalist, he apprehended the clouds over Nancy as huge water plants, the enemy planes as larvae or fat black water beetles, the trenches as the little scars on a tree trunk when the bark falls away. (In the Legion, the trench had been *le boyau,* the bowel.) Once, over the Argonne Forest, coming up under the "lee keel" of a "fat Boche," he felt like "a dory alongside a schooner." The German fighters, though, were like "sharks." Seven times before the last time, those sharks ripped at his wings and sent him to the ground.

He couldn't help it. The metaphors came out of his imagination, out of needs playing on realities, and they had been formed long before the war. Besides, he seems to have known that the distances were fast closing: Metaphors and realities, seeming and substance, were wheeling toward one another out of the sky. He certainly knew he was going to be killed. "Of course I shall never come out of this alive," he wrote his uncle William Astor Chanler. And a French friend of his father's remembered: "Someone once asked him if he would go on in France with his art studies after the war. ... a sort of vagueness came over his look, as he just repeated slowly, 'After the war ... ,' without adding another word."

He was killed on 23 June 1916. His father heard the news from the head farmer at Sylvania, listening with no visible show of emotion, saying only, "That's good." It was good. Victor had died on an errand of mercy and in an act of rescue. That morning he had taken off from Luxeuil to bring some oranges to a comrade who was recovering from his wounds at a nearby hospital. Then, over Verdun, he saw two planes from his squadron being attacked by a pack of five Germans. He climbed for altitude, putting the sun behind him to blind his adversaries, then dived. Smoothly, the German pilots parted to let him pass, then caught him in a cross fire, probably killing him instantly. His plane crashed behind enemy lines, but his body, like that of some fallen warrior on the plains of Troy, was returned to his unit. He was one of the first American aviators to die in the Great War, almost a year before the United States entered it. He was buried on 4 July 1916, after a funeral at the American Church in Paris. His sacrifice was honored by tributes from all over the world. Later, in a panegyric all his own, published in the *Atlantic Monthly,* his father wrote: "To what better use could these young heroes and all this amassed wealth have been put? It was for this that they existed."

War is the ultimate in the series of ordeals, beginning at boarding school, going on to the trial by Nature, through which the Old Rich discover their personal powers and enter at last into the line of descent and succession that marks their place in time. Of course, not every war, or arm of warfare, provides Old Money with an equally satisfactory ordeal. Each class has its own war: wars of obedience for plebeians, wars of calculation for the entrepreneurial bourgeoisie. Old Money makes war distinctively, invidiously its own when conditions provide an opening for sacrifice, when the class as a whole and its individual members may give of themselves freely and ardently. "Why do I want rich men to hate each other?" cried Bertrand de Born in the twelfth century. "Because a rich man is much more noble, generous and affable in war than in peace." The sentiment passes on down through the centuries, inspiring John Jay Chapman to write in 1897: "I tell you the kind of man I am thrives only on romance. In real life he does murders, loves, revenges, heroisms and crimes. He gets into places where no human agency can reach him. How much good is he? For business, for politics, for anything but poetry and possibly war?"

From the viewpoint of the Old Rich, World War I was the most satisfactory of America's wars: so many of them figured in it, so preeminently and voluntarily. In the Great War of St. Paul's School, for example, Victor Chapman was by no means the first to die, only the first aviator. George Williamson, a writer and lawyer, was killed fighting with the British near Ypres on 8 November 1914: the first S. P. S. graduate and first American college graduate to die. André C. Champollion, an artist and conservationist, was killed fighting with the French in the Lorraine on 25 March 1915: the second "old boy" and second American college graduate to die. The school would also have a "last" on its roll of honor: Hobey Baker was one of the last American fighter pilots to be killed, in 1918. In the end, 762 alumni served in one arm or another of the United States military or its allies, out of about 4,000 living graduates. Forty-eight died, their names inscribed under the Angel of Death in the antechapel.

Long before the United States entered the war, in schools, colleges, clubs, and summer resorts, wherever Old Money lay thickest, there was a breeding ground of warriors. St. Paul's was typical. Each week throughout the 1915–16 school year, some eloquent testimonial of the war was read to the boys in chapel or published in the school paper. They heard letters from the Harvard graduate who drove the "noble Ford" that the school had subscribed to through the American Friends Service Committee. Just before his death, Victor Chapman wrote a vivid description of a bombing raid into Germany. Julian Allen wrote of the suffering he'd seen as an aide at the American Hospital at Neuilly. David King sent a grim report of a battle at Verdun where his battalion, after losing 1,500 men in one day, spent three more days under constant bombardment, like "250 mice in a cracker tin." All through the fall of 1916 and early winter of 1917, Tommy Hitchcock plotted how he might leave the school and join the Lafayette, even though, at sixteen, he was still underage. With the help of Theodore Roosevelt, a family friend, and with a bit of fudging about his birth date, he was accepted later that spring, the youngest flier in the French corps. (On the steamer, Hitchcock read a book his mother had given him, Victor Chapman's *Letters from France,* edited by John Jay Chapman.) What Dr. Drury saw in all this, of course, was David with his "homing affinity for things that are difficult and daring and fine." When the country at last declared war, in 1917, it must have seemed to the rector, clergyman and classicist that he was, that Athens and Old Testament had finally come together—in the medieval church militant. As in the Middle Ages, when at Mass the knights remained standing during the reading of the Epistle (for Paul also was a knight), so, from 1917 on, Drury loved to think that he had found a purpose for his school that forever saved it from being a "country club." The school, he preached, was "not to be a dispensary for cripples, but an armory for soldiers,—a place all glistening and clanging with breastplates of righteousness, swords of the spirit, and helmets of salvation."

It was the same, whatever breeding ground of the Old Rich one named. The Great War, especially in the years before the U.S. entered the fray, was a class reunion. After a visit to the volunteer officers' training camp at Plattsburgh, New York, Chapman wrote his mother:

Of course no end of people you know are there. By the way, forty-three men from the Porcellian. This is very remarkable. The Porcellian is a small club—and when 1400 men volunteer out of the

100,000,000 in America—forty-three of them are from the Porcellian. This seems to my mind to show that the Porcellian really does amount to something—which I have never believed.

Vincent Astor came down to Washington to see his cousin Franklin Roosevelt, then assistant secretary of the Navy. The sense of a common past was almost palpable at that meeting. Twenty years earlier, at the outbreak of the Spanish-American War, Vincent's father had visited Theodore Roosevelt, Franklin's cousin and Eleanor's uncle: he, too, an assistant secretary of the Navy. And both Astors had come on the same errand: to offer the yacht *Nourmahal,* and themselves, to the war effort.

Reunions abroad were even more poignant. Tommy Hitchcock's letters home were full of news gleaned from friends and relatives he met while on leave in Paris. He cannot visit the grave of his French cousin, killed at Verdun, because the corpse is still lost in the mud. Quentin Roosevelt (Theodore's son) has wrecked his motorcycle. He has gone to the theater with Gilbert Winant—a favorite master of his at St. Paul's, the future Democratic governor of New Hampshire, FDR's ambassador in Britain (and Hitchcock's boss) during the next war. The Old Rich discovered each other even in the provinces. Victor Chapman wrote that a girl had spoken to him in a café at Nancy: "'Tiens, je connais un Américain de l'Ambulance. Son nom de famille ne reviens pas, mais tout le monde l'appelle Villie. C'est un type le plus charmant, le plus gentil que je n'ai jamais vu.' Of course it was Willie Iselin." Of course. In the theater of this war, in the lobbies at any rate, the beneficiaries of Old Money could meet "everyone."

And not just "old boys," but older men and women too. The war had hardly begun in August 1914 when the better Paris hotels, like the Crillon, began to fill up with all sorts of the Old Rich, all eager to volunteer their services to the Allies. Anne Morgan, J.P.'s daughter who had dressed as Pocahontas at the Bradley Martin Ball, funded and for a time commanded her own fleet of ambulances. Margaret Chanler Aldrich came to see what she could do. Other women served as nurses' aides at the American Hospital, perhaps with Harvey Cushing, the Massachusetts General Hospital's great neurosurgeon (and Babe Paley's father). In some of these older men and women, the ardor to give of themselves was almost too painful to express. In late August, for example, Robert Bacon—a great Harvard athlete in his time, later a Morgan partner and Theodore Roosevelt's assistant secretary of state for Latin America and his ambassador to France—wrote his wife from Paris in an agony of frustration:

> I seem to be conscious of a feverish desire to do something for somebody, with not enough aggressiveness or ability to make it worthwhile. . . . [P]erhaps it's weakness, a lack of the preeminent attributes of the masculine animal. . . . I can add nothing to my children's moderate inheritance, either material or moral. They must fight the fight for themselves and my dream of being, sometime, somebody to serve as an inspiration, and to awaken a big ambition, is past. I am even inarticulate and cannot explain to them the truth.

Here was citizenship indeed: a longing to sacrifice for posterity. Later, in December 1916, on his way back to France after a summer of officer training at Plattsburgh, Bacon made explicit the link between the ordeal of war and the corrupting influence of wealth. "The world—*our* world—is not lucky enough to be snuffed out as was Pompeii. We have got to go through a long sickening decadence. . . . Come away . . . and let's really give up something. The children and the grandchildren will be the better for it."

World War I was the Great War for Old Money in part because it provided outlets for such spirits, but also because it made possible— for the last time before H. Ross Perot and Ronald Reagan made it so again—to bend private wealth to purposes that were supposedly the prerogatives of states. The American Ambulance Corps was the most broad-based of these efforts. One committee under the direction of Mrs. Robert (Cowdin) Bacon raised $2 million for the corps at schools and colleges all over the East. The most glamorous effort, practically a private army, was the Lafayette Escadrille itself. Almost entirely a creature of Old Money imagination, it was first conceived by a benign conspiracy of upper-class Foreign Legionnaires, middle-aged Francophilic American millionaires, and a member of the French Ministry of Defense, who was alert to the propaganda possibilities of sending highly visible Americans to fight and die for the cause of France. Among the older men involved were William Astor Chanler, Victor Chapman's uncle and an old Roosevelt and Wister intimate from the Porcellian; Augustus Jacacci, a Harvard-educated banker and Morgan partner; and, later, William K. Vanderbilt. Vanderbilt continued paying Lafayette pilots a stipend even after the original Escadrille was absorbed and bureaucratized as the Lafayette Flying Corps. The younger men present at the creation of the famous squadron included Norman Prince of Groton and Harvard, a Hitchcock family friend from Prides Crossing on Boston's North Shore; Eliot Cowdin of St. Paul's and Harvard, Mrs. Robert Bacon's nephew; and William Thaw II of Yale, a cousin of Harry K. Thaw, the murderer of Stanford White. (Harry was still in the news in the early years of the war, denying that Evelyn Nesbit was carrying his child, asserting his support for women's suffrage.) Prince, Cowdin, and Thaw spent a few months in the winter of 1915 touring the men's clubs and schools of the eastern seaboard, where they spoke of the beauties and perils of flying, and of America's duty to make sacrifices for the Allied cause. Norman Prince, not long after Victor Chapman, made the supreme sacrifice. Cowdin and Thaw survived.

The Lafayette Escadrille occupies a special place in the epic of Old Money's ordeal under fire. Sacrifice derives its redemptive value from being voluntary. In that sense, the first three years of World War I were all sacrificial wherever the scions of Old Money fought, in the trenches or in the air. But the essence of trench warfare was industrial, not "natural" or outdoorsy at all. It was also anonymous, its units no more composed of free and equal citizens than was a box of machine-gun bullets. "The generals are the wholesale packers," a friend of Tommy Hitchcock's wrote, "and the soldiers the retail butchers. They are all the hired assassins of the demagogues who are the puppets of ignorance, bigotry, and greed."

The Lafayette offered an escape into the past from this bourgeois war, to the romances of chivalry and the romance of cavalry. The *pilote de chasse* has a helmet, a steed, a squire to care for the steed, and he sallies forth alone or in a small company of equals—all like the knight or cavalryman of yore. The Lafayette Escadrille was probably the most thoroughly photographed, written about, and filmed fighting unit in history, and hardly a story or caption was ever composed about them that didn't salute them as a cavalry or knighthood of the air. (The metaphors seemed irresistibly appropriate as late as the Vietnam War, when Tom Wolfe published an article on carrier-based Navy jet pilots entitled "Jousting with Sam and Charley.")

The assimilation of fighter squadron and cavalry, one to another, was completed on the ground. There, as usual, envy blinded the envious to their own virtues but provided insight into the weaknesses of the envied. Infantrymen focused on the cavalrymen's ease (riding when others walked) and on their relative riches (their arms and uniforms

were privately subvented and expensive), but their envy arose, too, out
of a sense that the effectiveness of mounted men against massed foot
soldiers was almost entirely a matter of animal fear and social deference—in other words, almost entirely imaginary. Infantrymen had
known at least since Agincourt that if they kept their courage, they
could slaughter men on horseback as easily as they could slaughter
horses. And with this, they were able to pick out the most salient
characteristic of the mounted warrior—his incredible stupidity. It was
stupid to ride against a square of riflemen, even more stupid to ride
against machine-gun fire, as in the opening days of World War I. Naturally, as horses grew wings like Bellerophon, envy went to work on
their new riders in much the same way, scorning the luxury of the
pilots' lives on earth even as it mocked the imbecile recklessness of
their combats in the sky.

Old Money had no trouble choosing which side it was on. The
difference, always crucial to the imagination of the Old Rich, was the
difference in aristocratic liberty. Trench mice had none of it: they lived
and died by impersonal technical forces beyond their knowledge and
will. The cavalry of the air, on the other hand, was always perfectly
free to fight or not to fight. Before takeoff, the pilot might have engine
trouble; aloft, he might lose his squadron, or duck into a cloud, or
crash-land in a hayfield; back at the aerodrome, he could say that the
hunting was poor, he'd had no luck. The choice was his. Like no other
modern warrior (except for the spy, perhaps), the pilot can still truly
be said to *give* battle—just as, if it comes to that, he gives his life.
Asked once by a fluttery Parisian hostess what medals he had still to
win, the great French ace Guynemer replied, *"Le croix de bois, ma-
dame."* A few days later, it was his.

World War I was also a Great War for the Old Money class because
of the clarity with which its beneficiaries saw what they were making
their sacrifices for. It was not their country, or democracy, or liberty: it
was European civilization, the Old World—the Platonic heaven from
which the Old Money curriculum took its ideal forms. It was the man-
ual in which they had studied their social graces and virtues. It was
the great court, or antique shop, to which they went to acquire the
costumes, furnishings, art, taste and sensibilities, and in many families
the very blood, with which to adorn their lives and make a class.

Tendering the gift of their lives, Old Money sealed with its blood
its long struggle to become part of history. Not history as "progress"

but the great legacy of the past. Chapman, even before Victor's great sacrifice, considered this an accomplished fact:

> The myth of America as a promised land is finished. We are going to be taken back into the fold. We are Europeans, European history, both past and present, is our history, and Europe's future is our future. The thought of this allies us with every form of intellectual life in Europe and destroys at a blow the mind-killing theory on which we have all been brought up,—namely, that America has a private destiny of its own, a fate distinct from Europe's fate.

The entrepreneurial imagination might prate of America's destiny, a destiny manifestly as bright and promising and endless as a hustler's. Old Money would speak of a whole world of old nations, America at last among them, and it would speak of fate, of ends shadowed by tragedy.

Jack Chapman was not the only Old Money man to understand America's ordeal in World War I as a way by which the country might come into the kingdom of historical reality. So did Willard Straight, an adopted son of the class who married Dorothy Whitney and with her founded the *New Republic*. In the spring and summer before the Armistice, Straight's letters home had been as full of "social" gossip as Tommy Hitchcock's had been before he was shot down behind German lines and imprisoned. Much of the chat was about whether Quentin Roosevelt should marry Flora Whitney, Dorothy's cousin, given the likelihood that Quentin, then a fighter pilot with the American Army, would be killed. In July, he was killed, his father responding to the news much as Chapman had done to the news of Victor's death. "My only regret is that I could not give myself," said the old Rough Rider. Straight himself would die shortly after the Armistice, of pneumonia, at the Hotel Crillon in Paris, with Walter Lippmann and Daisy Harriman at his bedside. Old Money sacrificed many lives in their Great War. But, like Straight, they knew for what they gave. After a visit to Langres Cathedral on Easter Sunday 1918, Straight wrote to his wife:

> The white & golden & red-robed figures moving to and fro—the curling smoke of the incense—the crowd ... the chanting of the choir boys—the pealing of the giant organ—now free & reverber-

ating—now distant & plaintive ... And the thought of what it all meant—sorrowing, worshipping folk—the soldiers of France and America—in this centuries old cathedral in the heart of France—all the tradition that clustered about it—of past wars—of past deeds of valor—of past struggles for liberty. The thought that in sharing their struggle—we were winning the right to share again in all that had gone before.

If any one man can be said to have carried the imagery of the warrior's ordeal from the First to the Second World War, it was Tommy Hitchcock. A scion of Old Money whose line went back on his father's side to the buccaneer speculation of the Gilded Age and on his mother's side to Brahmin Boston and cosmopolitan New Orleans, Hitchcock was sent at an early age to the Fay School, then to St. Paul's; otherwise he spent every waking hour outdoors, mostly on horseback, at his family's places in Westbury, Long Island, and Aiken, South Carolina. He was just eighteen, though already with one or two "kills" to his credit, when he was shot down over Germany in 1918. He redeemed this (to him) ignominious end of his fighting career by a celebrated prison-camp escape, in which he made his way, on foot and at night, hundreds of miles along the Danube to Switzerland. After the war, he went to Harvard, where he was a member of the Porcellian, and thence for a term or two to Oxford. In the 1920s and 1930s, the so-called Golden Age of Sport, Hitchcock was almost as famous a figure in polo as Bill Tilden was in tennis or Bobby Jones in golf. In the matches against England or Argentina, forty thousand people used to come out from New York to the Meadow Brook Club to see him play. No one, certainly no American, ever played better.

When war again broke out, he was married (to a Mellon heiress), with four children and a promising career at Lehman Brothers. At thirty-nine, he was too old, as he had once been too young, to volunteer for World War II's Lafayette Escadrille, the Canadian-British Eagle Squadron. (His nephew Averell Clark did join the Eagle Squadron, and went on to become one of the most decorated fighter pilots of the Eighth Air Force.) Hitchcock himself enlisted right after Pearl Harbor, serving as air attaché at the embassy of his old St. Paul's mentor, Gilbert Winant, but repeatedly trying to get himself transferred to combat flying. He never succeeded, despite Old Money connections that went at least as far up the chain of command as Robert Lovett, under secretary of war for air. What he did succeed in doing, partly thanks to those same connections, was to facilitate the deployment of one of the most crucial planes in the European theater, the P-51 fighter escort. He was killed probably as he would have wished, certainly as his class ideals made possible: on a volunteer mission on behalf of others. In 1944, a mysterious flaw had turned up in the P-51 and Hitchcock undertook to help find and correct it. It was not his job at the time; above all, test piloting was not his job. On 12 April 1944, he took an experimental P-51 B up over Salisbury Plain to test its stability in a dive. He did not pull out of it. He was posthumously awarded the Legion of Merit, the Bronze Star, and the Distinguished Flying Cross; his widow received a personal letter of appreciation from Franklin Roosevelt, much the same sort of letter, indeed, his parents had received from Roosevelt twenty-eight years earlier, when Hitchcock had gone to a Navy "preparedness" camp on Plum Island and Roosevelt was assistant secretary of the Navy.

Among his contemporaries—not only his social peers like Averell Harriman but his would-be social peers like Scott Fitzgerald—Hitchcock was an upper-class icon, largely because of his polo playing. Ralph Lauren is not the first marketeer (though having run it into the ground he may be the last) to exploit the imagistic possibilities of polo as a "class act." The Olympic sports of track and field, boxing, and wrestling have slightly better antecedents than polo, but none is older or more aristocratic. Wherever there are horses, there are men, and in Persia women too, playing polo; and from Persia to the Indian raj to the British Army to the New World, polo is the sport of the "country" or aristocratic side of Old Money's imagination, just as America's Cup racing belongs to the "city" or patrician side. There is also no sport that more graphically illustrates the means and objectives of Old Money's ordeals. The man on horseback is a primal image of command and self-command, grace and power united at last. Add other men to the tableau, set them in perilous contest with one another on a field as broad and beautiful as the plains of Troy or the battlefields of Tennyson's "Idylls," and the iconic echoes are strong enough to resound in the coldest New World entrepreneurial heart. There is also a sense in which polo is truly unpurchasable. It's not the expense: sailboat racing, certainly long-distance ocean racing, is just as expensive but nowhere near so "exclusive." The problem is time. Polo is the most difficult game on earth, requiring the horsemanship of a Genghis Khan, the anticipatory sense of a hockey player, and the hand-eye coordination of a pool shark; to play it well, therefore, one has to have always—past perfectly—played it. As easily as the entrepreneurial imagination grasps the class significance of polo, and perhaps aspires to it, just as easily does the game elude the aspiration. The entrepreneur cannot learn it without looking ridiculous. All he or she can do is buy the clothes associated with it—polo coats, button-down shirts (an Argentine invention), and the rest of the kit.

In Tommy Hitchcock, the imagery of the poloist and the *pilote de chasse* came together. He was deficient in the graces, as "country" aristocrats often are, sloppy in dress and awkward in manner; but he possessed in full measure the virtues valued by his class: modesty, loyalty, and magnanimity. The last, in fact, he carried into the politics of polo, opening it up (over the protests of a few of his class) to anyone who wanted to play: to Westerners, cowboys, and rich Jews. His friends worshiped him. Douglas Burden said of him: "His life was controlled by a directness of purpose. There was never anything remotely ambivalent about him. He always seemed to know just what he wanted to do, and when he made up his mind, he did it." William Jackson, a Wall Street lawyer, later with the CIA, recalled with awe how Hitchcock had once very nearly killed him on the polo field, then rescued him. After riding him off the ball so hard that Jackson's horse fell to its knees, "Tommy reached across with his left hand, still holding the four reins, and pulled me back in the saddle. And in the next split second he hit a near-side back-hander [the most difficult stroke in the game] far away in the opposite direction." Averell Harriman, with whom Hitchcock played in a victorious campaign against the Argentines, said of him that "he brought out the best in all of us, whether we were good, bad or indifferent. He never shouted ... but encouraged his teammates in every way by his own excellence." David Bruce, who shared an apartment with Hitchcock in London during World War II, went so far as to call him the only "perfect" man he'd ever met.

Fitzgerald's friendship with Hitchcock was purely social (they seem to have gone to a lot of the same parties in the early 1920s) and probably slight. But the novelist claimed the warrior-athlete for his "pantheon of heroes" and claimed him for a friend—his only rich friend, he said (in reply to the charge that he was nothing but "a suck" around the rich), apart from the Gerald Murphys. He also left a life-like, romantic portrait of Hitchcock in the character of Tommy Barban in *Tender Is the Night*. Barban's role in the novel wouldn't have altogether pleased Drury: the aim of this David, after all, is to make off with Dick Diver's wife. Nevertheless, Barban exists for much the same purpose in the novel as David does in the sermon—as a warning and reproach to everyone else. In *Tender Is the Night,* everyone else is in passage to pitiable self-destruction or vulgar self-selling. Nicole Diver, the bred-in-the-bone heiress of Old Money, is as morally and psychologically weak as any other poor little rich girl. Dick Diver, her husband and psychiatrist, is an adopted son of the class and well on his way to being corrupted by its money. The lives of this pair are depicted in the usual terms one would expect from a mentor or critic of the class. They are graceful but inconsequential, lovely but unreal. Barban enters this party to highlight the weightlessness, the lack of traction in the men, and to awaken Nicole, slumbering in the narcissistic stupor of her social graces. Fitzgerald didn't have to choose a soldier-adventurer for this role. He might have reached for another stock character in the Old Money gallery, a figure of patrician probity like Squire Montague in Twain's *The Gilded Age* or Lambert Strether in James's *The Ambassadors.* Instead, he brings on stage a figure of Homeric antiquity: a man whose "simplicity of . . . ideas" combines with a "complexity of . . . training" to create what is the only thoroughly purposeful male character in the novel. Fitzgerald once said that he often felt for the rich "not the conviction of a revolutionist but the smouldering hatred of the peasant" and that he could never stop thinking that "at one time a sort of *droit de seigneur* might have been exercised to give one of them my girl." Barban is that *seigneur,* but in the circumstances of this novel the exercise of his *droit* looks less like a rape than a rescue.

In the Second World War, the fighter pilot was now joined, iconographically, by the seaborne cavalrymen of the PT boats and the destroyer escorts, and also, at least in the person of General George Patton, by the earth-shattering cavalrymen of the tank corps. The European literature of the Great War also helped redeem foot soldiering for the Old Rich—not in the Army, to be sure, but in the Marine Corps. The Marines were and still are tremendously appealing to Old Money. It is an all-volunteer force, of course, and one solely dedicated to the hard reality of combat. But it was also the service, as my friend Edwin Morgan once pointed out to me, where the children of the rich could "rejoin the United States"—rejoin, that is, the children of the poor: they, too, volunteers. As an ordeal, the Marine Corps continued to exercise its sway over the upper-class imagination right through the Korean and Vietnam wars. Even in peacetime, even today when Old

Money's romance with war has either cooled or turned into a warlike romance with peace, there are Old Money parents who think wistfully of the Marine Corps as the perfect way to endow their lightweight children with a little *gravitas*.

World War II also introduced a wholly new form of service to the Old Rich—new to them, at any rate—neither in the skies above nor in the seas and jungles below, not even on the front lines. It was underground and behind the lines, in World War II's OSS and the Cold War's CIA, that the Old Money class finally came into an inheritance of all the glamour and peril they had been reading about for years in the work of such Old World romancers as John Buchan, Compton McKenzie, and H. C. McNeile, the creator of Bulldog Drummond. The honor roll of the OSS-CIA between 1941 and 1975, by which time age and discouragement had pretty well decimated their ranks, reads like an alumni bulletin of a St. Midas or an Ivy League school: Allen Dulles, Arthur Schlesinger, Jr., Tracy Barnes, Thomas Braden, James J. Angleton, Desmond FitzGerald, Archibald Roosevelt, Kermit Roosevelt, Robert Amory, Richard Bissell, Frank Wisner, Richard Helms, et al. And those names are only the ones most famously connected with the organization. There are scores of others, as diverse a collection of people as William F. Buckley, Jr., Peter Matthiessen, and James Chace, for example, who wittingly or unwittingly did "a little work" for the CIA when they went to Europe or Latin America after graduation from college.

The OSS-CIA, being voluntary, was assimilable to the ethos of citizenly sacrifice. It was also very dangerous, or could be, as in the behind-the-lines action seen by Merrill's Marauders (Philip Weld) or Chennault's Flying Tigers (Joseph Alsop), both of which carried out "intelligence" missions. For most OSS-CIA volunteers, however, the deepest appeal of this service lay not in its likeness but in its contradistinction to the classic arms of war. Cord Meyer had experience of both and appreciated the difference. A St. Paul's boy and a Yale man, later a Harvard Junior Fellow, Meyer underwent a terrible ordeal in the battle for Guam. Badly wounded, he lay on the battlefield and reflected, or so he claimed later in his memoir, on why he had joined "so dangerous a service." It was because he had wanted "to redeem by personal valor a lost consistency of purpose." Now, as he lay dying, he prepared to "accept the consequences." The language would have been perfectly familiar to Victor Chapman or, indeed, to Meyer's own father, who had flown with Quentin Roosevelt in the Great War. Later, having recovered from his wounds, Meyer discovered that there was a realer reality to be faced than death under fire. The reality of his memoir's title, *Facing Reality,* was in the realm of ideas: democracy versus tyranny, whether of the right or the left; or liberty versus coercion, whether economic or political. He joined the United World Federalists, then the CIA, where he had particular responsibility for such ideological services as Radio Free Europe and the Congress for Cultural Freedom (the latter my own sometime employer, as it happens).

There was something noble about this movement from an ordeal of the body to an ordeal of the mind: a sort of modernist nobility. A spook's story is a modernist romance. The contest has now moved indoors. It is no longer physical but intellectual. The peril includes a willed suspension of the very virtues—honesty, loyalty, sportsmanship—that the ordeal is meant to "prove." And the stakes have shifted: They have become almost completely performative, subject to hardly any win-or-lose measurement. This is the nobility (and the modernism) of the move: that the prince and princess now try their capacity for rule and self-rule under a sort of moral and spiritual fire, where *tyche* holds out the risk not merely of one's own tragic death and suffering but of others' as well. Many Old Money men of the CIA cracked under this ordeal. James Angleton froze in the paranoid Manichaean certainties of "free" versus "communist" systems. Many others muddled through until they killed themselves or were struck down by midlife heart attacks and alcoholism. The cost to their fellow citizens was incalculable, like the actions of all citizens, good and bad.

But there was also something ignoble about the ordeal by "intelligence." It represented a striking retreat of the Old Money imagination from the public to the private world. As Frederick Seidel puts it in a poem about upper-class CIA men:

> Public servants in secret are not servants,
> Either. They were our gods working all night
> To make Achilles' beard fall out and prop up
> The House of Priam . . .

The CIA, when it was dominated by Old Money, was a patrician preserve, not an aristocratic one. My great-grandfather would have felt perfectly comfortable there: a place where prudent, knowledgeable, indeed *knowing* men could help to preserve the nation's patrimony without the let or hindrance of those who had not yet "evolved." It was a place already half given over to the entrepreneurial mind: not to greed, perhaps, but to fear and the sowing of fear. It is just as well, for Old Money if not for the nation, that it has now passed altogether into the hands of the middle classes.

The challenge to the Old Money imagination today, "real" war having become quite unreal (at least for the proving of princes), is to discover what William James called for at the turn of the century—a "moral equivalent of war" to combat the "effeminacy" and "trashiness of fibre" which he supposed the love of luxury was spreading throughout all classes of the civilized world. But there is no question about what the imaginations of most Old Rich have come up with. It is neither distinctive nor edifying, being postwar America's most unifying political passion, after the pursuit of happiness. For most of its heirs and heiresses, most of the time, Old Money's moral equivalent of war is just like everyone else's. It is the great cause, not yet a Great War, of anticommunism.

AFTER THE ORDEALS

One contingency to which Old Money makes itself vulnerable, when it submits its children to princely ordeals, is the possibility that the results may be subjected to rational economic measurement. The ordeals are a production system, more accurately a reproduction system, whose output may be compared to its input, its benefits to its costs, its risks to its probabilities of success, and so on through the strange series of ordeals that Market Man prepares for *his* children.

Fortunately for the Old Rich, perhaps, the question of how well they or the system survives those econometric ordeals is moot. The imagination still reigns wherever Old Money makes its presence felt: the social imagination of Old Money, intermittently blinking on and off, or the more commonplace, therefore steadier fancy of the entrepreneurial mind. But both, in point of fact, see mostly failure in the issue of Old Money's princely ordeals. In the New World, the little angels of inherited wealth continue their free, well-subsidized fall through trackless space.

This failure is especially obvious to the insight of envy. The swing of perception—from blinded, admiring envy to clear-eyed, malevolent envy—goes back and forth in the work of all three of America's most snobbish writers, Fitzgerald, Marquand, and O'Hara, but most famously in Fitzgerald. Tom Buchanan, for example, is a malevolent representation of Tommy Hitchcock, just as Tommy Barban is a rather admiring representation of the same man. Buchanan is the Meadow Brook *seigneur* who doesn't have to exercise his *droit* over the novelist's girl or Gatsby's; he simply, effortlessly, got there first, and Daisy is his by precedence. (Daisy is the Old Money girl the entrepreneurial imagination loves best: a beautiful nonentity, with nothing but money in her voice, waiting only for the rough caress of the self-made man to bring her to sensual life, to put her mouth, as it were, where her money is.) Everything about Buchanan declares him the sort of man that the American go-getter can comfortably despise. It's in the "effeminate swagger" with which he wears his jodhpurs and hacking jacket, the "cruel" body beneath the jacket, his "arrogant" eyes and "supercilious" manner. Most despicable, of course, is his carelessness. He is careless with what was given him, his girl and his body: He neglects the one for his mistress and abuses the other with booze. He is careless of the lives and well-being of the less fortunate, driving recklessly through people's lives like a sporting lord.

Old Money recognizes this character from a different angle. He is the icon of nonchalance gone bad, everything the ordeals of boarding school, nature, and war were meant to forfend. Tom Buchanan gives nightmares to the mentors of St. Midas; he even strains the vaunted loyalties of his classmates. People like him make up what one old Grotonian once described as a representative sample of his form: a bunch of "cheats, drunkards, lechers, panhandlers, suicides." They are what a friend of mine from St. Paul's, Geoffrey Gates, calls Locust Valley Rednecks. They are what the Old World's Old Money would recognize as the New World version of the shit-kicking, peasant-abusing rural aristocrat. His political views, insofar as he has any, are fascistic. He hates and fears Jews, patronizes and despises blacks, sees decadence and decay everywhere except in the mirror, is secretly thrilled by the more brutal exploitations of Market Man, and has for a religion not the patrimonial worship of nature but the banal night horrors of anticommunism. The only hope for this man, as even his mother sometimes suspects, is the coming of another war. In war, Tom Buchanan has a chance to become Tommy Barban or, better yet, to make the supreme sacrifice and die in glory.

But these two (or three, counting Daisy) do not exhaust the imaginative possibilities of the human performances that can issue from Old Money's ordeals. In truth, as far as the class's perceptions are concerned, the performative ideal dictates that each beneficiary shall decide on his (or her) own whether the passage through boarding school, the great outdoors, and war has led him into full and rightful possession of his self and his estate, or whether it has left him where he began, floating on his unearned money.

Nevertheless, Old Money has its heroes, as does Market Man, and many of them are clearly marked by their ordeals. I think of a man named George Cadwalader, St. Paul's School '57, Yale '61, a former career officer in the Marine Corps who retired from the service after being wounded in Vietnam. I know nothing about Cadwalader except what I have read about him and by him in the school alumni bulletin. Still, there's enough there, I should think, to qualify him for heroic Old Money status, and in rather specific Old Money terms. What he did—after graduation, after Labor Day, after the war—was to set up a reform school for delinquent adolescents on Penikese Island, the last and smallest of those Elizabeth Islands of which the Forbeses' Naushon is the first and largest. Some of the Old Money sources of this undertaking are obvious: the location of the school (and the fact that it is a school) in a place of great natural beauty and some peril; the definition of the educational experience as a reduction of life to real, pre-money necessities (the boys farm and fish their own food, build and maintain their own primitive quarters, etc.); the evident construction of *his* experience, though he doesn't put it in these words, as a social act for the public good, a giving of the self to the city; and the rather dismissive tone he takes toward those base specialists "the social scientists," whose province of delinquency he is happy, as an amateur, to invade. There is even a touch of nonchalance in the opening sentence of his article: "Fourteen years ago, some friends and I abandoned our various careers to found a school for young male delinquents on a remote island off the Massachusetts coast."

But perhaps the subtlest clue to where George Cadwalader came from on his way to his estate on Penikese Island is in his understanding of what makes these children of poverty the way they are. It is very much like what makes the children of riches the way they are:

> What they do has no identifiable influence on what happens to them. Whether they are praised, punished, or ignored depends more on the erratic moods of unstable adults or the often equally mercurial intervention of officialdom than on anything they do themselves. In an unpredictable world, their only guide to behavior is simply to

satisfy the impulse of the moment. A childhood that never gave them the chance to make consistent connections between cause and effect leaves them feeling powerless to influence the course of their lives.

The usual social-scientific understanding of these boys, as Cadwalader sees it, is to presume that their thievery, violence, and self-destruction are rational choices (or "adaptations") they have made after doing a rational cost-benefit analysis of their environment. To him, after a while, it looked like the random behavior of people whose training and economic circumstances give them no sense of their weight and traction in the world, no sense of the cost or consequence of their actions, no sense of personal power.

But Cadwalader's qualifications for upper-class heroism don't rest on his understanding. They rest on his actions, and on the ideological context of his actions. Far and away the most striking thing about the attitudes that this former soldier brings to his city-state on Penikese Island is his view of "success."

> The Penikese Island School began by attracting the kind of publicity that quixotic pursuits of this kind always get, particularly if they occupy picturesque locations. The coverage we received contained all the predictable superlatives. Our "no-nonsense" curriculum was "unique." Our staff was "dedicated," and our students were quoted talking earnestly of "turning themselves around."
>
> All of this was true.
>
> Yet when, five years later, we did a survey involving interviews with as many as we could locate of our first 100 students ... we discovered what, by then, we had already begun to suspect. All but 16 had not turned themselves around: 84 had gone on to lives destructive in varying degrees to themselves and to society.
>
> Among those 84, most were survivors who had mastered the chameleon-like ability to adapt instinctively to whatever an unpredictable fate threw at them. This is why so many of them did so well at Penikese.

He goes on to express something close to scorn for those who "inflate claims of success"—the supervisors of the Penikese Island School in the Massachusetts state government, for example. Cadwalader is an Old Money hero because he judges what he is doing by his own standards of personal performance. These standards are noneconomic: "no hospital would make less effort on behalf of a patient having only a 16 percent chance of success ... every boy who comes to us is a potential member of that 16 percent ... statistics provide an incomplete picture of actual results ... we may [reduce a kid's] capacity for crime from murder to car theft—and that is progress, even if it will never show up in the statistics." But such standards are more than noneconomic. They admit what economic measures never can, that the fate of lives like those boys' may ultimately be tragic, and here, ultimately, is Old Money's last best escape from the nemesis of futility. It is in the recognition, like Cadwalader's, that the well-lived life, in an overwhelmingly economic world, is neither tragic nor comic but some combination of the two. It is, as he says, "quixotic."

Most graduates of St. Midas, however, return from their summer vacations on the coast, or from their wars, to rather more banal estates than Quixote's, and there must find something to do with their lives. Two roles await them, the patrician and the aristocratic, one relating more or less directly to the caretaking of their family patrimonies, the other a much riskier adventure into public life. There is no question about which role is inherited by most of the Old Rich. It is the patrician.

The patrician manages, preserves, enhances, and passes on the gift of wealth to his posterity, and, often, to the nation's as well. Most of that wealth, as I've said, is in various states of liquidity, an amorphous agglomeration of paper possessions, much of it stashed away in trust funds. But there's a significant sector of the Old Rich patriciate whose heirs and heiresses come into something very close to real estates. Sometimes they are businesses—newspapers, for example, or even large industrial corporations. More often, though, they come into traditions of patrimonial management that are strongly institutionalized enough to contain the liquidity of the assets and to withstand the temptations of a free fall through freedom, or a fuck-you ride down the river.

CHAPTER SIX

Hazards of
Old Fortunes

While all minds were struggling to right themselves, the boy
still moved steadily forward, with high port and confident
mien; he had never halted from the beginning; and while the
tangled minds still floundered helplessly, he stepped upon the
platform, and the mock king ran with a glad face to meet
him and fell on his knees before him and said, "Oh, my lord
the king, let poor Tom Canty be the first to swear fealty to
thee and say, 'Put on Thy crown and enter into thine own
again!'"

Mark Twain, *The Prince and the Pauper*

WHEN NED MCLEAN, the second generation of his family
to own the Washington *Post*, lost the paper in 1932 to Eugene Meyer, no one in the capital could have been less
surprised than Alice Roosevelt Longworth. She had known Ned since
she was a debutante living in the White House, and even when he was
a young man everything about him had promised disaster, both for
himself and for the estate he would succeed to. It was in his receding
chin, as she was quick to point out: that fateful sign of "weak character" for which Roosevelts, like all Old Money people, anxiously scan
the faces of their progeny to this day. It was also in his training. Mrs.
Longworth did not phrase it in these words, but the fact is that Ned
had never been obliged to pass through any of the ordeals that the Old
Money curriculum prescribes. On the contrary, his parents had tried

very hard to spare him all that. His mother used to bribe his playmates to let him win at Parcheesi. His father, hearing that he was at home in bed with a cold, once sent him a note that read: "Tell Pop the truth, how are you? ... Everything is going all right here at the *Post*. All you have to do in the world is keep well. Pop will take all the responsibility. I am only holding the *Post* for you."

The worst fears of Old Money—and the most gleeful expectations of New—came true in Ned McLean. He became an alcoholic. He fell victim to "urination syndrome," an unfortunate malady he shared with another newspaper heir, the New York *Herald*'s James Gordon Bennett, which compels its victims to pee in open fireplaces, potted palms, ladies' reticules, any convenient place so long as it be in full public view. He also lost his kingdom.

The loss seems to have devastated his wife more than it did Ned. Dynastic feeling ran strong in Evalyn Walsh McLean. Recalling her high hopes in 1916, the year Ned finally came into his estate, she wrote: "I wanted him to have the admiration and acclaim that go with greatness. I wanted him to rule his father's fortune ... , and above all else I wanted our sons to be fit to play and work with the leaders of the nation." It took Ned sixteen years to bring ruin to the *Post*. In 1924, in the single most important decision a publisher has to make, he appointed as editor of the paper a conservative journalist called George Harvey, then at the bibulous end of his career, and awarded him a salary of more than half the *Post*'s annual profit. Then in 1928 Ned cut loose from Evalyn, his last best anchor in reality, and moved to Hollywood, where he set up house with Rose Douras Davies. Perhaps he hoped to acquire a little of the "admiration and acclaim" that attached to William Randolph Hearst, whose mistress, Marion, was Rose's sister. At any rate, Ned and Rose had a good time. In 1931, they spent $100,000 on a brief holiday in Europe. In 1932, the *Post* went bankrupt. Evalyn, a considerable heiress in her own right, tried to save the paper for her sons. At the auction, she bid $660,000 for it. Eugene Meyer, an adopted child of Old Money who had gone to Yale and made a fortune of his own in investment banking, bid $800,000 and won.

Dynastic aspiration has run as high in the Meyer family as it did in the McLean family, and so far with rather better success. Under the publishership of Donald Graham, son of Philip and Katharine (Meyer) Graham, grandson of Eugene Meyer, the paper is now in the third generation of family ownership and management. Donny, as he was called as a boy, was eight years old in 1954, when his father and grandfather finally succeeded in taking over the *Post*'s one remaining major competitor, Cissy Patterson's *Times-Herald,* thereby acquiring a dominant position in Washington's news and print-advertising markets. It had been a hard struggle. Time and again they had tried to buy out their rival, only to be rebuffed either by Miss Patterson or by the principal owner of the paper, her cousin Colonel Robert McCormick, publisher of the Chicago *Tribune.* Why the isolationist, pro-McCarthy McCormick finally agreed to sell out to the internationalist, liberal Meyer was put down by one observer to the fact that they were both "Yalemen who had earned their 'Y' in life after graduation" and to the fact that Meyer had "shown himself under stress to be a gentleman." Be that as it may, within the Meyer-Graham family the takeover was an event of overwhelming significance. The *Post,* said Meyer of his grandson, was now "safe for Donny."

With so much expected of him, and with so much to be given him, Donny Graham was encouraged to prove himself through virtually every ordeal on the Old Money curriculum. True, he was sent to an Academy boarding school rather than a St. Midas one, but this may have meant no more than that his parents preferred him to run the risk of becoming tough and graceless rather than weak and graceful. Perhaps it was better thus: At least one chronicler of his early career, the journalist Maureen Orth, suggests that at one point at Harvard he was tested so severely that an education in the more delicate values of the social virtues and graces might have undone him.

The ordeal took place at the editorial offices of the Harvard *Crimson,* the student newspaper where Graham had volunteered to compete for a position. As a modern bard, Orth is careful to emphasize that a post on the *Crimson* is not like the Sword in the Stone, a power that yields only to a mysterious, indwelling sign of divine right. The *Crimson,* Orth says, is a "highly charged daily ... an elite meritocracy." These are magic words, chosen to suggest that Graham might have competed for the job incognito, for all the influence his future kingdom would have on his judges. Nevertheless, one day a group of staffers got together to play a trick on him: They fed him a phony story. Graham was not fooled. Then they played another trick on him: phony page proofs. That was enough. It was time to show the envious world what stuff Donny Graham was made of.

"Okay, you guys," he is supposed to have "teased," to use the bardic formula, "I'll buy any paper you're on just for the fun of firing you."

It was a memorable moment, apparently. One of the *Crimson* staffers, Joe Russin, later told Orth: "That's when I realized here was a guy who was going to have a lot of responsibility." Another of those who came to mock and stayed to admire was "blond and brainy Mary Wissler," who later became his wife.

Donny Graham went through more ordeals, of course, at war and in police intelligence. Orth's account stresses the time he spent on his own two feet—at boot camp, in Vietnam, in Washington as a gumshoe, and later, "in spite of being the heir to a $500,000,000 media fortune," walking to and from the bus stop to work. This was the usual drill for a child of Old Money—following Antaeus, lest one be tempted to follow Peter Pan—but it had some different features. One was the importance of Harvard.

Harvard's usefulness to Old Money does not exhaust itself in class-membership functions. Harvard has always offered its own ordeal, its own version of "reality," its own way of giving form to freedom—the contests in the classroom and elsewhere, where children of wealth compete to prove their excellence. Nobody who's "got it made" has to strive for A's at Harvard, or go out for the varsity, or try for the lead in undergraduate plays, or (like Donny Graham) "comp" for the *Crimson,* or do much of anything except get by and get into the Porcellian Club. Everything is optional, as most things always will be for these children of the rich. Thus a good deal of honor, if not merit, attaches to an achievement like Donny Graham's.

But merit opens up the more important feature of Graham's Harvard ordeal. Merit is an elastic concept, but in a liberal society it ought not to fit very well on someone who gets what he wants by saber-rattling his inherited money-power. "Okay, you guys, I'll buy any paper you're on just for the fun of firing you" is a perfect example of an infamous contravention of liberal doctrine, which the Harvard philosopher John Rawls calls "to each according to his threat." Yet there's an Old Money sense in which such a remark is indeed meritorious. Not the threat itself, which even as a "tease" is repulsive, but the capacity to make it. Russin, the young man who suddenly realized what sort of kingdom this prince was heir to, got closest to the true merit of Graham's *grossièreté.* This was no ordinary rich kid they were testing here, no usual trust-fund preppie, whom Harvard likes to admit for Old Money's sake and its own historic tone. Graham was that rare issue of Old Money who inherits, as Russin noted, "responsibilities," not just freedoms; things to do, not simply ways to be; powers, not only options. Donny Graham's estate, in short, was "real," and what made him "real" enough to inherit it was the willingness to use the powers that came with it. That's what Donny Graham's ordeal at the *Crimson* proved: that he was willing to take power.

Graham's story points to the single most fateful distinction among scions of the Old Money class: the distinction between those who are born to a powerful functional estate in life, in practice most often a business, and those who are born merely to money. Inevitably, the money inheritors are a vast majority. Whatever wealth-generating enterprise it was that initially carried the family into history, the chances are that it did not continue under family management for more than the proverbial three generations. One study has shown that the attrition rate of family businesses in America—enterprises, that is, for which there's evidence that the founder intended to pass them on to the next generation—is about 80 percent in the first-to-second-generation transfer, and again 80 percent in the second-to-third-generation transfer. Even if executive power does manage to get passed on for more than three generations, the usual imperatives of fiduciary management will have long since dictated some diversification of the family's assets. The Old Money class is overwhelmingly a *rentier* class. It lives off the income of inherited capital, or, as Brahmin Bostonians like to have it, the income of the income of the capital.

It is this circumstance that gives Old Money its peculiar position in American society. It is a highly invidious position, also a highly problematic one, invidious because unearned income brings with it all those freedoms, options, and choices that for most Americans constitute the American Dream; problematic because those freedoms exert a terrific centrifugal force on the spirits of their inheritors, constantly threatening to shoot them out into trackless space. The Old Money curriculum is designed to foreclose this fate, of course. Its breeding in the courtesies and graces, the toughening realities of its ordeals, are supposed to lift its beneficiaries above the moral and aesthetic ugliness of the marketplace, but at the same time to discipline their freedom, giving it shape and vigor and the moral content of "character." Too often, however, the curriculum seems unavailing. The centrifugal force of freedom, the great double-edged gift of unearned wealth, is simply too much for it.

This is the context that gives the inheritance of power in a truly functional estate its great distinction. What Donny Graham inherited with the publishership of the Washington *Post,* Old Money would describe in many ways: a seat, a domain, a kingdom; or a responsibility,

an obligation, an honor. But however it is described, the most important distinction between what he got and what his brothers and sister
got is that they came into freedom while he came into a tangible,
seriously consequential working relationship with his fellowmen.
Against this, all the "realities" of the Old Money ordeals seem adventitious, make-believe—in the worst sense of the word, *gratuitous.*
Against this, too, the striving of the self-makers seems unnatural. Graham did not have to *make* his relationship with the *Post;* it already
existed: actual, historical, and deeply rooted in the economic life of his
community.

It is the historic givenness of this sort of estate, its stability and
objective reality in the lives of others, that make it so meaningful to
Old Money. The essence of the Old Money project is family continuity.
The project seeks to score a generational line through (and slightly
above) the turbulence of striving and struggling that is life in a liberal,
entrepreneurial society. It seeks to be a triumph of history, the family's
history, over time. But the Old Money family cannot carry this project
alone. The generational line, if it's to be of more than a genealogical
interest, must figure in public and be drawn through other institutions
than the family. This is the purpose, obviously, of cultivating a distinctively Old Money *presence* and of keeping up memberships in distinctively Old Money schools and clubs. A functional estate could be just
another stage on which to figure, another institution to belong to, but
it can also be more than that. It can enable a child of Old Money to
inherit a place that's *in* the economic world without being *of* it.

This possibility gives a kind of grounding to the family's hopes for
continuity between generations. A typical expression of such hopes is
contained in a letter that Theodore Roosevelt, then a Harvard freshman, received from his father in 1876, not long before the elder Roosevelt died:

> It has always seemed to me as if there were something peculiarly
> pleasant in the relations between a father and a son, the enjoyment
> of the father is so great as he cares for the boy and sees him gradually
> becoming a reasoning being, his mind and his physique both devel-
> oping under his care and training.... As he approaches manhood
> the boy enjoys relieving his father of part of the responsibilities
> which he has borne until that time, and these cares prepare the boy
> to take the father's place in the great battle of life.

What responsibilities? *What* place? In most Old Money families, including the Roosevelts, sentiments like these have no clear referent in the everyday economic world that everybody else lives in. When the elder Roosevelt died, there was no business for Theodore or Eliot (never mind their sisters) to succeed to, no employees to be kept working, no plans to be made and carried out. There was merely a shapeless bundle of "investments" to be looked after as time permitted and the market demanded. A functional estate like the Washington *Post* would have given this father's feelings a grounding in economic actualities.

But this does not exhaust the imaginative possibilities of a functional estate. It's conceivable, for example, that a family enterprise should come endowed with the aura of the *familias*—that little state of classical antiquity which was composed of family and retainers, and of buildings and other forms of property, all laid out on a determinate spot of the earth. This fancy is agreeable enough in itself. It gives a kind of aesthetic coherence to the estate, almost as if it were "landed." More important, however, is the domestic political theory that the *familias* brings with it: the idea of a *pater* and *mater* to whom fate and the gods give absolute authority for the conservation and well-being of the estate. From Bracton in the Old Regime to Blackstone and Bentham in the New, jurists cautioned postclassical *patres familias* to hold fast to the purse strings lest they lose purse and family all together. Bentham put the issue most bluntly:

> The same power [of making a will] may be considered as an instrument of authority, intrusted to individuals for the encouragement of virtue in their families and the repression of vice.... Clothed with the power of making a will, which is a branch of penal and remunerative legislation, [the proprietor] may be considered as a magistrate appointed to preserve good order in that little state called a family.... By means of an order not payable till after his death, he procures for himself an infinity of advantages beyond what his actual means would furnish. By continuing the submission of children beyond the term of minority, the indemnity for paternal cares is increased, and an additional assurance against ingratitude is secured to the father; and though it would be agreeable to think that such precautions are superfluous, yet ... [in] the rapid descent of life, every support on which a man can lean should be left untouched, and it is well that interest serve as monitor to duty.... [The] influence of this [will-making] power, established in society by the laws,

tends to form general manners, and general manners thus formed
determine the sentiments of individuals. This power given to fathers
renders the paternal authority more respectable, and those fathers
whose indigence does not permit them to exercise it, unconsciously
profit by the general habit of submission to which it has given rise.

Even in this great theoretician of liberalism there was a yearning, perhaps even a need, to preserve some ground for that patriarchal or
paternalistic authority which it was the historic task of liberalism to
destroy. The further irony is that, in America anyway, the *patres* who
could best afford to preserve that authority were among the first to
throw it away. Trust funds are a tax dodge, a flotation device to lift the
beneficiaries of the rich above the hazards and vulgarities of the marketplace, but they also work to subvert the parental authority that
Bentham, and many political and economic liberals after him, have
been so eager to retain—at least in the family. Imaginatively, then, an
inheritance like Donny Graham's recalls a Benthamite "little state"
where all is orderly and secure, and all the "citizens" are well-
mannered, thanks to the power of the *pater* to cut everybody off.

In yet another flight of fancy, the family enterprise becomes a feudal estate. Under feudalism, powers and dominions, statuses and functions, rights and responsibilities—all issued from the estate to which
one was born, arranged in beauty and fixed forever, like the Great
Chain of Being hanging from the Hand of God. Liberalism remembers this arrangement as an insufferable restriction of the liberty, potentiality, and mobility (always presumed to be upward) of the
sovereign self. Entrepreneurialism remembers it as a system of entail,
as an insufferable restriction on the free marketability of property. But
Old Money remembers the special relationship to the things of this
world, land particularly. Old Money cannot forget the *particule,* that
"de" or "von" that symbolically tied a family to a determinate piece of
land, grounding it in the only (apparently) immortal thing that men
know, the earth itself. The relationship was not ownership as capitalism understands it and as free markets make possible. It was a relationship, almost ontological in depth, of reciprocal possession. A
person was *of* his property, as the property was *of* him (and, in many
places, her as well). For such a form of property there could be no
money value, no market. Alienating such a possession, selling it, was
literally inconceivable, like the idea of selling one's name.

Needless to say, not all family enterprises recall such feudal arrangements, but most large ones do, and the rhetorical language of the arrangements is still very much alive. Journalists helplessly describe heirs presumptive to corporations as "crown princes," and the heirs themselves rarely object to the comparison. Edsel Ford, suffering through an ordeal at one of Ford's subsidiaries in Australia, was once asked whether his fate didn't promise greater power than Prince Charles's. "Yeah," said Edsel. "I suppose that's right."

Only the Fourth Estate, however, confers automatic elevation to the nobility. Most businesses that stay under family management and control for more than one generation deal in goods that are staples of life, or close to it. Thus there are clusters of family enterprises in the grain industry (Cargill); beer, wine, and spirits (Coors, Gallo, Bronfman); fuel (oil and gas "independents" in the Southwest); and shelter and construction (Tishman, Turner, Bechtel). But news is also a staple in a commercial culture and a democratic regime. Moreover, it's a staple that its purveyors have been increasingly able to market under near-monopolistic conditions. This has made newspapers extremely attractive to takeover by other corporations—some of them public like the Gannett Company, but others family owned or dominated, like the Washington Post Company itself, or the New York Times Company, or Dow Jones & Co. Nevertheless, if the family can withstand takeover bids, hostile or otherwise, the paper's dominant position in its market can help the cause of continuity.

Newspapers are also attractive properties to inherit. They are very profitable: The average return on investment for a metropolitan daily is about 16 percent. Then, too, they bring with them extraordinary powers. Like other corporate commanders, publishers decide whether to change the means of production: whether to automate, for example. They decide on mergers and acquisitions. They decide where to build new facilities and when to close down old ones. These decisions can make their businesses (and families) a laughingstock of the industry, or the pride of the nation.

But a newspaper publisher's powers go far beyond these. A newspaper affects the reputations and life prospects of every individual, institution, product, work of art and commerce, every idea it chooses—or does not choose—to touch. Daniel Defoe, the first modern journalist, once said that "he who would be great must first be popular." Newspapers are the toll collectors of the modern traffic in popularity, and to a large extent its manufacturers and bankers as well. That's because newspapers promote, and earn profits from their promotions. Art, labor-saving devices, fads or fashions, deeds of service, acts of notoriety, feats of prowess, styles and life-styles, any vehicle by which someone might *make* himself, and/or make himself rich, needs the media to raise it from the ruck of anonymity. "Known" and "noble": the two words have the same root. Newspapers have the power to ennoble in the only sense that a democracy recognizes as legitimate—by making known. No wonder inheritors of newspapers are always being touched up with a bit of the purple and reinstated in some Old Regime. Their employees are often the first to do so, as in this passage from Theodore White:

> One used to be able to see them in the flesh in unforgettable display at the *New York Times'* annual reception ... when the A.P. each spring gathers publishers from around the country for its annual meeting. The Sulzberger family would receive as befitted the Grand Dukes of Manhattan, Arthur Hays Sulzberger sitting in his chair, his consort, Iphigene, standing beside him, both nodding graciously and extending their hands to the other noble families of the realm as they strode proudly in. There were the great personages from out-country, the Grand Duchesse of Los Angeles, Mrs. Norman Chandler; the Grand Duchesse of Washington, Mrs. Philip L. Graham; there were the earls, counts, countesses, of lesser but still courtly blood—the Taylors of Boston, the Binghams of Louisville, the Fields of Chicago, the Pulitzers of St. Louis, the Ridders of the Midwest. They were to be distinguished by bearing and disposition from those publishers [of] ... commercial enterprises where family lineage was either absent or, like the Newhouses, too fresh in power to have acquired patina. As politicians and diplomats watched, the great family figures would circle, flanked by small courts of their own famous writers, stars, or editors. If swords, costumes and decorations had been permitted, one might have transferred the personages to a levee in the Hall of Mirrors—and they would have been at home.

It would be hard to say whether the tone of this passage owes more to its author's snobbery, his sycophancy, or the circumstance of his adoption by the Old Money class. All were applicable, for Theodore White was a born hero-worshiper, a sometime newspaper employee, and a Harvard man. Still, every cliché he used, from the Sulzbergers' "gracious" presence to the Newhouses' "commercial" and patina-less "lineage," tells of the astonishing infectiousness of Old Money's social imagination. Journalists seem to pick up this way of thinking about their bosses even when they hate them. At the Washington *Post,* for example, following the printers' strike of 1974, a consultant was called in to find out what had gone wrong. Katharine Graham was publisher then, having succeeded to the publisher's chair when her husband killed himself, and her strong antiunion stand had not endeared her to the help. "Phil Shot the Wrong Graham" proclaimed one of the signs on the picket line. Nevertheless, it was clear to the consultant that Mrs. Graham had aroused among the printers, not the rivalrous antagonism that one might expect of "countervailing" power in a liberal regime, but the bitterness of unrequited fealty that one might expect of dependents in a feudal regime. "To most of the employees," the consultant wrote, "[Mrs. Graham] has something of the aura of a hereditary monarch. They regard the internal life of the WP as a political struggle for her favor. To most of them she is a benevolent ruler who would resolve all controversies in their favor providing she was aware of the facts."

Mrs. Graham has had a slightly different image of herself over the years, it seems, but a no less "feudal" one. Recalling once what it had been like growing up as she had, in a salon dominated by her fiercely intellectual mother, she told an interviewer: "I thought I was this peasant walking around among brilliant people." Her marriage did not improve things much: The peasant was brought indoors to become Phil Graham's maid. "He was so glamorous that I was perfectly happy just to clean up after him. I did all the scutwork. . . . I was always the butt of family jokes. You know, good old Mom, plodding along." But eventually the day arrived when Cinderella came into her kingdom, not by finding her prince but by losing him—first to insanity, then to suicide. For days thereafter she couldn't get out of her mind a scene from *The Vagabond King,* "when the suddenly enthroned vagabond— for the first time dressed in royal robes—descends the great stairs, slowly and anxiously, tensely eyeing on either side the rows of archers with their drawn bows and inscrutable faces." She needn't have worried. Back and forth the royal images flew, but not like arrows. Soon, to McGeorge Bundy, Mrs. Graham seemed to have transcended the musical stage and achieved the substance of history. "The most powerful woman in the world since Queen Victoria," the former knight of Camelot once described her.

Needless to say, few of these relicts of the Old Regime, rhetorical or historical, have escaped the destructive attentions of the American revolutionary tradition of 1776, neither Adam Smith's revolution of efficiency in the service of greed, nor Thomas Jefferson's revolution of independence in the service of freedom and mobility. No sooner had the Declaration defied George III as a "tyrant . . . unfit to be the ruler of a free people" than revolutionary liberals discovered that royally proportioned wealth could also tyrannize a free people. As John Taylor of Caroline warned in 1814: "If wealth is accumulated in the hands of a few, either by feudal or stock monopoly, it carries power also; and a government becomes as certainly aristocratical by a monopoly of wealth as by a monopoly of arms." From there the ideological line runs fairly straight and true to Franklin Roosevelt's castigation of "economic royalists" in the 1930s. By that time, however, it had occurred to many people that feudal comparisons, while charming, were misleading. A more accurate language might speak of a "ruling class," and then perhaps of a second socialist revolution to complete the liberal one against George III.

This was an alarming prospect. To most Americans, socialism threatens liberal values of individual initiative in seeking one's own path to happiness, and of individual responsibility for one's failure or success in attaining it. Socialism also threatens to wipe out great hereditary inequalities of wealth and power. The significant issue is not over the facts of rule—societies must have posts of command—but over who takes those posts and how they're recruited. If the "rulers" emerge from a small class of people who recruit their successors primarily from among their own weak-chinned and limp-wristed children or their retainers, then clearly the liberal revolution has bogged down in "aristocratical" government, and perhaps a socialist revolution is necessary. But if the command posts are held by a large class of people who recruit their successors as they themselves were recruited, from among meritorious and efficient strangers called professional managers, then no socialist revolution is necessary. At all the command posts of the nation, a revolution will already be continuously in progress, in which one group of professional managers rises up in response to the market for efficient management and overthrows another, less efficient group. As the liberal slogan has it: The revolution is dead! Long live the revolution!

The 1980s were a bad time for Old Money family businesses. Every day, in every sort of industry, *patres* of the functional *familias* were being overthrown, lines of succession interdicted, all by professional managers deployed by free markets in capital and talent, all in the name of greater efficiency. An excellent example is what happened in 1985–86 at the Richardson-Vicks Company, the family-dominated and family-managed maker of such old-time family remedies as Vicks cough drops and VapoRub. The company was a true Old Money domain. Its care and growth had been handed down in the family for four generations; relationships among family members were close whether they served the company directly or not; many of them summered in the same places, and once a year the whole clan gathered at a great picnic to honor their founder and celebrate their solidarity. But then in the early fall of 1985 Richardson-Vicks suddenly discovered that the British-Dutch conglomerate Unilever had hostile designs on its stock. To fend them off, family members in top management sent out urgent appeals to their relatives to strengthen their holdings in the company. The same appeal was sent out to the trustees of various family foundations, some two dozen family trust funds, and an employee trust fund, which all together controlled about 25 percent of Richardson-Vicks stock.

The relatives loyally stood fast, refusing to sell out their family heritage even as Unilever drove up its market value from $35 to $65 a share. They were betrayed by the trustees—their trustees, they must have thought, or trustees of *their* money, who were advised by *their* lawyers that recent court decisions mandated that they accept the highest free-market bid for the assets they held in trust, or else run the risk of being charged with a breach of their fiduciary responsibilities. With that, the family called in a white knight, Procter & Gamble, and sold out for $69 a share. Elderly aunts wept, the fourth generation of Richardson managers sadly prepared to give up their desks to professional managers, but the family as a whole, including the trusts, took $400 million to the bank.

There was a question, of course, of whether it still made sense to speak of "the family as a whole." The Richardson-Vicks takeover and liquidation sent shivers of apprehension throughout the network of American family businesses. It was said that recourse to the free money markets was no longer safe, not even if the family retained a 30 percent interest in the company, if some of that interest was held in trust. Trusts were the weak point, and the irony here was enormous. The more ancient a family's presence in a business, the more likely its presence will be in the form of trusts—those "inert mass[es] of wealth" that Gustavus Myers complained of. The law has commanded that they be inert no longer. The *Wall Street Journal* quoted "take-over experts" as saying that some of the most renowned family-dominated business domains in America were now at risk (even when they were under professional managers): Walt Disney, Du Pont, H. J. Heinz, Eli Lilly, Marriott, The New York Times, and Dow Jones. So were thousands of others, less well known. As a consequence, family companies have been looking frantically for ways to protect themselves—"going private," or tying up their stock in ingenious devices that Thomas Jefferson, for one, would immediately recognize as sophisticated forms of entail. It was not at all clear that they would be successful. A mergers-and-acquisitions man at Drexel Burnham Lambert was emphatic: Any company was vulnerable unless, as he put it, "51 percent of the company is in the hands of one person who is young, in good health, has money outside of his investment in the company, and doesn't live in a community property state."

Adam Smith would seem to have presided alone over most of these revolutions, with Thomas Jefferson nowhere to be seen. But if free-market efficiency explains the *coups d'état* at many Old Money domains, it does not explain them all, and many of them it never explains completely. Sometimes the presiding genius at the affair is Thomas Jefferson, with Adam Smith merely standing by. The most striking illustration of such a situation is the story of the 1986–87 takeover and liquidation of the Bingham domain in Louisville, Kentucky.

The Binghams belonged among Theodore White's "lesser but still courtly" lords of the press. They were Old Money. They had "lineage" and "patina." They cultivated Old Money's presence, values, and virtues, and supported its favored institutions. They had an estate in the country to match the one in the city. (It was called Melcombe, after a house in Dorset, England, where some sort of Binghams had lived since the twelfth century.) The children were sent east to school, to boarding schools, then to Harvard and Radcliffe. Summers, too, were spent in that "old" part of the country. Their properties included not only two newspapers, the *Courier* and the *Times,* but a television station, an AM and an FM radio station, and a printing company, as well as other well-diversified assets. These properties generated enough wealth to give the four surviving third-generation heirs unearned incomes of about $300,000 a year each—or more than ten times the earned income of the average American. Their parents, second-generation heirs, with a larger share of the family trusts, had even larger unearned incomes.

The Bingham drama began at the founding. Robert Bingham

bought the two newspapers with money he'd inherited on the sudden and somewhat suspect death of his second wife in 1918, less than a year after he'd married her. The money had come to Mary Lily Flagler Bingham equally fortuitously. One summer around the turn of the century, or so Harry Lehr's widow told the story, she had been a plucky little sewing woman on the domestic staff of Mrs. O.H.P. Belmont in Newport; the next day, thanks to the loss of a button, she had won the affections of Henry Flagler, the Standard Oil partner and Florida real-estate magnate. Flagler died soon after her marriage to him, leaving her very rich.

That was an accident. An accident of a different sort, full of por-tent for the end of the Bingham estate, was that Mary Lily Flagler Bingham was a feminist.

Nothing troubled the smooth first-generation transfer of the estate from Robert Bingham to his son Barry. Barry's siblings were not rival-rous. They allowed themselves to be bought out and happily departed for England. In the third generation, however, terrible things hap-pened. Within two years, 1964–66, two of Barry and Mary Bingham's five children were killed in violent, careless accidents. Jonathan, the youngest boy, was electrocuted while trying to feed some lights directly off a power line. Worth, the oldest son and heir presumptive, died on Nantucket when the surfboard he was carrying across the back seat of his Volkswagen was struck by a passing car; it snapped forward, breaking his neck. His place in the line of succession was taken by Barry junior, the second son. But no sooner had Barry junior been elevated to the publisher's chair on his father's retirement in 1971 than he was struck down with Hodgkin's disease, the same malady that had killed his grandfather.

He survived it. He might have understood it as part of his princely ordeal. Barry junior's is the classic fairy-tale ordeal of the younger brother. Worth had been their father's favorite; Nature's too, appar-ently. The father remembered him as a natural leader, a natural ath-lete, and a natural newspaperman. A sister remembered him, not inconsistently, as profane, reckless, and overbearing. Barry junior was a plump little boy, a tag-along, always (like Mrs. Graham) the butt of family jokes. He was also dyslexic. Still, he seems to have done what was expected of him by the Old Money curriculum, if not with "nat-ural" grace, then with character and determination. He went to board-ing school, got into Harvard, rowed on the crew, joined the Marine Corps. He suffered and sacrificed. And when his time came to take over the care of the estate, he proved worthy of the honor. In the years of his "stewardship," as he liked to call his rule, the papers added three more Pulitzer Prizes to the five they'd won in his father's day. True, profits at the papers were below industry averages, but the television and radio stations more than compensated for the difference.

Into this happy domain in 1977 came a sister, Sallie Bingham Ellsworth Iovenko. Since graduating from Radcliffe in 1959, she had been living in the East, first in Boston, then in New York. Twice married, twice divorced, now in her forties, she was the mother of three sons. She was a writer—or had been: She hadn't published anything in years—and in 1977 she decided to go home again. She said later that she was "demoralized" and wanted "to be a little safer for a while." Perhaps she was one of those princesses who are defeated by their ordeals. She was certainly a revolutionary liberal—that is to say, in her case, a feminist.

Sallie was soon joined by her much younger sister, Eleanor, who had tried to "make it on her own" as a television producer and, like most people who do that, had failed. Eleanor was married, and soon had two children.

With his two daughters back in Louisville, Barry senior, their aging but still powerful father, decided to make room for them on the boards of directors of the family companies. It was the best he could do to give them some share in the governance of the sources of their wealth. It was not enough for Sallie. Indeed, from her new position on the boards, she probably saw herself as neither powerful nor free, neither in command of the necessities and realities that other people must live with, nor gracefully (or even disastrously) floating above them, but, rather, as humiliatingly dependent on the largesse of her *pater familias*. She wrote later: "[W]e rich women are uniquely handicapped in defending our rights, which may seem to belong to us only because of the charitable instincts of fathers and brothers. These rights are not rights but favors." She was talking about rights to power, and not just power over her trust-fund wealth (which in any case she soon discovered she had). She had wanted to be book editor of the papers, as her mother had been. She had got the job, but only after asking her father to intercede for her with her brother. Barry junior had objected to giving her that "right" (or "favor"), on the grounds that the papers already had a book editor, someone who had been awarded the post on her merits, not her birth.

Sallie's position on the boards also gave her to see the dark side of all that dazzling imagery of feudalism with which people like Theodore White loved to adorn families like hers. Her grandfather, she realized, had created a kingdom in which women were as submerged, at once included and subordinate, as ever the bourgeoisie was in the Old Regime: "We are not seen as individuals, because we are not there to be heard," she wrote. "And as a family's determination to pass on great wealth depends on exclusions of many kinds, depends, in fact, on its ability to set up and maintain a kingdom inside a democracy, the exclusion of women, who tend to see and hear too much, becomes crucial to the survival of the family and its institutions."

Adam Smith contributed something to her thinking as well. She complained of inefficiency: of "dividend payments lower than the current rate of interest," of "carefully selected trustees," and of trust funds whose "corpus" could be so tied up as to benefit children, "enriching them after our deaths." She spoke as if her share in the family estate were an "inert mass," and a badly invested one at that, which no one, least of all herself, could get at.

But in this she was quite wrong. There was nothing inert about her inheritance, and it had come to her in a way that nicely combined Smithian values of the free market and Jeffersonian values of independence. There were no hobbling entailments on it. No laws or wills or testaments, no iron-fisted *patres,* no George III, mandated her dependence on her family's kingdom, only her family's Old Money history and the traditions of loyalty and gratitude in which she had been bred. Thanks to Jefferson and Smith, she was freer than either of them had been—as free as Huck Finn to light out for the territories, and as free as a self-made man to take her money with her. In 1985, she decided to do both.

In the end, the struggle between her and her brother came down to the difference between the $32 million she wanted for her stock and the $26 million he was willing to pay for it. She denied that she was trying to destroy her brother's "stewardship" of the family domain. She admired the papers editorially, she said, and she harbored no subversive designs on her family's control. She simply stood on her rights to liquidate her share of the estate. She planned to use the cash to set up a foundation for Kentucky women in the arts, and if she intended to name the foundation after her step-grandmother, the little seamstress whose money had enabled the Binghams to enter history, why, she meant no more by that than a trope of poetic justice. All she sought for herself, really, was her freedom and her price.

Her brother might have been delighted to give her the freedom, but he balked at the price. Why he did so was puzzling. Professionals advised him that Sallie's demands were fair enough and that the family could well afford to buy her out. He still refused. "Winston Churchill said that wars are won by survivors," he told the press. "That's true of families, too. The survivors have got to move in and got to take over and got to do their damnedest, or one tragedy can wipe out a family tradition." His waxed RAF mustache, his regimentally correct suits, his flawlessly shined shoes, all spoke of loyalty and sacrifice dictating a life's course, keeping him going in spite of pain and discouragement. Or perhaps it was simply that he had concluded, like so many princes before him, that his ordeals entitled him to possess not only a kingdom but truth and justice as well.

With the battle deadlocked between Sallie and Barry junior, the balance of power was held by their father, as majority stockholder. Reluctantly he decided to liquidate the estate. In 1986, it was sold, piecemeal, for a total of around $450 million. The newspapers alone, the material base of their lordship, brought $300 million. That was the highest bid, and it came from the publicly owned, professionally managed Gannett Company. The losing bidder was the family-dominated Washington Post Company, which failed to bring the *Courier* and *Times* into its family of newspapers by a shortfall of about $50 million.

The Bingham holdings carved up, as estate lawyers say, into six major blocks of money. The senior Barry Binghams were to take about $106 million. The two children of Worth Bingham, Clara and Robert, twenty-two and nineteen years old, were to divide about $42.9 million. The junior Barry Binghams, with two girls, Emily and Molly, were to get about $45.6 million. Sallie, her three sons, and the Mary Lily Flagler Bingham foundation-to-be, were to share about $55.2 million. The family of Eleanor Bingham Miller were to have about $55.8 million. In addition, about $84.5 million was to go into a generation-skipping trust fund established by the family founder, to be dispersed to his surviving grandchildren (Barry junior, Sallie, and Eleanor) on the death of their parents. All these funds, of course, would come on top of whatever assets—diversified portfolios of stock, real estate, paintings, and so forth—the family members had acquired over the years with their unearned annual incomes. With the estate finally settled, no inertness would remain. All would be lively, liquid, movable wealth—the way it's supposed to be in a liberal, entrepreneurial society, and the way it is for most inheritors of Old Money.

But on 9 January 1986, the day the Bingham family enterprise was offered for sale on the free market, the chief concern of the two male Binghams appeared to be the future of the "traditions and principles," as one of them put it, of their two newspapers. In his written statement to the press, Barry senior tried to be reassuring. His metaphors seemed designed to suggest that the values he espoused could be transferred: "Our family roots in the community and the state are too deep to sever. We are determined to pass along the papers ... to owners who can be counted on to operate them at high levels of journalistic and civic responsibility. ... we trust that they will strive in their own way to strengthen the traditions we cherish." His words managed to imply that what he was doing with his family's inheritance was simply a bequest. He wasn't selling it for money; he was just going to "pass" it "along."

His son took a less complacent view. His statement accused his father of one of the most terrible acts in Old Money's code of honorable behavior: outright and deliberate disloyalty. "While my father has kind words to say for my stewardship ... ," Barry junior declared, "[i]t is difficult not to view [his] action as a betrayal of the traditions and principles which I have sought to perpetuate."

Immediate nonfamily comment on the dissolution was generally more restrained than Barry junior's in the matter of blame and more pessimistic than Barry senior's in the matter of traditions and principles. Many thought of the various benefits the Binghams had instituted at the papers over the years. Day care, maternity *and* paternity leaves, job sharing, all the benefits of a nurturing company culture were in place on the Bingham estate before they became the fashion elsewhere. Other people mentioned the company's extraordinary generosity to the Louisville community and the state of Kentucky. Five percent of the papers' pretax profits were each year set aside for "charitable giving." Reporters and editors recalled the budgetary generosity that their profession believes is necessary to maintain a paper's reputation for well-written, thorough, and extensive coverage of the news, and to keep it in the running for Pulitzer Prizes. It is a generosity that often requires financial sacrifice: ample space for editorial matter even when the advertising isn't there to pay for it; hiring policies that emphasize depth of human resources; editorial management policies that give plenty of time and discretion to reporters in the field; layout designs that are attractive (not vulgar); and of course nationally competitive salaries to attract the best practitioners in the industry. The

Binghams had always been ready, it was said, to sacrifice whatever was required to make their papers great. They could afford it, of course. The sacrifices might not even be sacrifices, economically speaking, but long-term investments that would eventually bring handsome returns.

The question was whether Gannett, a professionally managed, publicly held company, could afford the same practices. The answer seemed to be that it could not. However high or low Gannett's reputation is in the journalistic profession, however well or badly its newspapers carry out their "civic responsibility," what counts most at the end of the day is their reputation among money managers and their responsibility to their investors. Gannett has a high reputation in the investor community, among other things for rigorous cost control. In Rochester, New York, for example, the chain has two papers, with a combined circulation comparable to the Binghams' two Louisville papers. The difference is that the Rochester papers, with news staffs of around 200, earn profits of about 20 percent, while the Louisville papers, with news staffs of 337, in their next-to-last year of Bingham owner-management earned profits of 12.6 percent. The suspicion was that under professional managers and public owners, many of the employees on the former Bingham estate would be lucky to hold on to their jobs, never mind their paternity leaves and nationally competitive salaries.

A more significant issue in the imagination of Old Money was the regard in which the professionals and the public would hold their new property. The Binghams, the Old Rich said, held their newspapers in a very special regard that was unlikely to be duplicated by Gannett. No one was specific about the nature of this peculiar way of holding property, what its values are or where they come from. As one observer put it, the Binghams "consistently gave up profit when it interfered with principle or quality." Such a comment could be understood differently: "If it weren't for their money, they would have had to bend the principles and cheat on the quality just like everyone else." As I've said, nothing is easier in a commercial culture than to subtract a rich man's powers, including his moral powers, from his personal account and to credit them to his money.

Other comments on this special regard that Binghams and other Old Money families supposedly have for their property focused on the antiquity of the family and on its breeding. Their newspapers, said one longtime retainer of the family, Norman Isaacs, were like "damn few other newspapers: old family independence and the idea of public service. You don't get much of that." Isaacs's notion of independence, needless to say, implies little of what Thomas Jefferson had in mind in the Declaration, or in his long struggle against the evils of entail. Indeed, "old family independence" owes everything to a refusal of the sort of independence promised in the Declaration, and to an acceptance of entail.

Again, much depends on the nature of the estate. The inheritor of merely moneyed Old Money comes into something like a perfection of Jeffersonian independence: a wealth-generated freedom that his class may fear, and his rivals hope, will spin him out into empty space. Yet if the Old Money be grounded in a functional estate, in a working relationship with society, then this freedom can look like something else altogether: a wealth-protected independence of the corrupting exigencies of promotion and self-promotion, above the traffic in popularity. This is what passes for Tocqueville's "aristocratic liberty" in America. This is what, as Isaacs said, you "don't get much of." It is an independence of the tyranny of consumers—also known as the discipline of the marketplace—whether arrayed as consumers of things, of people (in the form of political candidates, for example), or of ideas. It is, again, fuck-you money.

But fuck-you money with a social conscience. Something like that is almost certainly what Norman Isaacs means by "the idea of public service." And behind that idea is another: that the Binghams' independence frees them to consult their own conscience and imagination in formulating their notions of what constitutes the public good. Their stand on desegregation, for example, a favorable one, was an egregious instance of the family's independence of public opinion on a matter concerning the public's own good. The papers' support for desegregation in the 1960s aroused fear and anger among middle- and working-class white Kentuckians. Stones were thrown through the newspapers' office windows, and harsh things were said about the Binghams personally. They were the things that angry, frightened (and in this instance racist) people usually say about those who tell them what to do without having to do it themselves. The Binghams favored the desegregation of schools, but they'd never sent their own children to public schools; they were prigs, cowards, weaklings. This is the common run of insults thrown at the hereditary rich, and the insults fell harmless at their feet. Secure in the knowledge that they were right, secure in so many other ways as well, the family held fast to their idea of the public good.

What is lost in a revolution like the one that severed the Bingham line in Louisville is not primarily a voice for this or that cause, party, or policy. Such losses occur, obviously. The Hodding Carter family sold out their progressive Delta-Times Democrat in Greenville, Mississippi—apparently without a qualm, for $20 million—to the Freedom Group, a small chain of newspapers owned by another family, the Hoileses, whose founder once attacked public education as socialistic. But it's quite conceivable that since then Gannett has picked up a Hoiles-like paper somewhere and turned its editorial pages in a slightly more progressive direction, or, as the professional manager would put it, "repositioned the editorial product to appeal to a broader base of readers." In the contests of ideas, losses and gains may even out. In any event, the days are gone when the head of a large newspaper chain can boast, as E. W. Scripps once did, that his editorial command makes him "at least 2 percent reponsible for all that is good or ill in the management of this great nation."

Then what was lost in Louisville, or, for that matter, at Richardson-Vicks? Two things, in the view of Old Money, both of them good for the public. One is the voice of history—history, to be sure, of a very old-fashioned kind: history as biography (and autobiography), moving to the pace and powers of individual human beings and not to the impersonal dictates of markets and masses. The good lost here is fundamentally aesthetic, as so many Old Money values are. In Old Money family businesses, there is a drama of idiosyncratic, even arbitrary, personality that unfolds in an intelligible narrative of human actions, not a demographic study of customer satisfaction. The other loss is perhaps more substantial. It is the loss of an object of *noblesse oblige*.

No figment of the Old Money imagination leads a more fugitive existence in this New World than the principle of *noblesse oblige*. Only three times in this century, in the time of Theodore Roosevelt, of Eleanor and Franklin Roosevelt, and of John F. Kennedy, has it managed to get some purchase on imaginations other than Old Money's.

The whole idea is deeply offensive to popular democratic ideology, almost deliberately so. *Noblesse oblige, richesse permet*. The invidious comparison, if taken seriously, could be devastating to the moral reputation of New Money, even to the morality of desiring to make New Money. Moreover, defenders of the idea often willfully confuse the *noblesse* that is a class and the *noblesse* that is a human quality. This leads far too easily to a justification of "aristocratical government," or worse. Yet, in fact, no concept better accounts for the various policies that the Binghams put into effect at the Louisville *Courier* and *Times*, the benefits, salaries, charitable giving, sacrifices of profit to principle and quality. A whole medley of sentiments and impulses and convictions lay behind them, including the gift ethos, the idea of public service, paternalistic care and maternalistic nurturance, and political and economic expediency. Summed up, this is *noblesse oblige.*

Furtive though it must be, hiding for the most part under the more acceptable ideal of public service, *noblesse oblige* occupies a spot very close to Old Money's heart. Mentors of the class especially like it: For one thing, it seems to accommodate that ancient Old Money endeavor to turn an inheritance of wealth into a true privilege, not just an advantage, in life. Second, *oblige* adds a strong supplementary strand of moral fiber, and a rather flattering romantic strand at that. New Money and No Money may totter along under the stick of Necessity, straining for the carrot of Self. Old Money dances to the music of Obligation.

In most Old Money families, however, there's a serious difficulty with *noblesse oblige,* the same difficulty that plagues their yearning for generational continuity. This is the lack of an objective correlative. Obligation to what? The answer is easy when there's a family enterprise to be taken care of. Obligation then attaches to the time-honored task of conserving the patrimony—the business. Sometimes the impact and scope of the patrimony—and hence of the obligation—will encompass the whole nation, indeed the whole world. And when this is the case, Old Money rises to extraordinary heights of *noblesse.* A classic example was provided by Eugene Meyer in a speech he gave on 5 March 1935, two years after he bought the Washington *Post*:

> The first mission of a newspaper is to tell the truth as nearly as the truth can be ascertained.
>
> The newspaper shall tell ALL the truth so far as it can learn it, concerning the important affairs of America and the world.
>
> As a disseminator of news, the paper shall observe the decencies that are obligatory upon a private gentleman.
>
> What it prints shall be fit reading for the young as well as the old.
>
> The newspaper's duty is to its readers and to the public at large, and not to the private interests of its owners.

In the pursuit of truth, the newspaper shall be prepared to make sacrifices of its material fortunes, if such a course be necessary for the public good.

The newspaper shall not be the ally of any special interest, but shall be fair and free and wholesome in its outlook on public affairs and public men.

Everything has come together here—well-bred graces and virtues, a readiness to sacrifice, a social conscience—all solidly grounded, but by no means unattractively immersed, in a real economic estate.

But for most inheritors of wealth, a patrimony like the Washington *Post* only begs the question. What is Old Money to do with its *noblesse oblige* when all it has to be obliged to is money? How can capitalists be held subject to the moral constraints of *noblesse oblige?* In short, what is Barry Bingham, Jr., to do now?

Old Money comes up at this juncture with the figure of the trustee— the trustee, in the first place, of one's family's capital. There has always been a touch of reluctance, even sullenness, in Old Money's admiration for the capitalist trustee—strangely so, given the part he plays in maintaining their class. Perhaps he's the less honored for being the more important. He is, after all, a persistent reminder of the most demoralizing suspicion that can come to an inheritor of wealth, the suspicion that without the invisible water wings of his unearned income, he would sink.

There are other faint shadows on the capital trustee. It is true that he deals in a "staple" at least as vital to the operations of society as grain and news. But it is a staple not easily assimilated to the more aristocratic forms of Old Money's social imagination. Capital is too protean, too liquid, too coolly abstract to relate to it, so to speak, nobly. To command capital properly calls on human qualities that Old Money often finds unattractive: calculation, secretiveness, skepticism. To Old Money tastes, the capital trustee must frequently come too close to the moral and aesthetic ugliness of the marketplace. Beneficiaries would sometimes rather he kept out of sight, like the money he cares for. Yet if the heart of Old Money's imagination is aristocratic, its head is patrician. Somewhere behind each grand and noble gesture, deed, or service there is a patrician standing guard over the well-diversified portfolio that forfends the possibility that the family should ever have to be self-made. He is the steward of their freedom, the conservator of their good fortune. In a capitalist society, it could hardly be otherwise.

For *noblesse oblige,* however, capital trustees need some form of wealth that has a more public dimension to be obliged to than the capital they hold in trust for their families. They find it in two forms. One is in such huge quantities of capital that its trusteeship necessarily has public consequences. The other is in the form of treasures—a child's, a family's, a pirate's, or a nation's.

The key figure here, the beau ideal of a specifically patrician *noblesse oblige* in the service of capital and treasure, is J. P. Morgan (1837–1913), the son of J. S. Morgan, a Hartford financier who before the Civil War established a highly successful international bank, based in London. (One of the elder Morgan's associates was the father of Endicott Peabody.) All patrician children of Old Money who take up a legacy of capital trusteeship, like David Rockefeller, for example, more or less consciously become the heirs of J. P. Morgan. Except for his great rival, Theodore Roosevelt, no man in the history of Old Money in America has been of greater inspiration to his class.

Old Money Society, the women especially, always remembered Mr. Morgan's nose, as veinous and colorful as a maple leaf in autumn. When Mr. Morgan came to tea, little girls were always cautioned by their mothers not to notice his nose. But they always did, of course, and inevitably one of them would say, "Do you take milk or lemon with your nose, Mr. Morgan?" But everyone else in the founding age of Old Money remembered his eyes. They were like my great-grandfather's eyes, "glinting black"; like John D. Rockefeller's, which "took you all in." They glitter out of Edward Steichen's portrait of him like a fox's. Lincoln Steffens went to see him one day on Wall Street without an appointment (anyone could do this, apparently: the great man worked in a cubicle on the main floor, in full public view) and ever afterward he remembered the terrible "glare" of the banker's eyes.

His performance equaled his presence. In the memory of Old Money, Morgan was not just another big dealer in the financial markets; he was a stern but understanding *pater familias,* who took the whole economy of the country as his "little state." More than Theodore Roosevelt, and to most of their social equals far more properly, Morgan imposed discipline on the reckless New Money of his day, organizing fratricidal rivals into smoothly interdependent combines of productivity, which soon dominated the world. Old Money likes to recall that wherever the great banker chose to exert his influence, on the railroads, on the steel industry, it was to bring reason, order, and some measure of probity to the destructive competitions of immoderately selfish men. He was a gentleman, born and bred in the courtesies and values of the attractive life, and he surrounded himself with gentlemen. To this day the various banking institutions that bear his family's name continue to favor the products of St. Midas schools, Harvard, and the Porcellian and AD clubs. He passed on the patrician traditions he had inherited and embodied, not only to his younger associates but also to his son, J. P. Morgan, Jr., who succeeded him at the bank in 1913. The son spoke for the father when he summed up their code of business ethics: "Do your work; be honest; keep your word; help when you can; be fair."

Again and again, the patrician strain in Old Money returns to the elder Morgan's matchless combination of personal and institutional powers, on the one hand, and the tastes and values of a gentleman on the other. The fascination is particularly noticeable in an elegant popular biography by Frederick Lewis Allen, a Groton and Harvard graduate who was for many years editor of *Harper's Magazine*. In Allen's exposition of Morgan's career, the "kingly" powers of the man are seen as at once redeeming and being redeemed by social sensitivities and generous impulses, which ordinarily have no place in the business world. In Morgan, the gentlemanly ideal finds an incarnation that is of decisive consequence. Toward the end of his life, reluctantly testifying in Congress as to the source of his great power, he was asked:

> "Is not commercial credit based primarily upon money or property?"
> "No, sir," said Morgan; "the first thing is character."
> "Before money or property?"
> "Before money or anything else. Money cannot buy it. . . . Because a man I do not trust could not get money from me on all the bonds in Christendom."

There was plenty of room here for *noblesse oblige,* even for sacrifice. What Old Money likes best to remember are the occasions when Morgan "saved" the United States economy from disaster. As Allen recounts the first (and least complicated) drama, all during 1894 there had been what President Grover Cleveland called "an endless chain" of gold withdrawals. By January 1895, the run on gold was continuing at such a rate that the Treasury would be exhausted within a few weeks. Floating a public bond issue was a possible solution, but risky inasmuch as it had been done only a few months before; a second issue might reveal the government's peril, thereby panicking note holders into more withdrawals. Besides, as Morgan told the President, it was too late for a second issue.

He spoke to Cleveland, according to Allen, with "tremendous certainty," and there was no question about who was in charge of their meeting. Cleveland saw nothing in Morgan that was dubious, he recalled later, only "a man of large business comprehension and of remarkable knowledge and prescience ... of clear-sighted, far-seeing patriotism." Rapidly a plan was devised whereby in exchange for Treasury bonds the government would buy gold from a syndicate headed by Morgan. The President had only one last request: the banker's personal guarantee that the gold he proposed to purchase would not go the way of all the gold before it—to Europe. After a moment's thought, Morgan committed himself to shore up the credit of his country. His syndicate made a profit of about $250,000—"a modest recompense indeed," notes the biographer, "for saving the credit of the United States."

Trusteeship of capital could reach no higher height than this, and would not after 1907, the year when Morgan again, in Allen's words, "exercise[d] the functions of a central banking system" to save the credit of his country. But from then on, despite the best efforts of my great-grandfather to institutionalize Morgan's paternalistic role in a sort of private Federal Reserve system, it was the obligation of the United States government to save the credit of banks, not of bankers to save the credit of the United States government. This is not to say that an Old Money banker's public services were thenceforth doomed to be negligible. No one could believe such a thing who contemplated the career of David Rockefeller, whose foreign (loan) policy of "saving" the credit of other nations' governments, politically and financially dubious though it may now appear, was an indispensable adjunct to his country's; or who followed the activities of Felix Rohatyn in "saving" the credit of New York City. But never again after Morgan would a private banker so dominate American capital markets that he could deal with a President of the United States, as Roosevelt said of him, as one "rival operator" with another.

Even if banking had been diminished in its opportunities for service or trusteeship (or for setting the gentlemanly tone), J. P. Morgan's career would still be exemplary, for another form of wealth called forth his magnanimity quite as much as capital, and it does the same for those who follow in his footsteps. This wealth is treasure. J. P. Morgan is as towering a figure in the collection and care of treasure as he is in the collection and care of capital.

Old Money hasn't yet come up with a neat definition of treasure. Nor has anyone else, that I know of. The British economist Roy Harrod describes something he calls "oligarchic wealth"; the American economist Fred Hirsch argued for something he called "positional [in the sense of social position] wealth"; and in Old Money's notion of treasure there is something of both these concepts. A treasure can be a good or a service; a building or a landscape; a work of art, a performance, a tradition, an institution—or a human being. It is the "real" part of the patrimonial estate. But what the treasure has to have, beyond "reality," is a certain moral and aesthetic elevation. A treasure is or should be of disinterested delight and enjoyment, an object of love. A treasure is something that should be thought of, if only metaphorically, as a gift—a gift of God, of Nature, of history, or of men, whichever agent seems most plausible and persuasive.

Treasures are always limited in quantity, and most are in some sense unique. Two of the most treasured treasures of Old Money, for example, are Old World manuscripts, books, prints, and drawings, which Morgan especially fancied, and New World wildernesses and creatures of the wild, the particular love of Theodore Roosevelt. The Old World produced only so many illuminated manuscripts, and by the same token, Nature's God made only so much coastline in Maine, only so many Badlands in the Dakotas, only so many mountain ranges in Nevada—they, too, vulnerable to random depredations. Likewise the gifts of men in history. To list only those institutions that Morgan served: only one Harvard has come down to us out of the past, one Metropolitan Museum, one Metropolitan Opera, one New York Yacht Club, one Wadsworth Atheneum in Hartford, one Cathedral of St. John the Divine in New York, one St. Paul's Cathedral in London, one American Academy in Rome. (There was also only one American Museum of Natural History and one Groton School, institutions more often associated with Roosevelt than with Morgan, but that Morgan also served, the first as treasurer, the second as founding trustee.) That was Morgan's list. Any patrician scion of Old Money has his or her own.

A treasure, in Old Money's view, must also have the power to transform anyone who sees it, anyone who gives to it some measure of his or her energy and imagination. Aesthetically, morally, even socially, a treasure changes the way people think and feel about the world and themselves. In this sense, the prospects in Roosevelt's national parks are no different from the contents of Morgan's library, or from a Groton training. The transformation must be for the better, obviously; toward the good; and for an Old Money class in a predominantly New Money, market-driven society, a change toward the good is almost always a change *back*. Forward change, up-and-down change, technological progress and social mobility, the ceaseless turbulence of markets and the endless hustle of selves—all these transformations are what Old Money has daily to command, to rise above, at least to ignore. In their treasures, therefore, the Old Rich seek to be transformed by the immutable, to be renewed by the old, to be changed by the changeless. That's why it is usually only on the margins of the class—women, or among relatively New Money—that there are people who collect, or feel any sense of trusteeship for, contemporary art. Contemporary art represents change; it moves to the moods of fashion and its movements are measured, for all to see, in markets. What Old Money demands of treasure is just the opposite: that it mirror and confirm the central faith of the class curriculum, which is that some things endure, *must* endure.

Inevitably, then, the obligations of treasure-trusteeship carry with them opportunities to exercise two dramatic impulses trained in the class ordeals: rescue and self-sacrifice. Walter Benjamin maintained that the true collector redeems his acquisitiveness from avarice by his quixotic intention to save the objects of his desire from utility, the usual, vulgar fate of desired objects. Benjamin also argued that the most agreeable way of coming into possession of things is by inheritance. The Old Rich treasure trustees would not contest this proposition. A social system has grown up under their auspices that accomplishes both the rescue from utility and the possession by inheritance. The system works at two levels: the basic private patrimonialization usually begins with the family founder, who collects treasures for himself and for the inheritance of his descendants; in the more extended form, the treasures are gathered up and given over from the system of use and exchange, an economic system, to be made safe in a system of gift and curatorial care, a social system.

Treasure being what it is, and the basic obligations of trusteeship being what they are, it should be obvious why Old Money considers itself especially well qualified to assume this form of *noblesse oblige*.

Statistics have no index of Old Money, of course, but some figures are suggestive of it. A 1969 survey of 156 museum trustees, for instance, revealed that 60 percent were graduates of Ivy League colleges and 40 percent were Episcopalians. More recent figures would undoubtedly show a loss for the Episcopalians and a gain for the Jews, but probably no loss for Old Money as a whole. Trusteeships are also famously hereditary, at least as hereditary as family businesses. Even in a city like New York, a place famously hazardous to old fortunes, as late as 1979 the board of the Metropolitan Museum reserved seats for the Morgan family, the Astor family, the Whitney family, the Rockefeller family, and (the so-called media seat) the Sulzberger family. Morgan's seat was in its fourth generation in the line of descent. In a smaller city like Providence or Seattle, say, every cultural, charitable, and environmental organization will be held in trust by predominantly Old Money hands.

As usual, it must be pointed out that they can afford it. The costs of trusteeship are not so great for the hereditary rich as they are for the self-making. But even if they were, there is always that ancient longing in Old Money beneficiaries actively to welcome a cost as a sign of their reality and as a rein on their freedom. Trusteeship is one of the few things they can do that allows them to share in the work of the larger society without becoming part of it—indeed, while still remaining in many ways antagonistic to it.

Beyond that, Old Money's claim to trusteeship rests on the obvious congruence, even identity, of the ambitions it has for its families and the needs it perceives for its treasures. Old Money's imagination understands treasure in the same way it understands the family, that primary treasure of the class: as an entity that describes, or should describe, a more or less smooth line of descent through time. Like families and family businesses, a treasure has a history, and Old Money families are practiced in history. They know that history holds far more hope for immortality in beautiful objects, sublime landscapes, and useful institutions than it does in rich families. Who better, therefore, to hold things in trust than those who hold themselves in trust? The duty of preservation is best served when compounded with a long history of self-preservation.

This is true, Old Money would argue, even when the treasure to be preserved is in no way its own. Yet there is a sense in which the treasure often *is* its own, and a sense, too, in which the class can turn this circumstance to advantage in advancing its special claim to trusteeship. For example, one of Morgan's recent successors as a trustee of the Metropolitan Opera (as it happens, Tommy Hitchcock's step-daughter-in-law), Mrs. Alexander Laughlin, Judy Walker, as she was, once remarked of Anthony Addison Bliss's fine (as she thought) stewardship of that frequently troubled treasure: "Tony Bliss grew up in that house [the Metropolitan] and has a real feeling for it. He knows its moods, the way you know your own home—the maid, the butler, who needs jollying." It was unfortunate, of course, that in her first condescension to the press (a duty to which Morgan would have taught her to give short shrift), Mrs. Laughlin raised Old Money's famed obtuseness to new heights of sublimity. Not long after she spoke, the Met was brought to its knees by a striking musicians' union, which could hardly decide whether to be more offended by Bliss's treating it like a servant or by his paying it like one.

Nevertheless, Mrs. Laughlin's mortifying remark does express a key presumption of Old Money's claim on trusteeships, the presumption of precedence, of having been there always. It doesn't matter where *there* is—the Met or Northeast Harbor, the Morgan Library or the Grand Tetons, Harvard College or a landmark building on New York's Upper East Side—Old Money was there before anyone else. The claim to precedence is also, as we know, a claim to knowledge, to past perfect knowledge, to *gnosis*.

If this sounds preposterous, as it usually does to Old Money's chief rivals for trusteeships, professionals and *nouveaux riches,* the class will fall back on feeling, the "real" feeling that Mrs. Laughlin said was Tony Bliss's. What is that feeling? It is gratitude, generosity, attachment—a congeries of sentiments sustained by the culture of the gift and often summed up as loyalty. This is the class's most persistent claim to sit in trusteeship over treasures—its loyalty to the treasure, to the cause of its survival in history. All the values of the Old Rich are mobilized, perhaps even justified, in trusteeship. Invidious as the graces and virtues may be, they are social values, and nothing could be more social than the milieu of the trustee. This is true in at least two ways. One of them is what John Jay Chapman expressed in a letter he wrote to Dr. Drury of St. Paul's, that "*social life* [is] at the bottom of every form of art" (his italics) and that America's lamentable "artistic incapacity" is the fault of the "deadness and feebleness of our social life." In this Old Money view, it's not just the invisible, all too lively hands of the market that must be kept away from the treasures held in trust; it is also the dead hands of professionals, experts, scholars, pedants. Chapman went farther in his loathing of professional scholars than most beneficiaries of Old Money would dare; he could afford it, being not only the social equal of the beneficiaries but the intellectual superior of many professional scholars. Hidden away in the upper class's special claim to trusteeship is the secret conviction that the best caretakers of priceless things are priceless people—people who are in some sense the social equals of the things they've been charged to preserve.

Of course, there must be more to it than that, as J. P. Morgan would have been quick to insist. There must be money. The best defense against the enemies of treasure is money. And Old Money people find as many reserved seats on boards of trustees as they do because they know, gnostically, how to socialize money. Their social knowledge of where their kind of money is, their past perfect familiarity with those who have it, the ease with which they can call on it, more than makes up for their relative poverty, as individuals, with respect to New Money. They can also claim that their presence on a board is extremely attractive to New Money as well. Nothing so encourages the generosity of a hesitant *nouveau riche* benefactor than the prospect of dining with Douglas Dillon or Brooke Astor. Old Money trustees stand in the receiving line of the gift culture, so to speak, giving to the self-made givers a gracious promise of social equality to come. It is fitting and useful that they be there.

Chapman proposed St. Francis's idea of heaven as the sort of social life in which the arts would flower, a place "all glowing and jolly, merry, joyous." His choice of saint was inspired: St. Francis the nobleman, well-born and well-bred; St. Francis, whose vow of poverty, as enjoined on the order he founded, came to be underwritten by the first trust fund in history; St. Francis the patron saint of conservationists and environmentalists, the trustees of Nature, Old Money's most favored object of *noblesse oblige*. God's more obvious works have always attracted the wealth, wisdom, and work of Old Money, and the root of this concern is as social as any other. The conservationism of Theodore Roosevelt's generation of the class was born of their trips "out West," but conservationism would have stagnated in nostalgia if it hadn't been kept vigorous and focused in such gentlemanly clubs as the Boone and Crockett—which required of new members that they shoot an animal on each of the five continents—the Explorers Club, and so on down the generations to the environmentalist associations of today, such as the Audubon Society, the Nature Conservancy, the Wilderness Society, the Sierra Club, and the like. Many of these groups are not simply social but *invidiously* social. Just as smoothly as the social foundations of the arts and private education (the visiting committees of museums, for example; or the alumni and parent associations of Harvard and the St. Midas schools) in time confer Old Money status on New Money, and confirm it in legitimate or adopted beneficiaries, so many of the environmental groups do. The roots of Old Money environmentalism go back to the most fiercely protected of all the treasures of Old Money, their summer places on the coast of Maine, their "camps" in the Adirondacks, their ranches out West. It was an inspiration of the same order as Chapman's that prompted Gary Trudeau, an adopted child of St. Paul's and Yale, to give his endearingly dithery upper-class congresswoman, Lacey Davenport, an upper-class husband, Dick, whose only passion in life seems to be for wild birds. In this couple's social circles, the care and feeding of birds is as noble an obligation for Mr. Davenport as is the care and feeding of constituents for Mrs. Davenport. St. Francis would have approved.

It isn't only in its milieu that treasure trusteeship is social; its objects are social as well. Treasures in Old Money's view have a public dimension, like newspapers and capital, if only because they are the focus of acquisitive desire. They also have a private dimension, of course: the solitude created by their aura of pricelessness, signifying their transcendence of earthly markets. And what trustees do, in essence, is to help determine the boundary between the two dimensions. (Trustees have never been the only factors in this historic task—there are laws and, increasingly in the last generations, professional managers, many of Old Money background.) In the last analysis, however, the boundary is the issue—a notional circle whose circumference is determined by whatever balance of fear and magnanimity possesses the trustees at the center, and by whatever balance of deference and desire agitates the public on the periphery.

For the trustees, there's no question on which side the balance of feeling falls. It is fear. In the whole history of Old Money stewardship and the whole patrician strain of *noblesse oblige,* fear is the dominant emotion. Nor is there any question about the source of the fear. Like their model Morgan, like my great-grandfather, patricians fear the public; by the same token, patrician trustees fear for treasure at the hands of the public. Good *God,* here they come! The public as voracious consumer, as follower of fashion, as vulgarian and ingrate, as the bully boy of democracy, as a worshiper of celebrity and a truckler to

professionalism. The public, in short, as a middle class. Phobia is not
far behind.

The patrician's fear of the people has little to do with a self-maker's
fear of being confused with the people he came from. Patrician fear of
the people depends on a quick and constant sympathy with the objects,
environments, and institutions whose fate patrician trustees believe to
be bound up with their own. If they don't want "millions" of people
in their museums, parks, or schools, it's for the same reason that they
don't want millions of people trampling their lawns or poring over the
books in their libraries or fouling up the plumbing in the big house
overlooking the bay. These things remind them of change, which reminds them of the fragility of their Old Money project. But above all,
these things are ugly. Fundamentally, the patrician trustee's fear of the
public is the anticipatory revulsion of the easily wounded narcissist.

Their fear, however, is contested by their magnanimity. Where it
comes from is hard to say. Perhaps it emerges from that "deeper" impulse which Marc Bloch described as moving the lords of the Middle
Ages to share even their privileges with their vassals:

> In a society in which so many individuals were at one and the same
> time commended men and masters, there was a reluctance to admit
> that if one of them, as a vassal, had secured some advantage to him-
> self he could, as a lord, refuse it to those who were bound to his
> person by a similar form of dependence. From the old Carolingian
> capitulary to the [Magna Carta], the classic foundation of English
> "liberties," this sort of equality in privilege, descending smoothly
> from top to bottom of the scale, was to remain one of the most fertile
> sources of feudal custom.

Perhaps, rather, their magnanimity has its source in the even more
ancient reflex of hospitality; perhaps it lies in the brighter side of narcissism, its expansive vanity. But wherever it comes from, Old Money's
sense of obligation to its treasures is touched with generosity. Aristocrats and demagogues, types frequently united in the same person,
accuse patricians of confusing their prerogatives as trustees of things
with the tyrannical rights of owners over things. But this accusation is
usually false. The circles that patrician trustees seek to maintain
around their treasures are never utterly closed. They cannot be. They
are open to the future, to lines of descent and succession, and they are
not, as Orestes Brownson shrewdly observed so long ago, individualistic. They are social.

Nevertheless, in the endless struggle over the boundary around the treasure, the instinct of patrician trustees is to be conservative. Ideally, Old Money trusteeship is a sorting and matching system in which each particular form of treasure gets the trustees whose balance of fear and magnanimity, or squeamishness and hospitality, is most appropriate to its preservation and enjoyment. In practice, however, it is rarely clear what the proper balance should be.

But some things are more clear than others. Seldom in history has patrician trusteeship had to suffer more vulgar, more insistent, or more destructive offenses against its ethos than during the administration of Ronald Reagan. In his presidency, a secretary of the interior gleefully opened the national parks and forests to the marketplace, an EPA administrator exposed the environment to further pollution, and a secretary of education heaped ridicule on Harvard. Toward the end, Reagan went so far as to support a withdrawal of the gift of free admission to the Statue of Liberty, the only *national* symbol of magnanimity, hospitality, and giftedness in the United States. This nauseating performance was a perfect example of what happens when the entrepreneurial imagination runs amok, conscious of neither society nor posterity.

Other conservationist issues are more difficult to judge. The best-known example is the question of how to respond to the deluge of appreciative desire for the fine arts—no trickle-down, this—that daily inundates America's museums with millions and millions of people. At one level, the astonishing popularity of beautiful artifacts of the gift culture is gratifying, calling forth a measure of magnanimity from even the most jealous of patrician trustees. (To aristocratic directors of these museums, of course, men like Thomas Hoving and J. Carter Brown, popularity is like the sound of bugles to Theodore Roosevelt, or the prospect of election to Franklin Roosevelt. It encourages them to ever greater feats of blockbusting, ever more generous shows of hospitality to the millions.) At another level, it is a disaster. In the first place, it has enormously driven up the costs of treasure trusteeship—labor costs, insurance costs, time costs, acquisition costs, and so on. Second, these rising costs have introduced an unattractive form of economic necessity into the temples of the gift. The costs have to be paid with money. Not time or talent, not "character," just money, more and more money, and this in turn has forced open an ever-growing corner of the temple to the marketplace. The money changers have had to be let in to set up shop—called, with bitter irony, the museum "gift" shop. Most dangerous of all to the J. P. Morgan tradition of trusteeship, museums have had to seek the support and protection of governments. Governments, as Reagan showed, make unreliable trustees. Governments do not often end up in the hands of gentlemen, and even when they do, as in the case of the Roosevelts and Kennedy, or as in the case of my great-grandfather's successor as the senatorial guardian of the arts, Claiborne Pell, they seem to end up in the hands of aristocrats—gentlemen who are more apt to consult the needs of their vassals than the good of their treasures.

In other areas of Old Money trusteeship, the boundary issues are not so dramatic or pressing, but just as problematic. Certain strategies of environmental protection, for example, are already causing skirmishes on the periphery that may lead to all-out warfare. Year after year, beneficiaries of Old Money and their adopted classmates have been giving thousands and thousands of acres of scenic and wilderness treasure to such trust agencies as the Nature Conservancy, the Audubon Society, the Maine Coast Heritage Trust, the (Massachusetts) Trustees of Reservations, and the like. One way of presenting this strategy is to describe it as the creation of a new system of national parks, parks too small or remote from public desire to necessitate government trusteeship. Old Money favors this presentation, for it recalls the glory days of patrician concern with the environment around the turn of the century, the days of Gifford Pinchot and his energetic patron, Theodore Roosevelt, and it plays on the themes to which the class is most responsive—voluntary sacrifice ("giving something," "giving something up"), antagonism to change and the preservation of innocence, hostility to the market, the many-generational view of time and the historical view of the public good.

But another way of describing this strategy is to call it the most flagrant attempt to reinstitute the system of entail since Thomas Jefferson got rid of it. Disregarding the fact that a stretch of coastline is now being kept wild and natural, or that a mountainside has been saved for its deepest ecological purposes, or that an island may now and forever resound to the cry of the loon, this view reminds us simply that these properties have been taken off the market, entailed, rendered (as Gustavus Myers would put it) into "inert masses" of wealth that no one will be able to make something of again.

All up and down the granite coast of Maine, in the White Mountains of New Hampshire and the Green ones of Vermont, there are towns in which parcel after parcel of sometimes prime residential land is being lost to the tax collector. The cry goes up that the summer people, not content with keeping the private sector on starvation wages, are now determined to starve the public sector as well—schools, police, fire department, and so on. Not far behind the public of local government is what might be called the rear guard of the self-made men, people on the make who want what the rich have—a house with a view of Penobscot Bay, for example. Their numbers combine with their desires to drive up the price of scenic land enormously. The land trust strategy only makes a bad situation worse, cutting down on the available shorefront, say, even as it enhances the social and economic values of shorefront property.

For the moment anyway, the land trust strategy seems safe from the covetous middle classes. Yet Old Money's treasures as a whole never are. Trusteeship requires constant vigilance, and on all fronts—the tax front, the rights front, the market front—for the initiative rests with the public. So far, the patricians have held their own and preserved, against great odds, the aura of pricelessness and the opportunities for their own disinterested delight.

What they have occasionally failed to do is to suppress the emergence of "traitors to their class"—those public-minded aristocrats sometimes produced by the Old Rich whose presumption is that *their* administration of government will be a stronger and more equitable trustee of the nation's patrimony than the private agents and agencies of the patriciate, and whose definition of the patrimony is sometimes broad enough to include, besides capital and treasure, the human resources represented by the people.

The first of these traitors was Theodore Roosevelt. If J. P. Morgan was the Silver Spoon Age's ideal type of the patrician, Roosevelt was its aristocrat. They had to clash, and not merely iconographically. By 1904, TR appeared determined to bring the corporate forces represented by Morgan, his "rival operator," under some sort of governmental control. It was for their own good, he confided to his friend Owen Wister. "They had much better accept me. . . . I am on their side. I believe in wealth. I belong to their class. They had much better accept me, instead of some Bryan who'll come along and ride over them rough shod." Wister offered Roosevelt a formulation of the problem that cast government in the role of a wise but liberal parent: the *pater,* so to speak, of the patricians. "I think the Government should allow them to protect themselves from themselves," Wister said to his old

Porcellian brother. Roosevelt eagerly seized the phrase. "'Themselves from themselves!,' he exclaimed. 'Yes. Precisely!'" Some days later (or earlier; Wister isn't sure which), the Gridiron Club staged a confrontation between Morgan and Roosevelt, which remains, as Wister recalled it, one of the great moments in the annals of Old Money.

> What hardly could have been anticipated was the dramatic climax which Roosevelt brought on, carried utterly out of himself by his own intensity. After referring to the unstable temper which he believed the country at large to be in, he came to the steps which he and his advisors were trying to take in order that confidence might be restored and general security established. As he went on, advocating and justifying [his] remedies ... he suddenly turned, walked along the table to where Pierpont Morgan sat, and shook his fist in Morgan's face, as he concluded: "And if you don't let us do this, those who will come after us will rise and bring you to ruin."

There, hypostatized in the public leader's fist and the private banker's nose, is Old Money's intramural quarrel between the aristocracy and the patriciate. Under TR, nothing more sensitive than the nose—though what a nose!—was in danger. Roosevelt asserted government's claim to a seat on the board, and from then on the claim gained grudging but growing acceptance, especially as Market Man came to see it as potentially advantageous to his own projects. The patriciate, too, came to concede the claim, but not until it was, as TR predicted it would be, ruined. It wasn't the sort of ruin he'd envisaged. No uprising of the people brought it around, only a catastrophic downfall of the market. And the rough rider of the storm was no commoner like William Jennings Bryan, but another aristocrat, of much the same background as himself—in fact, another Roosevelt.

CHAPTER SEVEN

The Prince
and the People

As long as the king lived he was fond of telling the story of
his adventures, all through, from the hour that the sentinel
cuffed him away from the palace gate till the final midnight
when he deftly mixed himself into a gang of hurrying work-
men and so slipped into the Abbey and climbed up and hid
himself in the Confessor's tomb, and then slept so long that
he came within one minute of missing the coronation altogether. He said that the frequent rehearsing of the precious
lesson kept him strong in his purpose to make its teachings
yield benefits to his people; and so, whilst his life was spared
he should continue to tell the story, and thus keep its sorrow-
ful spectacles fresh in his memory and the springs of pity
replenished in his heart.

Mark Twain, *The Prince and the Pauper*

THIRTY YEARS AFTER the clash between J. P. Morgan and
Theodore Roosevelt, there was another great rendezvous with
enmity between an Old Money aristocrat and the patrician
wing of his class. In April 1935, only halfway through Franklin Delano
Roosevelt's first term, the New Deal seemed dead in the water, with
the old skipper from Campobello, his compass spinning, apparently at
a loss over how to get it going again. The first one hundred days had
restored courage to the country; something was at last being done. The
Civilian Conservation Corps, the Public Works Administration, the
Civil Works Administration, and the Works Progress Administration

had sopped up a little unemployment around the edges, but one fifth of the work force was still idle, and the national income was still half of what it had been in 1929. Moreover, the key instruments of recovery, which Roosevelt had counted on to pull the productive system out of the slump—the NRA, the AAA, and other agencies—were under attack in the courts and in Congress; and if they went down, knowledgeable observers were saying, the administration seemed to have nothing to propose as alternatives.

Meanwhile the President himself was at sea. He was cruising on Cousin Vincent Astor's ocean-going *Nourmahal,* and no one in the whole country was more pleased to hear it than Senator Huey Long of Louisiana.

For three years, indeed for most of his forty-two years, the Kingfish had been getting himself elected to office by saying that the basic sufferings of the American people, the Depression above all, came about "because a handful of men in the United States own all the money." From this analysis the simple solution suggested itself, Share Our Wealth, and Huey had been flogging his program on the radio, in the Senate, and to Roosevelt himself. With Roosevelt he had little success, as we have seen; with the Senate even less, despite the almost pedantic solemnity, complete with display cards, with which he lectured his colleagues on the vanishing middle class. With the people, however, he was steadily gaining popularity. The same rich-baiting rhetoric that had endeared him to the folks down home in Louisiana seemed just as effective in the Middle West and West. Are the rich complaining that Share Our Wealth will cut their inheritances to a million dollars? Huey would ask. Yes, they are! "One measly, lousy, slivery million dollars? That means that if one of those birds stepped under an electric fan to cool off he wouldn't be getting but about four dollars a minute while he was doing it. That means if he went to bathe and shave, he wouldn't be but about five hundred dollars richer by the time he got his clothes back on." Why was it that Roosevelt did nothing to share the national wealth more equitably? Huey shook his head and claimed not to understand.

But he did understand, or thought he did. It was because Roosevelt did not want to redistribute *his* wealth or that of his friends. And the proof was right out there, floating around somewhere on the deep blue sea. The ship of state was a millionaire's yacht, its guest of honor a so-called aristocrat. But he was an aristocrat without a title, and the Kingfish resolved to give him one. On 22 April 1935, he rose from his seat in the Senate and acclaimed "Prince Franklin, who, when he wanted to study the problems of the Depression, had himself invited to go cruising on the yacht *Nourmahal* owned by his millionaire friend Vincent Astor, and therefore should be known as the Knight of the *Nourmahal!*"

Knight (or Prince) was not the only title Huey gave the President. He also called him "Stalin." No cruise on a yacht lay behind this sobriquet; rather, it was Roosevelt's establishment of the National Recovery Administration. If Huey was Jeffersonian-Jacksonian enough to rail against concentrations of wealth in the hands of the hereditary rich, he was also Jeffersonian-Jacksonian enough to resent the engines of that wealth being taken over by the state. Huey filibustered "Stalin"'s NRA for fifteen and a half hours, a heroic performance that actually won him some sympathy from those who might have had better reason to fear him. During the night of his filibuster, the Senate galleries were packed with socialites in ball gowns and black tie, who came to hear the rich-baiter gloss the Constitution. ("Some of 'em," Will Rogers joked later, "thought he was reviewing a new book.") But the sympathy was misplaced. Huey was no friend to the already rich, only to the would-be rich. His fundamental argument against Roosevelt was consistent: The Prince and Stalin were up to the same old trick, as he saw it. For whether Roosevelt was defending his rich friends from a just redistribution of their wealth or proposing a "communist" takeover of the means of production, he was effectively foreclosing the middle classes from their rights, as given them by the Declaration of Independence, to pursue opportunities for happiness through individual, on-your-own-two-feet self-enrichment.

"Every Man a King, No Man with a Crown," Huey's slogan, was borrowed from William Jennings Bryan, whom Theodore Roosevelt had said would ride roughshod over the rich unless they accepted him. Now thirty years later, another Old Money President was faced with this new champion of populism: a noisome little man in a white suit who wasn't content to dilute the golden patrimonies of the rich with silver but wanted to confiscate large pieces of their unearned wealth and give it to the poor. Long was probably never the threat to FDR, or to FDR's generation of the rich, that Bryan was to TR and his generation. Still, by April 1935, he was receiving more than a quarter of a million letters a month in support of SOW, and there were SOW clubs in every state, with 4.7 million members. More ominously, even so "responsible" a political leader as Senator George Norris, the great

Progressive Republican, was calling for some sort of redistribution of hereditary wealth. It was a matter of "preserving our civilization," he said in a February speech. Drawing the ancient popular distinction between money and property, he went on to explain that redistribution "does not mean that we should take the property of A and give it to B. It only means the taking of money from the estates of the very wealthy, where it can perform no real service for humanity, and the giving of it ... to all the people, from whence it was originally taken and under whose laws it was accumulated." Norris even cited the same "estate" that incited Huey Long's raillery, the Astor estate. There's not "one laborer in the city," brooded the senator, "who has not contributed his mite to the Astors out of the sweat of his brow."

To the knight-sailor of Campobello Bay, the political message of this redistributionist pressure was clear enough. For some time, the New Deal had been drifting to the right. A purge of liberals had begun in the AAA bureaucracy; the NRA was not pleasing the labor unions; wages in the public-works programs were being cut back; and the Social Security program being readied for legislation would never be described as sharing our wealth. More amusing, there was a marked improvement in the level of invective on Roosevelt's side of the debate. Harold Ickes said that Long was suffering from "halitosis of the intellect, if he has one." Hugh Johnson, head of the NRA, lumped Huey's SOW with Father Coughlin's National Union for Social Justice and called the mix "a magical financial hair tonic put up by a partnership of a priest and a Punchinello, guaranteed to grow whiskers on a billiard ball overnight." All this was reassuring to patrician Old Money. In every medium at its command—which included virtually all media—patricians expressed their tentative satisfaction with the course of the ship of state. FDR was doing the sensible thing, as *Time* expressed it, putting "recovery" ahead of "reform." From the skipper's point of view, too, the political prospects looked fair. The gale kicked up on his right in the early months of the New Deal was dying down.

On his left, however, if that's where Huey and the other redistributionists actually belonged, another storm was brewing. The Knight of the *Nourmahal* knew what to do. When the wind is pressing you down on the lee shore, safety lies in the teeth of the gale. So Roosevelt tacked left. To gain the open sea, he proposed to take away some of the money of the rich.

The legislation had been on his desk since December, in the form of several proposals for an inheritance and gift tax. Like some policy-makers before and since then, Roosevelt's advisers believed that an inheritance tax, combined with a gift tax to discourage *in vivo* dodges of the inheritance tax, is the most equitable way to promote the redistribution of wealth. The tax falls on the beneficiary; the richer he already is, the greater the tax. Thus the testator is encouraged to make out a will that distributes his money more generously—to impecunious cousins, for example, or outside the family altogether, to charities and other nonprofit institutions.

Raymond Moley thought the whole idea a terrible mistake. Moley had been a friend and adviser of Vincent Astor's as well as of Roosevelt's; he was, in fact, soon to leave the White House to become editor of *Newsweek,* the recently purchased vehicle of Astor's bid for press lordship. Moley told Roosevelt that the tax plan seemed a crudely opportunistic soak-the-rich gesture that would avail him nothing on Wall Street, where he needed all the support he could get. The President dismissed the argument. He didn't seem to have realized, or perhaps he simply didn't care, that such a tax would have an effect on him and his family—or families like his. To Governor Herbert Lehman, for example, descendant of a grand old German-Jewish family whose wealth was considerably larger than the Roosevelts', he wrote: "Past records seem to show that the larger the estate the greater the success in avoiding inheritance taxes. . . . [He meant estate taxes; only a few states have ever passed true inheritance taxes, and the federal government never has.] If everybody were as honest as you are, and as I try to be, the problems of Government would be easier, especially in connection with the richer members of the community!"

Who, exactly, he had in mind here is difficult to divine. FDR's class consciousness was probably as well developed, but certainly no better developed, than Uncle Ted's. For Roosevelts, "the richer members of the community" constituted two categories: "old families" like their own who had kept their money, and new families who had made their money more recently. These categories were cross-cut by two others: those who had a social conscience and those who did not, and on *this* score FDR was probably very skeptical of the *nouveaux riches* and more than skeptical of the old families. If they had ever had a social conscience, it was surely gone by the spring of 1935. The proof of it, he was proud enough to suppose, was that most of these people—the people he'd grown up with and gone to school with—were now unalterably opposed to his programs and to him. In May, he asked Felix Frankfurter to write a tax message on inherited wealth for delivery to Congress in mid-June.

At about the same time, he called in a reporter from the Hearst organization to explain what he was doing:

> I am fighting communism, Huey Longism, Coughlinism. . . . I want to save our system, the capitalistic system; to save it is to give some heed to the world thought of today. I want to equalize the distribution of wealth. . . . To combat Longism and similar crackpot ideas it may be necessary to throw to the wolves the forty-six men who are reported to have incomes in excess of a million dollars a year. This can be accomplished through taxation. . . . The thinking man, the young men, who are disciples of the new world idea of fairer distribution of wealth, they are demanding that something be done to equalize this distribution.

The Old Money themes in this odd declaration are barely discernible, but they are there. The rescue motif is familiar, even if the object to be rescued is a system, and the market system at that. There's also the suggestion of disinterestedness—an aesthetic notion of statecraft as the writing of history, perhaps—in the President's appeal to the *Zeitgeist* and the "thinking young men," as though he himself were only the appreciative amanuensis of this "new world idea." Then, too, there's the astonishing idealism of his proposal for an *equal* distribution of wealth; nothing in his political situation pushed him to go so far as that, not even Huey. FDR's egalitarianism here, sloppy or cynical as he may have been in expressing it, is more or less consistent with Periclean notions of civic equality, and not at all with entrepreneurial notions of starting-line equality. Finally, there's that distressing passage about throwing the forty-six rich men to the wolves. A Renaissance prince is revealed here and, in his reckless candor, a New World prince too. To simplify the message, it comes down to this: To keep Huey Long from slavering around the back door of the White House, it may be necessary to throw him a hunk of my cousin Vincent Astor.

When FDR's redistributionist proposal was read to Congress on 19 June 1935, the next day's *Times* announced the news in a four-column headline: "President Asks Inheritance Taxes and Other Levies on Big Fortunes." Subheads announced: "Tax Move a Big Surprise / Concentrated Riches Hit / House Applauds Message." Indeed loud cheering did in fact break out in the House chamber at the reading of the phrase "redistribution of wealth." The senators, among whom the patrician (and would-be patrician) element was rather more heavily represented, listened in silence. Behind the President's chair, Huey Long strutted and smirked in his white suit.

FDR's tax message—reasonable in argument, elevated in tone—called on old traditions of the polity. He quoted TR, for example, the TR who had fulminated against "the inheritance or transmission ... of ... fortunes swollen beyond healthy limits," who had seen the life of "hopeless decorousness," ending in alcoholism and death, of his brother and Eleanor Roosevelt's father, Elliott Roosevelt. The TR whom FDR quoted was the TR of the performative ideal, the strenuous life, the New World agon that was meant to prevent the wastage of people like Elliott Roosevelt:

> Our aim is to recognize what Lincoln pointed out: The fact that there are some respects in which men are clearly not equal; but also to insist that there should be an equality of self-respect and mutual respect ... and at least an approximate equality in the conditions under which each man obtains the chance to show the stuff that is in him compared to his fellows.

Franklin Roosevelt also tapped into Southern republican fears of oligarchy, like John Taylor of Caroline's:

> The transmission from generation to generation of vast fortunes by will, inheritance or gift is not consistent with the ideals and sentiments of the American people. Great accumulations of wealth cannot be justified on the basis of personal or family security. Such inherited economic power is as inconsistent with the ideals of this generation as inherited political power was inconsistent with the ideals of the generation which established our government.

The message was sparse in details. FDR did not presume to define a "vast" fortune, any more than TR had presumed to define a "swollen" one. It was thought that $10 million was the statistical "moment" the President had in mind to start the levies, but he was silent on how severe the taxes would be. There was one nice touch. The new tax revenues would be used to balance the budget, an objective devoutly desired by Old Money's patricians. There were no "homesteads" or "grubstakes" in the message, as there were in Huey's SOW, for example, and nothing so radical as a guaranteed annual income, or so feckless as a state-mandated leisurely work week. This was a serious, responsible proposal.

Even so, in the days after the reading of the message, the question that kept being asked was whether the President was really serious about these proposals. Several patrician newspapers hoped (and many reformist politicians feared) that in the end only an effigy of Vincent Astor would get thrown to the wolves. FDR himself was not available for comment. He was at sea again, this time on the White House yacht *Sequoia,* to see the Harvard-Yale boat races at New London, Connecticut. Franklin junior was rowing for the Harvard Junior Varsity that year, and of course the races were a high point of the Old Money social calendar. "I'm off to the New London boat races," FDR had written to William Bullitt, his ambassador to the Soviet Union, just before leaving, "and am much afraid that you damn Elis will sweep the river."

In New London, the early morning of 21 June 1935 was overcast and foggy, but when the wind came around to the southeast, the sun appeared, the fog lifted, and the fleet was revealed. The *Sequoia* was surrounded by hundreds of boats: slim, powerful tenders, whose brass and brightwork gleamed in the sun; catboats and schooners, the working vessels of Arcadia fitted out for the summertime ordeals of the rich. Among them all, the big yachts rode at anchor like chaperones at a debutante ball. There were at least sixty vessels in the 100–250-foot range, from Charles E. F. McCann's 248-foot *Charlena* to Ogden Mills's *Avalon,* Ernest Dane's *Vanda,* Mrs. William L. Harkness's *Cythera,* Cornelius Vanderbilt's *Winchester,* Alfred B. Sloan's *Rene,* Edward S. Harkness's *Stevena,* and so on down to a 150-foot yacht from Texas owned by a Dr. John R. Brinkley and called, to the derisive laughter of the avatars of good taste around her, the *Dr. Brinkley II.* The *Nourmahal* was missed, as was her owner. (Vincent was commodore of the New York Yacht Club that year, but his half-brother, John Jacob VI, whom everyone called Jackasster, was the only Astor in the news that day. He'd been seen at Bailey's Beach in Newport, having just retrieved *the* Mrs. Astor's diamond ring from an enraged former fiancé.) Still, even without the *Nourmahal,* a *Times* reporter happily noted that the yachts at New London composed the largest flotilla of private vessels ever assembled. Old Money, he might have added (but didn't), was doing very well in the Depression.

As the President had feared, the damned Elis swept the river, carrying Franklin junior and the JV's with them. The next day, while Mr. and Mrs. Roosevelt journeyed on to Hyde Park, the Senate of the

United States met briefly to consider the President's inheritance tax measure. Huey Long monopolized the session with the reading of a "letter" in which he acknowledged that if the President were truly serious about redistributing the wealth of the rich, then not only would the people be relieved of their oppressors but he, Huey, would be relieved of his mission. The press agreed with him. "However hard it comes," said the Los Angeles *Times,* "the Kingfish must perforce applaud." None of these newspapers, needless to say, approved of the President's tax plan. Many of their owners were the guardians of sizable patrician estates, great slices of which the tax measure would toss to the wolves along with Vincent Astor. Nevertheless, the papers all appeared to take comfort in the hope that Roosevelt might actually be up to no more mischief than playing politics with images—or effigies. To *The New York Times,* for example, it seemed obvious that the intention of the whole exercise was to buy off the left until after the election. The proposal was so vague as to rates, structure, modalities, and so manifestly inadequate to its proclaimed task, balancing the budget, that it couldn't be serious.

The *Times* was not wrong. The old Knight of the *Nourmahal* didn't even bother to wait until after the election before he began to back away from his proposal. When Senator La Follette of Wisconsin (the first state, incidentally, to have an inheritance tax) asked for FDR's support in pushing through the tax measure as an amendment to pending legislation, thus bypassing the House, the President told him to go ahead. But when La Follette gathered twenty-two votes, FDR asked his conservative leaders for the impossible. He wanted a bill before the summer adjournment, he said, but he wouldn't accept one that had been written in haste. The inheritance tax provision seemed particularly worrisome. Having earlier assured one great inheritor, Herbert Lehman, that the honest rich wouldn't pay any more in taxes under the new bill than they had under the old, he now confessed to another, his Hyde Park neighbor and secretary of the Treasury Henry Morgenthau, that he wasn't sure where he stood on the bill. "I am on an hourly basis, and the situation changes momentarily." By July, he had withdrawn his call for a bill before adjournment. Like TR's proposal before it, nothing ever came of FDR's inheritance tax.

In none of this did the Knight show signs of a willful betrayal of his class. The old sailor was simply trying to regain his political freedom—perhaps, indeed, his aristocratic freedom—by beating out to sea. Why, then, did they hate him so, those preposterous patrician clubmen of Peter Arno's cartoon, going down to the Bijou to hiss Roosevelt? Not all of them, of course. Most of those who did were roughly of his own generation, my grandfathers' generation, and even they were not solidly against him by any means. My grandfather Tweed supported him until he came up for the controversial fourth term, and though my grandfather Aldrich never voted for the man, he never had much enthusiasm for his opponents, either. He condescended to like Willkie: He even named one of his Sealyhams for Willkie. In my father's generation, Roosevelt was considered a great man, if also (as a great man should be) a slightly dangerous one. By my own generation, he was acclaimed almost as though he had never left the patrician fold.

Even Vincent Astor remained loyal to him. Few people like being thrown to the wolves, even in effigy, so there were no more cruises on the *Nourmahal* after 1935. (The first had come right after the election, in February 1932.) Yet the cousins parted on cordial terms. For some time, Astor had yearned for press lordship. He was one of the bidders in the auction for the Washington *Post,* losing to Eugene Meyer. He bought instead a weekly called *Today,* sharing the cost and deficits with Mary Harriman Rumsey, Averell's widowed sister and an old friend of Eleanor Roosevelt's. *Today* eventually changed its name to *Newsweek* and so eventually became part of Donny Graham's patrimony, but for as long as Astor owned it, he supported it generously. He made Raymond Moley editor. FDR blessed the new magazine, inviting his two old friends to Hyde Park. There he posed with them for a photographer and gave each of them a dollar to become the first subscriber. *Today* did not always subscribe to FDR, however. Whenever, in its view, the skipper from Campobello departed from a course that lay equidistant between the "predatory rich" and the "predatory poor," a comfortable Old Money course, they refused to follow. Otherwise, between the two cousins, loyalty prevailed. Vincent always voted for Franklin, and Franklin never again spoke of throwing Vincent to the wolves.

Still, there is no question but that most of FDR's class, for most of the time he was in the White House, feared and loathed him, as they had his ruinous uncle-in-law before him. In her biography of his eldest son, Mrs. Theodore Roosevelt, Jr., tells of young Ted making the rounds of Wall Street offices trying to sell bonds to "old friends of the family" after his father the Rough Rider started riding on the trusts. He got nowhere. The job was humiliating enough—*selling,* for pity's sake, how low could a Roosevelt sink!—but beyond that it was clear to young Ted that these men, for his father's sake, hated him. In 1935, they hated FDR even worse, and it is a curious matter why.

In a sense, the question answers itself. FDR really did save these people from themselves, and no one likes to be rescued, least of all from oneself. To be thus rescued is to surrender to one's rescuer a good deal of one's power and, for a time, one's dignity. The patricians of Old Money hated Roosevelt because he appeared to them as the symbol and instrument of their disgrace in the eyes of their countrymen. Before the Depression, they could well have believed that they enjoyed more or less complete control over the national aggregate of private patrimonies, much of it their own, plus all the quasi-public treasure under their trusteeship in the Great American Museum. Their hegemony had been disputed, of course, but not by some reckless "cousin" who had gone into politics and unaccountably managed to become President of the United States. Their traditional rivals for power, as the patricians saw it, were the makers and shakers of the marketplace, the champions of Market Men. (Another rival was the politically conscious working class, Marxism's candidate for ultimogeniture; even though, in the New World, working-class consciousness is even more diluted by the dream of possibility than upper-class consciousness.)

With the coming of the Depression, however, the patricians received a blow from which, as a *patronat*, they have never recovered. The blow, as the flotilla at New London bore witness, was not to their pocketbooks—in the long multigenerational run the trust-fund rich and their capital trustees usually have more to fear from inflation than from recession or depression—but to their pride. The Depression struck the patricians where they were most proud of themselves, at their prudence and self-discipline. As trustees of patrimonies, they were trusted (not only by their immediate families) to maintain a safe, respectable distance between themselves and the capital entrusted to them, and the tumultuous fear- and greed-driven marketplace. As a matter of statistical fact, they probably did. But as a fact for the imagination, their performance in the interwar years looks like an ignoble mess. The symbolic figure here, as every Old Money beneficiary knows, is Richard Whitney, the Groton-Harvard-Porcellian former president of the Stock Exchange, who went to Sing Sing for stealing from the funds entrusted to him (by, among other families and institutions, the New York Yacht Club and the New York Stock Exchange itself). The news of Whitney's betrayal was possibly even more shocking to Old Money than the news of Alger Hiss's rather different sort of betrayal many years later. My great-uncle Winthrop Aldrich, I've heard it said, went to the bathroom and "puked" when he heard about what Whitney had done. Whitney's specific crimes were forgiven him by his Old Rich friends; his name remained on the rolls of the P.C. and Endicott Peabody visited him in jail. But much worse than his sins was his attitude. It had always been bad, even before he got caught embezzling. Asked what he thought of the regulations that Roosevelt had forced on the stock market through the SEC in order to curb speculation, Whitney took exception: America, he said, had been built on speculation. He had a point, but to Old Money it was a hideous and vulgar entrepreneurial point, better left unsaid.

Whitney was a perfect example of a failure of the princely ordeal, a Tom Buchanan of Wall Street, a gambler, a cheat, a thief: a man whose indulgence in the *plaisir aristocratique de déplaire* had nothing brave or noble or eccentric about it. The troubling thing was that people like Whitney were showing up everywhere, not only in imaginations like Scott Fitzgerald's but in the class's own picture of itself. Old Money's gallery had always included unflattering family portraits, most of them variations on the nightmare of personal powerlessness: the chinless wonder, the simpering debutante, and so forth. But the 1920s saw the addition of one or two more: the drunk, for example. Samuel Eliot Morison suggested that Prohibition revolutionized Old Money's traditional drunken behavior. Before Prohibition, a gentleman was expected to hold his liquor, which is why he got "stiff" with the effort (ladies, of course, were not allowed to get drunk at all); after Prohibition, there was a pronounced relaxation of the "stiffness" and of the double standard, and it became permissible, if not actually amusing, to get uninhibitedly drunk. The new portraits in the Old Money gallery begin, then, with another Peter Arno cartoon: the handsome couple in evening clothes languidly wrapped around a lamppost, their eyes dulled with surfeit, their mouths rippling with incontinent joy. The portraits go on, with obituary photographs of Harry Phipps, perhaps, or David Kennedy, or any one of the many Old Money beneficiaries who never came back from their last free fall in freedom.

Between the mug shot of Richard Whitney and the blurred snapshot of one's own out-of-focus self, there is the photograph of J. P. Morgan's son Jack, who was called down to Washington to testify on the causes of the Depression and was then persuaded to pose for the press with a dwarf perched on his knee. Morgan had no one but himself to blame for this ignominious blot on his patrician image. But with respect to the class's image, Old Money would have to be more than human, or less than American, if it didn't concentrate the fury and frustration of its disgrace on an enemy within. This they did. The enemy within was the perfidious Roosevelt, traitor to his class.

Yet FDR was not that. He was only an aristocrat. But what *that* was, and still is, is deeply unsettling to the patrician wing of the Old Money class. First of all, there is something unsocialized, almost undomesticated, about him. It is not a question of his manners—the social graces animate the presence of aristocrats as well as they do the presence of patricians, and promise even more. It is a question of his social virtues. The aristocrat doesn't seem quite trustworthy; he lacks prudence; he might even be called careless. Pictorially, he seems "right" only outdoors or in some doubtful battle—noble or shameful, one can't be sure.

The dangers of this aristocratic presence are very clear, at least to patricians, in the case of John F. Kennedy. Kennedy's social virtues seemed to exist only in a public dimension, on the scale of the city, so to speak; in private, the dimension of most concern to patricians, his behavior seemed dangerous, for he displayed that reckless sense of invulnerability which mentors of the class know to be one of the most toxic effects of the costless life. To his admirers, whatever sort of money they came from or aspired to, the President's womanizing, his cruelty to his retainers (especially those whose adoration or dependency prevented them from "teasing" him back), and the somewhat affected vulgarity of his language—all this was more than compensated for by his charm, his humor, the magnanimity of his public policies and utterances. But to patricians—wherever they stood with respect to his policies, however much or little they might be moved by his utterances—Kennedy's private behavior was ominous. So, in somewhat the same way, was Nelson Aldrich Rockefeller's. Aristocrats are dangerously uninhibited men: like David the King and Tom Buchanan, they are sensual, ruthless, and intemperate. New Money presidents like Nixon and Reagan, products of their own entrepreneurial imaginations, usually destroy themselves in fear and greed—the classic nemeses of the self-made life. To patricians, messy endings like theirs are merely distasteful. Had Kennedy lived, had Rockefeller ever gained the White House, both might have destroyed themselves in the classic manner of Old Money—in moral carelessness, in nonchalance gone bad. To patricians this is worse than distasteful; it is terrifying.

Kennedy might have been a decadent aristocrat, but neither of the Roosevelts gave much promise of that. Still, to the patrician members of their class, both Teddy and Franklin seemed unsteady in their loyalties, immodest in their presentation of self, and wildly experimental in their conduct of the affairs of state. There was something unseemly about the way TR seemed to court the attention of the public. The Harvard dandy, the ridiculous frontiersman in his Leatherstocking suit, the bespectacled cowboy-cavalryman with his gauntlets and pistols, all these gave way in the end to the demagogic politician with his portly strut, squeaky voice, and the ragtag militia of his teeth. If FDR was never so ludicrous, it was because he was so much better-looking. I remember my two grandmothers, the Countess and Grandma Aldrich, being quite emphatic about his looks. "But how handsome he is!" they would say. "What a marvelous smile!" My grandfathers thought he was *too* good-looking. That smile was the smile of vanity, yet another sign of untrustworthiness.

Such aesthetic judgments, as usual with the Old Rich, blurred into moral-political ones. The poseur TR and the vain FDR became the unpredictable and opportunistic TR and the sinisterly suave and evasive FDR. How could one trust the wealth of the United States to a man who, like TR, couldn't seem to make up his mind whether he was a trustbuster (the mildly progressive Republican Roosevelt) or a protector and would-be director of trusts (the New Nationalist Roosevelt)? By the same token, how could one trust the restoration of the wealth of the United States to a man who, like FDR, seemed ready to try anything and everything, without regard for principle or tradition (never mind the sensibilities of dignified men)? Patricians know—they have always known—what is good for the polity. To them, nothing was more disturbing than the aristocratic Roosevelts: they were frighteningly royal in their reckless pandering to the people, their antic tinkering with public policy, and (above all) their high-handed presumption of authority over their cousins. (If Kennedy did not arouse fear to the same degree, it was because his policies were not so erratic; most of them, indeed, had become the policies of the patriciate. His presumption of authority was the same, however, and aroused the same indignation.)

In a way, the patricians' enmity for their aristocratic cousins is the enmity of the grownup for the child or adolescent. Those who knew the two Roosevelts and Kennedy, for example, never ceased to be astonished at how puerile they were. Henry Adams called TR "pure Act," and while the remark had scholastic overtones and a disparaging intent (TR hadn't Henry's intellectual attainments, but he was the only President since John Quincy Adams to come even close), it also pointed to an obvious truth about Roosevelt. Boys are "pure Act," and TR was a boy and delighted to admit it. He said once, of an adventure he was about to go on late in life, that it was his last chance to be a boy again. FDR's sense of humor was scandalously childish, and if he hadn't been crippled by polio his animal spirits would have rivaled Uncle Ted's. He was vacationing at Campobello the day before he came down with the disease, and he began the morning by marshaling his children to help beat out a forest fire, then took them on a two-mile run, then took them swimming in the freezing water of the bay, then, finally, led them on another run home. JFK's "vigah" was legendary—no man except TR did more to celebrate the strenuous life—and his humor was also hopelessly "immature," at least as patricians understood it. He liked horsing around and playing practical jokes; he loved to talk about women and sex, and to do more than talk. Politics is a fine playground for temperaments like these. Children love attention; politicians get it. Children have endless curiosity, quick sympathy, and the attention span of fleas; politicians need all these qualities. Children are relatively, foolishly, free of anxiety; so must politicians be, if they're ever to get any sleep. Finally, children (boys especially) love contests and games, preferably ones where the rules are fairly flexible, the stakes in prestige high, but the downside risk low. That may not be an exhaustive description of American politics, but it's one way of looking at it, and maybe the best way if the contender wants to win and keep sane. Patricians, however, often find it appalling that government, that vital and sensitive safeguard of their liberties and their patrimonies, should be vulnerable to seizure as the plaything of grown-up babies.

The patrician wing of Old Money also nourishes a subtler form of enmity for "aristocrats." It is the enmity that those who suspect themselves of powerlessness nourish for those who have overcome such doubts. It is the enmity that the reflective always have for the active. It is the enmity of irony. Eleanor Roosevelt used to tell the story of how she and Franklin once went to tea at the house of Henry Adams— "Uncle Henry" as he was to them—just across the street from the White House on Lafayette Square. Franklin was assistant secretary of the Navy at the time, and it seems he rattled on about his plans to do this and that for the country. It isn't important what he said; what Eleanor never forgot was how deprecating Uncle Henry was. "Young man," she remembered him saying, "I have lived in this house many years and seen the occupants of that White House across the square come and go, and nothing that you minor officials or the occupants of that house can do will affect the history of the world for long."

The Roosevelts were not downcast. To Eleanor, Adams's "pessimism" was just "an old man's defense against his own urge to be an active factor in the world." That was too generous. In the more aristocratic circles of Old Money, the received wisdom was that Henry Adams's urge to be an active factor in the world, never very strong to begin with, had long since expired in a sour and squeamish disgust. Oliver Wendell Holmes, Jr., the warrior-scholar and old Porcellian "brother" whom TR had appointed to the Supreme Court, once told Owen Wister that if "the country had put him on a pedestal I think Henry Adams would have rendered distinguished public service. . . . He wanted it handed to him on a silver plate." What TR himself thought of Adams is less clear. He admired him for his intellect, his learning, and his *History of the United States in the Age of Jefferson and Madison,* and often invited him to dine at the White House. Wister, a much more patrician figure than the President, placed the *Education* among the classics of American literature, "where the pages of Emerson and Poe and Whitman and Hawthorne are to be found with *Huckleberry Finn."* TR would never have done that, for he hated "pessimistic generalization," as Wister paraphrased him. It undermined his own somewhat tenuous hold on optimism, and, as Wister pointed out, "a man can not be a leader unless he is an optimist."

Irony is a great enemy of the aristocratic impulse among the Old Rich, both the aesthetic irony that sees the comic distance between substance and seeming, actor and performance, actuality and imagery, and the historic irony that flows, as it probably did with Henry Adams, from too vain a devotion to the historical project of an Old Money family, and too skeptical an intelligence to believe in it. For the patrician, these ironies can be a source of wit and solace, making disappointments bearable and self-pity "attractive." But for the aristocrat, they can be crippling, historic irony especially. It can turn the cherished Old Money notion of fate into an argument for passivity—sometimes a "poetic" argument, as in Adams's *Mont St. Michel and Chartres;* at other times, as in the *Education,* a "scientific" one. In either case, fate (or history) becomes a force that men struggle with, amusingly or pathetically as the case may be, but always in vain.

But irony can also be beneficent in a political leader. Aesthetic irony leads to laughter and a mocking sort of tolerance, not only useful for a prince but a blessing for his people. "They [Jack and Jacqueline Kennedy] both so rarely show any emotion, except by laughter," said Benjamin Crowninshield Bradlee, Kennedy's Old Money friend and (later) the Grahams' editor. But laughter is what the White House servants said they missed after the Theodore Roosevelts moved out, and laughter is what they said they welcomed when the Franklin Roosevelts moved back in. "When I got back," said the man who drove the *nouveaux riches* Hoovers to the station as the Old Rich Roosevelts began to settle in, "I found the White House transformed during my absence into a gay place full of people who oozed confidence." Of course, the envious always point out that Roosevelts and Kennedys can afford to ooze confidence. They have money, high social standing, good looks (some of them), good manners, influence in high places, and now power—everything that most Americans have to struggle for all their lives and often do not get. Old Money irony at its best is in some sense a response to that perception, accepting it and turning it into a metaphysical joke. "Life is unfair," said Kennedy. This was gloomy news when Jimmy Carter delivered it, but when Kennedy spoke, it was bracing, and somehow his words and his laughter felt like a tonic. FDR's smile had the same effect, lifting hearts with his courage but also, unmistakably, with a hint of mischievous laughter.

The aristocratic figures cut by the Roosevelts and Kennedy suggest minds that are simultaneously hopeful about human ingenuity and skeptical about human possibility, and they suggest temperaments in which high spirits play constant light designs on a dark ground of pessimism and sadness. A sense of the ironies of history, the histories of families as well as nations, might contribute to those qualities. It can do more. It can protect the political leader from taking his country and its cause too solemnly—as, for example, Jimmy Carter did. Even more important, it can protect him, and the rest of us, from identifying the country's cause with his own.

Fundamentally, though, corrosive irony like Henry Adams's bears witness to deeper hostilities to the aristocratic project than can be accounted for by personal spite or *fin de race* sensibility. This is the characteristically patrician fear of the public domain as a stage of personal performance. Ever since the massive enfranchisements and antiaristocratic rhetoric of the Jackson Era, Old Money has had difficulty imagining any public role for its beneficiaries other than that of the (private) trustee. Before Theodore Roosevelt came along, very few Old Money people ever went into politics at all. All the most discerning nineteenth-century visitors to this country, from Tocqueville to Bryce, commented on the "fastidiousness" (Bryce's word) of the upper classes with respect to open political action on their own behalf, or anyone else's. (Covert action was something else again.) Government, said Mrs. Trollope, was something that respectable people left "rather supinely to their tailors and tinkers"—or to discreet and well-rewarded inside operators like Senator Nelson W. Aldrich.

There were many reasons for this withdrawal of the Old Money class from the public world. One is the irremediable fragility of the upper-class social imagination. William Waldorf Astor, Vincent's great-uncle, is a case in point. In the late 1880s, he twice tried to run for Congress in New York City's "Silk Stocking" district and lost both times. His opponent campaigned on the slogan "We have no landlord aristocracy here, thank God!" Astor came to a rather drastic conclusion. "America is not a fit place for a gentleman to live," he said. "Politics is closed to a man who will not seek votes in the Irish slums; it isn't easy to see why people of means remain here." Shortly thereafter he decamped for England, where he bought himself a lordship, founded a family of lords and press lords (one of the *Times,* the other of the *Observer*), and lived to see his son and daughter-in-law (Nancy Astor) handily win seats in the House of Commons.

England, naturally, is the lost paradise of Old Money's imagination, the country where Periclean Athens moved after the Peloponnesian War, mercifully leaving slavery behind. Even with his Porcellian pal in the White House, Owen Wister still lamented that America was not England, that he was not English:

[D]espite the protest of the President, [Robert] Bacon and I were of the opinion that our country offered no traditional and accepted career [of public service], such as England offered, to the college-bred gentleman; that, save in wartime, there was no market for [them]. The [gentlemen] of England entered the open doors of political service to their country, and had been the builders of the British Empire. Here the doors were shut in their face, and had to be broken open with such persistence and force, and with methods so disgusting to most decent men, that they either chose careers where business was on the watch for ability and gave it every chance, or turned to idleness and were ... simply wasted.

"Disgusting" is the most significant word in this passage. As a stage for performance, politics is attractive to Old Money, a way of getting close to the Periclean ideal of citizenship and the best possible arena in which to exercise the peculiar gifts of the all-round man. It is, in fact, a calling in which almost everyone considers having a lot of unearned money a positive asset. And finally, of course, politics is an ordeal, war by other means.

Yet it is also disgusting, or seems so to the patriciate. Part of the reason is their squeamishness, the prospect of having to consort with less magnanimous characters and more venal ambitions than their own. Fitzgerald parodies this view, perhaps unintentionally, in one of Amory Blaine's ruminations on his future after Princeton:

> He tried to imagine himself in Congress rooting around in that incredible pigsty with ... those glorified proletarians babbling blandly to the nation with the ideas of high school seniors! Little men with copy-book ambitions who by mediocrity had thought to emerge from mediocrity into the lustreless and unromantic heaven of a government by the people.

Old Money has always been more than half convinced that politics is not public service but self-service, just another place to feed, wallow, and waste, another place to make it.

The two Roosevelts and Kennedy consciously strove to combat this (to them) shameful revulsion of their patrician classmates with respect to politics. And they were successful for a time. TR even managed to get Wister out on the hustings. "Up and down the seventh ward of Philadelphia," the novelist wrote later, "I made speeches in stinking halls amid rank tobacco smoke to dirty niggers and dingy whites.... It was extraordinarily good fun, once you got going." Most Old Money beneficiaries know the names of the men who answered the appeal of their aristocratic cousins to the antique ideals of citizenship they all shared: Elihu Root, Robert Bacon, Gifford Pinchot, and Oliver Wendell Holmes, Jr., among others in the TR administration; Henry L. Stimson, Henry Morgenthau, Robert Lovett, Averell Harriman, George and Francis Biddle, Dean Acheson, Sumner Welles, and scores of others in the FDR administrations; McGeorge Bundy, Douglas Dillon, and a number of Harvard-made Old Money sympathizers in the Kennedy administration. More important is the number of young people (and their mentors) who were stirred by the example of these Presidents, or their appointees, to go into electoral politics—Adlai Stevenson, John Lindsay, Nelson Rockefeller—or to serve non–Old Money Presidents—Dean Acheson (again), John Foster Dulles, Elliot Richardson, Cyrus Vance, and many others. The Senate of the United States is full of more or less patrician politicians who took some inspiration from the three aristocrats, and seem to have survived immersion in the pigsty with their dignity and their class credentials intact: John D. Rockefeller IV, Edward M. Kennedy, John Heinz, Lowell Weicker, Claiborne Pell, John Kerry, John Chafee, Nancy Kassebaum, John Warner, and others.

Actually, a generational view of the Old Rich in active, open public service reveals that patrician disgust works quite as well to encourage as to inhibit them. In my great-grandfather's day, for example, Endicott Peabody was so revolted by what he saw happening to his country that he contemplated "a desperate charge" into politics himself. That was the noble impulse of one man, and not acted upon, but there seems to be something like a law governing these impulses. It's not a law that Henry Adams could have imagined: It's a law of market societies, not would-be traditional societies, and therefore it postulates cycles, not lines. Market societies are susceptible to cycles of appetite, of satiation and revulsion, and these cycles seem to swing political attitudes along with them, disposing a critical mass of the population now to the ideology and practice of self-service, now to the ideology and practice of public service.

The Old Rich may be especially sensitive to swings in these cycles. The swing from satiation to disgust, for example, announces that public-service politics, preeminently their sort of politics, may be coming back into favor among the common run of market-driven voters. It's a question of appetite. The patrician Old Rich enjoy feeding themselves on the sort of goods that markets provide, but for the most part, having already been given so much, they are easily satisfied. Consequently, they are quickly sickened by the feeding frenzies that periodically overcome their less contented fellow citizens. From this comes their usefulness as barometers of the political weather: Their rising gorges indicate increasing opportunities for public service, lowering gorges a time for withdrawal.

Of course, the key question is what it takes to turn a patrician stomach. In the first post–Civil War cycle, the appetitive phase of which began right after Appomattox, the orgy of entrepreneurial self-making in private life and self-service in public life had to run on for almost two generations before enough nausea accumulated to produce an opportunity for Theodore Roosevelt. Even at that, without the strange, cerebral, civic idealism of Woodrow Wilson, that Southern puritan and Anglophile, to keep it flickering, and without the challenge of World War I to fire it up again, TR's spirit of public service would have suffocated under the regime of that well-fed patrician William Howard Taft.

The second cycle was much shorter. Beginning right after World War I, the orgy lasted about thirteen years. Then Uncle Winthrop puked, announcing an opportunity for Franklin Roosevelt.

The third, post–World War II cycle is neater. The patrician withdrawal into private life began (as it always seems to do) during the administration of a man who in one way or another adopted the values of Old Money but could not convincingly adopt its imagery or persuasively articulate its performative and participatory ideals of citizenship. Harry Truman set off the patrician withdrawal, just as Wilson had done before him, just as Lyndon Johnson would do after him. Be that as it may, the post–World War II orgy that made way for John F. Kennedy lasted almost exactly fifteen years.

In the most recent cycle, it was easy to tell when the patrician gorge began to rise. Ronald Reagan installed an administration composed almost entirely of self-made men (men, indeed, who were determined to use their offices to make it), and by the end of his second term Reagan had fed a flock of torrent birds whose droppings nauseated patrician sensibilities as nothing had since the days of Richard Whitney. There is no question that enough of this disgust is shared by the larger electorate to make an aristocratic Old Money presidency possible. Significantly, perhaps, no aristocrat has appeared to take advantage of it.

The relationship between aristocrat and patrician is more complicated than I've suggested so far. Confrontations like the ones between TR and J. P. Morgan, and between FDR and Vincent Astor's effigy, are in danger of being overdramatized by partisans of the one or the other "cousins." The true relationship is, as one would expect, sibling rivalry. Arthur Schlesinger, Jr., wittily describes the antipathy between FDR and Senator Bronson Cutting, both of them Grotonians, both strong "liberals" or "progressives" or "conservationists," whatever label seems useful, as the sort of feeling two explorers might have if they'd run into one another in the same patch of jungle. The same dismay registers as: "What are *you* doing here?" when an Old Money aesthete encounters an Old Money athlete at the ballet. Old Rich old boys or girls are forever slightly miffed to note that someone else of their "background" is doing the same thing. In the rivalry of aristocrat and patrician, the stakes are much higher. TR got it just right when he said that J. P. Morgan treated him like a "rival operator." The field of operations is the public good, and the rivalry comes down to a contest between two visions of the proper guardianship of America's goods: private trustees or public trustees, the private power of wealth or the public (political) power of government.

Nowadays, this rivalry has become a striking example of cooperative antagonism. To protect the nation's patrimony and their own, patricians and aristocrats know they need each other. They know, too, that however antagonistic they may be, they have the same enemy: the rhetorical forces of the entrepreneurial imagination—individualistic, envious, exploitative, opportunistic. In this New World, the entrepreneurial rhetoric is overwhelmingly persuasive to most of their fellow citizens, people, after all, who can't afford to listen to any other rhetoric. With such a fearsome and powerful common enemy, patricians and aristocrats haven't had any serious disagreements since World War II. My grandfather wasn't the only Old Money old gentleman to look kindly on John F. Kennedy, and younger gentlemen like myself—young ladies too—actually adored him.

Nevertheless, structurally solid though their cooperation may be, there's still a good deal of antagonism between the two camps of the Old Rich. And the most contentious issues still revolve around the relationship of the aristocratic leader and the people.

The best approach to this issue lies through the princes' consorts, two of them anyway, Eleanor Roosevelt Roosevelt and (as she is now) Jacqueline Bouvier Kennedy Onassis. As an embodiment of Old Money tastes and social graces, the image of Jacqueline Kennedy (as she was) is so preemptive that it's hard to think of anyone else. Mrs. Kennedy entered the American imagination of wealth, even at the beginning, in radiant solitude. She is still doing it. For an instant she is motionless, seemingly transfixed by the public gaze, pinned like a photograph to a wall. Her great unblinking eyes widen, a slow smile parts her lips, her lean and rangy figure seems to concentrate, to gather substance and gravity, and at the same time to soften. She is composing herself. It is an act of will, but also of inspiration. Being blessed is to know one can bless. Inspired by grace, Jackie Kennedy knows she inspires grace around her. It is her gift. Click-whir, click-whir, click-whir, and the gift is given.

This queen belonged with Greeks long before she married Onassis. In Dallas, her first husband's blood on her dress, the great limousine speeding through the city, she was a queen of Troy:

> Andromache of the white arms
> held in her lap between her hands
> the head of Hector who had killed so many.

And then, with Hector dead and Troy fallen, she is carried off by Pyrrhus, Achilles' son, and wooed by him and pressed to become his queen. She marries Pyrrhus and goes to live with him on his island kingdom, and thereby remains true to herself, to her fate as an image of grace and queenly virtue.

This fate is simple enough as to ends: the maintenance of Old Money's standards of taste and behavior. But it is tricky as to means, for Mrs. Kennedy's performances roused the public to a high pitch of envy, teetering crazily between hatred and adulation. Naturally, much of the impact of her performance scored off her husband's. If she seemed an image of somewhat lacquered loveliness, of sometimes frivolous sensibility, it was only in contrast to his rough energy. But she overdid it; her performances were overplayed and overpublicized. She gave too much. She acquired too much. (Her acquisitiveness on behalf of the public was as great as her later acquisitiveness on her own behalf.) And she demonstrated too openly the sometimes embarrassing class fact that Old Money goes back to the Old World. To some patricians, it was as though she had never learned the lesson of the Bradley Martin Ball.

If the essence of Mrs. Kennedy's performance before the people was iconographic and theatrical, the essence of Mrs. Roosevelt's was corporeal and personal. Eleanor Roosevelt was not beautiful (though the discerning noted that her figure was), and she had as little flair as a Boston Forbes. When she went into the furniture business with enterprising female friends (not so much to make money as to set the example for other, less fortunate women), her company's product was described as "authentic copies of early American pieces." Mrs. Kennedy would have scorned such stuff. Indeed, most of Mrs. Roosevelt's Old Rich contemporaries scorned Mrs. Roosevelt herself. No one who knew her personally could fail to be struck by the contrast between the private woman and the public one. In private, to her family and friends, she seemed lonely, melancholic, puritanical, despairingly possessive, desperately controlling—a clinically perfect picture of the child of an alcoholic. In public, she was the image of sympathy and warmth, principle and strength: the image of a lady bountiful, and in depression, war, and peace, millions of her admirers cherished it. To those of her class who didn't like her or her image, or feared her husband's policies, Mrs. Roosevelt was a false and sentimental woman.

But after she discovered a way of making herself useful in the White House, she didn't much care what Old Money thought of her. She had found what aristocrats often do find: a solidarity with the people, which more than made up for what she lost (or never had) among her own kind.

Who were these "people," for her and many other aristocrats of the Old Money class? It is not the people that Pericles had in mind; his Athens was composed largely of citizens and slaves. Old Money's people are free. Not free in the Jeffersonian-Jacksonian or Adam Smith senses, and not free in the sense that Athens's citizens were. Old Money's "people" are free as emancipated slaves were, or as the urban proletariat is free (in Anatole France's phrase) to sleep under a bridge. The "people" of the Old Rich live beneath the market (as Old Money lives above it), or have little to sell there (as Old Money sometimes has nothing to sell except its money). They are people as an object of parental care and protection, as human resources at least as valuable as art and mountains, as possessors of civil rights, as troops, as posterity.

They are also the people as "reality," the reality that Old Money encounters on summer jobs, and for which they winter over at their summer places. More real, in fact. Too often, when the Old Rich go in search of the people, what they find is the middle class. The people they long for have a deeper, touchstone reality. They look for what Eleanor Roosevelt found, what post-1960s philanthropists like Sarah and George Pillsbury find today: slum dwellers, dark-skinned minorities, poverty-stricken women, Latin American peasants. For the Pillsburys, brother and sister founders of two "alternative" foundations, the Haymarket foundations of Los Angeles and Cambridge, the people's below-market status raises the hope that they can be organized as the Haymarket foundations encourage them to be organized, not for individualism and competition but for cooperation and community. Real people are thought to be real in their being somehow closer to the earth, to physical labor and to the certainty of weight and power that it gives. Jane Addams caught this sense of the Antaean reality of the common people in a remarkable passage:

> You may remember the forlorn feeling which occasionally seizes you when you arrive early in the morning, a stranger in a great city. The stream of laboring people goes past as you gaze through the plate glass window of your hotel. You see hard-working men lifting great burdens. . . . Your heart sinks with a sudden sense of futility. The door opens behind you and you turn to the man who brings you in your breakfast with a quick sense of human fellowship. You find yourself praying . . . that the great mother breasts of our common humanity, with its labor and its suffering and its homely comforts, may never be withheld from you. You turn helplessly to the waiter. You feel that it would be almost grotesque to claim from him the sympathy you crave. Civilization has placed you far apart. . . .

Jane Addams—whose New Money was getting Old through giving and through her going to Bar Harbor, Maine, in the summer—was the founder of an alternative foundation of sorts. And Hull House was not far from the scene of the riots and massacre for which the Pillsburys named their foundations.

Somewhere in the imagination of Old Money beneficiaries there's a longing for forms of human togethering that leap the social distances "civilization" puts between classes. Jane Addams's generation of women—Eleanor Roosevelt's too, and my stepmother's as well—found these forms in a variety of institutions: from the settlement house movement to the Public Education Association, from the Women's Trade Union League to the Consumers' League and the League of Women Voters. To one degree or another, these activities provided rich women with the ancient satisfactions of *in corpore* giving—the satisfactions of "the great mother breasts of our common humanity." Today's alternative foundations do the same for the current generation of women *and* men.

In any event, it was through this experience of community with the people that Eleanor Roosevelt discovered her role in the White House. She described it very well, if inadvertently, in 1940. She was trying to explain to her friend and biographer Joseph Lash why Americans should vote for Franklin rather than John Nance Garner. Lash paraphrased her words. Garner, she said,

> was a self-made man and in achieving success had become insensitive to the sufferings of others. He considered people in need of help failures and regarded all reform as a conspiracy to divest him of hard-won personally-achieved gains. The president, on the other hand, never having gone through bitter personal struggle to achieve wealth and prominence, had no such feelings about his possessions and privileges. He was sensitive to privation and suffering and, once he understood, would go to the limit to change things; the problem was to get him to understand and see a situation.

The passage is a classic summary of Old Money's claim, as against the entrepreneur's claim, on the political imagination of a democracy. But it is more than that. The aristocrat's lady is saying that FDR knew nothing, personally, of hard work, of success and failure, of struggle, triumph, and resentment—nothing, in short, of most people's lives in a market society. And she was right. Of the three presidential aristocrats, none had more than the briefest experience of the numbing discipline of boss, subordination, specialization and routine. It's a good question, in fact, what these men would have done with their lives, if anything, had they not gone into politics.

Mrs. Roosevelt went on to assert that this experience, or lack of it, leaves people like FDR "sensitive" to suffering and privation, yet somehow needing to be made to "understand" it. Her observation is one of the clichés of the imagination of wealth. Variations of it can be found from Tocqueville—"feudal institutions awakened a lively sympathy for the sufferings of certain men, but none at all for the miseries of mankind"—to the latest television work of dynastic fiction. It may even be accurate: In war, certainly, the aristocrat must be able to send men to their deaths without a qualm and afterward move among the bodies of the wounded and dying with genuine pity and concern for each one of them. Be that as it may, Eleanor Roosevelt found a clear vocation in the difference she saw in her husband between "sensitivity" and "understanding." It was she who would help him understand. She would take care of all those who were hurt and afraid. She would go out among them, in person, and stand by them in a gesture that would not fail to touch the heart of the aristocrat in the White House. Her somewhat worshipful biographer sentimentalizes the gesture, recalling

Michelangelo's Madonna of the Pietà, but not too much so for the millions who loved Mrs. Roosevelt.

Until coeducation came to St. Midas and Harvard, both sexes of the Old Rich tended to regard women as either wanton or indulgent: wanton with men and with treasure, indulgent with their children. Women were as potentially corrupting, debilitating, and degenerative as wealth itself. But just as wealth was also uplifting, nourishing, but firmly suppressed, so were mothers and other female lovers. The suppression was most violent among Old Rich women.

But a mercy that Old Money cannot openly abide in itself it can sometimes afford to give to others for whom fate has been less kind. History (or fate) must cooperate, of course, creating a depression to hurl huge masses of the less fortunate below the market, then a war to hurl most of the country above it. It must also tutor the masses to appreciate what a mercy like Eleanor Roosevelt's is. Old Money is not alone in its fears of mother love and queenly indulgence. The entrepreneurial imagination also puts mother love down, lest the self-made man be reminded of whence he came and be exposed for the impostor he is. "Tom's poor mother and sisters traveled the same road out of his mind," wrote America's closest student of imposture, speaking of the Pauper become Prince. "At first he pined for them, sorrowed for them, longed to see them, but later the thought of their coming some day in their rags and dirt, and betraying him with their kisses, and pulling him down from his lofty place, and dragging him back to penury and degradation and the slums made him shudder." The truth may be that No Money is the only money that can recall maternal feeling, or womanly mercies, without embarrassment. But there, precisely, was Eleanor Roosevelt's chance: to make not only her husband "understand" but her fellow countrymen as well.

"More than forty years ago," Roosevelt wrote his old rector at Groton, "you said, in a sermon in the old Chapel, something about not losing boyhood ideals in later life. Those were Groton ideals—taught by you—I try not to forget—and your words are still with me and with hundreds of others of 'us boys.'" The President did not specify the nature of boyhood ideals; he didn't have to. They are Periclean ideals of citizenship, courtly ideals of social grace and virtue, and knightly ideals of individual action. For the Old Rich as a class, and especially for aristocrats, the three sets of ideals relate dynamically to one another. They may be expressed in any number of ways—in sportsmanship or generosity, *pro bono* advocacy or philanthropy, sacri-

fices of life or treasure—but they will always be seen as "class acts."
Such acts are envied, and they are also subject to highly characteristic
interpretations by entrepreneurs. The harshest of these is the neoconservative's understanding of the "limousine liberal." As propagandists
of the "tougher" virtues, neoconservatives see every decent action of
the Old Rich as a response to the feckless prompting of limp-wristed
guilt.

Patricians often agree with them. The most devastating *mot* ever
said about Eleanor Roosevelt—that now she was in the White House,
she could take the whole world for her slum project—was reportedly
said by her first cousin, Alice Roosevelt Longworth. Patricians are sensitive to the irrational extremes to which imprudent heirs and heiresses
can take the ethos of the gift—of self, capital, or treasure. But aristocrats tend to be immune to the charge. Partly, this is because they are
reckless, impetuous, overly openhanded. But it is also because of the
way, at least since Theodore Roosevelt, they have placed their ideals of
just personal behavior in relation to ideals of just political behavior.
The issue, as TR understood, was one of equality. There would always
be ways, he suggested in his speech on inherited wealth, in which men
would be unequal. It is only just that society recognize some of those
inequalities: the inequalities of personal performance, in sports, arts,
politics, or even the marketplace. Injustice comes in, TR implied,
when society's recognition of these personal superiorities begins to tear
up the fundamental moral ground of citizenship in a democracy.

The common ground of self-respect and mutual respect among all
citizens is not only a test of the justness of the polity but also a program
of knightly political action for the Old Money aristocrat. He (or she)
must do everything he can to bring about a regime of egalitarian respect. If "guilt" has any part in this plan of action, it is implicit in the
recognition that the Old Money curriculum is neither legitimate nor
safe so long as anyone is kept out of it for lack of respect. This sort of
guilt looks rather like a combination of high idealism and low cun-
ning. And, by no accident, these are the most notable qualities in this
century's Old Money aristocrats in the White House.

Historically, a decent regard for equality of respect has pointed
aristocratic political leaders toward a liberal interpretation of the gift
ethos, not only in relation to capital (easy credit, welfare programs)
and treasure (environmental protection, state support of education and
the arts), but also to rights. The last was by no means a certain outcome
of the Old Money curriculum. On the contrary, as I have said, the

political training of the Old Rich, especially at St. Midas schools, militates against the recognition of civic or personal rights. As regimes for the promotion of virtue, these schools are always in danger of engendering in their pupils a taste for the most extreme forms of tutelary politics, whether the fascist politics of "blood" or the Russian-communist politics of commandeered work. Both these political forms have a fatal allure for St. Midas children: they seem virtuous and "real"; they offer clear-cut, drastic protection from the rich kid's fear of the free fall. Added to this, there's the well-known fact that the history of the world shows few instances where a class born to extraordinary civil and personal rights willingly shares them with less fortunate people without being forced to do so. Nevertheless, one such instance was the privileged class at the time of the founding of the United States, and the inheritors of that privilege, by and large, have continued the tradition. The Old Money class has seen to it that its own liberties are well defended by money, but in accordance with the ancient principle of the gift, they have usually been gracious enough to see to it that everyone else's liberties are protected as well—certainly not by sharing their wealth but often by sharing their rights.

What patricians fear about aristocrats in public power, especially aristocrats like Eleanor and Franklin Roosevelt, is that they will dissipate the patrimony of the country in maternalist mercy for the miseries of the world, and in paternalist indulgence of its crimes and follies. This patrician fear of the royal couple differs from the entrepreneurial fear of the same pair. It is founded on a different "selfishness" and a different notion of the possibilities of life in the New World. Patricians consider themselves trustees of America's capital and treasure; if any sector of the country is to assume parental responsibilities for "the people" and posterity, it should be their sector. The entrepreneur, by invidious contrast, tends to think of paternalism and maternalism—protectionism in all its forms—as another form of the dead hand of the past, a tyrannical interference with individual freedom. Patricians take a more (old) worldly wise view of life's possibilities. They know that life is never so fair, so meritocratic, as the entrepreneur would have it; they themselves are living proof of just how unfair it can get. But it is in their interest to know, too, that while this unfairness can be ameliorated, preferably by them, it cannot be undone. Fate, or history, is too strong. Patricians believe that perfect justice in one generation would mean bankruptcy for future generations—above all, perhaps, for the future generations of their own families.

There is one major theme in the aristocratic presence in public life that never fails to touch the patrician heart. This is the martial theme, the sound of war.

The weakness issue (really the inherited-wealth issue) is one of the most serious that aristocrats have to face in politics. Elites in America are predominantly composed of self-made men, people who find it difficult to believe that grace and power can coexist in the same person, who believe that grace must sooner or later enervate power, or power must sooner or later corrupt grace. This defines the aristocrat's major problem on entering politics. He must convince various key elites (by no means excluding Old Money members) that while he *belongs* in the chauffeur-driven limousine, he does not absolutely need it. In other words, for his class background (never mind wealth) to be seen as an asset, it must be shown that he has the stuff to walk on his own two feet.

All three of this century's aristocratic Presidents ran into this difficulty. Even at Harvard, TR had the reputation of being excessively dandified in dress and equipage. Out West and in his first years in New York politics, he was seen by many as a personification of the dude. FDR encountered the worst suspicions of his weightiness from members of his own class. To Oliver Wendell Holmes, Jr., FDR was for many years "a good fellow with rather a soft edge." Endicott Peabody voted for Hoover in 1932, mostly on the grounds that he didn't think Franklin sufficiently aggressive to deal with the country's problems. Walter Lippmann thought him agreeable enough, but without any discernible qualifications for the job other than a strong desire to have it. William Phillips, a Grotonian and a Harvard man who had known FDR in Washington during World War I, said of him, in the unmistakable accents of the patrician trustee: "He was likeable and attractive but not a heavyweight, brilliant but not particularly steady in his views. He could charm anybody. . . . He was always amusing, always the life of the party, but he did not seem fully mature." As for JFK, when he began his campaign for the presidency, the only people who thought him "man enough" or serious enough for the job were (possibly) a few members of his family, a few more of his retainers and friends.

War, needless to say, is the solution to the aristocrat's weakness problem. It seems very unlikely, for example, that patrician Old or entrepreneurial New Money would ever have rallied to FDR's standard if it had never been raised in war. As it was, the Old Rich rallied to him even before Pearl Harbor, doing all they could to help him make the case to a selfishly "economic" people that America should once again come to the rescue of the Old World and its values. War did even better rhetorical service for TR and JFK. No warriorlike images were ever more carefully cultivated than those of the colonel of the Rough Riders and the lieutenant of PT-109. Ben Bradlee, a friend of Kennedy's rather as Astor was a friend of Roosevelt's, tells a classic story of how war can be deployed in the cause of showing a rich kid's strength to disbelievers. Kennedy had just begun the race for the Democratic nomination, and Bradlee had arranged for him to be interviewed by some *Newsweek* editors and writers. The meeting began at the Links Club, a patrician establishment occasionally favored by J. P. Morgan when he was alive; it then adjourned to the New York Turtle Bay brownstone of the journalist Blair Clark, who was, like Bradlee, a St. Mark's and Harvard graduate.

Bradlee begins his story on a note of stunning upper-class ingenuousness. He announces that there will be "vulgarity" in his account. Some may be shocked, he says:

> Others, like Kennedy and myself, whose vocabularies were formed in *the crucible of life* in the World War II Navy in the Pacific Ocean, will understand instinctively. There's nothing inherently vulgar in the legendary soldier's description of a broken-down Jeep: "The fucking fucker's fucked." Surely, there is no more succinct, or even *graceful,* four-word description of that particular state of affairs. [My italics.]

Bradlee then goes on to describe how JFK laid to rest certain people's doubts as to his toughness:

> Crusty Hal Lavine, who had been covering presidential campaigns for *Newsweek* before Kennedy was a junior Congressman, asked him what he was going to do that would convince the skeptics ... that he wasn't "just another pretty boy from Boston and Harvard." Kennedy was enjoying himself, despite the heat he was getting, and he turned to Lavine and stopped him cold by saying, "Well, I'm going to fucking well take Ohio, for openers." Not only had none of the editors heard a presidential candidate express himself that way, but

all of them knew that taking Ohio would in fact impress the skeptics, and they were impressed with Kennedy's conviction.

Khrushchev and Castro were not impressed, and it's hard to imagine that crusty Hal Levine was. To make the case for a man's masculinity on his ability to talk dirty is not an easy task. Still, it was an advantage of JFK's imagery over Nixon's that his naval career culminated in the heroism of the PT-109 story while Nixon's culminated in a series of jackpots he won playing poker.

The martial theme is a *leitmotiv* of Old Money. "My line of politics is war-war-war," said John Jay Chapman. He added a typical qualifying clause: ". . . with an ideal of absolute good humor and self-control." Henry Stimson, a partner in Elihu Root's law firm, FDR's wartime secretary of war, a model public servant for McGeorge Bundy, and a preeminent architect of America's postwar policy of "collective security," once recalled that he had never been so "wonderfully happy" as when he caught a whiff of gunsmoke and cordite in World War I. In a long career of private trusteeship and public service, Stimson was always proud of what he called his "combat psychology." Joseph Alsop, TR's great-nephew and a World War II partisan of Chennault and Stilwell in China, in 1962 composed a passage of matchless upper-class nonchalance in the face of war: "Watching the new green [foliage] cover a box bush," he wrote, "is just as exciting as watching the progress of the anti-guerrilla effort in South Vietnam. But in the reporter's trade, alas, the anti-guerrilla efforts have to be covered more intensively than the old earth's annual effort of self-renewal." JFK once asked Bradlee, speaking of Nelson Rockefeller: "Where was old Nels when you and I were dodging bullets in the Solomon Islands?"

> To set the cause above renown,
> To love the game beyond the prize,
> To honor, while you strike him down,
> The foe that comes with fearless eyes.

To less ardent spirits, or to entrepreneurial imaginations busy with prospects of making it, sentiments like these are terrifying. They suggest a class of people so disinterested and disciplined that they will fight without hope of gain, and kill without hostility. To the Old Rich, however, such sentiments are deeply moving. It's not just that war offers them a priceless but redemptively costly image of personal power to balance the image of personal grace. The matter is more complicated, perhaps more tragic, than that. In the social imagination of Old Money, there's a sickening distance between the Athenian polity of free and equal citizens and what they see as the actual American polity. War closes the distance. War brings Athens to America. The tragedy is that it also brings death. Today, war and the imagery of war is more tragically equivocal than it ever was. At the same time, no more than they ever did, do moral or civic equivalents of war have the imaginative appeal of "real" war. There might be a war for peace, or another for Nature: two wars worth fighting for posterity, and ones that would seem to have far greater hold on the hearts of the Old Rich than they do on the hearts of the would-be New Rich. But no Old Money prince or princess has appeared in the public arena to take the lead in those wars.

This is unfortunate, for a war of peace and the health of the planet will require great courage, and if TR, FDR, and JFK are a guide, the special gift of Old Money aristocrats in public life is the gift of courage: the courage to face the contingencies of starting-line equality and opportunity in a New World. People must be brave in the land of the free. Courage was certainly the great gift of FDR to his fellow citizens, and he began to give it even before he was inaugurated.

Roosevelt's April 1935 cruise on the *Nourmahal,* which Huey Long had such fun with, was not the first time he had accepted an invitation from Vincent Astor to go to sea. The first was in January 1933, between his election and inauguration. His shipmates on that occasion included Astor, another cousin, Kermit Roosevelt, and the valued retainer Raymond Moley. They were bound for Miami, where Roosevelt was to accept the salutations of the city on 4 February.

"The Hasty Pudding puts to sea," Boss Flynn of the Bronx was heard to say, as the *Nourmahal* left the dock at New York. It was a shrewd crack, as far as it went. Vincent Astor was a Harvard sophomore when his father went down on the *Titanic,* with $2,700 in his trousers pocket and a heavy gold chain on his waistcoat, and Vincent had loved him as boys sometimes do whose fathers are kind but often absent, and whose mothers are often present but seldom kind. His mother was Ava Willing, a beauty of old Philadelphia family, whom Robert de Montesquiou once described as *"nonchalante et froide,"* and she thought Vincent unattractive. He was. His height (he was six feet four) was his most impressive feature. Otherwise he might have sat for Savage's bitter portrait of an English peer—"the tenth successor to a foolish face"—or for Alice Longworth's portrait of Ned McLean. Yet he was a sensitive man, intelligent, well-read, and decent. He married well—three times: to Helen Huntington, Mary Cushing (Babe Paley's sister), and Brooke Russell Marshall, the best and brightest of the three, who stayed with him until he died, in 1952. He also did well, in the best patrician tradition, by doing good. "Every dollar," he used to say, "is a soldier that does your bidding." He bid them freely into the political wars: He was an early and generous supporter of Al Smith, contributing $35,000 to his presidential campaign; and by 1932, when Cousin Franklin was the candidate, he was a member of the Democratic party's Finance Committee, raising money and giving of his own (another $35,000) to the triumphant cause. There is evidence that Vincent entertained some small hope of reward for his largess; in particular, that he wanted to be made assistant secretary of the Navy, like TR, FDR, and even TR, Jr., before him. It was not to be.

Kermit Roosevelt was something of an oddity among his siblings. TR's children generally regarded FDR with the jealousy of poor relations who watch desserts they believe their own go to the less deserving. Ted junior, for example, through Groton and Harvard and on into public service, tried terribly hard to be a worthy successor to his father's name. But it was no good. His character seemed all pursed up in a little rictus of manfully repressed fear. Kermit was more casual, at least on the surface, charming, quite good-looking, and married to a rich, beautiful woman—Belle Willard, as she was. Yet there was something demonic about him, as there was about all the Oyster Bay Roosevelts, as though he didn't feel fully alive unless his world was heavy with challenge, struggle, extreme danger. He had been in the Great War, of course, all three brothers had. But he had not been wounded, as Ted junior and Archie were. He named his son after Quentin, the brother who had been killed. (The son Quentin would be killed too, in the next war. Another son, Kermit junior, went on to serve in the OSS, then with the CIA in Iran, where he was the engineer of Mossadegh's downfall and the prop of the young shah. The nephew Archie junior had a very similar career, culminating as David Rockefeller's liaison with the shah. Archie junior is also, as it happens, an uncle of mine by marriage.) Kermit senior seems to have passed the years after World War I pining for some sacrifice that would save his life by costing it. Maddeningly, the sacrifice eluded him. In World War II, Archie senior was wounded again, on Guadalcanal; Ted junior was killed; but Kermit survived. At the end of the war, stationed in Alaska, he killed himself.

Different as they were, in personality and in the fates that birth and breeding held in store for them, the three cousins of the *Nourmahal* had much in common. They shared everything that was most constitutive of Old Money culture—its sense of time and place, of what moral dangers their lives held out for them, and where their performative duties lay—and this shared culture gave them a full measure of that ineffable belongingness which is the most comforting aspect of inheritances like theirs. They knew each other's houses almost as well as they knew their own. Astor's Ferncliffe and FDR's Hyde Park were part of the same natural social landscape, the same stretch of the Hudson River, which had dominated the imagination of New York's Old Money since before the Revolution. Indeed, American property couldn't come any closer to the ideal of the *familias,* or to a proprietorship *en particule,* than it did with Astor's and Roosevelt's country estates. For these "places" they felt a pride that was indistinguishable from the pride they felt for their forebears, their posterity, and their selves. (FDR's concern for his estate was, as one might expect of an aristocrat, rather imperialistic: During his years in the White House, buying at Depression prices, he added two thousand acres to the six hundred he'd inherited.) Kermit inherited nothing of his father's real property, but he and FDR shared memories of the patrician brownstone in the city where Franklin's mother and father had first met, and where Franklin and Eleanor had married, with Uncle Ted giving away the bride and Endicott Peabody performing the service.

The *Nourmahal* docked in Miami, as scheduled, on 3 February. Vincent had been "a dear and a perfect host," FDR wrote his mother during the cruise. The next day, Roosevelt, with his shipmates in the car behind him, passed through the city in a motorcade. For the next fourteen years, FDR made a similar progress through other cities hundreds and hundreds of times, and the sight of him—his fine strong chin in the air, the famous smile at once challenging and wickedly pleased—never failed to pick up the spirits of the crowds. But that February he was still a stranger, as, in a sense, the people were to themselves. It was the third year of the Depression. Promise, possibility, the ever renewable newness of the New World, had dried up as never before. Independence was revealed as a euphemism for loneliness, if not a lie. Americans, one third of them unemployed, were puzzled, angry, full of self-reproach and fear. Miami was the first sortie among them of the man they had elected to make things right again. As one Old World observer had written: "When a poor boy who has become a millionaire [Herbert Hoover] is followed at the helm of state by a rich man who seldom earned anything himself, then it is as clear as in a fairy tale which of the two is destined to play the role of St. George."

It wasn't that clear, not yet. The dragon had still to be slain, the rescue performed. But the imagery was all in place.

As the motorcade streamed through the streets, Vincent Astor had a premonition of what was to come, wondering aloud at the frightful risks a leader ran in showing himself to the people. Minutes later, an unemployed bricklayer by the name of Giuseppe Zangara fired several shots at the President-elect. He missed his target, hitting the mayor of Chicago instead. Roosevelt was utterly calm, as though such incidents were to be expected: a shot ringing out among the cheers, like the one that hit Uncle Ted in the chest twenty years before. (Or, as we might say, like the one that killed John F. Kennedy thirty years later.) TR had finished his speech, stanching the blood with his handkerchief. FDR acted with the same graceful courage. He ordered the car to the hospital and stayed with the dying mayor to see that he was well looked after. Only then did he return to the *Nourmahal*. There, as one historian put it, Moley and Astor and Kermit Roosevelt slowly awakened to the fact that the new President would be a man truly without fear.

In the end there may not be much more to the special gift of aristocrats than the old image of casual grace, of effortless belonging-ness and buoyant gaiety, riding easily above the fretful turbulence of a people trying so very hard, each so very much alone, to make them-selves new. The image is wispy, occasional, the creature of a starveling fancy that must illuminate plain and common things in this New World—families, time, money—and has only ill-remembered appa-ritions from the Old World to do it with. Worse, the image can't seem to stand by itself. Its light must have a field of darkness, some dull impasto of despair with a glint of violence flashing through. Without fear, the image lacks shape and substance, and dissolves into the pale, thin air of American possibility. With it, the image comes clear, and so does the gift of courage.

CHAPTER EIGHT

Hemingway's Curse

"Let me tell you about the very rich," F. Scott Fitzgerald begins the third paragraph of his 1926 short story "The Rich
Boy." "They are different from you and me." To which, in the
most quoted put-down ever delivered to the pretensions of
the American rich, Ernest Hemingway is alleged to have
replied: "Yes, they have more money."

THE UNITED STATES is the country where it's not supposed
to matter who your father is. This supposition lies behind
every figment of the entrepreneurial imagination. And because the entrepreneurial imagination colors so much of the peculiar
promise of American life, the dismissal of fathers helps to define a
great deal of what this country is. At the same time, of course, it does
matter who one's father is. His wealth or poverty, his race, his culture
and education, the work he does, his address—never mind what sort
of man he is or whether he's much of a presence in your life—all these
factors are as fateful for the drama of one's life as anything can be in a
New World.

Yet that is the question, isn't it? In the whole world, the United
States is the country where fate—or history, genes, environment, the
forces of contingency, which fathers and mothers serve as proxies and
agents—lies lightest. An acquaintance of mine, trying to seduce a
pretty girl in a San Francisco bar, learned in rapid succession that the
girl used to come from the Bronx, used to be a hairdresser, used to be
Jewish, and, somewhat disconcertingly for my acquaintance, used to
be a man. Such are the possibilities open to the entrepreneurial imagination in a New World. There are others. This is the country where

a man (or woman) does not have to accept other people's opinion of him, or even his own opinion of himself. He or she can be a drunk, a criminal, a pauper, and, with effort, amnesia, and imagination, change it. This is a country that belongs to men of confidence and to confidence men. Self-forgiving, self-forgetting, self-asserting, self-improving, every man's a king in America's kingdom of means: means of change, means of possibility, means of making oneself and everything else new and better.

Such a country could only come about through the miracle of markets: financial markets to create wealth, skill markets to "make" men and women, goods and service markets to whet appetite and satisfy need. In such a country, any class that tries to stay above market, like any class that is kept below market, has a hard time becoming visible. The only thing that people will see of such a class will be what provides the class with a palpable connection to the market: its money or lack of it.

Hence the bane of Hemingway's Curse. The only commonly acknowledged difference between the nonrich and the rich is their money. Intermittently, in the flashing green light of imaginations like Fitzgerald's, other qualities will be visible, but for the most part, the only thing America sees in its Old Rich is their riches.

As a vision of the good life, Old Money has very little appeal to the American imagination of wealth, to the various visions that Americans have of what money can buy. It doesn't appeal to poor people, or to the "hard" middle class, or, except stroboscopically, to the only people who might easily afford at least to entertain it—the self-made champions of the marketplace, the entrepreneurs. Why has Old Money's construction of the good life so little appeal?

At the rather basic level of appearances, Old Money is a *social* class, which means that it appears only in representations of the social world that are dense, thick, full of chiaroscuro effects. In America, such representations are widely believed to be either depressing or invidious. Rightly so. A dense social consciousness undoubtedly inhibits a lively sense of the individual self, eager to take responsibility for pursuing its own path to happiness. A thick sense of time knits together the lines of those who came before us and those who come after us, our own boys and girls. But in the process time itself slows down, stifling opportunity and the grasp of opportunity, changing history from a one-directional progress to a series of spirals, one generation describing much the same trajectory as the previous one, successors advancing beyond predecessors only to the measure of their performances and the seasons of their lives. The chiaroscuro effects of the composition are too disturbing.

Besides, there are so many more agreeable ways to represent the world. There's the psychological way, for example, which offers a range of visions that goes from the self-improvement shelf of the nearest bookstore to the soundproof room of the primal scream therapist to the tragicomic agon of the Freudian couch. All, of course, center on the self and the bettering of the self, and that's one reason why the psychological picture of the world is competitive with Old Money's. But there's another reason, which is that psychology offers a kind of modern, "scientific" romance to take the place of the old-fashioned, fairy-tale romance of life according to Old Money. Not only does psychology unmask the Old Money mystique of generational descent and succession, and demystify Old Money's ordeals—it does all that, in spades—but it subverts Old Money's representation of the way we make our way in the world: It replaces one narrative line with another—dramatically quite as engaging as Old Money's, but more manipulable as to plot and character, and less offensive (or defiant) with respect to the marketplace.

It is the marketplace that seems to represent the most agreeable picture of life to Americans. In its image, Americans are happy to see themselves as a gathering of individuals who are present to each other as producers of work—ideas and artifacts and performances, candidacies and celebrities, lines of credit and bottom lines, goods and services—and as consumers of other people's work. To Old Money, this is a dismal picture, but to those who love it, it has everything one might want, including moral cachet. If society must judge its members, let it judge them by what they contribute to society and by what they choose, in pursuit of their own definitions of happiness, to take from it. The process of judgment also offers people an identity—two, in fact: the name of the form of "human capital" they rent out on the producers' market, and the name of their feeding pattern. "What do you do?" asks the stranger on the plane. He or she means, among other things, at least subliminally, "What is your place and heft in the marketplace?" The stranger will remember, better than one's family name, the name of the contribution one makes: medical services, plumbing supplies and repair, toilet articles, kitchen utensils, art objects. That is one identity: not Herb the father, or Herb the son, or Herb the citizen, but Herb the purveyor.

The other identity is a new sort of class position, triangulated through one's taste and income and yielding a specific class behavior as a buyer. Market researchers and media trendmongers—the stranger on the plane too, if he's with it—have such identities for people, more precise, and happily much less fateful, than anything the social imagination, whether Old Money's or Marx's, could devise. One is a pool-and-patio man, or a preppie, or a zip code 02138 woman, or a yuppie, or a DINC, or a "special interest" voter. Americans are what they produce, they are what they consume, and anything else they are, after market hours, can be identified psychologically. Old Money hardly appears in this larger gallery of American representations of life.

The market has thus seeded the language with some of our most basic metaphors. It has also found its way into our most sophisticated thinking about the uses of power and freedom. To buy or not to buy, that is a question decision theorists have now elaborated into a strong and versatile technique of choice that is almost as miraculous as markets themselves. Risk analysis, cost-benefit analysis, probability theory, various new forms of accounting: These tools of choice already dominate the teaching of business schools and schools of government— including, preeminently, the John F. Kennedy School of Government at Harvard. They are rapidly becoming de rigueur in all the other graduate schools that shape the way Americans make decisions for (and sometimes with) other Americans: law, medicine, public health, architecture and town planning. There's nothing obviously wrong here—they certainly do not dispense with "values," as their students (above or below the market) sometimes allege. On the contrary, like windmills or airplanes or sailboats, they need the breath of life— which is to say values, passions, goals, visions—to make them work. Their language can even be translated into the romance of contingency, which the Old Rich fancy: a romance of risks and hazards, powers of will and horrors of consequence, with a courageous and magnanimous decision-maker all alone, facing a tragic choice. Still, the fact remains that the metaphors are those of the marketplace. This will cost that; if you buy this, then you also buy that, and for a great measuring device of life, the metaphor makes all the difference. Yet that is one choice—the choice of metaphor—that sovereign consumers don't get to make in the marketplace of decision theory.

Hemingway's Curse also settles on Old Money's representation of itself: the part of the canvas, at any rate, where one finds depicted all

those lightweights, empty suits, free-falling angels, drunks and druggies, fuck-ups and fuck-offs, who figure so prominently in any honest
roll call of Old Money alumni and alumnae. Contemplating the risks
of buying into that life-style, even the most socially imaginative self-
made man might hesitate. The bottom-line benefits, to him or to his
family, don't look as though they would stack up against the downside
costs.

The most curious issue, however, is how Hemingway's Curse has
affected the Old Rich themselves. They have continually brought it
down on their own heads. How they have done this and continue to
do it is the most pathetic, vicious turn in the story of Old Money in
the New World. They did it and are still doing it by mismanaging and
misunderstanding the problem that faces any upper class with pretensions to exemplify what it considers high standards of taste and
conduct to other members of society—the problem of exclusion and
selection.

According to the logic of Old Money's own values and principles,
there is only one way the class can legitimize its ascendancy over and
above the riotous flood of wanting and working that constitutes the
"hard" life of the middle classes. That is to be a beacon, showing the
more successful of those storm-tossed strivers the way to a more gracious, edifying, and socially responsible life. It is true, of course, that
an exemplary class can be a model of evil as well as of good. Senator
Norris, the Progressive Plainsman who supported both Roosevelts'
proposals for an inheritance tax, argued this case on behalf of the work
ethic:

> It is contended that sons and daughters who have grown up in idle-
> ness, when they come into great fortunes, will spend their money in
> lavish living, in debauchery, in gambling, and through disgraceful
> and illegal methods soon dissipate the fortune, and the dangers of
> the concentration of wealth are thus avoided. . . . [But] when the man
> in the street sees the man high up in wealth or position doing dis-
> reputable things or leading an immoral life, he feels justified in fol-
> lowing in his footsteps. . . . he raises his children in an atmosphere
> of impurity, and, instead of being a useful and upright citizen, he
> becomes a member of the great derelict army.

On the whole, however, the Old Rich prefer to emphasize their
powers of uplift over their powers of debauchery. Perhaps debauchery
is too much to hope for. Uplift, in any case, offers better grounds for

class self-justification. Even Jefferson would have had little quarrel with this view. In his scheme for Virginia's education system, he envisioned elementary schools for all, the rich paying according to their means, the poor according to theirs, or not at all if they hadn't any. However, every two years or so, at the grammar-school stage, tests would be administered to the poorer students "by means [of which] twenty of the best geniuses will be raked from the rubbish annually, and be instructed, at the public expense, as far as the grammar schools go." Jefferson does not expect that the rich will be raked onto this rubbish heap; quite the reverse, money will provide the same sort of educational buoyancy for the rich as "genius" does for the poor. "Those whom either the wealth of their parents or the adoption of the State shall destine to higher degrees of learning, will go on." To arrange otherwise would be to infringe on freedom of opportunity. What President Eliot of Harvard, Herbert Pell, and E. Digby Baltzell did was to expand Jefferson's scheme to include all the other curricular institutions of the upper class and to turn the "raking" process into an argument in favor of inherited wealth and status.

This position is one side of a continuous debate within the Old Money class, a debate, indeed, that each member of the class often has with himself or herself. It is the liberal side, liberal in the sense of generous. It is also the conservative side, in the sense that it seeks to preserve a curatorial class and its inherited values against the revolutionary opportunism of market men and the marketplace. It is the discriminatory position as well, in the sense that it will not cast its pearls before swine. Finally, it is the side of tolerance and optimism, in the sense that it is prepared to consider all grist for its mill, and all wheat as good for the world, but it is equally the side of intolerance and pessimism, in the sense that consideration is a far cry from acceptance. In short, it is selective.

The other side, obviously, is exclusive. Exclusivists are many other things as well—stuffy, squeamish, stingy, and staid, for example—but mostly they are afraid. They are afraid of almost everything that America is. They imagine America as a vast stream of men, women, and money—swelling, heaving, rolling along, always on the verge of breaching its channel and flooding the lovely structures where they, the Old Rich, feel so at home. The club man in his red leather armchair is especially prone to this nightmare, and for him, characteristically, not only his graces and virtues are in danger but all of Western civilization:

How New York has fallen off during the last 40 years! Its intellect and culture have been diluted and swamped by a great flood-tide of material wealth ... men whose bank accounts are all they can rely on for social position and influence. As for their ladies, not a few ... looked as if they might have been cooks or chamber maids a few years ago.

So wrote George Templeton Strong, a most clubbable man, describing the epochal wave of self-made men whose origins he thought he descried, in the time of Jackson, and which he saw gathering irresistible force in the inflated economy of the Civil War. Thirty years earlier, right in the middle of the Jacksonian flood, the historian George Bancroft had occasion to examine the human material it had deposited in the highest house in the land:

The number of ladies [at the White House reception] was small; nor were they brilliant. But to compensate for it there were ... men not civilized enough to walk about the room with their hats off; the vilest promiscuous medley that ever was congregated in a decent house; many of the lowest gathering around the doors, pouncing with avidity upon the wine and refreshments, tearing the cake with the ravenous keenness of intense hunger; starvelings, and fellows with dirty faces and dirty manners; all the refuse that Washington could turn forth.

A century and a half later, Ronald Reagan was in the White House. Jacksonian ideals of frontier capitalism were once again riding tall in the saddle. Once again, too, the great stream of men and money was in flood, leaving infestations of self-made men and women on society's tangled banks. Now the lamentations of Old Money and its admirers were not for the Eden of the Federalists or of the Silver Spoon Age but for a social era that fantastically managed to owe something to both these antediluvian gardens and to one even older—the Camelot of John F. and Jacqueline B. Kennedy. "Mrs. Kennedy," one critic has written, "remained attached to an older tradition of aristocracy and obligation, of the moral exchange between the affluent and the less fortunate. The high-society followers of Mrs. Reagan and [Diana] Vreeland celebrate aristocracy as posture, as external trappings, and as luxury without responsibility."

But typical complaints from the Old Money class are rarely marked by the tone of robust revulsion one hears in Bancroft's remarks, or by the somewhat romantic nostalgia of the contemporary critic's analysis. Instead, there's usually an unmistakable tone of squeamish self-pity. It's as if the Old Rich saw themselves as the help-ess victims of a violated privacy or an insidious disease.

The disease is an affliction of their wealth: something always appears to be eating it away, and often is. In the radical entrepreneurial imaginations of men like Orestes Brownson, Gustavus Myers, Ferdinand Lundberg, and G. William Domhoff, each in his own time, the institutions of inherited wealth, combined with capitalism's oligopolistic tendencies, concentrate America's wealth, power, and opportunity in the tight grasp of a self-reproducing and largely impenetrable ruling class. There are patricians who wish this were so. Herbert Pell (more aristocrat than patrician) wrote during the Depression:

> Property in this country is drifting . . . into the pockets of those who can keep it and out of the hands of those who can merely acquire it. . . . It is obvious that the standards of the "keeping" class will be different from those of the "getters" and on the whole that they will be better for the country at large. The keepers' hearts may be harder, but their fingers are less nimble; the average person is more likely to profit from the steadiness and order of a conservative and honest community than he is from the tortuous career of a Napoleon of finance.

But to most beneficiaries of Old Money, the "drift" of property is more an erosion than a concentration. It starts to seem that way beginning with the death of the founding father. In America, he has almost always divided up his fortune more or less equally among his children, daughters as well as sons, and this principle of primitive communism is usually carried out in subsequent generations. From the outset, then, a patrimony inherited is a patrimony divided. And the divisions do not end there: divorce and remarriage, widowhood and remarriage, all the perils of mixing love and money break up patrimonies as easily as *per stirpes* bequests by dying paters and maters.

The sense of erosion is quickened by Old Money's well-cultivated attitude toward the uses of the patrimonial capital. The "keeping class" in actuality is the small group of patrician trustees who "keep" the money; everyone else is "kept"—all of them: aristocrats, free-falling angels, fuck-you-sayers, St. Midas students, warriors, conservationists, ladies bountiful, philanthropists, newspaper proprietors. They are kept free, but they are also often kept ignorant of what's happening to their money. Many of them do not want to know. Others want to know but persist in a trained incompetence so thorough they wouldn't understand the subject if they were tutored in it for a month. Even if they did understand it, the trust device would render their knowledge purely gratuitous, like so much else in their lives. In any event, this massive ignorance of the source of their freedom does not conduce to a confident appreciation of their capital's steady growth in security and amount. Nor is confident appreciation always warranted. The keeping class is not always clever enough to manage the tension between asset growth (or stability) and asset security. As prudent men, they usually opt for security, which in times of inflation (as in the last twenty years) is a virtual prescription for patrimonial erosion. Thus, whether out of ignorance or out of knowledge, the Old Money state of mind is seldom at ease with respect to its money. The flood seems to be bearing it away.

It is the same with the class's patrimony in treasure. The house in Dark Harbor, Maine, or the Duncan Phyfe dining room, or the art that was too personal to be given to the museum—all these emblems of precedence, once "priceless" in value, are suddenly discovered to have very grand prices indeed. The admiring, covetous envy of New Money for the property of the Old pushes up its market value to heights of unendurable temptation to sell. This is a dreadful moment in a family, when greed, disaffection, or the insidious encroachments of a felt poverty tear the veil of sentiment to reveal the obscene market value of one of its treasures. It is the moment when a social treasure, however restricted in its enjoyment, is exchanged for the guilty joys of a free, individualized possession of cash. It is a moment of liberation, but also of liquidation, and it compels a descent into the onrushing torrent of money—and possibility.

Economics may hold the key to Old Money's sense of being eaten away, but something else entirely holds the key to its squeamishness and self-pity. It is the metaphor of family, the understanding the Old Rich so often have of themselves not as a social class but as an extended family.

As much as a class is composed of money and imagination, it is also composed of memories. These memories are very intimate, and fragile, and we want them to be safe. Thus Old Rich class consciousness is filled with stumbling recitations of the *Anabasis,* the feel of grass tennis courts under bare feet, an embarrassing performance in the Tavern Club play, a coming-out party at Hammersmith Farm ("everybody" was there), the steamed mirrors at the Racquet Club, a sudden access of love for a class of poor black children, the color of Penobscot Bay under a northwest wind (wine dark, surely), or, after the awful coherence of a chapel service at St. Paul's School, the heartening glory of sunlight on the snow. Many of these memories revolve around rituals powerfully connected to the sequence of dramas in human, not just upper-class, life. As they move along through the successive stages of the Old Money curriculum, its beneficiaries give ceremony and significance to the turning points in their lives, and a continuity between the generations, that is almost unknown among the mobile middle classes. Going "up to school," getting elected to "the club," taking his "seat," wherever it may be, the Old Money boy follows his father in a nicely graduated, fittingly celebrated progress (or so his mentors may hope) toward a responsible patrician manhood. For girls, the stages on life's way are less well-marked; or rather, since the passing of Society, they are less well-marked by gender. Sallie Bingham's revolution was not without cause.

In fact, for many of us in Old Money families, class institutions served virtually all the functions of the ideal "affective" middle-class family, teaching us everything from self-respect to sexual hygiene. Our schools and yacht clubs and "natural" men and women were our parents, and as parents they were at least as good and occasionally better than the ones fate provided. Thus while there's little excuse, still less any justification, for the exclusivists' squeamishness and self-pity, there's a certain pathetic inevitability about it.

Old Money's exclusivists want to protect these deeply intimate treasures, as well as more public ones, from the rising flood. Their most characteristic anxiety is the anxiety of violated privacy, for their memories are family memories. New Money, they imagine, is sensual, prurient money, and it wants to join the family. It wants, in the familiar phrase, to marry one's daughter. "Business dangled on high a protean prize, and each man saw in it what he longed for most," wrote Henry Dwight Sedgwick in the 1930s:

> The avaricious man beheld bags of gold piled high in safe-deposit vaults; the glutton smelt the fumes of Haroun-al-Raschid's kitchens; the lecher caught sight of feminine forms fresh from the salt-sea foam; the socially-minded fingered the jingling keys that unlock aristocratic doors and bedizened clubrooms; those born in hardship lay on imaginary beds of luxury.

Hysteria follows, and the sound of slamming doors.

But the worst is yet to come: the worst nightmare for the class, but also the worst wound that the class persists in inflicting on itself. This is the fact that since the 1840s, Old Money has always been able to flesh out its image of the flood of sensual money with even more terrifying images of a flood of strange, barbarous, or "ethnic" money. In a curious way, for Old Rich heirs and heiresses to be effectively cursed by Hemingway's Curse, they must have been cursed with one or another or all of the virulent varieties of ethnocentricity: Athenian xenophobia, British racialism, Brahmin Bostonian anti- (Irish) Catholicism, any one of a number of possible anti-Semitisms, and the traditional American anti-black racism. The "family" metaphor for the class, in other words, must be understood as being itself a metaphor for the "race" of White Anglo-Saxon Protestants.

Henry Adams is the representative figure of this disgrace, and a winter evening in 1850 was the pivotal moment. Uncle Henry describes the scene with a fondness for the lost ebullience of his boyhood that seems more characteristic of Mark Twain than of the self-styled last of the line of Adams. Note that the "Latin School" boys in this outbreak of class warfare are the rich residents of Beacon Hill, while their opponents come from the then mostly Irish slums to the south of Boston Common:

> Whenever, on a half-holiday, the weather was soft enough to soften the snow, the Common was apt to be the scene of a fight, which began in daylight with the Latin School in force, rushing their opponents down to Tremont Street, and which generally ended at dark by the Latin School dwindling in numbers and disappearing.... One afternoon the fight had been long and exhausting. The boy Henry, following, as his habit was, his bigger brother Charles, had taken part in the battle, and had felt his courage much depressed by seeing one his trustiest leaders, Henry Higginson—"Bully Hig," his school name—struck by a stone over the eye, and led off the field in rather a ghastly manner. As night came on ... [a] dark mass of figures could be seen below, making ready for the last rush, and rumor said that a swarm of blackguards from the slums, led by a grisly terror called Conky Daniels, with a club and a hideous reputation, was going to put an end to the Beacon Street cowards forever. Henry wanted to run away with the others, but his brother was too big to run away, so they stood still and waited immolation. The dark mass set up a shout, and rushed forward. The Beacon Street boys

turned and fled up the steps [of the Beacon Street Mall], except
Savage and Marvin and the few champions who would not run. The
terrible Conky Daniels swaggered up, stopped a moment with his
body-guard to swear a few oaths at Marvin, and then swept on and
chased the flyers, leaving the few boys untouched who stood their
ground.... [T]he boy Henry had passed through as much terror as
though he were Turenne or Henri IV, and ten or twelve years afterward when these same boys were fighting and falling on all the
battle-fields of Virginia and Maryland, he wondered whether their
education on Boston Common had taught Savage and Marvin how
to die.

Irony prevails, of course, undercutting everything in sight—Henry, his
brother, Conky, even Savage and Marvin's gift of their lives in a "real"
battle for the Union cause, compared here to a snowball fight on Boston Common. Irony also ensures that the passage shall contain no suggestion of the deep shock that the coming of people like Conky Daniels
had delivered to the more prosperous citizens of the Athens of
America.

In fact, Henry Adams was later inclined to treat Irish slum-
dwellers with something like magnanimity. "The obvious moral," he
wrote of Conky Daniels's sparing the lives of Beacon Hill's best and
bravest, "taught that blackguards were not so black as they were
painted." But the generosity was not typical—not of Uncle Henry and
not of most beneficiaries of Old Money, then or now. There was certainly no generosity in his response to another group of immigrants,
the Jews. In the Jews, money seemed to Adams more than sensual; it
became lascivious. In the Jews, the entrepreneurial imagination was
not just unnatural but preternatural. So with the Jews the struggle was
historic, and far less romantic (or "real") than a snowball fight: "Not a
Polish Jew fresh from Warsaw or Cracow—not a furtive Yacoob or
Ysaac still reeking of the Ghetto, snarling a weird Yiddish to the officers of the customs—but had a keener instinct, an intenser energy, and
a freer hand than he—American of Americans, with Heaven knew
how many Puritans and Patriots behind him." In the Jews, the *fin de
race* memoirist descried not only the triumph of the marketplace but
the defeat of Henry Adams.

It is not always Jews whom the Old Rich see to be threatening
their allegedly "family" values. My grandfather Aldrich's loathing of
the Irish, for example, was so great that he had no trouble making

common cause, as he saw it, with Jews. Jews—the ones he knew, any-way—respected the graces and virtues that he did, and the same insti-tutions: Harvard, the Museum of Fine Arts, the Tavern Club. Moreover (and this was all to the good), they were quite rich enough to afford these institutions and virtues. For most of the WASP Old Money class, however, anti-Semitism is the most salient manifestation of their "family" fears and loathing. It is qualitatively different from their anti-Catholicism or anti-black racism. It is more like a deadly rivalry—not over which set of values captures the soul of America but over which ethnic group wins custody of Old Money values. If Jews are an obsession with the WASP Old Rich, and they are, it is not because they spell the destruction of the things Old Money holds dear but because the WASP Old Rich half-suspect that Jews take better care, can afford to take better care, of the patrimony than they can.

Anti-Semitism has always been endemic in the Old Money class. Racism against blacks is relatively recent. Historically, the Old Rich view of blacks was somewhat remote, as in this vignette drawn by the historian of Society Dixon Wecter:

> [At] the Union Club of New York, before removal from Fifth Ave-nue to its present quarters at Park Avenue and 69th Street had in-validated its old custom of viewing the town from behind its plate-glass window ... [a] favored sport was to bet upon the number of Negroes who would pass ... during a specified time. A member ... once had the good luck to meet a parade of colored delegates starting far up Fifth Avenue. Hastily calling a taxi he arrived at the Union Club and with great success bet all comers on the apparently insane proposal that 500 Negroes would pass within the next half hour.

At least until the 1950s, the view was much the same from behind the ivy-covered walls of the Old Money educational system. Harvard and the rest of the colleges would take qualified blacks if they applied, but generally speaking these institutions no more considered themselves obliged to serve as a beacon of good manners and social virtue to black people than Ole Miss did. The St. Midas schools, being officially Chris-tian and Protestant communities, were in a somewhat more awkward position. Unlike the nondenominational colleges, they could exclude Jews and Catholics on religious grounds, but blacks were not so easily disqualified. Blacks were Christian and Protestant; more and more of them, in fact, thanks to aristocratic missionary priests like Paul Moore, were Episcopalians. This left the schools bereft of any reason to keep blacks out, other than ethnocentric revulsion. Neither Groton nor St. Paul's accepted blacks until the mid-1950s, or about the time the public schools of Little Rock, Arkansas, were forced by the government to do the same.

At Groton, the news that the school would accept one black boy set off one of the most wretched scandals in Old Money history. Francis Minturn Sedgwick, Henry Dwight's son and Edie's father, was one of those beneficiaries of the class whose love of his own image soared effortlessly beyond the narcissistic to the pornographic. When he learned that the school would soon enroll a black, he wrote a letter to his fellow alumni, fraudulently signing it with the rector's signature, which informed them that the new admissions policy would hence-forth reserve half of the places at the school for blacks. Sedgwick was a vicious man. But the people who read his letter were not vicious, and their response to it is not known to anyone but themselves. Still, we may safely assume that many of them were sympathetic to Sedgwick's follow-up letter explaining his hoax. He declared that he harbored no prejudice against Negroes. Negroes were welcome—he personally had welcomed them—at Harvard. But Groton was "family," in his view, much more so than Harvard, and Negroes had no place in the Groton family.

Bigotry has been a continuous disaster for the Old Money class. Some heirs and heiresses, believing in Old Money's mission to uplift the entire nation, might even go so far as to consider it a disaster for the country. But if so, it is a disaster of quite a different sort than what E. Digby Baltzell imagines it to be. Baltzell, following many others, argues that there should be a place in society, a kind of withdrawing room, for representatives of civilized authority: *all* civilized authori-ties—Jew and Gentile, Catholic and Protestant, black, white, and yel-low—so long as they cherish the values and principles of the upper class. The argument is for a class—an aristocracy, as Baltzell calls it—not a caste, which is what ethnocentrism leads to. It is an argument for a ruling class, for a "certain throne," as Lippmann revealingly put it.

In an entrepreneurially minded society, this seems to me a most unpalatable proposition, and, in a supposedly democratic polity, a very dangerous one. A more acceptable, safer one is the case Old Money makes for an ascendant *social* class, a class with a social imagination that sees a use for history, a place for *pietas* and posterity, a significance for citizenship, and an end for the strivings of Market Man.

But WASP ethnocentrism dooms an ascendant social class even more surely than it dooms a ruling class. White Anglo-Saxon Protestants happen to have been the first group of rich men to import into American society the class values characterized as Old Money. But there is nothing in those values that genetically marks them as belonging to white Anglo-Saxon Protestants. Inherited wealth certainly isn't WASP; nor are graceful manners, sportsmanship, the gift ethic, the ideal of performance, the impulse of self-sacrifice, or the idea of *noblesse oblige*. Pericles was a Greek. The "higher" courtesy was best described by Castiglione, an Italian. Old Money values are not Christian, either; far from it. St. Midas Christianity is never very Christian. If it isn't a bland disguise for race and class prejudice, it is a mixture of Stoic ethics and Pindarian celebration. In short, Old Money's curriculum is not an ethnic or tribal or family *curriculum*. It is, or might have been, a class curriculum.

The difference between class values and ethnic ones is a difference in the fatefulness of accidents of birth. In (entrepreneurial) theory and in practice, Americans can do anything they want with their ethnicity: love it, leave it, trivialize it, hate it, forget it. The only thing they can't do with it is aspire to it, or "make it." Ethnicity is a social space as dense, thick, and richly figured with dark and light as Old Money is, even more so. It's as Old World as Old Money is, even older. Thus ethnicity is more fateful than any class, and it can never be a goal of one's becoming, not even in America. Class, by contrast, seems almost optional, voluntary, even (very quietly) purchasable.

If Old Money is not a class, the fault is almost entirely that of the precedent, preeminent, prior WASPs. Much of the history of the Old Rich can be written as a squeamish withdrawal from the barbarian hordes that began more than a century ago to make their way into Old Money's schools and residences. St. Paul's was founded in 1854, by a Brahmin Bostonian, as a school far away from the city where the urban rich might gather their children among their own kind, away from the likes of Conky Daniels. Boston Latin was a public school, but after the Irish appeared on the scene, it wasn't a Brahmin kind of public school. Chestnut Hill, Massachusetts, supposedly the first "exclusive" suburb, was founded for much the same reasons and by exactly the same sort of people. The countryside around Westbury, Long Island, a favorite suburban enclave of New York's Old Rich to this day, was bought and settled by Tommy Hitchcock's father and my friend Edwin Morgan's grandfather in the 1880s. Sooner or later, in every old city in the land, the Old Rich followed the same line of retreat—defending their rear with any protectionist ploys they could think of and the law allowed—out of the Athens of America into suburban bastions of ethnics like themselves.

Greek Athenians, it must be said, behaved as ethnocentrically as the American ones, though they stood and fought the alien swarms. They did not abandon the city. The WASP Old Rich did, for the most part, and the shift was ruinous for their ideals of citizenship. Generation after generation of Old Families might stream through the social densities of St. Paul's and Groton, might even emerge with lively social consciences, but so long as they streamed in from Far Hills or Ipswich or Malvern or Sewickley, and back out again, the lessons of Pericles and David the Philistine-killer went the way of their school learning. They got thin and spotty. And once this pattern was established—a migratory pattern from suburb to school to summer place to daytime "seat" in the city and back again—class consciousness was bound to become equally thin and spotty.

The timorous withdrawal of the WASP Old Rich into suburban enclaves did not encourage the Irish, Jewish, Italian, or black rich to give up their ethnic identities for an Old Money class identity. Besides, there were (and are) all the other reasons for refusing this class identity in America: the threat of weakness and degeneracy, the fear of rejection, the "stupidity" of the gift ethos, the onerousness of *noblesse oblige,* and, above all, exposing oneself and one's family to the disturbing influence of other people's envy. Still, over the years the WASP Old Rich have observed generation after generation of rich non-WASPs who seem to aspire to the Old Money class, regardless of its WASP appearance. Excluded (or insufficiently selected) by the guardians of the Old Money curriculum, they established their own curriculums—schools, summer resorts, clubs—and bred their own patricians and aristocrats. They also established their own suburban enclaves and cultivated their own ethnic consciousnesses. Still, it seemed that these non-WASPs not only wanted to imitate WASP culture but yearned somehow to *be* WASP, as if they had always known that Old Money values were class values. But this knowledge the WASP Old Rich have always been reluctant fully to admit. It is too threatening. To concede that "other people" might entertain the same values as they imagine they do is to give up a large part of the exclusivist option. So long as they can go on confusing ethnic and class identities, for so long, it seems to them, they and their daughters can feel safe from the lascivious intrusion of sensual money.

The trouble with this line of defense is that it works only in those areas of life where exclusion has some chance of success—friendships, marriage partners, choice of suburb and resort, and the like. Wherever selectivist principles operate, on the other hand, the confusion of ethnicity and class has a catastrophic effect—on the confused. This means that catastrophe has become increasingly a regular feature of WASP Old Money. Selectivist principles have been the rule for a long time now at all the most valued institutions of the Old Money curriculum— Harvard and its social equivalents, the more meritocratic clubs, the boards of the most prestigious museums, hospitals, "land trusts," and the like. Thence these principles filter down into all the intimate recesses of Old Money life. The result has been an outbreak of the most fearful whining and wailing since Henry Adams complained of his life prospects. Upper-class WASPs are an "endangered species," they say. Asked about Old Money, they complete the confusion: "Old Money? I'd say it was on the way out, wouldn't you? Like the snail-darter." Even people who should know better fall into this catastrophic way of thinking. John V. Lindsay, an aristocrat once, was not long ago interviewed by the late Charlotte Curtis of *The New York Times*:

> Asked about the power of New York Wasps, the former Mayor just laughed.... "They're an endangered species," he said, as if he weren't one. And, more seriously, that while they are perceived as having tremendous power, they're down to a few commercial banks, hunks of real estate, corporate chairs, culture boards, and their clubs. "You realize you can't call any other ethnic group by its pejorative name," he said. "But you can say 'Wasp.' As if they didn't bleed."

This is what comes of supposing that Old Money priorities and presumptions belong to a "race" rather than to a particular way of imagining relations between men, money, and society—a vision of the good life that can be grasped by anyone who thinks he or she can afford it. Lindsay's last remark violates every class standard of grace and virtue he was taught, never mind every common standard of intelligence. It is disgraceful and stupid to suppose that "WASP" belongs in the same category of ethnic slur as "nigger" or "kike" or "spic." Yet that sort of perversion of the social imagination is almost commonplace among Old Rich WASPs. And the effects of the perversion go beyond the personal disgrace it brings down on "nice" people like Lindsay. Ethnocentrism like theirs and Adams's has the further disastrous effect of reducing Old Money's entire class project to the level of a competition for "market share."

A good place to see this competition, and its results in the erosion of Old Money dignity, is on the campus of a St. Midas school anytime before that dreadful April day when Harvard and its social equals send out their messages of acceptance or rejection to the boys and girls of Old Riches. Harvard's admissions policies started it all, in a way, ratcheting up their standards so high that the Old Money children risked being raked into the same heap of rubbish that once contained only poor kids. These higher admissions standards forced St. Midas, as we have seen, to raise its own, which in turn forced similar action on every "country day" in the rich suburbs. And as Harvard (et al.) were determined to apply the standard of the All-Round Man not only to the selection of individual applicants but to the composition of its student body as a whole, this meant a shopping list: so many ice hockey players, so many premed students, so many blacks, so many Californians, so many musicians, so many children of alumni. The composition of an Ivy League class is in fact one of the most formidable displays of studied nonchalance in the repertoire of Old Money; it needs to be, to avoid the pit of "quotas" and the pendulum of equal-opportunity violation.

But if Harvard had a shopping list, then St. Midas had to deliver the goods. Soon the schools discovered, to their horror, that they were in the business of selling their students, and the students, of course, discovered that they were in the business of selling themselves. With that, the market mentality was upon them, with bottom-line thinking not far behind. Ethnocentrism comes in to define the market as a zero-sum game, with every Harvard acceptance of a black, say, entailing the rejection of a WASP. I remember a conversation I had several years ago with a WASP St. Midas's boy in whom envy was not only unattractive but totally uncalled for. He was talking about how many kids in his class would get into "the Ivies":

> Take this guy in our class. He's got it all—good grades, captain of the track team, plays an instrument, handsome, popular. If they'd wanted a black Superman they could have cast him for the part. Yeah, I admit, a black Superman might not play well at the box

office, but this guy's sure going to play well at the Harvard admissions office. Guys like me, and I've done pretty well here, we don't have a chance against guys like that. And the beauty part is that he's not one of those upper-middle-class blacks you find at so many prep schools. They found him on a little old chicken farm in Maryland someplace. Chicken shit to Harvard in one easy bound, how about that?

The same spite and resentment is squirming around in Lindsay's (or Curtis's) remarks about the WASPs' loss of "seats" on the board. Many worthy beneficiaries of WASP Old Money say the country's going to hell, meaning that they are losing "their" share of the great marketplace of life.

They *are* losing their precedent share of the Old Money curriculum, there's no question about that, and with it goes a decided loss in class status. This may account for one of the most ignominious marks that has ever been set against the class: that in the 1987–88 campaign for the presidency, the two most obvious Old Money candidates, George Bush and Pierre "Pete" du Pont IV, both ran on platforms representing a total surrender to the entrepreneurial imagination. Of the two, du Pont was perhaps the greater class traitor. He was certainly more aware of what he was doing, and did it better. There is not one area of public life, not one actual or potential public good, not one slice of the nation's patrimony (except for its museums, perhaps, and a small part of the great outdoors), that Pete du Pont would not give over to the custody of entrepreneurs in free markets. It is almost eerie how this inheritor of trusts and other assets worth at least $3 million (the figure was grudgingly allowed to grow as his campaign went on) singled out *dependency* as the most sinister evil facing the nation. He might have pointed to greed and fear, but he didn't. Pete du Pont's America is full of welfare families dependent on government handouts, high-school students dependent on drugs, farmers dependent on price supports, parents dependent on their local public school, old people dependent on government-insured Social Security, and, all over the world, millions and millions of non-Americans who are threatened, and threaten themselves and ourselves, with political dependency on the Soviet Union.

In each and every case, Pete du Pont would extirpate these vices through the discipline of the free competitive market: independent consumers fighting freely for the best deal, producers fighting freely to produce the best goods and services, men, women, and children fighting freely for the best educations, careers, jobs, and lives they can get. He would let farmers sink or swim in free agricultural markets within five years. He would let welfare dependents sink or swim on labor markets as soon as he could get laws passed: no work, no check, or else work for the state. He would give parents $600 or $700 a year with which to open up a market in education for their children. Finally, in a nice twist, he would take all high-school students caught with drug traces in their urine and deprive them of America's most cherished symbol of independence, their driver's licenses. Freedom is also his solution to the threat of communism. "We ought to help people fight for freedom everywhere in the world," he told a gathering at Harvard's Kennedy School of Government.

Du Pont was a traitor to his class not because he presented himself as a conservative, not even because he presented himself as the candidate of virtue (conservatives usually do). Old Money is always politically conservative—patricians are conservative with respect to ends and means, aristocrats with respect to ends alone—and likes to think of itself as a party of virtue. Du Pont betrayed his class, rather, in presenting himself as a radical partisan of the marketplace and of the single virtue of toughness—"what it takes to make it in this world." For all his trumpet calls to get tough with the Soviets anywhere in the world, he was also a candidate of fear. But the best sign of his class background was his extremism. In Pete du Pont, the American people caught a glimpse of Tom Buchanan running for office, weakness hidden behind a breastplate of righteousness, careening through other people's lives while sure of the invulnerability of his own, his carelessness carefully packaged and marketed as "toughness." As Governor Bruce Babbitt once said, laughing, du Pont was the sort of fellow who, when his roof sprung a leak, tore down the house.

But then, of course, Pierre Samuel du Pont IV could afford to tear his house down; he could always build another. Hemingway's Curse struck again, in front of millions of citizens. With that sally, Babbitt brilliantly revealed that between him and Pete du Pont, between all the other residents of this New World and all the Pete du Ponts, the only difference was a difference of money. So it was with most of the Old Rich in the Age of Reagan, the New Age of the Entrepreneur. Most of the time, the class lay down before its historic antagonist like a bored housewife before a promising encyclopedia salesman.

. . .

Even so, in America it clearly does matter who your father is. It mattered to me. In the end, the best and brightest beacon of the Old Money class may be the one with which I began, *pietas*. And for *pietas*—perhaps for all the virtues and values of the class—no money is required.

In a sense, my feelings for my father are composed of piety (or impiety) and nothing else. He entered my conscious life when I was ten—too soon or too late for much of anything else. Suddenly he was there, back from the war in the Pacific, his presence emanating such tremendous authority he might have been Odysseus and I a timorous Telemachus. I never got over the shock, and for the rest of his life (he died in 1986) I tried to keep him at a safe distance. This was easy. For nine months of the year I was at boarding school or college; on vacations I often went to see my mother or godparents in another city. More important, for most of the overlap between their lives and mine, my Aldrich grandparents and I carried on a shameless family romance—of the Freudian sort, that is. My grandmother always used to say that I was old enough, or she young enough, for me to have been her fourth and youngest child, and as my actual mother was (by her own cheerful admission) a decidedly unmaternal woman, I was delighted to share my grandmother's fantasy and add to it my own. She also spoiled me rotten. My grandfather lent himself to the arrangement for motives of his own. What they were may be imagined from the fact that my grandfather retired from the practice of architecture (at the age of forty-five or so) about the time my father took it up, and from the fact that they barely spoke to one another from then to the day my grandfather died, forty years later. My own motives were, as I've said, fear. I feared my father, my grandfather was enraged by him; the situation offered a neat parallel to the alliances of nations, whereby the enemy of my enemy is my friend. Also, my grandfather and I got on well temperamentally. I loved him and he loved me. He, too, spoiled me rotten.

Another circumstance made it easy for me to keep my distance from my father and made it even more important: this was his stature as a public man. My father had a successful career as an architect, but I do not believe that his designs, with one or two exceptions, ever met his own standards of personal performance. Nor did his watercolors,

which he took to market toward the end of his life. But architecture
and painting, like sailing, were aspects of his private life, facets of his
all-roundedness, as his teachers at St. George's School might have put
it. It was his public life as a citizen that he was proudest of and where
he most intimidated me. It seemed to me that he was always attending
meetings: trustee meetings, town meetings (in Marblehead, where he
moved to his grandmother's house after the war), meetings in Boston
with public officials and private patricians for God knows what civic
purposes, meetings at various schools and colleges for which he did
the master plan. In the 1950s, he and his friend Jerome Rosenfeld
mounted in Boston's Public Gardens an Arts Festival, free to all, that
brought contemporary art to that graphically benighted Athens of
America, as well as free performances of ballet, poetry, and theater.
For all these contributions he received his share of honor. After he
died, the town of Marblehead named the new high-school auditorium
after him. He had not given it to the town; he campaigned for it from
his (elected) position as chairman of the Planning and Zoning Board,
and the money was the public's money.

He was an active man, and so the distance between us was not
hard to keep. This presented a certain problem when the time came
for me, his eldest child and only son, to give a eulogy in his memory
at Trinity Church in Boston. The problem was how to honor both the
father who terrified me and the man whom I admired, without being
embarrassing about the one or distant about the other. In a burst of
inspiration, I decided to commend his life as an example to *his* grandchildren. Only later did I think to call this by its right name—*pietas*.
At his funeral, this is what I said:

> The Bible has no story so full of your grandfather's life as this
> one from the Book of Kings:

> And it came to pass when they were gone over that Elijah said unto
> Elisha, Ask what I shall do for thee after I be taken away from thee.
> And Elisha said, Let a double portion of thy spirit be upon me. . . .
> And Elijah went up by a whirlwind into Heaven. And Elisha saw it,
> and he cried, My father, my father. . . . He took up also the mantle
> of Elijah that fell from him.

> I'd like to put it to you that the relationship of Elijah and
> Elisha was that of a grandfather and grandchild. We know
> from the Bible what we also know from experience, that they

weren't father and son. Parents and children stand too close to each other for mantling. Mantles must be freely given and freely taken up, and where the generations touch, the touch is too intimate, too searching, too exigent for freedom. But between grandparents and grandchildren the distances seem just right: the timing is good and so is the perspective.

Of course, there has to be a mantle as well, but in your case there is. Your grandfather let it fall last week. He let it fall for you. It's yours to take up if you want it.

Think of him now as Elisha. What kind of a person must one be to be Elisha? Your answer will depend a good deal on what kind of person you are. My guess is that you are decent, intelligent, fair-minded American persons; and if this is so, then I daresay the first thing you noticed about Elisha is that he had the gall ... to ask for a double portion of spirit. Who did he think he was? What kind of mantle is this, that it goes to people who want more than their fair share?

Your grandfather would have understood this response, but it would not have deterred him. Make no mistake: your grandfather had an outrageous appetite. And not only for spirit. He wanted powers, honors, admiration, respect. . . .

Of course, most people want these things. But your grandfather wanted more of them than most people do, and wanted them more. Many fair-minded Americans might say that such a man was greedy. But in his case you would be wrong. Greedy people don't simply want things. They need them. They need power, for example, to feel courageous; they need admiration to feel loved; they need honors to feel self-respect. Your grandfather was not one of the needy. He had love, power, courage, self-respect—had them already, so to speak. He asked for the double portion not because it completed his emptiness but because it complemented his wholeness. He claimed it as his due. He claimed it just because he had it already.

This reasoning is rarely persuasive to the fair-minded. Especially in America. America is the country where you're not supposed to have anything "already." Here in this New World you're supposed to make it all, earn it all, from scratch. Americans do not take kindly to people who have, as they say, "got it made" from the beginning.

But your grandfather had a different view. He thought it

was the task of one's life to make the most of whatever one had, without worrying too much about where it came from or why it had come to oneself rather than to someone else. He understood that his double portion might easily be perceived as an injustice—in some sense it was an injustice. But he did not apologize, nor did he try to explain. On the contrary, he loved everything that had been given him, everything he'd taken up, everything he was. He was blessed, and knew it. Indeed, there were times—when you were nearby, for example—when he felt he could bless.

But if your grandfather was never embarrassed to ask for his due, neither did he ever, as the sickening slogan goes, "want it all." He knew there were other people in the world who wanted things just as badly as he did, by no means the same things. It is true this often seemed to fill him with vast astonishment, but rarely did he look with contempt on the people who opposed him, and never with disdain on their right to do so. Whether or not his double portion was just, he always tried to use it justly. Only in that way could he earn the mantle that he took up from Elijah.

Who his Elijah was I don't know. Possibly it was his grandfather, the first Nelson W. Aldrich. But whoever he was, there's no question about what his mantle was. It was the mantle of a public man, a person who spends his life in and for the public world.

What does that mean? Though he wouldn't have put it quite this way, to live a public life means to be ultimately concerned with public goods—what they are and how they may be realized and protected. The public goods that concerned him especially were matters of beauty and ugliness, but that is not important. The mantle is for leading the life, the life of concern for the public world.

Your grandfather would not have said he made sacrifices to lead that sort of life. It was almost instinctive in him. He had an inner, private life—as full of ambivalences, fears, and personal satisfactions as anyone else's. The difference was that his view of these things was fundamentally impatient. He used to tell me that the most important moments of his day were the four or five minutes he'd lie in bed after waking up in the morning. It was then that he decided what he wanted to get done that day. Think of it. Four or five minutes to commit himself to a course of action. Four or five minutes entirely untroubled by the sort of analyses that Freud taught us to make of life, or Darwin, or Marx. Untroubled by whole centuries of Christian guilt. Your grandfather was not quite a modern man. He was almost purely Greek; that is to say, a citizen.

For his children, it was not always amusing or comforting to be brought up by a public man.... Growing up with a father like him was a complex experience, exhilarating and exhausting, discouraging and inspiring. One was always on stage, performing as best one could, in every way one could—intellectually, aesthetically, politically. In every way, that is, except the economic. It was the one sort of performance he didn't care about. With a public man you are always in public.

Here is the significance of all those dinner-table seminars you found so astonishing. What was astonishing was not their violence, intensity, or length, not even their subject matter: questions about public goods—the Vietnam War, civil rights, poverty, education, Reaganomics. What was astonishing was that we were the only people there. For as far as he was concerned, all of Boston was there, all of America, the whole world. He wanted everybody to be sitting there with us at the dinner table, debating what was good for them and what was bad. He behaved the same way in restaurants, in planes, even on the street. Suddenly he would reach out for another person's conception of the good.

There was more to his publicness than talk. He loved talk, but he loved action more. I could tell you about the actions of this public man—about what he did in and for his city, his town, his country—but I think you know all that. The important point is about the mantle. It is made up of talk and action, the talk redeeming the action from force, the action redeeming the talk from futility. There must be both. He would have wanted you to know this. It explains why, if you would take up the mantle, you must first ask for a double portion of spirit. You will need it to wear the mantle.

Do you want it? Many people wouldn't touch it. Many people tend to think of the public world as a place where they have to go to fight for themselves. And they can be extremely critical of the double-portioned. Your grandfather's way of dealing with this problem was rare and effective. It had to do with his spirit. He was a very tolerant man. Tolerance is a great and vital virtue in society, despite what neoconservatives will tell you, but it needs an animating energy, if it is to be a personal virtue in a public man or woman. Tolerance must be more than "openness"; it must be an embrace.

In America, the republic of change, your grandfather welcomed change and adored his country. He reveled in the variety of its people, their cultural differences, their economic conflicts, their political exertions. He never condescended to anyone. In his own way, this double-portioned man was an egalitarian. That was the sort of tolerance he had: embracing, insatiably curious, generous, performative. He couldn't wait to go out into America, to mix it up there, and to invite it home.

He never supposed that the public world was his. To him it was a place to be contested, and any citizen had the right to contest it, so long as the rules were respected. In that sense, the public world was like the coastal sea which all his life he loved, first to race on, then to cruise, finally to paint. His sea was marked off by buoys that set the course of the contest, to navigate by, to get us where we want to go, and to tell us when we've got there. But his sailing was more than that: more than clashes of will and directions of desire. He saw great beauty in it, and craft, and intelligence. He saw the wind and the weather, the line of shore—things one couldn't do anything about, things he might have called God. He thought of it all— the public world, the sea—as a great and exciting gift. The only ignoble thing was not to know what to do with it, not to go out into it, and not to pass on one's love for it.

So there is the color and texture of the mantle my father left for you. There, too, the qualities of spirit that are needed to take it up. The ancient Greeks believed, and I think he believed, that happiness is to act justly and to see the birth of a grandchild. He acted justly and saw the birth of more than one grandchild. I know he wished that sort of happiness for you.

"Democracy" in America, Tocqueville observed, leaves the rich with their property but deprives them of their pride. If by "democracy" he meant all the forces that nip New World aristocracies in the bud, then envy must be included as one of the forces, now awarding the rich man with the coveted powers of wealth, the next minute denying him any personal power whatever. Freedom is another such force, riches being more often defined as facilitating personal freedom than as providing a focus for social obligation. Markets are another, the markets that dissolve patrimonies and flood old social settlements with new people and new money. Finally, there is the force that Tocqueville arrived here too soon to observe—ethnicity, the fact that most Americans, when they imagine themselves socially, not economically, imagine themselves in a society organized more by race or national origin than by class.

These forces don't so much humble the Old Rich as drive their pride into furtive whispers of expression and private corners of activity. They have created what at times looks like a cryptoclass. Aboveground, commercially available to all, there is a set of images of what Old Money might have been and might still be for those who "buy it." Belowground, there are the actual members of the class, the born-and-bred and a few converts. This situation leaves the public wide open to the entrepreneurial imagination, with its starting-line equality, market freedoms, econometric knowledge; its justice of just deserts, its ethos of competitive self-reliance, and its keen nose for what people *want*. All this offers, to most Americans, more promising visions of the good life, or happiness, than Old Money does.

But the situation is not such a good thing for Old Money: not for its individual members, not for its generational families, and not for its supposed *mission civilisatrice*. So long as the class's actual composition remains underground, with only intermittent breakthroughs into public awareness—and those racially "exclusive"—then the class is available to others only in the commercial model, so to speak, or else in the cryptic experience of nudges, innuendos, and hidden rituals, most of them virulently ethnocentric. In the long run, this spells doom for any social class consciousness in America. Market Man will be triumphant then, alone in the field, with no place to go, socially speaking, except his ethnic group, and no one to think of, economically speaking, except his interest group. Old Money will then cease to exist, even in the minds of Marxists and fascists, as a class-based culture of values, virtues, and vices.

With that, these values, virtues, and vices will become what perhaps they always were, not the heritage of a class but the legacy of particular families: families like mine, begun with some great crime or success, and continued on with a conscious sense of custom and obligation. For this no class is needed, really, not even a great deal of money. All that's needed is *pietas*.

Notes & Index

Notes

As my subject is the images that have gathered around one American elite, Old Money, and as I am a member of that elite, it is probably inevitable that the most important sources of the observations and anecdotes in this book have been the conversations I myself have provoked, not always intentionally, on the subject of "people like us" or, just as often, "people like *you*." These conversations, together with a near lifetime of alert reading, have yielded a personal collection of popular clichés, stereotypes, animadversions, flatteries, epithets, favorable insights and fatuous biases, shrewd insights and ignorant prejudices about the social class into which I was born, a collection without which this book wouldn't be what is is—or I, in part, what I am, for that matter. I have noted here only those books and articles from which I have quoted particular passages, turns of phrase, or stories, and have credited only those authors whose ideas I feel I've done some justice to, not merely those who have inspired me. The latter, in any case, should be obvious.

CHAPTER ONE : MY FOUNDING FATHER

5   *There was a biography:* Nathaniel Wright Stephenson, *Nelson W. Aldrich: A Leader in American Politics* (Scribner's, 1930).

6   *The books were:* Matthew Josephson, *The Robber Barons* (Harcourt Brace, 1934); Ferdinand Lundberg, *America's Sixty Families* (Vanguard, 1937); Karl Marx, *Capital, and Other Writings* (Modern Library, 1932).

10   *Letters of Nelson A. and Michael Rockefeller:* Quoted in Peter Collier and David Horowitz, *The Rockefellers* (Holt, Rinehart & Winston, 1976).
"Very like leaves . . ."; "Hippolokhos it was": Homer, *The Iliad,* trans. Robert Fitzgerald (Doubleday, 1975).

11   *"The example of my grandfathers":* Quoted in Collier and Horowitz, *The Rockefellers.*
Nelson W. Aldrich was raised in: This account of my great-grandfather's life, all except the details of the deal that made him rich, is taken from Stephenson, as are all quotations from his letters.

13   *"Everybody was at work trying to make money":* Quoted in Russell B. Adams, Jr., *The Boston Money Tree* (Crowell, 1977).
"That's the American way": quoted in *Fortune,* 25 May 1987.
"I feel now more than ever": Quoted in Collier and Horowitz, *The Rockefellers.*

15   *Many states in the United States:* This account of Rhode Island state politics around the turn of the century relies heavily on Lincoln Steffens, "Rhode Island: A State for Sale," *McClure's,* February 1905.

20   *"In pursuing personal power":* In Jerome Sternstein, "Corruption in the Gilded Age Senate: Nelson W. Aldrich and the Sugar Trust," *Capitol Studies,* Vol. 6, no. 1.

21   *The stronger reason for his decision:* My account relies on Sternstein's paper.

23   *"The enclosed refers to the stock":* Quoted in Sternstein, "Corruption."

26 *"Here," gushed a writer:* E. L. D. Seymour, "The Aldrich Estate at Warwick Neck," *Country Life,* February 1919.

27 *"new" aristocracy whose "errors":* Henry James, *The American Scene,* ed. W. H. Auden (Scribner's, 1946).
"keep the buildings": Quoted in Seymour, "Aldrich Estate."

CHAPTER TWO : THE COMPOSITION OF OLD MONEY

30 *is said to have been a "Brahmin":* E. Digby Baltzell, *The Protestant Establishment* (Random House, 1964).

32 *"A man of inherited wealth":* William Graham Sumner, *The Challenge of Facts, and Other Essays* (Yale University Press, 1914).
"There is, indeed, good reason": Friedrich A. von Hayek, *The Constitution of Liberty* (University of Chicago Press, 1960).

33 *"The family, rather than the individual":* Quoted in Baltzell, *Protestant Establishment.*
"Again and again I have said": Quoted in Henry Dwight Sedgwick, *In Praise of Gentlemen* (Little, Brown, 1935).

34 *Herbert Pell's views:* See my "The Senator Attired for Running," *New England Monthly,* June 1984.

35 *"When it became known that Martin A. Seigel":* John Crudele, "Fallen Deal Maker," *New York Times,* 15 February 1986.

37 *on those same meeting grounds:* See, for a definition of social class as a "circle of friends and potential friends," Randall Collins, *Conflict Sociology* (Academic Press, 1975).

38 *"What . . . is this American system?":* *The Works of Orestes A. Brownson,* ed. Henry F. Brownson (AMS Press, 1966).
"[I]nherited concentrations of wealth": Irving Kristol, "Taxes, Poverty, and Equality," *The Public Interest,* Fall 1974.
the Great American Museum: Karl E. Meyer, *The Art Museum: Power, Money, Ethics* (Morrow, 1979). See also George Steiner, "The Archives of Eden," *Salmagundi,* Fall 1980–Winter 1981.

39 *"The next regular step":* Henry Adams, *The Education of Henry Adams* (Houghton Mifflin, 1918).

41 *"Aubrey . . . neither knew nor cared":* Norman Podhoretz, *Making It* (Random House, 1967).

42 *St. Midas:* F. Scott Fitzgerald, "The Diamond as Big as the Ritz," *The Stories of F. Scott Fitzgerald,* ed. Malcolm Cowley (Scribner's, 1951).
"most imperious necessity": Alexis de Tocqueville, *Democracy in America* (Knopf, 1948).

43 *As Fitzgerald noted:* F. Scott Fitzgerald, *This Side of Paradise* (Scribner's, 1970)

44 *The Bradley Martins' notorious ball:* See Dixon Wecter, *The Saga of American Society* (Scribner's, 1970).
"F. Townsend Martin . . . once wrote": F. Townsend Martin, *The Passing of the Idle Rich* (Doubleday, Page, 1911).

45 *"It is simply appalling":* Quoted in Elizabeth Drexel Lehr, *"King Lehr" and the Gilded Age* (Lippincott, 1935).

47 *"radiant body":* Thorstein Veblen, *The Theory of the Leisure Class* (Random House, 1934).

48 *"In a great doorway":* Ralph Pulitzer, *New York Society on Parade* (Harper, 1910).
"The opera gives Society": Ibid.

50 *A story is told of the late John Hay Whitney:* See my "Rumors of Power and Wealth," *Rolling Stone,* 6 October 1977.

54 *"Improvised Europeans, we were":* *The Letters of Henry Adams,* ed. Worthington Chauncey Ford (Houghton Mifflin, 1938).

55 *Joseph Alsop:* Joseph Alsop, *FDR* (Viking, 1982).

But money, in a tangled sort of way: For this relationship, see Lucy Kavaler, *The Astors* (Dodd, Mead, 1966); Harvey O'Connor, *The Astors* (Knopf, 1941).

57 *The charming Jacksonian hero:* Quoted in Judith N. Shklar, *Ordinary Vices* (Harvard University Press, 1984).

Every emergent family in history: See Fustel de Coulanges, *The Ancient City* (Doubleday, n.d.).

58 *a list of the largest fortunes in America:* Stanley Lebergott, *The American Economy* (Princeton University Press, 1976).

Marshall Field's was the most stunning of these legacies: Gustavus Myers, *History of the Great American Fortunes* (Modern Library, 1936).

59 *Trusts may run for no more than:* The exposition is taken from Robert F. Dalzell, Jr., *Enterprising Elite: The Boston Associates and the World They Made* (Harvard University Press, 1987).

61 *the Boston Associates:* The account is given in Ibid.

65 *John J. McCloy, Jr., for example:* Walter Isaacson and Evan Thomas, *The Wise Men: Six Friends and the World They Made* (Simon & Schuster, 1986).

67 *"I was lucky to come from a family":* Letter by Charles S. Boit, '49, reprinted in the *Bulletin* of the Fund for SPS, October 1978.

CHAPTER THREE : CLASS ACTS

72 *Born to a provincial manor ... Paley's introduction:* William S. Paley, *As It Happened* (Doubleday, 1979).

75 *To Lady Diana Cooper:* Diana Cooper, *The Rainbow Comes and Goes* (Houghton Mifflin, 1958).

77 *Cleveland Amory tells the story:* Cleveland Amory, *The Proper Bostonians* (Dutton, 1947).

79 *"In our ordinary moods":* Richard Bennett Hovey, *John Jay Chapman: An American Mind* (Columbia University Press, 1959).

"The flapper is deceased": Quoted in *The Romantic Egoists,* ed. Matthew J. Bruccoli, Scottie F. Smith, and Joan P. Kerr (Scribner's, 1974).

80 *"Thirty years ago":* See Leonard Baker, *Brahmin in Revolt* (Doubleday, 1972).

83 *In Arthur Schlesinger's account:* Arthur M. Schlesinger, Jr., *The Age of Roosevelt,* Vol. II (Houghton Mifflin, 1960).

Fitzgerald, after having Dexter Green: "Winter Dreams," *Stories of F. Scott Fitzgerald.*

J. P. Marquand has one of his envious: John P. Marquand, *Thirty Years* (Little, Brown, 1954).

the sheer restfulness: quoted in Paul Aron, unpublished article on Choate.

84 *"'Tis the perpetual promise":* Quoted in Sedgwick, *In Praise of Gentlemen.*

"divine assurance": Veblen, *Theory.*

"an expression of the relation of status": Ibid.

85 *Emerson:* In Sedgwick, *In Praise of Gentlemen.*

"Why, you're as good as I am!": The observation is Brownson's, in *Works of Orestes A. Brownson,* though not the attribution of such feelings to "aristocrats."

86 *"Come down to it":* Mark A. deW. Howe, *John Jay Chapman and His Letters* (Houghton Mifflin, 1937).

I think of the day when Senator Huey Long: My account is taken from T. Harry Williams, *Huey Long* (Knopf, 1970); and from Schlesinger, *Age of Roosevelt.*

88 *"If people are rude to you":* Brooke Russell Astor, *Footprints* (Doubleday, 1980).

90 *"character" and "personality":* My description of the distinction I owe to Timothy Dickenson.

91 *Market Man has not been well regarded:* George Gilder, *The Spirit of Enterprise* (Simon & Schuster, 1984).

92 *Endicott Peabody:* Frank D. Ashburn, *Peabody of Groton* (Coward, McCann, 1944).

95 *"I've got some prodigious operations on foot":* Mark Twain and Charles Dudley Warner, *The Gilded Age* (New American Library, 1969).
Samuel S. Drury: Roger W. Drury, *Drury and St. Paul's: The Scars of a Schoolmaster* (Little, Brown, 1964).

97 *Harvard Medical School wanted:* Frederick Lewis Allen, *The Great Pierpont Morgan* (Harper, 1965).

99 *Katharine Graham:* Her remark is quoted in Chalmers M. Roberts, *The Washington Post* (Houghton Mifflin, 1977).

100 *"Time was called on a round":* Owen Wister, *Roosevelt: The Story of a Friendship* (Macmillan, 1930).

101 *"Sports require great physical gifts":* John Davis, *The Legend of Hobey Baker,* introduction by Arthur Mizener (Little, Brown, 1966).

102 *"The cultures of the past":* Jean-François Revel, *Without Marx or Jesus* (Dell, 1974).

104 *John Leonard ... "made friends with the Louvre":* John Leonard, "Private Lives," *New York Times,* 23 May 1979.
"Elizabeth's ... account of St. Paul's": Quoted in Howe, *Chapman.*

CHAPTER FOUR : THE REVENGE OF MARKET MAN

106 *The victim was William Graham Phillips:* My account of the incident is taken from Kenneth S. Lynn, *The Dream of Success: A Study of the Modern American Imagination* (Little, Brown, 1955).

108 *The young lawyer Samuel Rosenman:* Schlesinger, *Age of Roosevelt.*

112 *"There are a few cases like that of the Morgans":* Harlan Eugene Read, *The Abolition of Inheritance* (Macmillan, 1919).

113 *Titanesses:* Thomas Beer, *The Mauve Decade* (Doubleday, 1926).
Wilfrid Sheed: Wilfrid Sheed, *Clare Booth Luce* (Dutton, 1982).

115 *Field ... welded his fortune:* Myers, *Great American Fortunes.*

116 *not since the Dark Ages:* Pollock and Maitland, *History of English Law,* Vol. II (Cambridge University Press, 1968).

117 *Share Our Wealth:* Schlesinger, *Age of Roosevelt,* and Williams, *Huey Long.*
Consequently, "for the good of Humanity": Works of Orestes A. Brownson.

118 *The key document ... Thomas Jefferson's celebrated dismissal: The Life and Selected Writings of Thomas Jefferson,* ed. Adrienne Koch and William Peden (Random House, 1944).

120 *The natural term of any contract:* Garry Wills, *Inventing America* (Vintage, 1979).
Blackstone's passage: William Blackstone, *Commentaries,* Book II, Chap. 1, Sec. 2.

123 *"Six stallions, say, I can afford":* Goethe, *Faust,* quoted by Karl Marx in "The Power of Money in Bourgeois Society," *The Marx-Engels Reader,* ed. Robert C. Tucker (Norton, 1978).
"the arrogance of wealth": Foster Rhea Dulles, *America Learns to Play* (Appleton Century, 1940).

124 *"I began to dread rides":* Adam Hochschild, *Half the Way Home: A Memoir of Father and Son* (Viking, 1986).

125 *"only one gentleman stands ahead of me":* Quoted in Edmund Wilson, *The Pre-Presidential T.R.: Eight Essays (Doubleday, 1954).*

126 *"Having money is like being a beautiful woman":* Quoted in Katy Butler et al., *Robin Hood Was Right: A Guide to Giving Your Money for Social Change* (Vanguard Public Foundation, 1977).

129 *"The older I get":* Ibid.
George Bush has provided a wonderful example: Time, 3 December 1979.

130 *"I'll never forget":* Robin Hood.

132 *an intriguing item about Allan MacDougall: Alumni Horae,* Autumn 1986.

134 *Cost is not a figure:* See Charles E. Lindblom, *Politics and Markets* (Basic Books, 1977).

135 *William Randolph Hearst:* W. A. Swanberg, *Citizen Hearst* (Scribner's, 1961).

136   *Eleanor had occasion to write:* Joseph P. Lash, *Eleanor and Franklin* (Norton, 1971).

138   *"I remember at one of these meetings":* Robin Hood.

140   *Townsend Martin once observed:* Martin, *Passing of the Idle Rich.*

CHAPTER FIVE : THREE ORDEALS

144   *"After a couple of summers at Portofino":* Astor, *Footprints.*

145   *Woodrow Wilson . . . and Samuel Drury:* Drury, *Drury and St. Paul's.*

146   *Asked what they got out of [Exeter]:* *Exeter Remembered,* ed. Henry Darcy Curwen (Phillips Exeter Academy, 1965).

148   *John Jay Chapman:* In Hovey, *Chapman.*

149   *In his diary [Drury] railed:* Drury, *Drury and St. Paul's.*

152   *Kathy Cronkite:* Judy Klemesrud, "Kathy Cronkite: A Celebrated Father," *New York Times,* 30 March 1981.

154   *the Athens of Pericles' funeral oration:* Thucydides, *The Peloponnesian War* (Random House, 1934).

155   *"It is thought that the peculiar merit of Democracy":* quoted in Hovey, *Chapman.*

159   *"[T]he choppy seas around Newport":* Richmond Barrett, *Good Old Summer Days* (Houghton Mifflin, 1952).

160   *Owen Wister's story is typical:* Wister, *Roosevelt.*
     Nature even briefly blessed John Jay Chapman: Howe, *Chapman.*

162   *"[T]he west . . . I knew so well":* quoted in Wister, *Roosevelt.*
     "For a boy who is destined": Gerald W. Johnson, *Roosevelt: Dictator or Democrat?* (Harper, 1941).

164   *the story of Harvey Cheyne, a spoiled sprig of wealth:* Rudyard Kipling, *Captains Courageous* (Airmont, 1966).

165   *Dean Acheson, the somewhat dandified:* Dean Acheson, *Morning and Noon* (Houghton Mifflin, 1965).

166   *But in Eliot's memoir:* Charles W. Eliot, *John Gilley of Baker's Island* (Eastern National Park and Monument Association, 1978).
     that led Douglas Burden to write: Douglas Burden, Autobiography (unpublished).

169   *Victor Emmanuel Chapman was born:* *Victor Chapman's Letters from France,* edited with a memoir by John Jay Chapman (Macmillan, 1917).

173   *Bertrand de Born:* Quoted in Marc Bloch, *Feudal Society* (University of Chicago Press, 1964).
     "I tell you the kind of man I am": Quoted in Howe, *Chapman.*

174   *St. Paul's was typical:* See my *Tommy Hitchcock* (Fleet Street, 1984).
     As in the Middle Ages: Bloch, *Feudal Society.*
     "Of course no end of people you know": Quoted in Howe, *Chapman.*

175   *Vincent Astor came down to Washington:* O'Connor, *The Astors.*

176   *"I seem to be conscious of a feverish desire":* Quoted in James Brown Scott, *Robert Bacon: Life and Letters* (Doubleday, 1923).
     The most glamorous effort . . . was the Lafayette Escadrille: See Herbert Molloy Mason, Jr., *The Lafayette Escadrille* (Random House, 1964); *The Lafayette Flying Corps,* ed. James Norman Hall and Charles B. Nordhoff (Kennikat Press, 1964); William A. Wellman, *Go Get 'Em!* (Page, 1918); *Norman Prince,* a memoir by George F. Babbitt (Houghton Mifflin, 1917).

179   *"The myth of America as a promised land":* Quoted in Hovey, *Chapman.*
     So did Willard Straight: Account and letter from W. A. Swanberg, *Whitney Father, Whitney Heiress* (Scribner's, 1980).

180   *If any one man:* Aldrich, *Hitchcock.*

184   *Cord Meyer:* Cord Meyer, *Facing Reality: From World Federalism to the CIA* (Harper, 1980).

188   *George Cadwalader:* George Cadwalader, "Honing in on Delinquency's Cause," *Alumni Horae,* Spring 1987.

CHAPTER SIX : HAZARDS OF OLD FORTUNES

191 *When Ned McLean . . . lost the paper:* See Roberts, *Washington Post.*
193 *Maureen Orth:* Maureen Orth, "The Prince and the Paper," *New York,* 27 August 1979.
196 *a letter that [TR] . . . received from his father:* Quoted in John Milton Cooper, Jr., *The Warrior and the Priest: Woodrow Wilson and Theodore Roosevelt* (Harvard University Press, 1983).
197 *Bentham put the issue:* Jeremy Bentham, *Of Laws in General,* ed. H. L. A. Hart (Athlone, 1970).
199 *Daniel Defoe, the first modern journalist:* quoted in Francis Williams, *Dangerous Estate* (Longmans, Green, 1957).
200 *this passage by Theodore White:* Theodore White, *The Making of the President 1960* (Atheneum, 1961).
201 *"To most of the employees":* Quoted in Roberts, *Washington Post.*
 "I thought I was this peasant": Ibid.
203 *Richardson-Vicks:* See James B. Stewart and Michael Waldholz, "How Richardson-Vicks Fell Prey to Takeover Despite Family's Grip," *Wall Street Journal,* 30 October 1985.
204 *the Bingham domain:* See Alex S. Jones, "Bingham Family to Sell Media Holdings," *New York Times,* 10 January 1986; Jones, "Sale by Binghams Marks End of Era," *Times,* 13 January 1986; Jones, "The Fall of the House of Bingham," *Times,* 19 January 1986; Jones, "Gannett Gets Louisville Papers for $300 Million," *Times,* 20 May 1986.
206 *[Sallie] wrote later:* Sallie Bingham, "Biting the Hand," *Radcliffe Quarterly,* June 1986.
213 *Eugene Meyer in a speech:* Roberts, *Washington Post.*
215 *The key figure here . . . is J. P. Morgan:* See Allen, *Morgan.*
 Lincoln Steffens . . . "glare" of the banker's eyes: Lincoln Steffens, *The Autobiography* (Harcourt Brace, 1931).
219 *Walter Benjamin maintained:* Walter Benjamin, "Unpacking My Library," in *Illuminations* (Schocken, 1969).
220 *Metropolitan Museum reserved seats:* Meyer, *The Art Museum.*
224 *"In a society in which so many":* Bloch, *Feudal Society.*
228 *"What hardly could have been anticipated":* Wister, *Roosevelt.*

CHAPTER SEVEN : THE PRINCE AND THE PEOPLE

229 *there was another great rendezvous with enmity:* My account based on Schlesinger, *Age of Roosevelt;* Williams, *Huey Long;* Frank Friedel, *Franklin Delano Roosevelt* (Norton, 1971); and *New York Times,* 22 June 1935.
243 *Eleanor Roosevelt used to tell the story:* Lash, *Eleanor and Franklin* (Norton, 1971).
245 *"When I got back":* Ibid.
247 *"He tried to imagine himself in Congress":* Fitzgerald, *This Side of Paradise.*
248 *Endicott Peabody . . . "a desperate charge" into politics:* Ashburn, *Peabody.*
 It's a law of market societies: See Albert O. Hirschman, *Shifting Involvements* (Princeton University Press, 1982).
251 *"Andromache of the white arms":* Homer, *The Iliad.*
253 *"You may remember the forlorn feeling":* Jane Addams, "The Subjective Necessity for Social Settlements," *Philanthropy and Social Progress: Seven Essays* (Crowell, 1893).
255 *"More than forty years ago":* Quoted in Schlesinger, *Age of Roosevelt.*
258 For views of TR and FDR and JFK as "weak," see Edmund Morris, *The Rise of Theodore Roosevelt* (Coward, McCann, 1979); Schlesinger, *Age of Roosevelt;* and Benjamin C. Bradlee, *Conversations with Kennedy* (Norton, 1975).
260 *"My line of politics":* Quoted in Howe, *Chapman.*
 Stimson: Encyclopedia of American Biography, ed. John A. Garraty (Harper, 1974).
 Alsop: Quoted in Bradlee, *Conversations.*

261 *They were bound for Miami:* My account based on Schlesinger, *Age of Roosevelt,* and Friedel, *Roosevelt.* My portrait of Astor based on Kavaler, *The Astors,* O'Connor, *The Astors,* and Brooke Astor, *Footprints.* My portrait of Kermit Roosevelt based on conversations with family.

CHAPTER EIGHT : HEMINGWAY'S CURSE

265 *Hemingway's Curse:* The conceit of presenting Hemingway's shopworn riposte as a curse on old money I owe to Timothy Dickenson.
269 *"It is contended that":* Quoted in Richard L. Neuberger and Stephen B. Kahn, *Integrity: The Life of George W. Norris* (Vanguard, 1937).
270 *"Those whom either the wealth of their parents":* Life and Writings of Thomas Jefferson.
271 *George Templeton Strong . . . George Bancroft:* Quoted in Cleveland Amory, *Who Killed Society?* (Harper, 1960).
272 *"Property in this country is drifting":* Quoted in Baker, *Brahmin in Revolt.*
278 *Francis Minturn Sedgwick:* See Jean Stein, *Edie: An American Biography,* edited with George A. Plimpton (Knopf, 1982).
283 *du Pont:* See my "Pete du Pont," *Regardies* magazine, January 1988.

Index

A NOTE ON THE TYPE

This book was set on the Linotron 202 in Granjon, a type
named in compliment to Robert Granjon, but neither a copy
of a classic face nor an entirely original creation. George W.
Jones based his designs for this type on that used by Claude
Garamond (1510–61) in his beautiful French books, and
Granjon more closely resembles Garamond's own type than
does any of the various modern types that bear his name.

Robert Granjon began his career as typecutter in 1523. The
boldest and most original designer of his time, he was one of
the first to practice the trade of typefounder apart from that
of printer. Between 1557 and 1562 Granjon printed about
twenty books in types designed by himself, following, after
the fashion, the cursive handwriting of the time. These types,
usually known as *caractères de civilité,* he himself called *lettres
françaises,* as especially appropriate to his own country.

Composed by Graphic Composition, Inc.,
Athens, Georgia

Printed and bound by The Haddon Craftsmen, Inc.
Scranton, Pennsylvania

Typography and binding design by
Dorothy Schmiderer Baker